Andy Varipapa

Andy Varipapa
Bowling's First Superstar

GLENN GERSTNER

McFarland & Company, Inc., Publishers
Jefferson, North Carolina

ISBN (print) 978-1-4766-9333-0
ISBN (ebook) 978-1-4766-5244-3

LIBRARY OF CONGRESS AND BRITISH LIBRARY
CATALOGUING DATA ARE AVAILABLE

Library of Congress Control Number 2024013806

© 2024 Glenn Gerstner. All rights reserved

No part of this book may be reproduced or transmitted in any form or by any means, electronic or mechanical, including photocopying or recording, or by any information storage and retrieval system, without permission in writing from the publisher.

On the cover: Andy Varipapa, 1947 (Brunswick Bowling Products LLC/Varipapa family collection)

Printed in the United States of America

*McFarland & Company, Inc., Publishers
Box 611, Jefferson, North Carolina 28640
www.mcfarlandpub.com*

Table of Contents

Acknowledgments — vii
Preface — 1
Introduction — 5

One. Arrival — 11
Two. The Bowler — 16
Three. Husband, Father, Machinist — 23
Four. Lawler's — 29
Five. The Match — 35
Six. Tricks — 41
Seven. Hollywood — 49
Eight. Out in the Cold — 57
Nine. Andy Comes to Town — 64
Ten. Who's the Champ? — 74
Eleven. A New Kind of Tournament — 81
Twelve. The War — 88
Thirteen. All-Star Andy — 97
Fourteen. Back-to-Back — 105
Fifteen. Respect — 114
Sixteen. Traveling Man — 122
Seventeen. Television — 133
Eighteen. Boom, Jackpot, and Heartache — 142
Nineteen. No Slowing Down — 154
Twenty. Century Lanes — 165
Twenty-One. A Lasting Honor — 172

Epilogue	179
Appendix I: Tournament Victories, Awards, and Honors	187
Appendix II: Glossary of Bowling Terms and Acronyms	189
Chapter Notes	193
Bibliography	225
Index	237

Acknowledgments

The efforts of many people improved this book. My editor at McFarland, Beth Foxwell, corrected numerous rookie mistakes and offered thoughtful guidance as needed. Eric Hartman, Dr. Nick Hirshon, Dr. Tom Kitts, Larry Pitilli, Dr. Jake Schmidt, and Kari Williams reviewed drafts of my manuscript and provided valuable feedback and suggestions.

Several people took time to speak with me about Andy: Parker Bohn III, Nelson Burton, Jr., Jim Dressel, Norm Duke, John LaSpina, Larry Lichstein, Jim Lizzo, Mort Luby, Jr., Johnny Petraglia, Tom Rossman, Roy Ryan, Carmen Salvino, Joan Taylor Schliewenz, and Sam Zurich.

Those who assisted in other ways include Tom Adams, Phil Cardinale, Tom Clark, Elizabeth Clemens, Mark Gerberich, Brian Graham, Bob Johnson, Chris Keller, Len Nicholson, Jason Overstreet, Barb Pelz, Jeff Richgels, Kier Rouse-Perry, Arlene Shaner, Brandy Silva, and Aaron Smith.

Thanks to Kari Williams, curator and program manager of the International Bowling Museum and Hall of Fame (*www.bowlingheritage.com*). She and her staff tracked down articles and photographs featuring Andy from the IBMHOF archives, some almost 100 years old.

Finally, special thanks to the Varipapa family. I learned about "The Great Varipapa" by watching his films and reading newspapers and magazines. Lengthy discussions with Andy's grandchildren—Andy Ruffolo, Joe Ruffolo, Andy Varipapa II, and Susan Varipapa—educated me about the devoted husband, father, grandfather, great-grandfather, and friend. Many of the photographs in this book came from their private collections. I could not have completed this book without their assistance and unfailing support.

Preface

An inexorable link exists between sports and popular culture. As a college professor who studies sports, I have long been interested in studying that intersection. Given my love for the sport of bowling, I thought the life of Andy Varipapa provided the basis for an interesting research paper. More than any other bowler, and possibly more than any other athlete, Andy bridged sports and popular culture as a competitor and entertainer. Of course, if you read this, you can see that my project grew into more than just a paper.

Andy Varipapa is perhaps the most famous bowler who ever lived. He died almost 40 years ago but is still a towering figure inside and outside the bowling community. Born in Italy in 1891, he immigrated to Brooklyn in 1903. And like millions of immigrants before and since, Andy arrived at Ellis Island having never attended school and not speaking English.

His uncanny trick-shot artistry, showcased in several short films, fueled his rise to fame. Andy starred in the Academy Award–nominated *Strikes and Spares* released in 1934.[1] Millions of Americans saw Andy make an array of unbelievable shots. He converted the 7–10 split by throwing a ball with each hand. Andy rolled his 16-pound ball between the legs of nine nervous showgirls. He made spares by kicking the ball down the lane. And while he did not speak in the films, the productions gave audiences a glimpse of his natural charisma and fun-loving personality.

In their exhaustive *Historical Dictionary of Bowling*, Grasso and Hartman summarized Andy's impact on American popular culture: "During the 1940s and 1950s if you were to ask a non-sports fan to name a bowler, chances are they would say Andy Varipapa."[2] He traveled the country for 50 years giving clinics and exhibitions. He was the rare bowler who endorsed products outside the bowling industry, becoming a spokesperson for international brands, including Goodyear, Pennzoil, Pepsi-Cola, and Equitable Life.

After retiring from competition and cutting back on his exhibition schedule, Andy still received star treatment. In 1970, when Andy was 79, Richard Nixon named him to the President's Advisory Conference on Physical Fitness and Sports, which was created to advise the President's Council on Physical Fitness and Sports. He was the first bowler and the oldest athlete so honored. At age 90, he performed trick shots for a new generation of fans on the popular ABC television show *That's Incredible!* Andy died peacefully at age 93 in 1984, but his legend lived on. In 2015, more than 30 years after his death, General Mills made him the centerpiece of an advertising campaign for their iconic breakfast cereal Wheaties.

This book documents Andy's contributions to the sport of bowling and

American popular culture. It also highlights his accomplishments as a competitive bowler. He was a successful bowler before appearing in *Strikes and Spares*, but many of his rivals believed he "was nothing but a trick shot artist, a vaudeville performer."[3] Some called him the "Clown Prince of Bowling" because of his trick-shot prowess and affinity for showboating and trash-talking. He detested the name, declaring, "I consider myself an artist with a bowling ball."[4]

Andy channeled his skills into a career as an entertainer, one that made him a good living at a time when opportunities for bowlers to earn money were scant. Andy long considered himself the greatest bowler in the world and told anyone who would listen. He regretted that "most people know me for [trick shots] more than my professional ability."[5]

That perception changed in 1946 when, at age 55, Andy won the Bowling Proprietors Association of America (BPAA) All-Star tournament. Known today as the U.S. Open, the All-Star was the most prestigious and grueling bowling tournament of its day, a 100-game marathon contested over eight days against 144 of the best bowlers in the country. And for those who dismissed the notion that bowlers were athletes, Andy walked more than 30 miles and threw 12 tons of bowling balls that week to secure victory. After his win, he proclaimed, "This has been long overdue. It's about time that the world's best bowler was also the world champion."[6]

To prove it was no fluke, he won the All-Star again in 1947 and finished second in 1948, at ages when most bowlers had long since retired from competition. All-time bowling great Johnny Petraglia said his All-Star victories were "the greatest accomplishment in the history of bowling and one of the greatest in sports. Could you imagine Jack Nicklaus winning the U.S. Open two years in a row at age 56?"[7]

My interest in researching the life of Andy Varipapa originates from my friendship with his late son Frank, the owner of the local pro shop in my hometown of Mineola, New York. We bowled many "pot games" on weekday afternoons at Sheridan Bowl. I met Frank's son Andy Varipapa II when we bowled in the same league in 1980. After finding Andy's website documenting his grandfather's life, I contacted Andy II to discuss my idea of authoring a research paper about Andy.[8] When we spoke, he told me that no one had ever written a biography of arguably the most famous bowler ever. At that moment, I decided to write this book.

The idea of an Andy Varipapa biography is not new. In the late 1950s, Andy's daughter Lorraine Ruffolo set out to document her father's life. When two respected bowling writers passed on her request to write Andy's biography, she decided to author the book herself. At least six publishers rejected her proposals between 1960 and 1992. The publishers ranged from the biggest in the world (Harper and Doubleday) to others I had never heard of.

On the advice of one publisher, her original manuscript morphed into an instructional book, but later drafts returned to a straight biography. In the early 1970s, Andy approached his friend and longtime *Bowlers Journal* editor Jim Dressel and asked if he would write his biography. Busy with several other projects, Dressel turned down the offer. He said, "It was a big mistake. I've made a few of them in my life, and that's one of the big ones."[9] Ruffolo died in 2014, her book unfinished.

Andy II's sister Susan Varipapa saved her Aunt Lorraine's notes and drafts. I am thankful she did. Susan sent me four incomplete manuscripts, several dozen two- and three-page vignettes, and correspondence—about 200 pages in all. The material included private glimpses of Andy and information that never became public. Ruffolo's notes represent the closest thing we have to Andy's memoirs. Passages based on her work are cited as "Varipapa Family Papers" and fact-checked when needed.

Most of this book's source material originated in daily newspapers, starkly contrasting where most information is today. A search for "Andy Varipapa" via Google returned 139 unduplicated results, while that search on Newspapers.com yielded 25,492 matches. Unless otherwise noted, all newspaper articles in this book are from Newspapers.com, New York State Historic Newspapers, Newspaper Archive, Chronicling America, or TimesMachine.

You would not know it today, but bowling was once a staple of newspapers' sports sections. Most newspapers had dedicated bowling columnists, and Andy's bowling exploits received significant coverage. Journalists loved interviewing him. He was engaging, funny, and candid. Never at a loss for words, Andy admitted that he was "a talking machine."[10]

While few of his contemporaries are alive, I interviewed several people who knew Andy. Each stressed that he was a gentleman and treated everyone respectfully. They told stories about how he helped them and positively influenced their lives. Several said that Andy was like a second father or, in some cases, a second grandfather to them. The consensus is that Andy Varipapa was a lovely man.

In 1972, Andy was asked to identify his proudest accomplishment. He said without hesitation, "My seven grandchildren. They're all in college or about to go. What more could a man want who came to this country and couldn't read or write?"[11] Humble words from the man who once billed himself as "the greatest one-man bowling show on earth" and claimed he was "the best bowler I ever saw."[12]

Andy's braggadocio was part of a larger plan. Despite his lack of formal education, Andy was a shrewd marketer. His bold statements led to increased ticket sales to matches and exhibitions. Whether this quotation, often attributed to Muhammad Ali, is apocryphal is beside the point: *It's not bragging if you can back it up*. And Andy backed it up as well as anyone who ever laced up a pair of bowling shoes.

Introduction

Andy Varipapa was born in 1891. The world looked nothing like the one that existed when he died in 1984. His lifespan closely mirrored that of my maternal grandfather. Leon Frideman was born in 1890 in Hackensack, New Jersey, approximately eight miles west of Manhattan. His father, Conrad, a German immigrant who arrived in the United States shortly after the Civil War, raised Leon and his six brothers.

On July 13, 1895, the tornado that swept through what is now River Edge, New Jersey, left Leon and his brothers orphans. Conrad, age 49, was killed when the hotel he owned collapsed on him or he was blown out of its windows and projected head-first into a telegraph pole.[1] (My mother told me the latter, more spectacular version of the story.) My great-grandfather was one of three people killed. If tornados sound rare in northern New Jersey, they are. As of this writing, it is the only tornado that caused fatalities in Bergen County.[2]

Leon's oldest brother Grover, all of 10 at the time, became the head of the household. The seven brothers took care of each other. The 1900 U.S. Census identified Martha Frideman as their mother, but I understood she was not always around.[3] She died in 1905 when Leon was 15. My grandfather stayed in school through sixth grade when it was time to get a job to help support the family.

He had a knack for things mechanical. Leon was the guy who took apart a toaster and repaired it with some solder and toothpicks. In the early 1920s, he parlayed those skills into a job as a stationary engineer at a New York City sewage plant on Tallman Island in Queens. The plant still exists as a "wastewater treatment facility."[4]

Leon married Ida Fromm in 1914 and moved to Glendale, Queens, to raise my mom Vera and her older brother, Lee. Whatever bowling genes passed to me came from his family. Leon and Ida bowled regularly, but Uncle Lee was a local star. He made the finals of the *Newsday* Eastern Open in 1949 and 1952. Unfortunately, I did not get to know him very well. He moved to Las Vegas in the early 1960s and died of lung cancer at just 57 in 1972. My mother told me I looked and behaved like Lee: tall, handsome, and quick-witted (remember, this was my mom talking). We were also wise asses who enjoyed gambling. Whenever I won a few bucks bowling, she said, "Just like your uncle."

My grandfather retired in 1955 and relocated to St. James, a hamlet 45 miles further east on Long Island. He and Ida stayed busy. Leon tended his vegetable garden, repaired his neighbors' cars, and volunteered as the sexton at the St. James Methodist Church. He did all these things until his late 80s. When I visited, he pitched batting practice to me at the local ball field and took me clamming at the Head of the Harbor.

My visits to St. James were not all fun and games. My grandfather put me to work. I vividly recall mowing the lawn in the church cemetery, weaving the Lawn-Boy in and out of headstones. He died at 93 and, like Andy, never sat still and never took a moment for granted. It is why they led such long and productive lives.

I often marveled at what my grandfather saw during his lifetime. He lived through World Wars I and II and saw the Vietnam War fought live on television. The automobile was invented just before his birth. By 1915, he owned a car outfitted with a crank starter. When it broke down, as it regularly did, Leon repaired it on the side of the road, which was probably unpaved. He watched a complex interstate highway system be built and drove on it to visit his half-brother's family in Oregon in the late 1950s. Later, creature comforts like automatic transmissions and air conditioning appeared in his cars.

The only sport Leon paid attention to was baseball. He watched Walter Johnson, Honus Wagner, and Josh Gibson play at Ebbets Field, the Polo Grounds, or Yankee Stadium. He also lived long enough to watch Rickey Henderson, Tony Gwynn, and Cal Ripken, Jr., begin their careers.

Leon boarded an airplane only twice, the legs of a round trip from New York to Las Vegas in the late 1960s to visit my uncle and his family. He was 13 when the Wright brothers flew at Kitty Hawk and 79 when Neil Armstrong took his first steps on the moon. Leon watched the lunar landing on yet another invention not dreamed of at his birth, the television.

Throughout Andy Varipapa's life, which ended in 1984—a year after my grandfather's passing—he, too, saw all those changes. But more importantly for Andy, his birth coincided with a time when the relatively new sport of bowling was poised for extraordinary growth. An individual's innate talent and hard work determine success in any endeavor, but good fortune is always needed. At the very least, you must be in the right place at the right time. We all have the bad habit of playing the *what-if* game and wondering how our lives might have turned out had circumstances been different. For Andy, many moving parts had to be in place for him to become a well-known bowler, let alone the most famous of them all.

He was born in the tiny Italian village of Carfizzi on March 31, 1891. What if his father had not died suddenly at age 33? His family might not have ever immigrated to the United States. What if a truck had not broken his leg in 1919, just as he blossomed as a baseball player? The injury left his left leg slightly shorter than his right, ending any hopes of a baseball career. What if Andy had not settled in the Williamsburg section of Brooklyn just a few blocks from young James Melillo? The young bowling phenom motivated Andy to become a better bowler. When they met in 1904, Melillo, better known to bowling fans as Jimmy Smith, was on the precipice of becoming bowling's undisputed world champion.

Granted, we all have stories like Andy's and reflect on how events change our lives. Andy was fortunate to arrive in America when economic conditions were well suited for the growth of bowling. Our nation went through an industrial revolution only a couple of decades earlier. While immigrants' living and working conditions at that time were bleak, the industrial revolution set the stage for unprecedented economic growth.

Industrialization eventually shortened the workdays and increased the real wages of average workers. It gave them additional leisure time and disposable income. Once electricity was available in urban areas, indoor activities flourished. Working-class men (and later women) had time on their hands and money in their pockets. They looked for something fun to do that also satisfied their need for competition. And that something turned out to be bowling.

Golf and tennis enjoy wide popularity today, but in the 19th century, they were sports for the rich. Golf courses and tennis courts were accessible only to members of private clubs. Golf and tennis strictly adhered to the code of "British Amateurism," which appeared to promote practical virtues. First, athletes played for love rather than money. Second, gambling on the outcome of a game was prohibited. Finally, sportsmen played in a fair, dignified, and humble manner. Unfortunately, the code was little more than an insidious institution designed to limit sports participation to the upper classes.[5]

Fortunately, bowling did not originate in the United Kingdom and was not a country club sport. British Amateurism never constrained participation or its culture. Professionalism, gambling, and gamesmanship make bowling fun! Amateurism eventually disappeared from golf and tennis, but stereotypes die hard. Both sports struggle with the perception that they are elitist and non-inclusive. Meanwhile, bowling earned a reputation as a blue-collar sport. While modern bowlers bristle at that characterization, the fact is that working-class immigrants embraced bowling and helped fuel its widespread popularity.

When Andy was born in 1891, bowling as we know it today did not exist. That began to change in 1895 with the founding of the American Bowling Congress (ABC). Now known as the United States Bowling Congress (USBC), the ABC took a regional, disorganized sport, played under various rules, and made it a national, organized sport with consistent rules and equipment specifications.[6] It set bowling on a path that provided recreation for millions of Americans and gave its top performers, like Andy, a chance to earn livings as professionals.

Egyptians engaged in bowling-like activities as early as 5200 BC. Players used balls or other objects to knock down pins, but activities resembling modern bowling did not begin until the Middle Ages. English and Dutch settlers brought the game to North America in the 1600s, but not until the massive influx of German immigrants in the mid–19th century did the game become popular in the United States. Still, it was akin to lawn bowling or bocce. Bowlers used a ball that fit in the palm of their hands and played the game outdoors.[7]

Over the years, the balls got larger, and so did the pins. In 1840, an indoor bowling center, Knickerbocker Alleys, opened to much fanfare in lower Manhattan. Bowlers tossed wooden balls on clay lanes attempting to knock over nine pins. Indoor lanes soon opened all over Manhattan, and the sport spread to other large northeastern cities. Bowling became popular in midwestern cities with large German populations, such as Milwaukee, Detroit, and St. Louis.[8]

For the rest of the 19th century, bowling consisted of balls, lanes, and pins, but equipment and rules varied from venue to venue. The lanes were anywhere from 30 to 100 feet long (modern bowling lanes are 60 feet long) and made of clay or packed dirt rather than wood. Balls were of assorted sizes and weights, and so were the pins. While there was general agreement that 10 frames constituted a game, there was no consensus on how to keep score. Some versions of bowling allowed two balls per frame to knock down all the pins, while others allowed three.[9] One scoring system had a maximum score of 200, while the other system (still in use today) had a maximum score of 300.[10]

Even the number of pins varied. Early versions of bowling used nine pins, set up in a diamond shape, like in nine-ball billiards. Not long after indoor bowling became popular, some of the unsavory aspects of the game presented themselves. Bowlers drank, gambled, and fought among themselves. Religious and temperance groups urged politicians to outlaw bowling. In 1841, Connecticut became the first state to do so, and others followed suit.

This ban led to an oft-repeated story of how tenpin bowling came to be: soon after the law took effect, an enterprising bowling proprietor added a 10th pin, thus evading the ban on nine-pin bowling. The ingenious small business owner outsmarted pompous politicians and prohibitionists in this satisfying tale. Unfortunately, no historian has documented such a story.

The Connecticut law outlawed "any ninepin lane, whether more or less than nine pins are used in such play," contradicting the tall tale of the exculpatory 10th pin.[11] Laws or no laws, the tenpin version of the game caught on and the familiar sight of 10 pins set as a triangle became standard. Bowling's global governing body, the International Bowling Federation, still uses "tenpin bowling" to distinguish the sport from the nine-pin and five-pin versions.

Bowling in the late 1800s was not for the faint of heart. Today, bowlers expect automatic pinsetters, computers that keep score, food and beverage delivered to the lanes, and a clean and family-friendly atmosphere. These modern amenities did not arrive for decades. Places known today as "bowling centers" were "alleys" or "lanes," and most were extensions of saloons, fraternal halls, or billiard parlors.

Saloons were dark and dirty, their floors covered with sawdust and outfitted with spittoons, filled with cigar and cigarette smoke, and unwelcoming (if not downright hostile) to women. They attracted unpleasant characters and were sites of illegal and quasi-illegal activity, including gambling, loan sharking, and prostitution. Drunken brawls were commonplace. ABC Secretary Elmer Baumgarten said, "Bowling alleys were frequented principally by hustlers, touts, hangers on, cheap gamblers, and disreputable individuals…. The entire situation was disgusting, deplorable, disorderly, and chaotic."[12]

In 1875, leaders of bowling clubs in Manhattan met and formed the National Bowling Association (NBA) to standardize and regulate the sport. The NBA published rules, but they mattered little because most clubs and alleys ignored them.[13] In following years, an alphabet soup of new governing bodies appeared, but rather than uniting the sport, the various organizations fractured it even more.

Finally, in 1895, delegates from several cities met at Beethoven Hall in Manhattan and founded the ABC.[14] Unfortunately, the so-called "birth of bowling" is not as simple as the ABC later made it out to be. It was akin to how baseball executives convinced the public that Abner Doubleday invented the game in Cooperstown in 1839 (he certainly did not).[15] Delegates bickered, argued, and filibustered. Most importantly, bowlers from New York and Chicago did not resolve their differences and did not entirely do so until 1921.[16]

But the 1895 summit did lead to an agreement on playing rules that became standard nationwide. Delegates formulated basic equipment specifications: (1) lanes made of wood and 60 feet long from the foul line to the headpin; (2) balls can be any weight but are limited to 27 inches in circumference; and (3) pins are 15 inches tall.[17] They also voted to adopt the scoring system in use today: 10 frames, two balls per frame, and a maximum score of 300.[18] Despite haggling over issues that would not be fully reconciled for another 25 years, ABC delegates laid the groundwork for bowling's future growth.

The timing of the ABC's founding leads to the most intriguing *what-if* of all: if Andy Varipapa had been born 20 years earlier, he never would have become as famous as he was. Bowling would not have been ready for him. He would have channeled his formidable hand-eye coordination, strong work ethic, and engaging personality and been successful in another profession. But to the delight of bowling fans everywhere, Andy was born when he was and entertained us for 50 years.

He witnessed the industry and the sport grow before his eyes. The ABC held its first annual championship tournament in Chicago in 1901. Singles champion Frank Brill pocketed $55 (approximately $1,975 in 2023 dollars) for his efforts.[19] In 1921 the Petersen Classic in Chicago became the first individual tournament to offer significant prize money: $1,000 for first place ($17,045 in 2023 dollars).[20] Dozens of big-money tournaments sprang up across the country in the late 1930s and 1940s, including the Vogue Individual Classic in Detroit, the Waibel Singles Classic in St. Louis, and the Landgraf Classic in New York. The BPAA All-Star, which Andy won in 1946 and 1947, debuted in 1941.

After World War II, the popularity of bowling soared, at first spurred on by post-war economic prosperity and later by the invention of the automatic pinsetter.[21] The number of league bowlers grew from 1.1 million in 1946 to 6.9 million in 1963.[22] Between 1958 and 1962, in a bubble similar to Holland's 17th-century Tulip Mania, 3,259 new bowling centers opened in the United States.[23] That is an average of two per day! After having just 128 entries in 1938, the Petersen Classic attracted 14,144 entries in 1962. Winner John McDermott earned a cool $30,100 ($302,358 in 2023 dollars).[24]

The public began to pay attention to the game's best players. Stars were born. Bowling became a staple of network television programming, and millions watched the nation's best bowlers compete in various formats. *Bowling Headliners* was the first to air in 1948, followed by *National Bowling Champions*, *Bowling Stars*, *Make That Spare*, *Phillies Jackpot Bowling*, and local telecasts too numerous to mention.[25]

The popularity of bowling and its increased television exposure paved the way for the creation of the Professional Bowlers Association (PBA) in 1958. The founding players, led by sports agent Eddie Elias, set out to develop a national tour for bowlers like those for professional golfers and tennis players.

In 1959, the PBA sponsored just three tournaments in New York, New Jersey, and Ohio. By 1963, the PBA ran 37 tournaments in 27 states and another in Quebec. That year, Harry Smith earned about $75,000 ($743,537 in 2023 dollars) between prize money, endorsements, and his salary for being the house professional at Johnny Unitas' Colt Lanes in Baltimore.[26]

The first athlete to sign a seven-figure contract was not Willie Mays, Wilt Chamberlain, or Joe Namath. It was a bowler. In 1964, Don Carter agreed to a $1 million ($9.84 million in 2023 dollars) 10-year deal to endorse Ebonite products.[27] In

1965, Billy Hardwick won the inaugural Firestone Tournament of Champions and claimed the $25,000 ($240,764 in 2023 dollars) first prize. Jack Nicklaus earned just $20,000 for winning the 1965 Masters golf tournament.[28]

By the mid-1970s, ABC Television's weekly Saturday afternoon telecast of the *Professional Bowlers Tour* routinely drew more viewers than golf, tennis, NBA basketball, and NHL hockey. The first event of the 1982 season, the PBA Miller High Life Classic, drew an 8.7 Nielsen rating. In the same time slot, a men's college basketball game featured the two top-ranked teams in the nation. The broadcast of North Carolina (with freshman Michael Jordan) versus Virginia (led by player of the year Ralph Sampson) settled for a 7.9 rating.[29]

Bowling participation reached its zenith during the 1978–79 season when 9.8 million Americans bowled in certified leagues.[30] When Andy died in 1984, a sport that did not exist when he was born was the number one participation sport in the United States.[31] Hundreds of men and women earned their living as professional bowlers.

And Andy, more than any other individual, was the catalyst for this transformation. Others performed trick shots, but Andy brought them to a nationwide audience. Others toured the country, but Andy was bowling's first showman. Others taught bowling, but Andy was the first to reach thousands of students at a time. Others loved the game, but Andy made bowling his life's work. Others were popular, but Andy was bowling's first superstar.

ABC and PBA Hall of Famer Carmen Savino was a founding member of the PBA.[32] Salvino summed up Andy's influence on professional bowling: "In all sports, people tend to forget people from two or three decades in the past, and in fairness, they think of the new star, like Jason Belmonte in bowling," said Salvino. "And he deserves all the credit he is getting! But what Varipapa did for bowling, every star that came after him, we owe him a piece of our heart and a piece of our talent. He paved the way for us in a way that nobody else was capable of doing."[33]

Andy Varipapa is no longer in the conversation about who may have been the greatest bowler ever. That designation is reserved for players that followed him, such as Don Carter, Dick Weber, Earl Anthony, Walter Ray Williams, Jr., or Jason Belmonte. Andy may not have been bowling's most outstanding player, but he may have been its most important figure.

His influence was no more evident than in 1988 when *Bowlers Journal* named Andy their "Person of the Century." The editors based the honor on his "prodigious skill" and "becoming bowling's best and brightest ambassador."[34] ABC and PBA Hall of Fame journalist Chuck Pezzano wrote, "No person in any sport captured the attention, fancy, and imagination of friends, foes, and fans for as long as Varipapa did…. Andy was bowling's greatest showman and one of its best bowlers ever."[35] High praise for the man who arrived in the United States at age 12, uneducated and unable to speak English. His life story is fascinating.

One

Arrival

Andrea Antonio Varipapa was born on March 31, 1891, in Carfizzi, a small village in southern Italy. Andy never attended school in Italy, which was unsurprising since schooling was not yet compulsory. Many Italians did not understand the value of education, and the economics of 19th-century Italy were not conducive to mass education. The school system was highly decentralized, so a poor town like Carfizzi did not have the resources to provide schooling for children.

In 1972, Andy said, "In Italy, I never learned to read or write. In America, I could see you wouldn't go anywhere without education."[1] Nine years later, he added, "I went to all types of schools here [the United States], day school, night school, correspondence school. I couldn't get enough education to suit me."[2] Besides his lack of formal schooling and his dream of being a cowboy, little is known about the first 12 years of his life.[3]

Located on a hilltop in the Province of Crotone, Carfizzi (*Comune di Carfizzi*) is part of Italy's Calabria region, approximately 15 miles west of the Ionian Sea. If the Italian peninsula is a boot, Calabria is in the toe. Even today, Calabria is remote and sparsely populated. The region's largest city, Reggio di Calabria, has only 170,000 residents.[4] Naples—the closest major city, albeit more than 225 miles away—has a population of 913,000.[5] Carfizzi is still tiny in size and population. The village covers just eight square miles, and its population, approximately 1,343 in 1901, shrunk to just 524 in 2021.[6]

Andy described his father, Francesco Varipapa, as a "wealthy farmer."[7] The elder Varipapa was a farmer but not likely wealthy. At the turn of the 20th century, Italy's industrial revolution was just starting. While industrialization was taking hold in the northern cities of Milan, Turin, and Genoa, things were far different in the south.[8] The economy of Carfizzi in 1900 was typical of most rural towns in Calabria in that most residents earned their living via agriculture. Francesco died at age 33 in 1894. He left the family with some property of no immediate benefit to the family due to legal issues.[9] None of his wealth, if there was any to begin with, accompanied his family to the United States.

Given the political and economic climate of 1903 Italy, it is easy to understand why Andy's family emigrated. Turmoil consumed the Italian peninsula during the first half of the 19th century. In 1815, seven small states (including the islands of Sardinia and Sicily), each with a sovereign government, culture, and dialects, comprised post–Napoleon Italy. By 1850, numerous revolutions, insurrections, and wars consolidated the peninsula into three primary regions: Piedmont-Sardinia, the Papal States, and Two Sicilies.

Historians regard the years 1815 to 1860 to be the most controversial in modern Italian history. The determinants and motivations for the Unification (*the Risorgimento*) are still unclear.[10] In March 1861, Victor Emmanuel II of Sardinia was proclaimed ruler of the Kingdom of Italy, and Turin was named its capital city. In 1871, the capital moved to Rome, marking the birth of modern Italy.[11]

Unification created a national identity for Italy. However, the cultural elite of Piedmont-Sardinia defined its character. The North's political structure, foreign policy, and legal and social norms formed the basis of the Italian constitution.[12] Those in the South were disproportionally affected because of higher illiteracy and poverty rates than the North. Southern Italians were poor, oppressed, and held out little hope for change. The stage was set for the mass exodus of Italians that began in the 1880s and continued unabated until the 1920s.

From 1901 to 1910, more than two million Italians immigrated to the United States.[13] That was more than triple the number that arrived a decade before. Most came from the South and, like Andy, were illiterate.[14] In 1903 alone, of the 233,546 Italian immigrants that arrived at Ellis Island, 84 percent were from the South.[15] Andy and his family immigrated to the United States for the same reasons most other immigrants did. They wanted a better life, to live in a free society, and be protected by a constitution that holds individual rights paramount.

Andy offered various accounts about when and with whom he traveled to the United States. He arrived at age 12 or 13; in 1902, 1903, or 1904; with his parents; with his mother and stepfather; with his mother and one brother; or with his mother and two brothers. Even in Andy's own words, details varied. In a 1972 interview, he said he arrived at age 12 with his mother and stepfather. He confirmed that a year later but claimed he entered the United States at age 13.[16] In 1978, he said he was 12 when he arrived in the United States with his mother and two brothers, not mentioning his stepfather.[17]

Public records confirmed the details of Andy's immigration. Ships' manifests from 1900 to 1905 indicate that several Varipapa families immigrated via Naples from Italy to New York. They came from Andy's hometown of Carfizzi, or the village just south, San Nicola dell'Alto. Unfortunately, no passengers matched the names, ages, or genders of Andy, his mother, stepfather, or brothers.

Four factors complicated these searches. First, Andy's stepfather, whose birth name was Francesco Giuseppe Cardamone, was listed as either Frank or Joseph in future censuses. Who knows what name he might have used when he immigrated? Second, the 1910 census listed Andy as "Andrew Cardamone," the son (not stepson) of Joseph Cardamone, casting doubt on how Andy was listed on a ship's manifest.

Third, family members sometimes changed or truncated their surnames, either on purpose or by accident. For example, my grandfather's family went by "Fruedemann" in Germany but became "Frideman" upon entering the United States. Finally, handwriting can fool optical readers. The technology used to digitize these century-old documents is still a work in progress, so searches may not discover even correctly recorded names.

Andy's naturalization application, signed on July 27, 1910, stated he arrived in the United States aboard the SS *Sardegna* on May 14, 1903.[18] The *Sardegna* left Naples on April 29 and arrived at the Port of New York on May 13, 1903. The ship's manifest listed four passengers from Carfizzi: Concetta Fuoco, age 36, and sons Andrea

(Andy), age 12; Giuseppe (Josh), age 10; and Carmine (Carmen), age six.[19] Concetta's maiden name was Fuoco, and everyone's ages were consistent with their birth dates. She had $10 in her possession. So much for her late husband being wealthy.

The manifest did not mention Andy's stepfather as a passenger under any names he may have used. But the *Record of Detained Alien Passengers* record showed that "Gius. Cardamone, 54 Franklin St., Brooklyn," picked them up on May 14, so his stepfather immigrated to the United States before the rest of the family.[20] The evidence suggests that Andy's 1978 account of his immigration was accurate. He arrived in New York on May 13, 1903, with his mother Concetta, brother Josh, and half-brother Carmen.[21]

Andy's family settled at 145 Skillman Street in the Williamsburg section of Brooklyn, about two miles east of the Brooklyn Bridge. The family joined St. Patrick's, one of the oldest Roman Catholic parishes in the Brooklyn Diocese. They attended Mass two blocks west at the church on Willoughby Avenue. Concetta enrolled Andy and Josh in the St. Patrick's School for Boys grammar school.[22]

A 1900 article from the *Brooklyn Daily Eagle* provided a glimpse into stereotypes faced by Italian immigrants. The story noted that Italians were "industrious," and some had become "prosperous and own their own homes."[23] But it also said that Italians "are, despite popular impression, a cleanly race and are quick to learn ... although their apartments are somewhat crowded, the bed linen, the floors and the surroundings in general are the essence of cleanliness."[24]

Look past the implication that Italians are dirty and focus on the "quick to learn" comment. Many Americans believed that the children of Italian immigrants would never be educated because they were disinterested in school. This stereotype endured for decades for several specific reasons. First, if their parents were illiterate, they could not see the value of education. They may have believed it to be a vehicle for one to move up in social class rather than to develop human capital that allowed the child to get a better job later in life.

Second, many parents believed that education made them disrespectful of adults and undermined the father's position as head of the family. To some, schooling was a subversive activity.[25] Third, children were considered an important economic resource; if they were in school, they were not working.

Finally, getting a decent education was difficult for even a highly motivated immigrant child. Schools did not offer remedial classes for non–English speaking children, jammed 60 to 70 pupils in each classroom, and employed many teachers who bought into the "unwilling to learn" stereotype.[26] Some scholars have questioned the assertion that Italian Americans were disinterested in academics. But that cannot change the fact that in 1900s New York, Italian children aged 6 to 15 were the least likely to attend school.[27] Given the educational environment of the time, the fact that Andy went to school and learned how to speak, read, and write English was a testament to his strong work ethic.

Despite a commitment to education, Andy still needed to work to help support his family. He arrived in the United States during heightened public awareness of the horrors of child labor. While difficult to imagine today, parents viewed newborns as future wage earners. By extension, the more children a woman had, the better. In a rural setting, parents expected children as young as five to help on the farm by planting crops, harvesting them, feeding chickens, or mending fences.

Industrialization improved farm productivity, and in the face of the decreasing demand for labor in rural areas, families began to migrate to cities. Many children found work in factories—often out of the public eye—while some found work in the streets. Urban residents saw kids selling newspapers ("newsies"), shining shoes, and delivering messages and packages.

The Federal Government chose to leave child labor legislation up to the states. By 1903, New York State had weighed in on compulsory schooling and child labor. Children under 16 had to attend school. Businesses could hire children between 14 and 16 with proof of school attendance and could not employ any child under 14.[28] Employers routinely ignored these laws, as did parents. Without sufficient enforcement, school truancy and child labor were commonplace until after World War I. Despite being under 14, Andy began working soon after he arrived in Williamsburg.

It is unclear what Andy's first job was. In a 1972 profile, he said his first job was as a pinboy and suggested it was what got him interested in becoming a bowler: "Whenever the lanes were free, I'd practice."[29] He previously said his first job was as a butcher's delivery boy and that he spent "every cent" on bowling. One writer noted how his job performance suffered because of his bowling obsession: "The rump roasts, pigs' feet, sausages and other Brooklyn standbys often were late arriving to their kitchen destinations because Andy was looking in at the local bowling alleys."[30] In 1960 he explained that butcher boy was his first job, and he worked as a pinboy on evenings and weekends to make a few extra bucks, which seems the most plausible scenario.[31]

Pinboy ranked close to the bottom in the pecking order of unskilled jobs at the turn of the 20th century. Before the widespread adoption of automatic pinsetters in the 1950s, every alley required a person to set and reset pins as needed. The job was simple but required strength, stamina, and decent hand-eye coordination.

One game of bowling consists of 10 frames, and from the pinboy's perspective, each frame was the same task: (1) Set up 10 15-inch high, three-and-a-half pound pins one foot apart in the traditional triangular shape. (2) After the ball hits the pins, jump down from a perch above the pit and retrieve the 16-pound ball. (3) Place the ball on a four-foot-high return ramp and push it back towards the bowler with enough energy to move it 60 feet. (4) If the first ball knocked down all 10 pins, set 10 pins for the next bowler. (5) If not, remove any pins knocked down but remaining on the pin deck ("dead wood"). The pinboy repeated the procedure after the spare shot, returned the ball, cleared the pin deck, and reset 10 pins for the next bowler.

The typical bowler of the day averaging 150 might throw two or three strikes a game, so the process repeated about 17 times per game. A 1950s pinboy described his actions "as fast and nearly as well choreographed as a NASCAR tire change."[32] Good pinboys covered two lanes at a time, so two five-person teams bowling three games each translated to 30 games of work per shift for a pinboy. During 30 games, a pinboy had to jump into the pit about 500 times, set 10,000 pounds of pins, and lift 8,000 pounds of bowling balls, all in about two hours.

Working conditions for pinboys were poor. They usually worked underground, where it was cold and damp in the winter and hot and steamy in the summer. The pit was cramped, and the air filled with cigar and cigarette smoke. The most significant danger was getting clocked by a pin. Bowling balls travel up to 18 miles per hour, and when a round ball hits round pins, they fly in unpredictable directions. From their perch in the corner of the pit, pinboys routinely suffered bruised shins, split lips, dislocated fingers, lost teeth, and the occasional concussion. "I got hit really good right in the forehead," recalled one former pinboy, "and it knocked me out cold. I was laid out for quite a few minutes."[33]

For all this danger, pinboys were not paid very well. While a few busy establishments paid a weekly salary of $4 to $5 per week (plus a cot to sleep on), most pinboys received a piece wage. Pay differed slightly across the country, but a New York pinboy in 1903 earned one and a half to two cents per game.[34] On a busy night, a pinboy might handle 30–40 games, so depending on how many nights they worked, a good pinboy earned $3 to $4 per week. It does not sound like much, but it was in line with the 1905 national average weekly wage of $3.46 ($119.28 in 2023 dollars) for children under 16. However, it was far below the average adult male wage of $11.16 ($384.72 in 2023 dollars) per week and insufficient to compensate for the lousy working conditions relative to other occupations.[35]

Andy's career as a pinboy probably did not last too long. Working as a delivery boy, earning about the same wage, seemed like a more palatable alternative. While the streets of 1903 Brooklyn may have been dangerous, that paled compared to working in a stuffy basement, dodging flying pins, and being cursed at by drunken men. New York City weather notwithstanding, being outside, meeting different people, and earning a tip here and there was a better job for a 13-year-old boy.

Even if his pinboy career was short, it exposed Andy to the sport. Most of his rivals, including Frank Benkovic, Charley Daw, and Joe Falcaro, spent time in the pits, as did future all-time greats Don Carter, Dick Weber, and Earl Anthony.[36] Even Marion Ladewig, perhaps the greatest female bowler ever, worked as a "pinboy" in the 1930s.[37]

As proprietors adopted the automatic pinsetter in the mid–1950s, the job of a pinboy gradually became obsolete. The pipeline of pinboys who became great bowlers disappeared. During the bowling boom of the late 1950s, junior programs replaced pinboys as a vehicle to expose young people to the sport. The expansion of high school and college bowling programs did the same in the late 1960s and early 1970s.

An analogy is how the motorized golf cart changed the talent pipeline in golf. Before motorized golf carts, most professionals started in the caddie yard. All the great American professionals of the first half of the 20th century were caddies, including Ben Hogan, Walter Hagen, Gene Sarazen, Byron Nelson, and Sam Snead.[38] Had that profession not existed, there was no way that a dirt-poor kid like Hogan could become one of the greatest golfers ever. Andy's brief time as a pinboy exposed him to the sport that defined his life.

Two

The Bowler

A 1935 profile in the *Brooklyn Citizen* mentioned that Andy began bowling at age 14 at the Fraternity Hall alleys.[1] There were at least three Fraternity Halls in Brooklyn, but only one had bowling alleys. It was on the corner of Myrtle and Bedford Avenues, around the block from Andy's home. And like most all bowling alleys of the early 20th century, bowling was not its primary business.

Fraternity Hall hosted meetings, receptions, and dances for organizations such as the Foresters, Knights of Columbus, and American Legion. It housed four lanes as early as 1894, and the alleys differentiated Fraternity Hall from most other meeting places as it gave the meeting-goers something to do after the meeting ended.[2] Fraternal halls, saloons, restaurants, and billiard parlors used bowling alleys like pinball machines and video games in future years. They were amusements designed to get customers to spend more time and money inside the establishment (as *Space Invaders* and *Pac-Man* did for bar business in the early 1980s).

Modern bowling centers typically house 30 to 60 lanes. Early bowling establishments were tiny, some with just two lanes.[3] The median size of a center was, at most, eight lanes. Larger centers, with commensurately more significant investments in bowling, were the exception. The 24 lanes at Joe Thum's White Elephant Alleys in Manhattan made it the largest bowling center in the greater metropolitan area.

Brooklyn was home to several centers with 12 to 20 lanes: J.H. Heissenbuttel's Broadway Bowling Academy, Circle Hall, the Elephant Club House, Universal Bowling Academy, and the Superba.[4] A local trade publication suggested there were approximately 600 lanes in New York City.[5] If the median size of a bowling center was six to eight lanes, there were about 75 to 100 places to bowl when Andy took up the game.

Whether setting pins or delivering roasts, once Andy decided he wanted to do something, he wanted to be proficient at it. Coaching was nonexistent, so someone who wanted to improve their bowling watched others and learned by trial and error. Andy made a good decision when he decided whom to watch. One of his neighbors, just a few years older than Andy, caught his attention. James Melillo, a young phenom, began piling up victories against the local hotshots. He made a name for himself, but the name people remembered was not James Melillo but Jimmy Smith.

Born in New York City in 1882, Smith, like Andy, first saw bowling from the pit at Subway Bowling Academy at 65–71 Smith Street.[6] He spent just six months as a pinboy, after which owner Herman Ehler promoted him to delivery boy. Despite not being around the lanes as much, young Jimmy continued to bowl and honed his game.[7] Brooklyn newspapers noticed him as early as 1900, but his first big win was

Two. The Bowler 17

Pinboys at Subway Bowling Academy in Brooklyn, 1910. Jimmy Smith set pins here, and Andy worked in similar conditions at Fraternity Hall (photographer: Lewis Hine; Library of Congress, Prints and Photographs Division, National Child Labor Committee collection).

in 1902 when he defeated George Fraenkle to claim the Juvenile Championship of Greater New York.[8]

By 1904, Smith was the star of the Brooklyn team of the National Bowling League (NBL). The NBL was an ambitious experiment in which teams from Brooklyn, New York, Chicago, Philadelphia, Toledo, Buffalo, Pittsburgh, and Erie traveled to compete against each other during a three-month season.[9] The *Brooklyn Citizen* lauded his performance: "Jimmy Smith is easily the star bowler of the league … he has rolled eighty-four games in the league now, and has an average of something like 205, which is easily a world record."[10] Starting in 1905, he won the New York City individual championship for five consecutive years.

In 1906, Smith handily defeated Johnny Voorhies, then regarded as the best bowler in the city, six games to three in a best-of-11 match and became bowling's first "world champion."[11] He remained champion for 16 years, defending his title against challengers from all over the country. *Bowlers Journal* ranked Smith as the 14th greatest bowler of the 20th century, and there is little doubt that Smith was the best bowler of the first two decades of the 20th century.[12]

There are two versions of how young James Melillo became Jimmy Smith. The most often repeated account was clever but the figment of some sportswriter's imagination. When he first worked at the Subway Academy, he decided not to use his real name to stay one step ahead of his parents and the truant officer. He noticed the sign outside, "Smith Street," so when Ehler asked his name, he replied, "Jimmy Smith." But even if that happened, the ruse did not work. His father found out he played hooky from St. Patrick's and was none too happy about it.[13]

The version Smith confirmed in a 1936 interview was that as a 16-year-old, Ehler asked Jimmy to substitute on a team in an important match. When the scorer had trouble spelling his last name, he said, "We will just call you Jimmy Smith."[14] He bowled well during the match, averaging 195 and leading the team to victory. And just like that, he was forever known as Jimmy Smith.

Jimmy got lots of attention. Like all adolescents, Andy craved respect from his peers, and it seemed like being a good bowler was one way to get it. "I watched him play every chance I got," said Andy, "and I decided that I would become another Smith."[15] He even practiced during the day by tossing blocks of ice as if he were bowling outside the back door of the butcher shop.[16] While Andy eschewed Smith's down-and-in straight ball for a bigger hook ball, Andy copied his unconventional (for the era) four-step approach.[17]

The approach is what happens before a bowler releases the ball on the lane. The bowler stands holding the ball in front of them, eight to 15 feet away from the foul line. They walk towards the foul line, letting the ball swing back, then down, releasing it at the bottom of the swing, and following through. Bowlers take any number of steps before reaching the foul line. John "Count" Gengler, the mysterious hustler of the early 1900s, took just one step. Conversely, PBA champion Brian Kretzer took nine, 10, 11, or more, depending on how he felt on a given day.

When Andy started bowling, most players took three steps. The four-step approach was uncommon, and almost no one took five. In a three-step approach, the bowler must push the ball away from the body quickly, stand closer to the foul line, or take longer steps to achieve proper timing. (The bowler aims to reach the foul line with the ball approaching their ankle.)

Andy advocated two core principles in his instructional clinics: bowlers must stay relaxed and develop a smooth rhythm walking to the line. He believed taking three steps meant the feet and ball had to move too quickly. Using a four-step approach made it easier to relax and get in a rhythm. Later in his career, Andy adopted and advocated the five-step approach for others. It is the most common approach among today's top professionals.

It was not easy to gauge Andy's bowling prowess as a teenager. Newspapers published scores and occasional stories of everything from top travel leagues to challenge matches. Still, his first mention in a newspaper for anything related to bowling was not until 1918.[18] He certainly may have been an accomplished bowler before then, but his successes, if any, were local rather than citywide. In 1946, Andy said, "When I was about 20, I was a pretty good kegler. At 25, I was really great. But I was known only around my home neighborhood in the Ridgewood section of Brooklyn."[19]

When Andy began bowling, leagues and tournaments as we know them today did not exist. The competitions were ad hoc. When a bowler joins a league today, they commit to bowling for 30 to 36 weeks, on the same day of the week and time, starting after Labor Day and ending around Memorial Day. Leagues did not become common in New York until after World War I.

Tournaments were also rare. The only national tournament was the annual ABC Championships which rotated among various cities in the Midwest. The closest it came to the East Coast was Buffalo (1902 and 1914) and Pittsburgh (1909). The most typical form of competitive bowling was the "challenge match," when bowlers competed in a head-to-head contest. Matches could be one-on-one (singles), two bowlers (doubles), three bowlers (trios or triples), or five bowlers (team).

When well-known bowlers such as John Koster, Jimmy Smith, or Johnny Voorhies participated, newspapers enthusiastically promoted the contest and published the results. If the competitors were popular enough, proprietors charged admission and shared the proceeds with the bowlers. The participants always had "side bet," sometimes for $1,000 ($30,000 in 2023 dollars) or more. But for a relative unknown like Andy, his early bowling exploits happened in anonymity.

In his mid–20s, Andy set bowling aside to spend more time playing baseball and boxing. He cut back on bowling for two reasons. First, he became disillusioned by some of the seedier aspects of the game. Andy recalled that gamblers "were always putting up money to bet, and sometimes the gamblers would doctor the pins to get an edge on the man they were betting on."[20] Shenanigans did not end with pins. Pinboys were bribed to kick pins down, set them off-spot, or put grease in a player's thumbhole. Proprietors rigged lanes and approaches to benefit one player or another. Bowling in the early 20th century was about as reputable as cockfighting.

The second reason was the difficulty of becoming a professional. If bowlers wanted to make money, they had to bet on themselves. The PBA Tour was 40 years away, tournaments were rare, and sports sponsorship as we know it today did not exist. The only way to make money was to challenge another bowler to a match, specify the stakes and the conditions, and have at it. Andy explained, "I never cared much for the gambling part of match play bowling. I really didn't want to take money from other bowlers and I didn't want them to take mine. I wanted to be paid for my bowling talent."[21]

Years later, he recalled a story indicative of why he soured on bowling. Having beaten most local competitors, gamblers brought in a bowler known only as "Pittsburgh Joe" to challenge Andy. Details of the encounter vary, depending on who tells the story, but what is agreed upon is that Andy's friends placed big bets on him.

After losing the first two games, Andy wanted to quit, feeling bad for his friends and suffering from a sore thumb. Jack Sloan—out thousands of dollars—implored him to continue so he could get even. Andy won the next three games. Thinking Jack got even or maybe made a few bucks, he learned a valuable lesson. Sloan told him, "No, Andy. After the first two games I bet on Pittsburgh Joe."[22] Gamblers have loyalty only to their bankroll.

Pittsburgh Joe was Benny Cole, well-known in his hometown of Akron, Ohio, but unknown in New York. He remembered the match differently and said he came to New York to work at Barney Spinella's lanes. It was Cole, not gamblers, who set up the match. After beating Andy in the first two games, he got crushed in game three and realized he better take the money and run. "He began to hit the pocket with rifle-like accuracy," said Cole. "Varipapa really found the alleys. He murdered me in that one and I knew it was useless to continue."[23]

According to Cole, he was not introduced to Andy as Pittsburgh Joe. As Andy was leaving, he asked the stranger's name. "Just call me Joe," said Cole. "Where are you from?" asked Andy. Cole replied, "Pittsburgh."[24] Akron was a popular destination for Andy's future barnstorming, and whenever he saw Cole, Benny reminded him of when he got the best of the great Varipapa.

By 1910, Andy's family moved a mile east to 852 Hart Street, just off DeKalb Avenue, still in the Bushwick section. He still lived with his stepfather, mother, brother, half-brother, and four new half-sisters: Alice, Mary, Louisa, and Alvina. All were born in the seven years since the family arrived from Carfizzi. In his late teens, he took a job as a switchman on the Manhattan side of the Brooklyn Bridge. New York City had just begun to offer "through" service on the bridge as part of its growing subway system. Previously, a local train shuttled passengers from one end of the bridge to the other. He was likely hired when the city first needed switchmen on the bridge in 1908.[25]

The job of a switchman is just what it sounds like. They manipulate switches to ensure that trains travel on the correct track. In Andy's day, switches were mechanical and operated by a lever. Today, switching is electronic and fully automated. Switchmen were also occasionally responsible for coupling and uncoupling train cars. It was a dangerous job; injuries and deaths among switchmen were routine.[26] And, of course, putting the train on the wrong track spelled disaster.

At $9 a week, switchmen were paid more than pinboys or delivery boys. When Andy spoke about his days as a switchman, he always noted how the job made him a better athlete. He exercised by jogging back and forth across the bridge each day, strengthening his legs, which helped whether he was bowling, playing baseball, or boxing.[27]

The less time Andy spent bowling, the more he spent playing baseball, another sport he picked up after arriving in the United States. Andy said that at age 16, he put an ad in a Brooklyn paper that read, "Shortstop desires position with a semi-pro team."[28] Sure, Andy was confident and outspoken, but ads like this were common during that time. The Nassau Professionals responded and signed him to a $5 per game contract after a tryout.

Semi-pro baseball was popular in the early 20th century. In 1914, the Bay Ridge Athletics played in a stadium that seated 4,000 and played games each weekend from May through October.[29] Andy often said that his primary athletic ambition in his teens and early 20s was to become a big-league ballplayer. He also confirmed his distaste for some aspects of the bowling culture when he said, "I liked baseball better than bowling … you meet a nicer class of people."[30]

Baseball of the early 1900s was not exactly a genteel sport. Ballplayers and managers embodied a win-at-all-costs attitude and routinely fought with umpires, fans, and each other. They cheated, tried to injure opponents, and spewed insults that made longshoremen blush. For Andy to suggest that he met more reputable people playing baseball indicated how dreadful things were in bowling alleys.

Andy played under the pseudonym "Andy Bell," believing it was a more suitable name for a ballplayer, and because he "didn't think people would be able to pronounce Varipapa."[31] He was still playing shortstop and batting cleanup for the Professionals in June 1911, but Andy was looking for a new team by July.[32] He took out an advertisement in the Brooklyn *Standard Union*: "A fast all-around player and a heavy batter, formerly with the Nassau Professionals, wants position with a strong light semi-professional team. Has uniform. Andrew Bell, 852 Hart Street."[33] He must not have received any responses because he posted another advertisement with a new position three weeks later: "A good pitcher would like to finish the season with some light semi-pro team. Andrew Bell, 852 Hart Street."[34]

Andy Bell resurfaced in Brooklyn box scores in 1914 as a second baseman and right fielder for the Bay Ridge Athletics. In the following two seasons, he played

Andy, far right, with three unidentified Bay Ridge Athletics Baseball Club members, circa 1914. First known photograph of Andy (photographer unknown; Varipapa family collection).

third base and shortstop for the Cornelia Baseball Club and then second base for the Wayne Club in 1918.[35] He may have played for other teams at other times, but these are the only public mentions of his semi-pro baseball career.

His baseball playing days ended suddenly. In August 1919, a truck hit Andy while he was riding a bicycle, ending his baseball career. A compound fracture of his left leg left it a bit shorter than the right. It was a freak accident in many ways. He usually did not ride a bike but did so to speed up his commute during one of the many transit strikes that plagued Brooklyn in 1919.[36] Andy walked with a slight limp for the rest of his life, but fortunately, he still bowled like nobody's business.[37]

Andy's recollections of his semi-pro baseball experiences illustrate the difficulty of researching the life of someone born 130 years ago. He said (a) a semi-pro team signed him at age 16, (b) he played ball for seven years, and (c) his baseball career ended at age 28 due to a bicycle accident.[38] Obviously, one of those statements is incorrect. He also claimed that he played shortstop and was immediately placed in the cleanup spot in the lineup, making him the team's best fielder and most feared hitter.[39] It sounds just too good to be true.

This is not to say that Andy purposely misled his interviewers; it demonstrates how memories tend to fade over the years. It also illustrates the habit of embellishing one's past accomplishments. All of us are guilty of such transgressions, partly because it is a human condition to remember the good and forget the bad. Psychologists call it "rosy retrospection."[40]

Furthermore, Andy spent years making his living as an entertainer, and his performances included a well-rehearsed narrative. Psychologists suggest that the more attractive the narrative and the more astounding the stories, the closer the star feels to the audience.[41] Andy offered these exaggerations and embellishments to entertain and make a connection, whether he was talking to one person or one thousand.

Separating fact from fiction is challenging, with no one around to confirm or deny newspaper accounts. Consider Andy's boxing career. Many profiles mentioned boxing, baseball, and shooting pool as activities before he focused entirely on bowling. Most reported that Andy "dabbled" in boxing.[42]

His bouts ranged from two to six. Some articles said Andy won them all; others said he lost one or two; a few did not mention his record. One 1949 profile suggested he quit boxing because his wife was not a fan. In the "interests of matrimony," Andy put his gloves away.[43] A 1955 *Sports Illustrated* article stated that Andy won his first five bouts, took a thrashing in the sixth, and quit.[44]

He often stated he did not care much for the sport. In a 1950 radio interview, Andy said that after suffering a chipped tooth, "I thought to myself, this is no game for me, because after looking at those awful, ugly boxers, they look so bad, is this what I'm going to look like when I'm about 40 or 50 years old? So I quit."[45] He sometimes made light of his boxing experiences, quipping, "In bowling the pins go down but they don't hit back."[46]

Standing five feet, six inches tall, Andy the boxer probably had yet to reach his adult weight, usually reported as 180 to 190 pounds. Alternately described throughout his career as chunky, barrel-chested, husky, and even tubby, one cannot imagine him weighing much less than 150 pounds.[47] He likely fought as a welterweight, if not a middleweight, and faced taller and leaner opponents with much longer reaches. One cannot envision Andy dancing around throwing jabs. Instead, he put his head down, got inside his opponent, and flailed away with short uppercuts. He probably fought like a bull in a China shop, wreaking havoc with their more traditional styles. Whatever it took to get the job done!

It does not matter how long his baseball and boxing careers lasted and to what degree he was successful in those endeavors. What mattered is that after his leg injury in 1919, he put baseball and boxing behind him and focused on bowling. Fifteen years and one trip to Hollywood later, he was well on his way to becoming the world's most famous bowler. But that was a long way off. Andy still needed to learn the bowling skills and master the trick shots that made him a celebrity.

Three

Husband, Father, Machinist

Andy used his off-duty hours as a switchman to take classes at the nearby Pratt Institute and trained to become a machinist. At the time, Pratt was a trade school that offered certificates in art and design, mechanics, and engineering. Pratt awarded its first bachelor of science degree in 1936 and is still at its original 25-acre campus on Willoughby Avenue.[1] Andy probably enrolled in courses such as "Applied Mechanics," "Machine Design," and "Mechanical Arts."[2] With just an eighth-grade education under his belt, it is a testament to Andy's work ethic and ingenuity that he completed these courses.

Andy's training helped him land a job as a machinist with the Remington United Metallic Cartridge Company (Remington UMC) in Hoboken, New Jersey. In the initial stages of World War I, France, England, and Russia contracted with Remington UMC to provide them with two million rifles and 100 million rounds of ammunition.[3] These orders prompted Remington UMC to adopt a mass-production technology, which required the fabrication or retooling of thousands of machines, fixtures, and gauges.[4]

In 1915, Remington UMC manufactured firearms exclusively in Ilion, a small town (1910 population 6,588) near Utica in upstate New York.[5] Needing production facilities in more densely populated areas, Remington opened factories in Bridgeport, Connecticut, and Hoboken, New Jersey.[6] By 1917, the Bridgeport plant produced 5,000 rifles, and the Hoboken factory four million rounds of ammunition daily.[7] As a machinist, Andy designed, manufactured, and maintained the metal parts of the complex machinery used in the Hoboken facility. He found work at Remington because of the increased demand for ammunition, but a contributing factor was that he was not German.

In 1910, 27 percent of Hoboken's 70,324 residents were either German-born or of German descent, earning the city the nickname "Little Bremen."[8] Shortly after the United States entered World War I, the Federal Government declared that German residents were "enemy aliens." Some were arrested, others evicted from their homes, and most lost their jobs.[9] That anti–German sentiment might have been the break an inexperienced machinist like Andy needed to get his first job. Given all the indignities he and other Italian immigrants must have suffered in the early 20th century, it was ironic that, for once, being Italian helped Andy rather than hurt him.

Andy earned far more as a machinist than as a switchman. The International Association of Machinists (IAM), a union affiliated with the American Federation of Labor (AFL), represented the machinists at Remington UMC. While the IAM fell short of achieving their lofty objectives regarding pay and hours during the war

Wedding portrait of Vincenzia DeMartino and Andrea Varipapa, June 17, 1917 (photographer unknown; Varipapa family collection).

years, Andy benefited from working as a skilled craftsman in a union shop.[10] At Remington UMC, Andy made at least $21.60 ($513 in 2023 dollars) per week and was eligible for time-and-a-half overtime and double time on Sundays and holidays.[11]

Before taking his job at Remington, Andy met Vincenzia DeMartino, better known as Alice, who immigrated to the United States in 1905 at age seven. They married on June 17, 1917, and moved into Andy's apartment at 209 Palmetto Street in the

Bushwick section of Brooklyn. By then, Andy had lived in four different residences since arriving in the United States but always stayed within a mile-and-a-half radius from the corner of Myrtle Avenue and Broadway.

Andy and Alice wasted little time in starting a family. Daughter Constance (Connie) was born on July 23, 1918, followed by their son Frank on August 17, 1919. Needing more room for their growing family, Andy and Alice moved to 1232 Cypress Avenue in Ridgewood, Queens, less than a mile from their previous residence. Andy became a homeowner for the first time, sharing ownership of the four-family house with his stepfather Frank Cardamone.

While he had a good job at Remington UMC, Andy looked for one closer to home. His commute to Hoboken began with a subway ride to Manhattan followed by a train or ferry across the Hudson River to Hoboken. Travel time was at least one hour each way, if not more. The ramping-up of the war effort gave him a job opportunity in Brooklyn.

The Brooklyn Navy Yard (BNY) was located between the Williamsburg and Brooklyn bridges on the East River. Workers at the BNY built various vessels, including battleships, coal barges, and floating workshops. Convinced that the United States would join the Allies at war in Europe, the Department of Defense implemented a three-year plan to expand the nation's boat-building capacity. The Navy constructed new facilities and expanded existing ones, including the BNY. From 1916 to 1918, employment at the BNY grew from 6,000 to more than 18,000.

Specific to the war effort, the BNY specialized in constructing "submarine chasers." As the name suggested, these vessels were designed to seek and destroy German U-boats.[12] According to his draft registration card, Andy still worked as a machinist at Remington UMC as of June 1917. The BNY hired Andy during their rapid expansions of late 1917 or 1918.

His tenure at BNY began inauspiciously. Based on his experience at Remington, Andy was initially assigned the rank of machinist third-class. After his supervisor saw Andy's skills—or, more precisely, the lack of them—he demoted Andy to machinist fifth-class. The demotion prompted him to return to Pratt Institute and take some advanced courses. By 1920, he achieved the grade of machinist first-class.[13] It was typical of Andy to deal with the issue head-on. He was never one to settle for mediocre or even second best. Andy wanted to excel at whatever he did.

Andy earned the same hourly wage at the BNY as at Remington BMC. The Brooklyn Metal Trades Council represented the machinists, and Andy remained a member of the IAM.[14] (He carried his union card for years after leaving the BNY.)[15] But even at the same wage rate, Andy brought home a much bigger paycheck. During World War I, the BNY required workers to put in 10-hour rather than eight-hour days. The extra two hours of overtime resulted in a 37.5 percent increase in pay.[16] Long hours, yes, but with a growing family, Andy welcomed the additional income. And when he achieved the rank of machinist first-class, he earned 84 cents per hour, the top of the IAM pay scale, a handsome wage in 1920 America.[17]

Furthermore, the BNY was much closer than Remington UMC in Hoboken. From his apartment in Bushwick, he walked two blocks to the Knickerbocker Avenue station and caught the elevated BMT train that ran along Myrtle Avenue. After a 15-minute ride, he got off the Navy Avenue Station at the main entrance to the BNY, saving eight to 10 hours a week in commuting time. His job at the BNY also gave him time to bowl. In November 1918, he joined a league and resumed his bowling career.

The BNY Metal Trades League bowled Monday nights at the Rational Recreation Academy at 398 Fulton Street, close to the foot of the Brooklyn Bridge. Like virtually every bowling center of the day, it is long gone, now the site of a Gap Factory Store. Rational occupied a brand-new three-story building with 12 alleys on the first two floors and billiard tables on the third.[18] A novel aspect of Rational was that owner Frank Dwyer decided to give the so-called American (or Western) System of bowling a try.[19] (In 1918 America, anything west of the Appalachian Mountains was "western.") In the Eastern System, customers did not pay to bowl, a practice called "open play."[20]

Offering free bowling sounds odd. But recall that in the early days of bowling, alleys were extensions of saloons and banquet halls. Proprietors used alleys to lure patrons into their establishments and profited when bowlers purchased beer and spirits. In the West, where the American System was popular, alley owners charged players for each game bowled, so revenue no longer depended on how much customers spent at the bar.[21]

Rational charged bowlers 15 cents per game. With four cents going to the pinboy, Dwyer earned 11 cents of net revenue per game.[22] Given the cost structure of bowling alleys, the 11 cents represented pure profit because most bowling center expenses were fixed. Regardless of the number of games bowled, the owner had to pay rent, mortgage, insurance, taxes, gas, electricity, and water. Under the Eastern system, food and beverage income had to cover all those expenses.

If bar sales were no longer the primary revenue source, alley owners needed to find a way to fill the lanes. Like vacant seats to an airline, empty lanes do the bowling proprietor no good. The American System put bowlers on the lanes through the development of leagues. In the Eastern System, clubs organized bowling contests, and their members reserved lanes for a fixed time and competed. Club members bowled several games against each other in various formats as individuals or teams of up to five bowlers.

But the matches were strictly ad hoc: at the next meeting, players organized new teams and formats all over again, and much like pickup basketball games at the park, players showed up—or not—as they chose. Occasionally, members organized inter-club competitions, with the winning team receiving a trophy, medal, or sometimes cash. These contests created excitement among the club members, and local papers often published the results.

When bowlers join a league, they commit to bowling each week at the same time with the same format and teammates. In 1918, the most common league format was five-person teams, bowling three games weekly for 15 to 25 weeks from October through April. Like in other sports, leagues compiled standings and individual statistics. Structuring bowling around leagues had significant advantages over the club system for both bowlers and alley owners.

From the bowlers' perspective, the serial nature of a league provided season-long competition. As teams battled for wins, anticipation grew as teams chased the championship. It was like how inter-club matches created excitement among club members. But unlike those inter-club matches, leagues went on for weeks, creating rivalries between teams and bonding among teammates. The alley owner benefited by gaining more certainty about the number of games bowled daily. Leagues created more stable and predictable revenue streams and made it easier for managers to schedule the appropriate number of pinboys.

Not everyone embraced the "Americanization" of bowling. Customers are skeptical when they must pay for services that were once free. In the late 1970s, when adolescents (like me) suggested that their parents subscribe to cable television, they were told, *who in their right mind pays for television?* (Admittedly, I said the same about radio until Sirius/XM appeared in a new car.) A few establishments, like Orpheum Lanes, rejected leagues and continued to offer only open play.[23] But with hindsight, the move towards the American System was timely. On January 17, 1920, prohibition became law. Without beer and liquor sales, the Eastern system became untenable.

But even before Prohibition, Rational manager Lee Johns made his case for American bowling: "I thought, until I went West, that [the Eastern System] was the only way of conducting the bowling business. I know different now. The bowling game is better when conducted with the bar eliminated." Johns concluded that the Western System placed "bowling on a sound business basis instead of making it a catch-penny device for a barroom."[24] Whether anyone knew it or not at the time, the widespread acceptance of the American System was a watershed moment in the development of the bowling industry. Paying for games was essential if bowling were to become a legitimate, stand-alone activity.

League members typically enjoyed a social or business connection away from the lanes. Individuals did not simply wander into a bowling center and ask to join a league. Many, like the Metal Trades league, became known as "industrial leagues" because all members worked for the same company in the same industry. Other leagues hosted by Rational during the 1918–19 season included those organized by employees at Western Union Telegraph, J.P. Morgan, U.S. Steel, the American Stock Exchange, and the Edison Company.[25]

Clubs that wanted to bowl at Rational Recreation also needed to commit to the Western system, so the Iroquois Bowling Club, the Interboro Bowling Club, and the Inter-Church Bowling Club all pledged to pay for games.[26] The Metal Trades league ran 22 weeks from November 11, 1918, through April 14, 1919. Teams comprised employees from various departments at the BNY and included the Pipe Fitters, Pattern Shop, Boiler Shop, Riggers, and Electricians.[27]

Andy started slowly during the 1918–19 season. His first-night scores were just 152–162–133 for a 447 series—not even a 150 average—but his team won two out of three games from the Pipefitters.[28] On December 9, the fourth week of the league, Andy finally broke the 600 barrier by shooting 228–179–218 for a 625 series.[29] As the calendar year 1918 ended, Andy was averaging 180 after 21 games, and while modest by his future standards, it was the fifth-highest average among the 60 bowlers in the league.[30]

For most of the season, Andy bowled in the first position in the order (leadoff). Like a batting order on a baseball team, a bowling team's order is not random, at least not in a competitive environment. The team's best player usually bowls fifth in the order (anchor), the second-best player bowls fourth, the third-best bowls first (leadoff), and the remaining two players bowl second or third.

But these are guidelines, not gospel. For example, if the player with the highest average struggles under pressure, and another player is exceptional in the clutch, that player might bowl anchor. Performance in the 10th frame decides many games, so success often depends on a clutch performance by the anchor bowler. An animated and outgoing player sometimes bowls leadoff regardless of their average rank. Their passion can fire up the rest of the team. While it is unclear if Andy's dynamic bowling persona existed back in 1918, if it did, his enthusiasm made him a desirable choice as a leadoff bowler.

The Machine Shop No. 1 team was the class of the Metal Trades league and led almost wire-to-wire. They finished the season with a 55–11 record, four games ahead of the Outside Machinists No. 1 and the Riggers, who tied for second.[31] Machine Shop No. 1 averaged 886 per game, almost 30 pins per game higher than any other team. Their average was more than 250 pins per game higher than the last-place team in the league, Machine Shop No. 2, who finished with a record of 6–60. The wide variance in the standings resulted from a wide variance in talent. However, in 1918, the bowling community did not yet accept the idea of providing handicap pins to weaker teams to improve competitive balance.[32]

Andy finished the season with a 180 average, good enough for fifth highest in the league. Teammate Al Seivert had the highest average with 190; anchorman Robert Grauer finished third at 184. With three of the top five average bowlers in the league—and all 5 in the top 13—it is easy to understand why Machine Shop No. 1 won.[33] Andy's picture first appeared in a newspaper on May 9, 1919, in a *Brooklyn Citizen* photo honoring the Navy Yard Metal Trades league champions.[34]

Andy's finishing with one of the five highest averages in the league came with a significant benefit. Many industrial leagues fielded "all-star" teams to compete in matches and tournaments against teams from other leagues and companies. The BNY five-man team lost a match to the Morse Dry Dock team on April 6. But in the doubles match, Andy shot by far the best series—862 for four games, a 215 average—leading him and Grauer to victory.[35] Andy represented the BNY in the Grand Central tournament in April and the Rational Recreation tournament in May. While he did not win any of these events, Andy got a taste of high-level competition.

Andy's name was absent from the Metal Trades league recaps when the new season began in November. He was recuperating from the broken leg suffered in August, and when he returned to the lanes on December 29, he was not yet 100 percent. Andy bowled 135 in the first game and then sat out the rest of the set.[36] Returning to action on January 26, he bowled games of 155–112–120, followed by games of 147–128–135 a week later.[37] By the end of the season, scores reported in Brooklyn newspapers indicate an average of just 150 for 16 games, a very un–Varipapa-like performance.[38] There is no evidence that he bowled in any tournaments after the season ended, and other than a doubles match with partner Jack Sloan in April 1921, he did not bowl competitively in 1920 or 1921. The Metal Trades league disbanded after the 1919–20 season, a casualty of declining employment at the BNY.

The year 1921 was a significant one for Andy. When World War I ended on November 11, 1918, it was a matter of time until operations at the BNY slowed down. The Navy committed to keeping the facility running for at least two years to finish constructing new ships and repairing those damaged in the war. By late 1920, BNY employees were back to an eight-hour, five-day work week, and along with some across-the-board wage cuts, many employees quit for higher-paying jobs elsewhere. By July 1921, there were only 1,000 civilians left working at BNY.[39] Andy was among those discharged during those massive layoffs in early 1921. Since thousands of machinists were unemployed, finding a new job would be challenging.

Four

Lawler's

After being laid off at the BNY, Andy leased a billiards room at the Empire Bowling and Billiards Academy, 1821 Broadway in Bushwick. He knew going in that it was a temporary arrangement. Empire owner Joe Travaglia (better known as Joe Travis) gave him a five-year lease with no assurances of renewal.[1] One advantage of running the billiards hall was that there were 10 bowling alleys right next door, so Andy practiced anytime they were available.

Andy did what he needed to make ends meet while running Empire. He sold life insurance for John Hancock for about six months, but it was a tough gig in his neighborhood.[2] Andy may have been the best salesman since P.T. Barnum, but most residents in his territory rented small walk-up apartments and lived paycheck to paycheck. They did not have the means to purchase life insurance. He worked for short periods as a tile setter, a pipefitter, in a printing plant, and in a foundry.[3] Andy did not have time to bowl competitively but finally returned to the lanes in the fall of 1924.

In November, Andy partnered with Mike Tepedino in a season-long two-man tournament at Orpheum Lanes. Tepedino worked as an outside machinist at the BNY and bowled in the Metal Trades League with Andy during the 1918–19 season. He was a bowling prodigy, having rolled a perfect 300 game while still a teenager.[4] Andy and Tepedino won the league with 42 wins against 16 losses and earned $37.50 ($638.60 in 2023 dollars) and a gold medal for their efforts. Andy posted the highest average in the league at 189.[5]

His performance caught the eye of Orpheum Lanes owner Phil Spinella. Each year, Spinella captained the Orpheum Five team that participated in the annual ABC Championships (ABCs). He assembled teams that competed for eagles. (Bowlers refer to ABC titles as an eagle because a sculpted eagle sits atop every winner's trophy.) He invited Andy to join his team and travel to Buffalo to compete in the 1925 tournament. It was the first time Andy left New York City.[6]

The ABC holds its annual championships in a different city each year. The first was in Chicago in 1901 and has always used the same format. Bowlers compete in three events of three games each: singles (individual bowlers), doubles (two bowlers), and team (five bowlers). Chicago resident Frank Brill was the tournament star, winning the singles, finishing fourth in the doubles, and raking in $80 ($2804 in 2023 dollars) for his efforts.[7] Brill led the "grand average" list with a total of 1736 for nine games but earned nothing, not even a medal or a trophy.[8] Made official in 1906, the ABC "all-events" title was bowling's most prestigious until the BPAA All-Star tournament began in 1941.

Participation in the early ABCs was geographically limited. Buffalo hosted the 1902 ABC, the most easternmost site until New York City hosted the 1937 tournament. The ABCs did not become national until Los Angeles hosted in 1947. In 1901, of the 60 players who bowled all three events, 87 percent of them came from just three metropolitan areas: Chicago (24), New York (21), and St. Louis (7).[9] No more than two players entered from bowling hotbeds Milwaukee, Detroit, and Buffalo.[10]

As years passed, the number of bowlers participating, and the number of cities represented, gradually increased. Chicago hosted the tournament for the third time in 1924, and more than 10,000 bowlers from 18 states competed, compared to the 210 bowlers from nine states that participated in 1901.[11] The 1925 tournament marked the fourth time Buffalo hosted the ABCs and the third time the Broadway Auditorium was the venue.

Captain Phil Spinella must have believed that Andy was the weakest member of the team. First, each teammate won at least one major title or match. Spinella won the ABC doubles with his brother Barney in 1922. Harry Leavy previously won the Metropolitan championship, and Gus Cook once held the Eastern and Interborough titles. Anchor Harry Cohn rolled 11 perfect 300 games and beat the likes of Jimmy Smith and Jimmy Blouin.[12] Andy won nothing other than the Orpheum doubles.

Second, Spinella placed Andy number two in the lineup, a spot reserved for one of the two weakest bowlers on the squad. Finally, when five-man teams pair up to compete in the doubles event, there is always one odd man out. None of the other four bowlers wanted to partner with Andy, who bowled doubles with fellow Brooklynite Frank Reynolds, the odd man out on his team. Reynolds was talented but far less accomplished than any of Andy's teammates.

In the ABCs, bowlers compete in the team event on one day (three games) and the singles and doubles the next day (six games), or vice versa. The Orpheum Five bowled poorly in the Friday, March 27 team event. Cohn led with a 583, Andy shot 570, but no one else broke 531 for three games. The team finished with a 2,670 total.[13] Their finish was good enough to cash, earning $23 in a tie for 367th place, but miles behind the winners, Buffalo's own Weisser Blue Ribbons, who fired 3,028.[14]

On Saturday, Andy rolled games of 201, 168, and 245 in singles for a 614 total, earning him a tie for 305th place and a $14 prize. None of his teammates cashed.[15] In the doubles event, Leavy (635) and Cohn (638) put together a spectacular 1,273 total, good for third place and a $480 payday, finishing just 45 pins out of first.[16] Their performance illustrated how inconsistency across events makes for profitable tournament play. Leavy rolled just 484 in the team event and Cohn 482 in singles. Their all-events totals were nowhere near the cash line, but their outstanding performance in the doubles event made them the big winners.

Andy performed the best among the Orpheum Five. He rolled 621 in the doubles event, and with partner Reynolds adding 555, their 1,169 total earned them a tie for 213th place and $21.50.[17] His 1,805 all-events total, tied for 81st place, was worth $16. Andy, who always had a sharp memory for figures, recalled netting $113 ($1,959 in 2023 dollars) after expenses on the trip.[18] The extra money may have come from an arrangement in which teammates shared prizes (Cohn and Levy's big score in doubles helped) or winnings in side matches rolled before or after ABCs.[19] Andy's performance, while good, was a harbinger of things to come. He shot consistently well at the ABCs but never won an eagle in 38 tries.

Spinella brought Andy to the 1926 ABCs in Toledo. Spinella and Gus Cook returned, but Fred Kistenmacher and Chris Muller replaced Harry Leavy and Harry Cohn. Phil showed growing respect for Andy's ability by placing him in the anchor position.[20] The "new" Orpheum Five shot 2,709 to cash for a small amount. No one bowled exceptionally well; Spinella led the way with a modest 562.[21] Andy shot 623 with Cook in the doubles and added 607 in the singles for an all-events total of 1,778.[22] He cashed in all four events, but probably not enough to cover expenses. Andy did not bowl the ABCs again until the 1931 event in Buffalo.

After returning from Toledo, Andy began to compete regularly in tournaments and low-stakes matches. However, he knew his lease at Empire Billiards was expiring. The Varipapas moved from the home in Ridgewood that Andy co-owned with his father-in-law to a walk-up apartment at 74 Ralph Avenue in the Stuyvesant Heights section of Brooklyn. Andy and Alice welcomed a third child, daughter Lorraine, on November 9, 1924. Andy faced the prospect of having a wife, three young children, and no regular income to support them.

In 1916, brothers Ed and Jim Lawler purchased an interest in the Hancock Billiard Academy in the Stuyvesant Heights section of Brooklyn. By 1919 they bought out Hancock and renamed the business the Lawler Brothers Billiard Academy (everyone called it Lawler's). The brothers were among the best and most well-known billiards players in Brooklyn. When they enlisted in the armed forces during World War I, the news made the first page of the *Brooklyn Citizen* sports section, accompanied by their photos.[23]

Lawler's hosted tournaments and matches that featured the world's top pocket and three-cushion billiard players. Billiards was popular, and match results appeared regularly on newspapers' sports pages. Willie Hoppe, Ralph Greenleaf, Alfredo de Oro, and Jake Schaefer were household names. The fact that the Lawler brothers were two of the top players in Brooklyn gave the Academy credibility within the billiards community. Their participation in matches and tournaments—even those not held at Lawler's—was good for business.

In the summer of 1926, the brothers installed 10 bowling alleys on a vacant floor in their building and announced an October opening. However, neither knew much about bowling. Ed, the savvier marketer of the two, understood that Lawler's needed strong bowlers to represent them in matches and tournaments. If they did, the Academy could become as well-known for bowling as for billiards.

The Lawler brothers offered Andy the position of bowling manager, and he accepted. While he had little managerial experience, he was an up-and-coming bowler and could effectively represent Lawler's. But it was not like Ed just hired Andy to bowl. Andy refinished pins (made of solid maple in the 1920s), swept the floors, and learned the art of cleaning, shellacking, and waxing lanes.

Andy made an inauspicious debut during Lawler's grand opening gala in October. Leo Lucke, one of the best bowlers in New York, beat him soundly over six games, 1,337 to 1,251.[24] Sadly, it was one of the last matches that Lucke bowled. He contracted tuberculosis in early 1927 and never bowled again.[25] Andy regained his form in early November and starred in a competition against his former Orpheum teammates. While Lawler's lost the five-man match, Andy and his partner won the doubles match, averaging 214 overall. No other player averaged more than 200.[26] On March 28, 1927, Andy rolled his first 300 game—the first at Lawler's—in the final game of a handicap match against Dick Kraft, in which he averaged a healthy 250 for six games.[27]

With Andy on board, Lawler's entered a team in the Brooklyn Alley Owners Tournament. It was the toughest circuit in the borough, maybe in the entire city. Twelve three-man teams bowled in a different center each week against the best bowlers in Brooklyn. During the 1927–28 season, Andy's bowling achievements were headline news: "Varipapa Leads Lawler Team to Victory at Pins," "Andy Varipapa High Scorer in Alley Owners Tourney," and "Varipapa in Great Form."[28] When the tournament concluded in February, Lawler's finished 4th among the 16 teams, and Andy was the league's top player. His tournament-high average of 207.35 was more than 10 pins per game higher than Orpheum's George Stelter.[29]

Andy lost only one significant match during the season. In January, Mel Luft of Park View beat him by 88 pins in a 20-game tilt. The match was so close that Ed Lawler announced a rematch within two weeks, but as often happened in the improvised world of head-to-head bowling, there is no evidence of a rematch.[30]

Andy got his revenge on Luft in May. After the three-man tournament ended, the Alley Owners staged a 100-game singles tournament featuring the top bowler of each team. Luft (216.54) ended the tournament with a higher average than Andy (212.71), but the players' won-loss record, rather than pinfall, determined the champion. Andy coasted to victory with a 72–28 record, while Luft and Stelter tied for second at 65–35.[31]

Andy continued his outstanding bowling during the 1928–29 season. In June, he won a 10-game match against William Casey to claim the Long Island Championship.[32] Andy once again dominated the Alley Owner's tournament. He performed better than the previous year, posting the highest average of 211.90, more than 14 pins per game ahead of Stelter.[33] It is almost unheard of to be 1,000 pins clear of the second-best bowler over 72 games. The margin showed how Andy separated himself from his Brooklyn competition.

Most importantly, Andy's team won the championship in a runaway. Lawler's 52–20 record was eight games ahead of Farragut Lanes and Mayfair Bowling Academy, whose teams tied for second.[34] In 1929, the Alley Owners' replaced the spring singles tournament with a doubles tournament, but the results were the same as in 1928. Andy won high average yet again, bowled the highest single game, and partnered with Charley Ritter to win the tournament. It was a hard-fought victory. After 72 games, Lawler's and Orpheum Lanes (captained by the owner ABC teammate Phil Spinella) tied for first place. Tournament rules called for a 10-game home-and-home roll-off to decide the championship. Andy again showed that he was the class of the league, averaging 221 and leading Lawler's to a convincing 421-pin victory.[35]

The only bowling Andy did during the 1929–30 season was the annual Alley Owners' tournament. Some owners lost interest in supporting the league; only eight teams competed compared to 16 in the first season. Andy won high average again but was far from his dominating self. He averaged just 197.2, and Lawler's finished a distant third behind the champions, Bay Ridge Academy.[36] The league was in danger of folding, having dwindled to eight three-man teams, so the alley owners revamped the tournament for the 1930–31 season. It returned to five-man teams, bowled two nights per week (Monday and Wednesday), and featured 10 alleys. They even advertised the league in Brooklyn newspapers.[37]

By 1930, Andy established himself as one of the best bowlers in New York City. While managing Lawler's, he immersed himself in bowling and benefited from being able to bowl as much as he liked. But he was at a crossroads. Andy wondered if he could make bowling his career or return to more traditional work in a machine shop. His wife Alice preferred the latter.

In the late 1930s, professional bowling as we know it today did not exist. There were not enough tournaments for bowlers to make a living from prize money alone. Bowlers made money in challenge matches, but Andy was opposed to gambling for a living. There was also the risk of losing money in those matches. Even if backers supplied most of the capital, these were dollars that Andy could not afford to lose. Andy picked up some extra money by giving lessons at Dwyer's Academy in Manhattan, but with three kids and a mortgage, making ends meet was not always easy.

A select few, like world champion Jimmy Smith, were popular enough to draw big crowds at exhibitions and get paid handsomely. Andy needed to figure out how to get noticed without a world championship or ABC title. It turns out that the most successful exhibition bowler of the day had a unique quality that other top bowlers, including Andy, could not duplicate. She was a woman.

Floretta Doty McCutcheon was the first famous female bowler. And for several years in the late 1920s and 1930s, she was the best. Born in Iowa in 1888, she moved to Pueblo, Colorado, with her husband Robert and did not touch a bowling ball until she was 35. After being encouraged to bowl to lose weight, "Mrs. Mac" got serious about bowling in 1926 after attending a Jimmy Smith exhibition.[38] Emulating his smooth, controlled delivery, she bowled her first 300 game and 800 series within a year.[39]

When Smith returned to Colorado in 1927, he agreed to bowl against McCutcheon. Smith squeaked a win in their three-game set in Denver, 680–672, prompting Mrs. Mac to ask for a rematch, promising to do better. Smith agreed, and Mrs. Mac took full advantage, defeating the world's champion 704–697.[40] After the match, Smith called her "the greatest bowler I have ever seen."[41] The victory jumpstarted a new career for the 38-year-old homemaker when Brunswick hired her to travel and give exhibitions.[42]

And boy, did she travel. During the 1927–28 season, she averaged 191 for 789 games, and in 1928–29 199 for 871 games, including four 300 games.[43] In April 1930, Brunswick sponsored a "300 Club" tournament in Cleveland concurrent with the ABC Championships. The three-game sweeper was open exclusively to bowlers who rolled a perfect game on Brunswick regulation alleys. Brunswick entered Mrs. Mac into the event, and she did not disappoint. The only woman in a field of 139, McCutcheon finished fourth, shooting 678, just 28 pins behind winner Joe Kissoff.[44]

Crowds flocked to her exhibitions. Part of her attraction was she looked nothing like a bowler. At age 39, she was described as a "quiet, studious, smiling grey-haired little woman who just dropped her knitting."[45] Not powerful, tall, or physically remarkable, Mrs. Mac was a role model for women bowlers of all ages, shapes, and sizes. After tiring of the road in 1939, she opened a bowling school in New York and later one in Chicago. Between her traveling and brick-and-mortar schools, Mrs. Mac personally taught more than 400,000 people how to bowl.[46]

But Andy was not a woman, and he did not have the bowling resume of Jimmy Smith. Despite his dedication to schooling, he spoke with a thick Italian accent. So why would fans pay to watch him perform? He learned to perform trick shots like no one before or since. Bowlers, including Jimmy Smith, Count Gengler, and Mort Lindsey, entertained fans with trick shots after their matches since the mid–1910s.[47] These early trick-shot exhibitions were often little more than converting splits, which, while challenging for the average bowler, were easy for a skilled kegler. Andy was thinking bigger: "I designed most of them in my dreams, and one shot just led to another."[48]

As he developed his trick-shot repertoire at Lawler's, and long before bowling fans knew who he was, Andy heard from another New York bowler. At the time, Joe Falcaro was more well-known than Andy. He was the reigning world match game champion and, over the next 20 years, was the only bowler with as much confidence and braggadocio as Andy. Falcaro's call to Andy in late 1930 forever altered the trajectory of Andy's bowling career.

Five

The Match

A week before Christmas, in 1928, Ed Lawler announced a fund-raiser to aid Leo Lucke, still recuperating from tuberculosis in upstate New York. The highlight of the evening was a 10-game exhibition match between Andy and Joe Falcaro. Falcaro was the best bowler in New York and, within a year, became the world's champion.

Falcaro first garnered public attention by winning the New York individual championship in 1915 while still in his teens.[1] He won two consecutive Dwyer's Broadway Academy championships in 1927, pocketing $1,000 for each win.[2] He earned a national reputation in 1928 when he embarked on a "Cross-Country Marathon Bowling Contest." Accompanied by Sid Sherman of Toledo, the pair bowled 80 matches in 19 states.[3]

Born in Naples in 1896, Falcaro immigrated from Italy to the United States as a child. Like Andy, he arrived at Ellis Island with little more than the clothes on his back and the will to make something of himself. Like Andy, he was supremely confident and a showman, often jumping high in the air after strikes. Falcaro also shared Andy's penchant for talking about himself in the third person. In a 1946 *Saturday Evening Post* profile, he declared, "I've been playing the horses all my life and I must have lost a quarter of a million bucks on those damn things, but they will never have to run a benefit for Falcaro."[4]

But for all their similarities, their career paths and personalities were nothing alike. Falcaro never held a job outside the bowling industry, was unapologetic about being a hustler, and was proud that he was uneducated. He told anyone who would listen that he was a first-grade dropout and boasted that he learned to read and write on his own. Falcaro recalled all his triumphs but few defeats and claimed to have "made more money when I was sixteen than a college professor could count."[5]

Falcaro unabashedly encouraged crowds to cheer for him and heckle opponents during matches. Andy, too, bragged, boasted, and needled his opponents, but he did so with a twinkle in his eye. When Falcaro did the same, his comments came off as boorish. He referred to his marks as "fat Dutchmen," "chumps," and "bums."[6] A frequent radio guest, he instructed the host to introduce him as "New York's Gift to Bowling."[7] His behavior earned Falcaro the not-so-endearing nickname of "Chesty Joe."

But when Falcaro set aside all the nonsense and picked up a bowling ball, few were his equal. And more than anyone else, he had Jimmy Smith's number. Falcaro first challenged Smith when he was the reigning world champion. Falcaro, still a teenager wearing shorts, disposed of Smith in short order. Falcaro fired his first 300 game in a hastily arranged rematch in another victory.[8]

Smith took it well; not long after those losses, he told Falcaro about a dentist in Coney Island who looked like an easy mark. Falcaro hustled the dentist out of $640 and commented that he probably "went back to his office and tried to pull all the teeth on Coney Island."[9] He went on to beat Smith in 1924 (nine games), 1928 (30 games), and again in 1929 (30 games).[10] Unlike most opponents, Falcaro held Smith in high regard and considered him his bowling idol.[11]

Falcaro suffered from heart disease and died of pneumonia in 1951, just 55 years old.[12] Three years later, *Sports Illustrated* writer Victor Kalman—ignoring the adage which warns against speaking ill of the dead—penned what, on the surface, appeared to be a scathing profile of Falcaro. Kalman suggested that it was his bad attitude and behavior that had kept him out of the ABC Hall of Fame: "Falcaro had no respect for anyone but himself ... he profited richly from his own incognito forays into bowling's hinterlands. He did little to enhance bowling's prestige. He was often mixed up in all-night drinking bouts. His foghorn voice spouted profanity in a rich Italian accent."[13]

But the purpose of Kalman's article was not to bury Falcaro but to praise him. He suggested that voters look past his indiscretions. After all, he raised $10,000,000 in War Bonds during World War II, was among the first to teach women to bowl, and promoted the game tirelessly from coast to coast.[14] This is an issue that hall of fame voters in all sports grapple with: should off-the-field behavior—be it exemplary or reprehensible—influence the vote? Members of the Baseball Hall of Fame include racists (Ty Cobb and Cap Anson), drunks (Hack Wilson, Jimmie Foxx, Grover Cleveland Alexander, are just a few), and drug abusers (Tim Raines).[15] Despite his prickly demeanor, voters elected Falcaro to the ABC Hall of Fame in 1975.

The match on December 23 was informal and for a worthy cause, so there was a sense of nonchalance about it. But at the scheduled start time, Falcaro was nowhere in sight. After a short delay, a former Elk's Club champion, referred to only as Mr. Stern, substituted for Falcaro and proceeded to roll games of 150 and 157 to Andy's 227 and 225.[16] It was not much of a match.

Falcaro finally showed up and bowled five games, averaging 223.6. Andy bowled even better, averaging 234.6 for seven games without a game under 225.[17] The match ended after seven games instead of the scheduled 10, possibly because of the late start or because the results became irrelevant once Mr. Stern substituted for Falcaro.

But his showing up late may have revealed something about Chesty Joe's oversized and fragile ego. Of course, there may have been a legitimate reason for his delay. But given his personality, these are fair questions: Did he arrive late on purpose because he could not bear the thought of losing a match to Andy? Was the late entrance showboating? Was his cocky exterior a defense mechanism to hide his insecurities?

In 1928, it was illogical for Joe to fear Andy. Falcaro won $1,000 in the Dwyer's sweepstakes twice, bowled head-to-head matches against the best bowlers in the East, and placed high in the ABCs and the Petersen Classic. Andy's bowling resume included his 1925 and 1926 ABC performances, high finishes in the Alley Owners' Tournament, and not much else. Regardless of Joe's mindset, their match at Lawler's began their on-again, off-again relationship that lasted until Falcaro's death.

In 1929, Falcaro narrowly defeated Detroit's Joe Scribner 12,932 to 12,803 in a 60-game match to win the world match play championship.[18] In late 1930, Falcaro called Andy and asked him to be his partner in a match against two of the top bowlers in Philadelphia, Jim Murgie and Charley Reilly. Andy knew Falcaro in passing; they traveled together to the 1925 and 1926 ABCs, rolled the exhibition match at Lawler's, and crossed paths at some tournaments, but they never bowled as partners. Andy jumped at the chance: "Would I bowl with the champ? Boy! Was I tickled silly. Who'd miss an opportunity to team up with the best bowler in the country?"[19]

The 42-game match consisted of six blocks of seven games each, the first three at Dwyer's Broadway Academy in Manhattan and three more a week later at Bergman & Trucks Casino Alleys in Philadelphia. The stakes were $500 per man ($8,913 in 2023 dollars), and like many big matches of the day, spectators paid to watch (tickets priced at 50 and 75 cents), generating more revenue for the players.[20] Andy was a good local player but had accomplished nothing outside New York City. He had never even been to Philadelphia. This match was his big chance to make a name for himself.

Both teams insisted on tightly controlled playing conditions. Proprietors applied fresh coats of shellac three days before the event, and Andy recalled that "the pinboys wore gloves, new pins were used each seven games, and the alleys were [polished] before each block."[21] Fans filled Dwyer's to watch the first block on Saturday, November 22. The announcer introduced the players before the match: Falcaro as the world's champion, Murgie as the Philadelphia match game champion, and Reilly as the ABC champion.

"Everybody got this fancy introduction except me," said Andy. "The announcer said, 'Andy Varipapa from Brooklyn.' That's all he knew about me."[22] Admittedly nervous, Andy left the 6–7–10 split in the first frame and did not convert it. He spared in the second frame, then rolled 10 consecutive strikes, posting a score of 268. Falcaro added 180, Reilly shot 194, and Murgie 176, and the New Yorkers were off to a 78-pin lead that they never relinquished.

Andy continued an assault on the pins so memorable that he recited the details 50 years later: "I bowled 18 straight strikes. I can still remember my scores in every one of the seven games—268, 245, 257, 279, 279, 279, 214. I won. From then on, I was made."[23] When bowling ended that evening, Andy shot 1,821 for seven games, a phenomenal 260 average. Falcaro bowled well, posting 1,483, but the Philadelphia duo struggled: Reilly rolled 1,369 and Murgie just 1,278.[24]

Andy and Falcaro stretched their lead even further the next day. Andy cooled off a bit, shooting 1,550 (still a 222 average) in the afternoon session, but poured it on again in the evening, firing a 1,710 set. For the first 21 games, Andy averaged 242, Falcaro 220, and Reilly and Murgie 189 each. Incredibly, Andy and Joe won each game by an average of 82 pins and headed to Philadelphia with a commanding 1732-pin lead.[25]

On Saturday, November 29, Murgie put together an outstanding 1,709 set (a 247 average) in the fourth block. Combined with Reilly's 1,369, they cut 243 pins from the New Yorkers' lead but still faced a 1,489-pin deficit.[26] For unknown reasons, Charley Trucks, part owner of Bergman & Trucks Alleys, replaced Reilly before Sunday's action. Trucks was an accomplished player who tussled with the likes of Jimmy Smith, Charlie Daw, and Count Gengler during his lengthy career. Trucks bowled well in the fifth block, averaging 215, but that was not nearly enough to get the Philly team back in the match. Joe and Andy kept pace, surrendering just 12 pins.

With a 1,477-pin advantage going into the final seven games, the outcome was no longer in doubt.[27] When the dust settled, the New Yorkers prevailed by a staggering 1,626 pins. Andy's bowled spectacularly, finishing with a 233 average. Falcaro averaged 210, Murgie 208, and Reilly just 193 (which may be why he sat out the last 14 games).[28] After the match, sportswriters praised Andy. Newspaper articles described him as "the sensation of the match" and his performance as "one of the greatest exhibitions of bowling ever seen."[29]

Andy claimed that his performance solidified his resolve to continue his bowling journey. Years later, he said, "The birth of Andy Varipapa was on Nov. 23, 1930. Right up on 53rd and Broadway … after that, everybody knew who this Varipapa was. That's when my life started."[30] Despite his hot-and-cold relationship with Falcaro, Andy remained grateful. "I owe a lot to Falcaro for having the confidence in me," Andy said. "I knew I was good and he knew it, but it was still a great endorsement for me to have him select me in that match."[31] He added, "Without that break, I might have given up on bowling."[32]

It is easy to forget that Andy was just a few months shy of his 40th birthday when the match was held. He was not some young kid just starting his bowling career or life. Andy was married with three young children at home. At times, he must have wondered, how long can I chase this crazy bowling dream? He also had a mortgage, having purchased a home at 510 MacDonough Avenue, just a few blocks from the apartment he rented on Ralph Avenue. The home still stands on the corner of MacDonough and Patchen Avenues in the Stuyvesant Heights section of Brooklyn.

While Andy was doing well, personally and professionally, the nation was plunging into one of its darkest periods. Historical accounts often cite October 29, 1929, as the day the Great Depression began. But Black Tuesday was simply the peak of a selling frenzy that saw the Dow Jones Industrial Average fall 48 percent from September 3 through November 13.[33] A rapid decline in stock prices can affect the economy because if consumers feel less wealthy, they will spend less.

However, the Stock Market Crash alone did not cause such a crippling economic downturn. Economic historian Peter Temin wrote, "Given the magnitude and importance of this event, it is surprising how little we know about its causes."[34] To paraphrase Donald Rumsfeld, *there are things we don't know we don't know.*

Economists proposed several hypotheses. The Great Depression was caused by the 1929 market crash, increased tariffs, increased inequality in income and wealth, excessive debt, continued reliance on the gold standard, bank failures, and improper monetary policy.[35] History tells us that each has happened in isolation without significantly affecting the economy. Unfortunately, they all occurred simultaneously, with devastating results. Watch any episode of *Air Disasters*: a sequence of minor incidents causes most airplane crashes rather than a single catastrophic event.

Regardless of the causes, the Great Depression was real, and Americans suffered greatly. From 1929 to 1933, real gross domestic product fell by 27 percent, unemployment reached 25 percent, stocks lost 80 percent of their value, and 7,000 banks failed.[36] The Great Depression was the worst economic downturn in American history.

It is far more challenging to quantify the economic effects of the Great Depression on the bowling industry. At first glance, one might expect that the adverse effects on the bowling industry were more significant than in other industries.

Bowling is a non-essential activity, so a reasonable assumption is that funds previously spent on bowling shifted to essentials such as food, clothing, housing, and health care. Predictably, bowling participation decreased during the early years of the Great Depression. There were 23.2 percent fewer league bowlers in 1933 than in 1929.[37]

If the Great Depression had adversely affected the bowling industry, many bowling alleys would have gone out of business. Unfortunately, the available data provide no clear answers. There were 1,986 certified bowling centers in 1929 and 2,944 in 1933.[38] The fact that the number of bowling centers grew by 48 percent during the throes of the Great Depression is startling. But the data may be misleading.

The ABC reported the number of *certified* centers, meaning these alley owners paid a fee to ensure the lanes met ABC specifications. Uncertified centers may have certified to attract organized leagues to their establishments. Without conducting painstaking microeconomic research—city by city, center by center—it is difficult to determine how many bowling centers may have opened or closed each year.

Macroeconomic data does not provide clarity either. The U.S. Census Bureau first assigned bowling centers a unique North American Industry Classification System code in 1997. The category contains information about revenue, employment, capital investment, and other vital statistics specific to bowling centers. Unfortunately, in the 1930s, such disaggregated data was not tabulated.[39]

At the time, the U.S. Department of Commerce included bowling centers among several activities in the "recreation" group. From 1929 to 1933, personal consumption expenditures in the category declined from $4.331 billion to $2.202 billion.[40] That decrease of 49 percent was slightly greater than the 41 percent decline in expenditures across all industries. But this group included not only bowling but also toys, sporting goods, pleasure boats and aircraft, radios, records, spectator sports, musical instruments, amusement parks, movie theaters, parimutuel wagering, books, magazines, and flowers.[41] Because the category was a catch-all for almost any leisure activity, it is impossible to directly measure the impact of the Great Depression on the bowling industry.

One aspect of the bowling industry that appeared immune from the Great Depression was the high-stakes match game scene. Matches for $500, $1,000, and even $2,000 were commonplace, and after his coming out party in Philly, many involved Andy. Falcaro challenged any two bowlers in the country to meet him and Andy for any amount of money, and several teams accepted the challenge. After disposing of locals Barney Spinella (Phil's brother) and Mort Lindsey, the duo went on the road and beat teams from Detroit (Harry Gerloskie and Walter Schackett), Rochester (Tony Buonomo and Butch Hoefner), and Milwaukee (Charlie Daw and Frank Benkovic).[42] Matches were never for less than a $1,000 side bet.

Andy also bowled numerous singles matches and won most of them. He made national headlines during an exhibition match at the Charles Fritz Academy in Queens Village on January 17, 1932. After an opening 300, he reeled off games of 268, 279, 247, 299, and 259, a 275 average for six games. At the time, his total of 1,652 was a world record.[43] The wire service story announcing the record described Andy as a "local bowling instructor."[44] That performance led to Andy's first appearance in the syndicated cartoon *Ripley's Believe It or Not!* on March 10, 1933. Ripley paid homage to his world record score of 1,652 for six games, right next to the facts that "butterfly wings grow 3½ inches in 5 minutes" and "Marie-Henri Beyle, a French author famous under a German name, is buried as an Italian."[45]

A three-week stretch in 1932 best encapsulated Andy's hectic bowling schedule. On April 10, he was in Buffalo, wrapping up the final block of a 60-game home-and-home match with Ray Shultz. Andy collected $2,000 after averaging 212.2 and crushing Schultz by 939 pins.[46] On April 23, 24, and 25, Varipapa and Falcaro squared off in a 30-game match at Dwyer's, the site of their victory against Murgie and Reilly two years earlier. The good news for Andy was that he bowled superbly, averaging 252. The bad news was that Falcaro bowled better, averaging 255 and winning by 73 pins. During the match, each rolled *two* 300 games.[47] Years later, Chesty Joe said about his performance, "If it hadn't been me, I wouldn't believe it."[48]

Andy drove to Wilmington, Delaware, for an exhibition after a day off on April 26.[49] On April 29 and 30, Falcaro joined him in Rochester for a neutral-site doubles match against future ABC Hall of Famers Frank Benkovic and Charlie Daw of Milwaukee. Organized by sports promoter and Rutz's Bowling Hall owner Frank Rutz, 2,000 fans paid $1 each to watch Andy and Joe handily win the 20-game match by 552 pins.[50] And since they had not bowled enough, the pair stopped in Buffalo the following day for an exhibition before returning to New York.[51]

In September, news broke that Andy and Joe had come to a "parting of the ways."[52] One rumor was that their alignment with competing equipment companies broke up the team, but that made little sense.[53] Brunswick sponsored Falcaro for his entire career and Andy, too, until he worked with AMF after his competitive career ended. However, the news of their split was accurate: they never bowled another significant doubles match. There was always talk about them bowling against each other for high stakes, over 60 or 80 games. There seemed to be an agreement on the terms at times, but it always fell through. They retired undefeated as doubles partners.

Andy finished the 1932 season finishing fourth in the Thum's Individual tournament. While he did not win the event, he averaged 228.61 over 115 games, the highest in the league (won-loss record determined final standings).[54] Andy was busy and about to get busier. By 1932, the trick shot routines he practiced daily at Lawler's were polished enough that he was comfortable performing them in public. While his partnership with Falcaro provided him notoriety in the Northeast, his trick shots made him famous worldwide.

Six

Tricks

Andy Varipapa learned to perform trick shots out of necessity. "Everybody wants to hear about those trick shots," he said. "I had to invent these shots to make money. You couldn't make enough in tournaments in those days."[1] He reflected on his distaste for the gambling and shenanigans that permeated the match game scene. Andy did not want to have to bet on himself to make a living and did not aspire to the vagabond life of a hustler. "We didn't have professional bowling in those days," Andy said. "I wanted to get paid to bowl—and trick shots were the best way to do it."[2]

"I would lay awake at night and think up all kinds of stunts," said Andy. "Then, the next day I'd practice them."[3] Making those shots required pinpoint accuracy, and repetition was the only way to develop a requisite level of precision. Andy said, "I practiced so much my back would hurt."[4] Did Andy perform trick shots better than anyone else, before or since? He did. Did Andy become the most famous trick-shot artist in the world? He did. Was Andy the first bowler ever to perform trick shots? No, he was not. The genesis of bowling trick shots occurred decades earlier, thanks to bowling's sister sport, billiards.

Originally called "fancy billiards," trick shot exhibitions have been part of billiards since the early 1800s. Captain François Mingaud, a French army officer, sat in a French prison, convicted of little more than political outspokenness. With time on his hands, he invented and perfected the leather cue tip. Once released, he amazed audiences with his unprecedented control of the cue ball.[5] The leather tip made cue spin (English), the massé, and jump shots possible. Mingaud's 1827 book, *Noble Jeu de Billiard* (The Noble Game of Billiards), detailed 40 trick shots.[6]

His innovation marked the birth of "artistic pool." By the 1930s, future Billiard Congress of America Hall-of-Famer Charlie Peterson proved that a player with talent and personality could make a living giving trick-shot exhibitions.[7] Early reports of Andy's trick shots referenced the relationship with billiards, stressing the limitations of performing bowling tricks compared to billiards. A 1937 profile described Andy as "the Charlie Peterson of the trick-shot bowling world."[8]

Artistic Pool reached the masses in 2000 with the debut of ESPN's popular series *Trick Shot Magic*.[9] The show made stars of the greatest artistic pool players, including Tom "Dr. Cue" Rossman, Mike "Tennessee Tarzan" Massey, and Andy "Magic Man" Segal. Some shots were straight out of Mingaud's 1827 book. However, bowling trick shots never became institutionalized as they were in billiards. Fortunately, bowling did not require an innovation like the leather cue tip to get started. All it needed was a one-eyed hustler from New Jersey.

Garrett (Garry) Green was born in Hackensack in 1869. As a child, Green lost an eye in a cannon explosion.[10] Despite his disability, he became an outstanding athlete and finally settled on bowling as his sport of choice. In the absence of leagues and tournaments, Green built his reputation through challenge matches. Betting as much as $300 (more than $10,000 in 2023 dollars) per match, he must have won more than he lost. The *Passaic News* anointed him "champion bowler of Bergen County for several seasons" in 1893.[11]

His bowling life changed in 1901 after some visiting Buffalo bowlers called him out as a ringer. Green arranged a $100 match with one of the bowlers, introducing himself as "William H. Johnson."[12] Maybe the eye patch gave him away? In 1902, he announced his retirement, claiming that his notoriety was such no one wanted to challenge him.[13] But instead of retiring, he took his skills on the road, visiting Saratoga Springs, Buffalo, Baltimore, St. Louis, and Chicago. He eventually settled in Pittsburgh and, by 1904, acquired the nickname "Dead Center." He was the self-proclaimed "world's most colorful spare bowler."[14]

In Pittsburgh, he earned money organizing tournaments and, for a brief time, managed a bowling and billiards hall. Here, he began to monetize his fancy bowling as he traveled through Pennsylvania, Ohio, and upstate New York. He billed himself as "Dead Center Green, World's Champion Bowler."[15] Green claimed the title although he never challenged, let alone defeated, any great Eastern stars like Jimmy Smith, John Koster, or Johnny Voorhies.

One staple in his act was to bowl exactly any score under 175 upon request.[16] A fan called out a number, and Dead Center rolled it. Another of his stunts was to set up the seven, eight, nine, and 10 pins across 10 lanes and pick them off individually. He offered an even money bet—for any amount—that he could make all 40 shots.[17] Dead Center converted tough splits, including making the 7–8–9–10 with a single ball.[18] None of these feats qualified as "tricks" compared to what Andy did later, but Green became the first bowler to make money giving exhibitions.

The life of a traveling bowler was not an easy one. Green was a drinker, and by age 45, his lifestyle caught up to him. He died penniless in a Rochester hospital on February 7, 1915. His obituary noted that Dead Center was a big spender, having won and lost small fortunes throughout the country. But near the end, Green had to beg to round up the 40 cents needed to buy medicine.[19] His mother, brother, and two wives outlived him.

But his rise and precipitous fall led some to question if a bowler could make a living touring. Most of the top bowlers of the day either managed bowling alleys or had some other source of income. They could not survive on match winnings alone. Maybe Dead Center was not a great test case, given that he was an alcoholic and had no idea how to manage money.

If Dead Center Green was the king of fancy bowling for the first 15 years of the 20th century, Mort Lindsey was the successor to his throne. Born in Newark, New Jersey, in 1888, "The Moose" was a decorated bowler. He won three ABC titles, including the all-events crown in 1919. Lindsey was also a fearless match bowler. Unlike most rivals, he came from a wealthy family and usually backed himself in big-money matches.[20]

If Lindsey ever felt the pressure of bowling for his family's money, it did not show. He trailed then-world champion Jimmy Smith by 88 pins entering the final game of a 20-game match in 1922 and fired a 299 to win. In 1929, in a 60-game match with $5,000 on the line, Lindsey tripled in the 10th frame of the final game to defeat ABC Hall of Famer Billy Knox.[21]

His family fortune allowed him to buy a partial interest in a New Haven, Connecticut, bowling alley at just 23. He later owned centers in Stamford and Bridgeport. Lindsey won the Petersen Classic in 1934, was inducted as a charter member of the ABC Hall of Fame in 1941, and is the only bowler of his era enshrined in the International Jewish Sports Hall of Fame.[22] He competed at the ABC Championships well into his 60s and, at age 64, finished fourth in the annual *Bowlers Journal* tournament, a five-game sweeper which runs concurrently in the same city as the ABCs.[23]

Lindsey was well-suited to be a performer. He was "a delightful storyteller and admirer of good food," and his constant patter while performing trick shots kept fans engaged.[24] He was also a bit eccentric: during a 12-hour marathon match against George Kelsey in New Haven, they donned bathing suits to keep cool.[25] Lindsey was also an experienced billiards player. Artistic billiards shots required intricate and complex preparation and mesmerized audiences. Lindsey watched numerous billiards matches as a teenager, and the sport's trick-shot culture rubbed off on him.[26]

Lindsey probably learned trick shots when he toured the Midwest with Jimmy Smith in 1916. The previous year, Smith traveled with John "Count" Gengler, who entertained crowds after matches with displays of fancy bowling. Gengler was one of bowling's great characters of the early 20th century. Born in Luxembourg in 1877, he learned to bowl in Paris and relieved unsuspecting Parisians of their francs for several years.

Gengler continued hustling after arriving in the United States in 1914. Always resplendent in a vest and tie, he picked up his nickname from a pinboy who saw his walking stick and thought he was a European nobleman.[27] Between the formal attire, cane, one-step approach, French accent, and palm delivery, Gengler looked like a pushover to the locals. They had no idea he was one of the world's best bowlers.

The dapper Count continued his hustle until he was outed in a magazine article titled "Beware the Count."[28] Forced to go mainstream, he made a living touring, often as a shadowy wingman to the classy Smith. When introduced at Joe Thum's White Elephant Alleys in Manhattan, master of ceremonies Fred Biederbecke said he earned his nickname because "after each match, he's the one doing the counting."[29] Smith may have done a few trick shots as the reigning world champion but did not need to. He left those to Gengler, and when he teamed up with Lindsey a year later, Smith passed details of those routines along to his younger partner.

Newspapers first reported details of Lindsey's trick shots in 1921. His repertoire included converting tough splits (including the 7–8–9–10) and bowling exact scores over 10 frames.[30] So far, nothing that Dead Center Green had not already performed. But there was one shot where he set up 20 pins, lined up about 10 feet in front of the pin deck. Knocking them down was not particularly difficult with the pins frozen together (like billiard balls in a tight rack), but it looked impressive! It might have been bowling's first actual trick shot. Newspapers mentioned Lindsey's fancy bowling and trick shot artistry, but only after telling readers he was one of the nation's best bowlers.[31]

His talent caught the attention of John L. Hawkinson, producer of the Grantland Rice *Sportlights* short film series. Each film showcased a sampling of sports, some popular (football, baseball, horse racing) and many less so (jai alai, hurling, ice boating). On March 27, 1927, Pathé released *Weatherproof*, a 10-minute film dedicated to indoor sports. Segments included basketball, gymnastics, and bowling, featuring New Haven's Mort Lindsey.[32]

Like most silent films, *Weatherproof* no longer exists, but the film's copyright application does. The movie's shot list indicated that Lindsey first demonstrated a straight ball followed by a curve ball. Then came the tricks: he rolled his ball between two pins set with a quarter-inch clearance, converted spares with precision (such as making 5–7 split and leaving the 2–8 standing), made the 7–8–9–10 with a single ball, and finished with his 20-pin knockdown.[33] These were the same shots Lindsey had performed for years. In 1931, he appeared in another *Sportlights* short film, *Undercover* (or *Under Cover*). Besides featuring "Mort Lindsey, the world's champ fancy bowler," little is known about *Undercover*.[34]

Andy started by learning to convert difficult splits. The accompanying drawings show Andy's earliest shots, such as converting the 2–4–8–10, 3–7–9–10, and 2–3–7–8–9–10 splits. These early shots were like what Green, Gengler, and Lindsey had performed for years. Making a difficult split is not necessarily a trick shot; it is just a tough shot. And when entertaining a crowd, there is a substantial difference.

After mastering the split conversation, Andy developed complex shots no one had seen. The "double hook" was his very first. He laid the ball down in the center of the lane, aiming for the right gutter. Before the ball arrived, it changed direction and returned toward the left gutter. But before it got there, it changed directions *again*, traveling across the lane to cover the 10-pin.[35] The shot defied the laws of physics.[36]

Andy threw the ball about as well left-handed as right-handed, so he learned to convert the 7–10 split by throwing two balls, one in each hand. Later variations included "the crisscross," where the balls rolled down the lane like a double helix. In another, he converted the 7-pin on one lane and the 10-pin on the lane to the right.

Andy's shots kept getting increasingly creative. Instead of just converting tough splits, he invented new ones outside the boundaries of traditional bowling. The "flying dutchman" used two lanes. He set up the 7-pin on the left lane and the 10-pin on the right. On the left lane, he placed a pin about 15 feet away from the pin deck. When he pulled off the shot, that pin flew across the gutter to cover the 10-pin on the right lane, and the ball continued to cover the 7-pin. Later iterations raised the degree of difficulty by using *three* lanes.

Another favorite was the "tunnel shot." Twenty pins were set up on the lane, creating a tunnel for the ball to pass through. He threw his ball between the pins to convert the 7-pin. Andy used bowling balls as props for some shots, placing them three-quarters of the way down the lane and banked balls off them as if playing billiards.

These shots were spectacular. Syndicated columnist Al Demaree noted, "Some of [Andy's] trick shots would make the old Count turn green with envy."[37] PBA and USBC Hall of Famer Parker Bohn III still marvels at Andy's creativity and ability. "He was the king of trick shot artistry. Andy did things with a bowling ball that nobody back in the day even thought of," said Bohn III. "It's a shame I never got to

Opposite: **Andy drew this diagram of three difficult spares around 1930. Why he signed it upside down is anybody's guess (Varipapa family collection).**

Six. Tricks

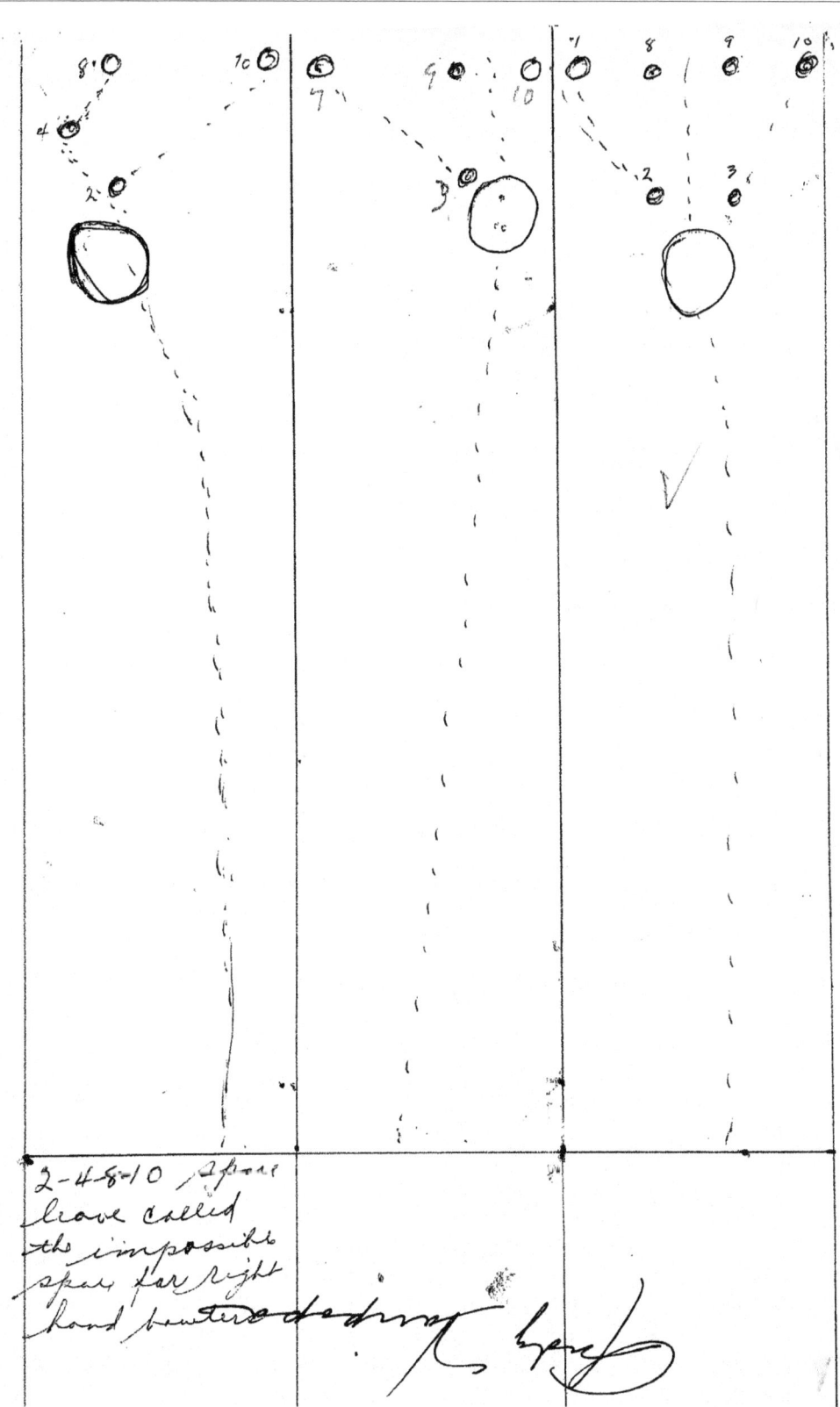

2-4-8-10 spare
leave called
the impossible
spare for right
hand bowlers

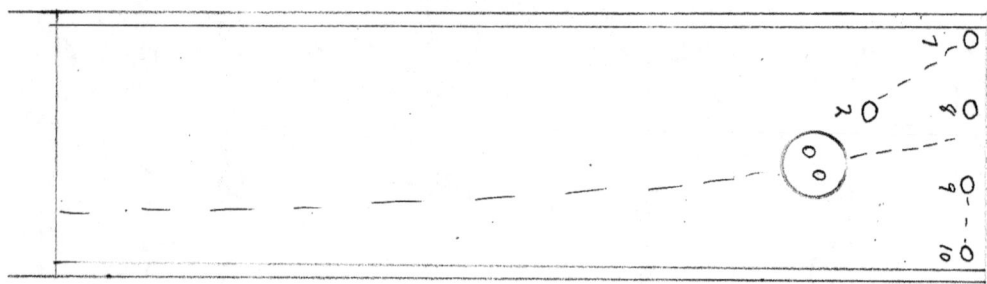

Andy's diagram of how to convert the 2-7-8-9-10 split. Lorraine likely added the typewritten caption, but it is unclear when Andy drew it. It could have been in the 1930s, but more likely closer to 1960 when Lorraine began work on Andy's biography (Varipapa family collection).

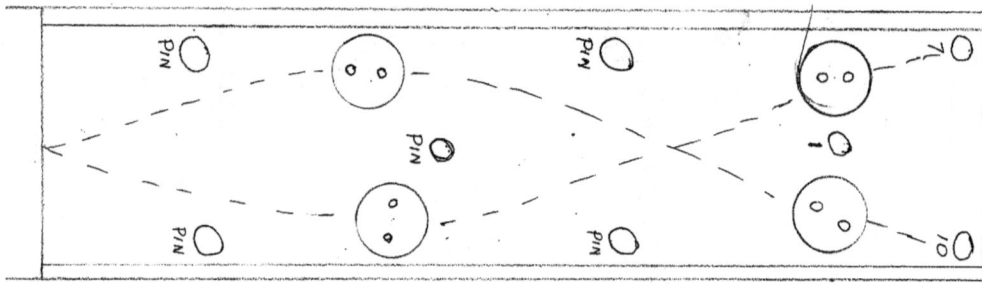

Andy's diagram of the "crisscross" shot with Lorraine's typewritten caption. He did not place pins on the lanes in *Strikes and Spares*. Andy added those years later to make the shot more visually appealing (Varipapa family collection).

watch the man perform those shots live. Because when you watch him on videotape, and see what he could accomplish, as a professional bowler I am still astonished to watch what happens."[38]

Precisely when Andy began performing trick shots in public is anybody's guess. He often bowled with Lindsey and Falcaro and probably did trick shots with them in 1930 or 1931. Jim Crover, a New Jersey bowling proprietor, claimed in a 1977 interview that he gave Andy his first opportunity to display his trick shots in a stand-alone exhibition.[39] In April 1931, Crover hosted Andy and Barney Spinella at his center, Perth Amboy Recreation, not to do trick shots but to bowl a 10-game match against each other.[40] They may have performed trick shots after the match, but Crover did not promote the appearance as a trick-shot exhibition.

Crover also claimed that he showed Andy how to perform many trick shots, including the double cross.[41] That is highly unlikely. At a Metropolitan Bowling Writers Association luncheon honoring Crover in 1978, Andy acknowledged that Crover was among the first to book him but said nothing about him teaching trick shots.[42] When Crover died in 1981, bowling writer Wes Bogle honored Crover as a tireless bowling promoter and called him the "father of organized women's bowling in New Jersey."[43] There was no mention of Andy Varipapa.

Mort Lindsey was the only bowler to grace the big screen until 1932, when Andy and Joe Falcaro appeared in the short film *Sport Slants No 5*.[44] Released on January 16, 1932, it was part of a series of 13 short films distributed by Warner Brothers and hosted by famous sportscaster Ted Husing. Like the *Sportlights* series, each *Sports Slants* film highlighted various sports. *Sport Slants No. 5* ran eight minutes and included segments devoted to bowling, jiu-jitsu, and backgammon. The bowling segment featured Andy and Joe performing what *Film Daily* called a series of "clever tricks."[45] An article promoting the film mentioned only Falcaro, which made sense since he was the world champion.[46] Nothing else is known about the movie, and it is unknown which shots Andy and Joe performed.

Specifics of Andy's trick shots first appeared in the March 25, 1932, edition of the Mount Vernon *Daily Argus*. The article stated that Andy's performance of trick shots drew "thunderous applause" from the crowd of 600.[47] The appearance marked the first time Andy was billed as "The World's Most Sensational Bowler," a soubriquet he used throughout his career. In December 1932, Associated Press correspondent Orlo Anderson wrote a piece describing Andy's trick shots and a photo diagramming his famous "tunnel" shot.[48] This article appeared in papers nationwide, and the word about the little Italian from Brooklyn who made amazing trick shots began to spread.

Trick shots excite us because they are unique. Bohn III said, "When I am doing trick shots, it is to entertain the fans … you try to go out there and do something the average person cannot do."[49] It is something Andy knew as well. PBA and USBC Hall of Famer Bob Learn, Jr., recalled Andy telling him, "Son, when you shoot a 250, some people might remember that in an exhibition. But when you make a really good trick shot, it leaves a lasting effect on them forever."[50]

The modern star best known for trick shots may be PBA and ABC Hall of Famer Norm Duke. He amassed 40 PBA titles, trailing only Walter Ray Williams, Jr., (47) and Earl Anthony (43). Duke is a throwback to bowlers of yesteryear because he was willing to bowl anyone, anywhere, for any amount of money. He also developed a love for performing trick shots at an early age.

Duke vividly recalls learning his first trick shot. After winning a substantial amount of money in a match near his home in Fort Worth, pro shop owner James Askins asked if he wanted to bowl some more. Duke bowled a lot already, so he begged off, but Askins proposed a wager: $200 that Askins could not shoot 140 or better while throwing a ball out of a towel.

After thinking briefly, Duke told him, "By golly, if you can bowl 140 out of a towel, it's worth $200 to see that."[51] Askins rolled 150 and won the bet. He then proceeded to relieve Duke of another $200 that he would not break 180 and another $200 that he would not break 210. While momentarily upset over being hustled, Duke quickly realized that if Askins could perform this trick, so could he.

Norm proved a quick study. After just 20 minutes, he figured out the basics and took the towel shot on the road. He won thousands of dollars from bowlers who believed, as he had, that no one can bowl consistently using a towel. The $600 lost to Askins turned out to be a worthwhile investment. The shot has been the highlight of his trick shot routines ever since. PBA and ABC Hall of Famer Nelson "Bo" Burton, Jr., said, "I've probably done more than a thousand exhibitions, and among the touring professionals I have taken with me, Norm Duke is the best."[52]

Sometimes, without warning, Duke will throw a shot out of a towel in a PBA pro-am, to the amazement of his amateur partners. Once, with the first 11 strikes in a row, he threw the final ball out of a towel. He struck to complete the perfect game.[53] Like Bohn III, Duke realized that if he was going to stand out as a bowler, he needed to do something unique. "I can't dunk a basketball. I can't hit a 400-yard drive," he said. "What I can do is bowl pretty darn well throwing it out of a towel. And it's fun!"[54]

A good trick shot artist needs to be able to make the shots and think on their feet. Andy admitted, "When you performed trick shots live, you couldn't make them all on the first or even second try."[55] Today, we marvel at incredible feats in many sports on YouTube, yet we wonder how many takes were needed. But live performances are without a net.

Billiard Congress of America Hall of Famer Tom Rossman, the winner of countless artistic pool titles, toured the world performing trick shots (and still does). He missed most of them. "I'm the only guy who missed more shots than he made and got paid for it," said Rossman.[56] He was ready with a seemingly endless supply of corny one-liners for when he missed, recalling that "I made a living for 33 years by telling bad jokes."[57] Rossman's point was that performing trick shots takes much more than being a good billiards player. Entertainment value is what fans pay to see.

Andy had the shots and the jokes to go with them. But he needed time to overcome his self-consciousness and "broken Brooklyneese" accent. "I had no diction," Andy recalled. "I knew the words but couldn't say them."[58] But like everything else, Andy worked hard on his delivery. He started by watching movies. "Westerns, comedies, love stories, I saw them all," he said. "I practiced the words as I drove to the next town. Maybe I'd drive 200 miles talking all the way—five or six hours straight. As a result, I now speak with perfect diction—like a Hollywood actor."[59] Andy did not have perfect diction—that was classic Varipapa hyperbole—but his quick wit and self-deprecating humor were well-received by fans.

Andy's trick shots began to pay dividends in 1933. He barnstormed around the Northeast, performing for ever-growing audiences. Andy still bowled matches and tournaments, but his status as a trick-shot expert spread far beyond Brooklyn. "The World's Most Sensational Bowler" made a good living from his performances, but a trip to Hollywood in 1934 made Andy a star. Many Americans who had never stepped foot in a bowling alley saw his amazing trick shots. Andy's impact on American popular culture became far more significant than anyone imagined.

Seven

Hollywood

Movies helped define American popular culture during the 1930s. Boosted by the widespread adoption of sound movies from 1929 to 1932, movie attendance more than held its own during the Great Depression. By the 1930s, 40 million of America's 130 million inhabitants were regular moviegoers, and movies accounted for 20 percent of all recreational spending.[1]

Short films (movies running less than 30 minutes) were integral to the theater experience. A ticket entitled a motion-picture fan to a feature film, a two-reel short, and several one-reel shorts. One-reel shorts ran less than 11 minutes and included newsreels, cartoons, music, travelogues, and novelties. Two-reel shorts ran between 11 and 22 minutes and featured popular acts best consumed in small doses (e.g., The Three Stooges).[2] Shorts were often the proving ground for up-and-coming performers, directors, and producers, deemed not yet worthy of a feature-length budget by the studios. Smaller budgets meant less risk, so studios sometimes allowed directors to try innovative ideas and technologies in short films.[3]

Theater owners did not necessarily want to show shorts. They ate up screen time and cost money to rent, but the studios gave them little choice. The "Big Five" studios—Metro-Goldwyn-Mayer (MGM), Paramount, 20th Century–Fox, Warner Brothers, and RKO—monopolized movie production and distribution. Their collective market power permitted them to engage in anti-competitive practices, including tying arrangements.[4] If an independent theater owner wanted to show *The Wizard of Oz*, MGM bundled its rental with shorts, cartoons, and newsreels. If the proprietor refused to rent the entire package, oh well, then no *The Wizard of Oz*. These practices were commonplace in the movie industry until 1948.[5]

While studios used tying arrangements to maximize profits, the practice ensured screen time for short films. In 1934, studios released approximately 650 shorts (88 from MGM).[6] But since box office data focused on features, it is impossible to determine how many people saw a specific short film. However, it is reasonable to assume that several hundred thousand moviegoers saw the average short.

Pete Smith was among those who saw *Sport Slants No. 5*, the short film Andy appeared in with Joe Falcaro. Born Peter Schmidt in New York's Hell's Kitchen in 1882, Smith held several jobs in the entertainment industry. He was a typist for the vaudeville players' union and wrote song lyrics before becoming a drama critic for *Billboard*. His enthusiastic reviews led several actors and producers to persuade Smith to move to Hollywood and become a press agent. Once there, he quickly retained 35 clients and ran the first independent publicity bureau in town.[7]

In 1925, Louis B. Mayer hired Smith to run MGM's publicity department. Smith worked with stars including Lionel Barrymore, Buster Keaton, Lon Cheney, Joan Crawford, Greta Garbo, and Spencer Tracy.[8] He transformed Mayer's public persona from a one-time junk dealer to the world's most famous studio president.

In 1931, the studio gave Smith 5000 feet of unused rodeo film and told him to "do something with it."[9] He edited the shots and added sound effects and his voiceover. The result was a well-received 10-minute comedy, *Wild and Woolly*. After receiving similar accolades from films based on raw footage of fishing, whippet racing, and cycling, Smith became a prolific short film producer.

Smith's background as a press agent served him well in his new job. He knew what the public wanted and produced one successful short film after another. He focused solely on comedy documentaries; according to some accounts, none lost money.[10] His films often covered sports, including golf, swimming, baseball, football, and auto racing.

Before retiring in 1954, Smith produced over 250 short films and received 16 Academy Award nominations (winning two). In 1953, he received a lifetime achievement award from the Academy "for his witty and pungent observations on the American Scene."[11] Smith may be the only short film producer with a star on the Hollywood Walk of Fame.

Smith wanted Andy to star in his new film, *Strikes and Spares*. It is unclear whether Smith set out to make a film about bowling and found Andy or decided to do a bowling film after seeing Andy in action. What is important is that he chose Andy, rather than Lindsey or Falcaro, to be the star of *Strikes and Spares*.

Lindsey had the talent to perform shots like Andy's. Released in January 1934, Pathé featured Lindsey in *The Super Skittler*. In just 90 seconds, he performed the tunnel shot, the flying dutchman, and converted the 7-pin by kicking the ball down the lane.[12] But unlike Andy, he performed with little emotion. And when he spoke, his New York accent was unmistakable. Ultimately, speech patterns did not matter because, like most Smith productions, the only voice in *Strikes and Spares* would be his. Smith reached out to the ABC, told them of his plan, and requested they contact Andy on his behalf.

In May, Andy received a telegram from ABC Secretary Elmer Baumgarten: "Can you come to Hollywood at once to show your trick shots in a movie short?"[13] Andy's first reaction was that the telegram was a practical joke. A movie? About bowling? And they will pay me $500? He did not take the telegram seriously. Finally, after some prodding by Alice and the kids, Andy called Baumgarten, who confirmed the request was genuine. This was no joke. He told Andy that Smith specifically wanted him and no one else. Armed with some leverage, he asked for expenses in addition to the $500, and the studio agreed.[14]

Ever practical, Alice asked, "What about the Thum's Classic?"[15] Joe Thum hosted the Thum's Individual Classic at his White Elephant Alleys in Manhattan since 1906. It was the traditional season-ending event for the city's top bowlers for several years, and the 1934 edition had just begun. Unlike one-day events, the Classic lasted for months. Each bowler rolled a best-of-11 match against each of the other bowlers (a round-robin), and the bowler with the best won-loss record was the champion. Past winners included Joe Falcaro and Mort Lindsey.[16] Andy was the defending champion. In 1933, he defeated Eddie Heineman in a roll-off after they tied with identical 11–1 records.[17]

Seven. Hollywood

In 1934, the field of 12 included every top player in the greater metropolitan area, including Falcaro, Lindsey, Chester Arnhorst, Eddie Botten, Ray Nolen, and Mike Shirghio. On May 20, Andy squeaked out a 6–5 win against Botten to move into first place with a 3–0 record.[18] When Ralph DeVito lost his match the following week, Andy sat alone in first place.

The tournament ran through early July, so Andy asked the league officers to postpone his scheduled matches until he returned from California. They denied his request, forcing Andy to forfeit his entry fee and any prize money if he did not bowl.[19] Despite Alice's concern, there was not much to think about. Andy earned far more from the film than winning the Thum's classic, so he dropped out despite the allure of a repeat.

Andy's daughter Lorraine recalled her and her siblings' excitement about the prospect of their dad making a movie. On the other hand, Alice was not looking forward to Andy being away for several weeks. He had traveled to exhibitions before, but Andy had never ventured west of the Appalachians, let alone California. He was never more than a few hundred miles from Brooklyn. Sensing her trepidation, Andy asked her, "What do you say, Al? Do I go?" Alice replied, "Why are you asking me? As if anyone could really stop you from doing anything you want to do."[20] She knew that once Andy made up his mind, there was no changing it. Andy prepared to go to Hollywood.

The trip created an inadvertent benefit for Frank. An athlete like his father, he lettered in football, basketball, and baseball, first at Richmond Hill High School and, later, at Adelphi Academy in Bay Ridge. And, like his dad, baseball was his favorite sport. He played on the sandlots every chance he got. But Alice loved the music and insisted he learn to play an instrument. Since her brother Frank was a violinist, her son Frank would be too. He was a much better athlete than a violinist.

Forced to sit through one of Frank's recitals the night before leaving for Hollywood, Andy sensed this was his chance to act. While never exhibiting an ounce of musical talent, he knew bad violin playing when he heard it. Andy announced as he packed his bags: "I've given the matter considerable thought, and I realize your mother has a great appreciation for the arts. But when I get back from California, that fiddle had better be a baseball bat!"[21] Lorraine recalled Frank jumping for joy and skipping to school that morning. She also knew the neighbors were jumping for joy as well. Six apartments shared the same air shaft and courtyard, and the neighbors listened to Frank's lousy violin playing for years.[22]

Andy left his apartment on a beautiful May afternoon and walked to the subway. With a suitcase in one hand and a bowling bag in the other, he boarded a train at Penn Station and was in Hollywood three days later. Los Angeles proprietor Eddie Cleckner met him upon his arrival, having arranged a few appearances for Andy during his stay in Los Angeles. An article promoting his appearance at Lynwood Lanes on June 1 was the first to report that Andy was filming a yet-unnamed movie for MGM.[23] On June 4, the *Hollywood Reporter* revealed that the move's name was *Strikes and Spares*, and shooting commenced on Wednesday, June 6.[24]

Andy met Pete Smith at the MGM lot where Brunswick constructed two alleys under a large tent, which served as the movie's sound stage. Smith told Andy there was no script, and they would make it up as they went along. Andy replied, "OK by me, Pete, that's how I like to work."[25] Andy performed his trick shots with director Felix Feist's cameras rolling, and Smith put the movie together in the editing room.

Andy performed his usual repertoire: kicking the ball for a strike, making the 7–10 split with two balls, the double-hook, and the flying dutchman Smith was particularly impressed with the tunnel shot and suggested a Hollywood modification. He asked Andy if he "could possibly use some real live pins instead of wooden ones?" Confused, Andy said, "Live ones?"[26] Pete told Andy he wanted to replace the pins with 10 showgirls, standing with their legs spread far enough apart to allow the ball to pass through. Smith wondered aloud if there was a danger of the ball hitting any of the young ladies' ankles. Ever confident, Andy snapped, "Of course, I won't hit them! Just get the girls, and I'll show you."[27]

Smith hired the girls and resumed filming. The description of the tunnel shot horrified the showgirls. Being hit with a 16-pound ball traveling 15 or 16 miles per hour would, at best, leave a bruise and, at worst, break an ankle. They must have wondered if this little Italian fellow with broken English could pull this off without hurting them. Andy practiced the shot with one girl at a time, but each jumped out of the way as the ball approached. Whatever Smith was paying them, it was not enough.

To the rescue came little-known actress Sally McKee, cast to throw a few shots during the film's opening sequence. She got the job in large part because she was a decent bowler. McKee stood on the lane, legs apart, and did not flinch as Andy rolled the ball between her legs several times. Gradually, the other girls came around until nine (one still refused) stood as Andy's ball rolled between their legs.[28]

The shot was the movie's highlight. Some advertisements for *Strikes and Spares* referenced the shot with one or more images of a showgirl. Andy repeated the "live" version of the tunnel shot for years, not with showgirls but often with the alley owner, who was often the only person with the courage to stand there. There were no reports of anyone ever being hit, but a close examination of *Strikes and Spares* suggests the shot was not as dangerous as it appeared.

When performing the tunnel shot with pins, Andy set them about 20 to 22 inches apart, leaving a gap of about 16 inches.[29] Considering the radius of a pin ($2\frac{3}{8}$ inches) and the diameter of a ball (about $8\frac{5}{8}$ inches), the setup left about a $7\frac{3}{8}$-inch margin for error. Even for a skilled bowler, a tiny target. And every once and a while, Andy missed the shot, like he did many others. But he knew a miss with "live pins" might hurt someone, so Andy gave himself more room.

A still shot from *Strikes and Spares* showed the first showgirl with her feet spread about 30 inches apart, leaving a gap of about 24 inches between her ankles.[30] The other women took roughly the same stance. This setup effectively doubled his margin of error to 15 inches. For context, a 15-inch target is slightly more than the $13\frac{3}{8}$-inch target needed to convert a single-pin spare.[31] Andy probably converted single-pin spares near the center of the lane 98 to 99 percent of the time. And if he missed, it was not by much. So yes, there was some danger, but not as much as anyone believed.

The movie started with Andy demonstrating some basics, such as the importance of keeping hands dry, wearing bowling shoes, and tossing a hook, rather than a straight ball. Smith scattered his comedy skits throughout the film. In retrospect, they looked corny, but so was everything else in 1930s cinema. The comedy was provided by Buster Brodie, playing a neophyte who falls while trying to bowl, gets his fingers stuck in the ball, and loses his toupee. McKee and an uncredited male appeared during the opening sequence, and veteran actor Ray Turner played "Sunshine," the pinboy.

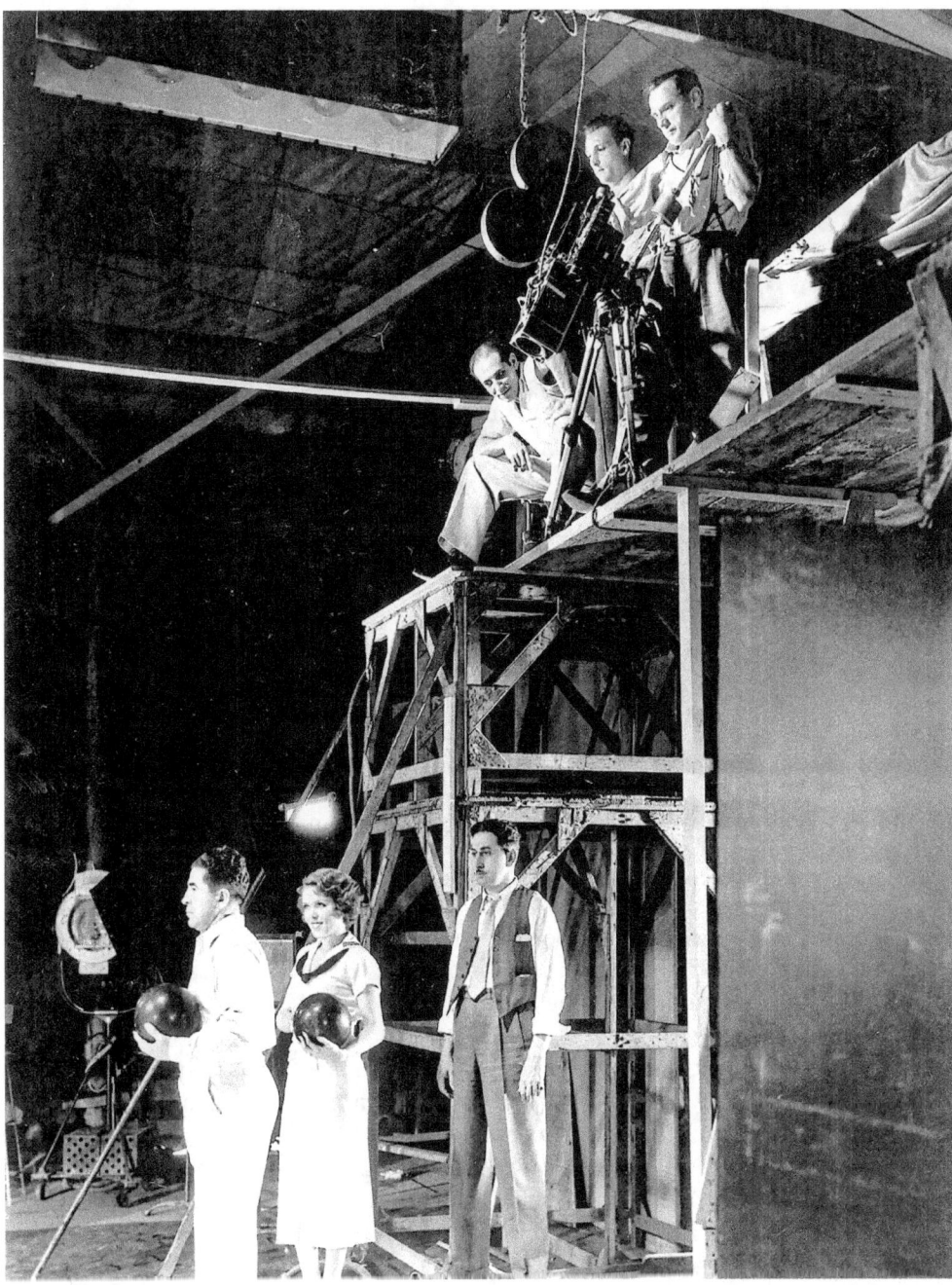

On the *Strikes and Spares* set, Culver City, California, 1934. Foreground (from left): Andy, Sally McKee, and an unidentified man. On the top at left, director Felix Feist looks on with two unidentified men (MGM photograph; IBMHOF collection).

Strikes and Spares, unfortunately, contains healthy doses of racism and sexism. Turner appeared in more than 500 films.[32] Unfortunately, being Black limited his roles to characters such as porter, bootblack, janitor, elevator operator, washroom attendant, and butler.[33] His performance as a pinboy in *Strike and Spares* is

On the *Strikes and Spares* set, Culver City, California, 1934. Andy was preparing for his "tunnel shot" with nine unidentified showgirls. Ray Turner is seated on the left (MGM photograph; Varipapa family collection).

cringeworthy. He smiles often, opens his eyes wide, laughs and claps, and is portrayed as subservient to white characters. Sadly, his role was indicative of the racial norms of 1934 America. It would be 24 years until Sidney Portier earned top billing in *The Defiant Ones*.

The tunnel shot scene displays sexism. Holding the ball, ready to roll his ball between 20 pins, Andy cocked his head and made a bit of a face, unsatisfied. Film magic replaced the pins with nine women wearing long dresses, and Smith's voice announced, "That makes it a little more interesting?" But presumably, because the women wore long dresses, Andy made another face. Smith asked, "Well, what's wrong? You want it a little more interesting?" So again, movie magic transforms the dresses into showgirl outfits with short shorts. Smith finally asks, "How's that, Andy?"[34] Andy smiles and nods approvingly. As Smith warns of the danger to the women's ankles, Andy rolls the ball through their legs and covers the 7-pin without incident. The spectacular shot draws a big smile and applause from Sunshine.

Smith finished shooting the film in about a week. After the wrap, Andy did not make any more appearances; he boarded a train and headed straight back to Brooklyn. He returned home on Monday, June 18, having been away for about three weeks.[35] In July, Pete Smith sent Andy a note: "We previewed the picture the other night, and it went over very big. You will be another Clark Gable after this is

On the *Strikes and Spares* set, Culver City, California, 1934. From left: Sally McKee, Andy, Buster Brodie (MGM photograph; IBMHOF collection).

released."[36] A bit of an exaggeration on Smith's part, but Andy became famous once *Strikes and Spares* hit theaters.

Early showings supported feature films such as *Belle of the Nineties* (starring Mae West), *Cleopatra* (Claudette Colbert), *Today Only* (Loretta Young and Cary Grant), and *Dames* (Dick Powell and Ruby Keeler). Early on, advertisements for features mentioned *Strikes and Spares* in passing, as they might do with any short film, and none cited Andy's name. On October 9, the Orpheum Theater in Madison, Wisconsin, noted *Strikes and Spares*, "Featuring Andy Varipapa, World's Most Sensational Bowler," as an added attraction to *The Last Gentleman*.[37]

Theaters began promoting *Strikes and Spares* independently and running advertisements in the sports section rather than the entertainment section. Later that month, the Strand Theater in Oshkosh, Wisconsin, advertised the film without mentioning the feature attraction: "Attention Bowlers: Hear Pete Smith's Detailed Story, *Strikes and Spares*, Featuring Andy Varipapa, World's Most Sensational Bowler."[38]

In November, local ABC associations and proprietors ran advertisements encouraging bowlers to see *Strikes and Spares*.[39] From Mansfield, Ohio: "Bowlers: Don't Fail to See Andy Varipapa, The World's Most Sensational Bowler, Featured in *Strikes and Spares*."[40] In Sheboygan, Wisconsin, the city bowling association coordinated the sale of discount tickets to the film at all local alleys.[41] Local officials repeated the strategy in cities with large bowling populations, like Chicago, Cleveland, Detroit, and St. Louis.

The proprietor of Blaney's Bowling Alleys in Pomona, California, offered a free ticket to see *Strikes and Spares* to anyone who rolled an all-spare game or threw five strikes in a row.[42] (Winners were welcome to stay and catch the feature movie, *The Count of Monte Cristo*.) Blick's Bowling Center in Atlanta ran a tournament that offered the winner a trophy and a ticket to the premiere of *Strikes and Spares* at the Loews Grand.[43]

Pete Smith foresaw these co-marketing opportunities. In July, he told the *Motion Picture Herald*, "There are 6,000,000 organized bowlers in the United States and they're the most rabid fans you'll find outside of a psychopathic ward…. The national body as well as the individual associations in the various cities throughout the country will go the limit in exploiting this picture."[44] He added, "The sensational plays by Andy Varipapa make good sports page publicity."[45]

Smith's marketing instincts were right on the money. Collectively, short films earned the derogatory nickname of "fillers." *Strikes and Spares* was anything but filler and became the rare short film that sold tickets independently. Nominated for an Academy Award in the Short Subject Novelty category, *Strikes and Spares* ran second to *City of Wax* (a film about a bee's life).[46] Financially and critically, the film was a rousing success.

Strikes and Spares made Andy a star. Fans recognized Andy from coast to coast. Even in places that were not exactly bowling hotbeds, an Italian immigrant from Brooklyn was a bigger drawing card than a comedian born in Oklahoma. In the Idaho Falls *Post-Register*, right beneath the commodities prices (the spot price of lard was 12.32 cents per pound), was a bold headline in colossal type: "Strikes and Spares—Andy Varipapa." Below, in much smaller type: "World's champion trick shot bowler at the Paramount with Will Rogers."[47] Hard to believe that just 10 years earlier, Andy was scraping together a living by renting a billiards parlor, selling insurance, and working as a pipe fitter. Now he was billed higher than Will Rogers.

After returning from Hollywood, Andy began preparing for upcoming exhibitions. He raised his appearance fee from $25 to $50 ($1,135 in 2023 dollars) as the demand for his services grew.[48] Alley owners made money from Andy's appearances in two ways. Some charged admission, and at 25 or 50 cents per person, even a modest crowd turned a quick profit. But the real value was getting people inside the bowling alley and creating new customers. Many proprietors did not charge admission, understanding that if the fans liked what they saw, they might join a league or spend money on open play.

Most proprietors recognized the long-term value of a Varipapa appearance. Getting just one bowler to join a league was worth at least $10 for the season, and what if the bowler stayed for years? A $50 fee sounded like a worthwhile investment. With hundreds of fans showing up to watch, getting just a few new bowlers recouped Andy's fee, and several dozen more was not out of the question.

Most of the proprietors he spoke with over the summer had no problem paying him the $50, and he looked forward to a profitable year. He did not know that his decision to raise his fee would ruffle the feathers of the president of the Bowling Proprietors Association of America (BPAA). The resulting controversy almost ended Andy's barnstorming career just as it was getting started.

Eight

Out in the Cold

Like most years, Andy took the summer off in 1934. Bowling alleys were quiet in the summer because few were air-conditioned. It was all for the best because otherwise, Andy might have been on the road 12 months per year! In July, he received a letter from Elmer Baumgarten which told him how everyone at the ABC was pleased with *Strikes and Spares*.[1] The ABC planned a membership drive in the fall, and the film played an essential part in its growth strategy. Andy agreed to help by encouraging bowlers to join the ABC whenever he performed.

Soon after, BPAA Secretary John Bauer wrote to Andy and described their new grassroots initiative. The BPAA planned to hire several star bowlers to travel the country and give exhibitions and clinics designed to grow the game. In the wake of *Strikes and Spares*, Varipapa was the most recognizable name in bowling, and the BPAA desperately wanted him to be part of the tour. Of course, Andy already toured on his own, but working for the BPAA meant they scheduled and promoted his appearances. All he had to do was show up and perform. Andy wrote Bauer, agreed to join the tour, and requested that the BPAA send him a formal proposal for his review and signature.[2]

In October, BPAA Treasurer and Director of Exhibitions Louis Petersen wrote to Andy with details. Andy would begin touring on November 15 and be booked solid for six months.[3] But there was a problem. While Andy commanded $50 per appearance, the BPAA offered just $15 plus expenses. Insulted, Andy told Petersen he would participate in the tour only if they met his price.

In Petersen's reply dated October 23, he expressed disbelief that Andy turned down their "wonderful offer," adding, "if you feel that you are bigger individually than our Association, that will be your problem later and not ours."[4] Petersen agreed to pay Andy the same rate as the current world champion (Otto Stein of St. Louis) and not a penny more. Petersen closed by imploring Andy to reconsider and to "take care of this matter at once."[5]

The next day, a letter from BPAA president Leo Schueneman arrived. His tone made Petersen's correspondence appear cordial. Schueneman, too, was "shocked" that Andy refused to sign up and asked, "I wonder if you fully realize what you are doing?"[6] He accused Andy of breaking a promise to participate.

But the most stunning part of the letter was a not-so-veiled threat. "Remember that 90% of the large [bowling centers] throughout the country are members of our National Association," wrote Schueneman, "and surely if you do not hook up with us, the feeling amongst them will not be any too pleasant towards you and they may refuse to book you if go out on your own."[7] Schueneman threatened to prevent Andy from appearing at any BPAA-member bowling center unless he fell in line.

Schueneman continued: "Be reasonable—do not kill off a good proposition that is being offered you, because after it is all said and done, you may be out in the cold if you act too independent ... many a good man has fallen down on account of trying to be stubborn."[8] Then, after calling Andy greedy, dishonest, and disloyal, he closed by writing, "I hope you understand the spirit of this letter and I hope I may hear from you with a favorable answer."[9] Oh, Andy got the spirit of the letter, all right. *You may be out in the cold.* If there was even the slightest chance of compromise, Schueneman's condescending letter closed the matter.

Schueneman was right about one thing: Andy was stubborn. It was no longer about money but honor. Petersen and Schueneman accused Andy of going back on his word, despite knowing full well that Andy was not agreeing to anything before reviewing the terms. About the worst thing anyone could do was question Andy's integrity. At an appearance in the 1950s, the master of ceremonies asked Andy when he started bowling. When Andy replied, "In 1905," the MC blurted out, "Really?" To which Andy snorted, "What do you mean, *really*? When Varipapa says something, it's the truth!"[10] Petersen and Schueneman underestimated Andy's resolve. He refused to join the tour.

The BPAA announced its promotional tour in September. The initial roster included Hank Marino, Otto Stein, Joe Miller, Jim Murgie, Joe Bodis, and Marie Warmbier. One article noted, "An effort was made to sign Varipapa of New York for the tour but he rejected the contract."[11] All six were great bowlers—Marino, Stein, Bodis, and Warmbier are Hall of Famers—but none had Andy's star power. They were not entertainers. They did not possess Andy's charisma and flair. And most importantly, none were movie stars.

Excluded from the BPAA tour, Andy had to figure out how to go it alone. Under pressure from the BPAA, alleys in the Midwest that previously booked Andy were no longer interested in his services. Several loyal proprietors continued to book Andy in the East, where the BPAA had less influence. But he needed to make more appearances to make ends meet. There were expenses on the road. Andy drove hundreds of miles, ate at restaurants, and stayed in hotels. He wanted to send his eldest daughter Connie to college, and Frank and Lorraine needed an education too. What Andy needed was someone to book and promote his appearances.

In October, Andy hired Al Cirillo, a vaudeville comedian who performed under the stage name "Windy Jones."[12] He was the perfect person because he filled two roles. Primarily, he was Andy's manager and used his show-business connections to book events all over the northeast. Second, Cirillo often became part of Andy's show. Many of Andy's trick shots were complex and took time to set up. Andy improvised, but it was more entertaining when Cirillo juggled pins, took pratfalls, and told jokes to fill the time. Occasionally, Cirillo had some of his old vaudeville friends join him and perform a skit, "Elmer's First Bowling Lesson."[13]

Cirillo was something of a bowling renaissance man. He did a little bit of everything. In the 1940s, he served as managing editor of the *Bowling News*, bowling editor of the New York *Daily News* and the *New York Enquirer*, and host of radio shows on WBYN in Brooklyn and WMCA in New York. Cirillo later was the vice president of an advertising agency, the public relations director of a bowling apparel company, and the manager of Bethpage Bowl on Long Island. Not all at the same time, mind you. Today, Cirillo may be best remembered as the producer and host of bowling's first television show, *Bowling Headliners.* The show was a template for future bowling shows and sports television in general.[14]

Thanks in large part to Cirillo's diligence, Andy appeared all over the Northeast: Poughkeepsie, Kingston, and Rochester in upstate New York; Newark, Paterson, Hackensack, Long Branch, Vineland, and Passaic in New Jersey; and Pittston, Bristol, Scranton, and Palmyra in Pennsylvania. In January 1935, Andy spent a week in Rochester as the feature attraction of the city's "Learn to Bowl Week." He appeared in nine bowling centers in seven days.[15]

Andy's appearances were big news wherever he went. Newspapers promoted his arrival weeks in advance. Stories and advertisements highlighted Andy as the star of *Strikes and Spares.* With rare exceptions, there were three stages to an Andy Varipapa performance. First, he offered some bowling tips, focusing on his keys of relaxation and rhythm. Second, he accepted the challenge of some local bowlers. Finally, he performed trick shots. If time permitted, he stayed and gave one-on-one instruction to anyone who asked. Appearances sometimes lasted eight hours. Andy displayed incredible stamina and energy.

Andy was far from a natural showman. Hard to believe, but he once thought of himself as an introvert. Recalling his big 1930 doubles match with Falcaro, he said, "In those days I didn't talk—I just made strikes. Now I'm a talking machine."[16] Early in his career, sportswriters commented about his modesty. In 1947, he recalled, "For years, they wrote about 'Unassuming Andy.' Now I'm a showman. That blushing violet stuff didn't pay off."[17] As noted in Chapter 6, Andy worked tirelessly on his speech and diction, honing his routine during the long hours in his car. One can picture people passing him on the highway and wondering *who is this guy is talking to*?

Andy became more outgoing and confident as his English improved. Before long, the blushing violet wilted, and "The Great Varipapa" blossomed. Sportswriters sought him out because Andy liked to talk, had a great sense of humor, and was candid. Byron Schoeman of the *Bowlers Journal* described Andy as "an individual in a nation of conformists, a no-man in a chain gang of yes-men … he stands on his own feet, does his own thinking and asks no favors of anyone. Take him or leave him, just as you like."[18]

Andy knew having the press on his side was beneficial: "I always had a tremendous respect for the press…. The reporters called it as they saw it and I appreciated the value of the printed word."[19] Over the years, Andy filled reporters' notebooks with quotations like these:

- "I'm the world's most known bowler, the most photographed, the most popular."[20]
- "I'm the most skillful, talkative, and controversial bowler who ever lived."[21]
- "Why is Varipapa the best in the business? Because Varipapa lives bowling, that's why!"[22]
- "I was the most knowledgeable. The most skilled. The most versatile. The most durable. There'll never be another Varipapa."[23]
- "The most sensational bowler in the world is Andy Varipapa."[24]

Like any good performer, Andy could think on his feet. His time alone in his car prepared him for almost any situation. Just before he attempted a difficult trick, a fan yelled, "I never saw that done before!" Andy quickly replied, "That is because you have never seen Varipapa."[25] Right on cue, he made the shot on his first try.

In La Crosse, Wisconsin, Andy noticed three priests seated in the front row at all three shows. Andy typically performed the same tricks, with the same jokes, at every appearance. After his final performance, one of the priests approached him and asked if he was doing the same shots at his next stop in Black River Falls. Andy replied, "Father, when you go to a different town, do you change the prayers?"[26]

Hecklers stood little chance of rattling Andy. In Beloit, Wisconsin, one fan gave Andy a tough time and began to disrupt the show. After starting their games with doubles (two strikes in a row), Andy left a split in the third frame, and so did his young opponent. Andy turned and told the crowd, "He's a real gentleman. Refused to take advantage of me and triple when I didn't."[27] Then the heckler's voice pierced the air: "All the bowlers in Beloit are gentlemen!" Andy walked over to the heckler, looked him in the eye, and asked loudly, "And what town are you from?"[28] The crowd roared as his tormentor's face turned beet red. He was silent the rest of the night.

As Andy's confidence grew, he became more candid. He always spoke the truth, even when it hurt. ABC Hall of Famer Bob Strampe bowled an exhibition match against Andy in 1943 at his father's alleys in Estherville, Iowa. In 1977, Strampe recalled, "Once Andy saw me, he said, 'You'll never make it, son.'"[29] Andy did not like his grip, where he tucked his pinkie under his hand rather than spreading it out, which was Andy's preference.[30] Strampe used Andy's comment as motivation: "Varipapa saying I wouldn't be any good was all I needed … bully for you Andy, I'm *going* to make it." After winning the 1964 BPAA All-Star, Strampe reminded Andy about that day: "I turned to Andy and said, 'Hey, Andy, I made it!' He and I became great friends."[31]

Andy had a similar critique of a young Dick Weber. In 1948, Andy told Weber, "Kid, you've got to get a bigger wrist. You've got to have a bigger wrist to bowl good."[32] Weber recounted the story in 1966 while discussing how he dealt with slumps. Rather than listening to the advice of veterans, Weber watched and spoke with the young stars of the PBA. His philosophy was that while the old timers were set in their ways, young players were more open-minded. He put little stock in the opinions of veterans, so rather than brooding over his skinny wrists, Weber continued to practice and became one of bowling's all-time greats.[33]

For Andy, his big, blunt talk was a way of drawing fans' attention. Once he got it, he worked on getting them to love the game as he did. "The game is my religion," he said in 1972, "and I'm like a preacher spreading the gospel. I just can't resist trying to make it easier for somebody who doesn't know what he's doing."[34] Award-winning Syracuse bowling writer Ed Reddy first viewed Andy as a loudmouth, in a Joe Falcaro-ish way. But after he met Andy, he changed his tune.

Reddy wrote, "When you got to know him better, you found out that he had been the greatest … and you realized how much he added to any gathering."[35] He learned that Andy simply wanted to entertain fans and get them to love bowling as he did. He lauded Andy's "good-natured acceptance of any chance to make a speech and his ability to fend off any criticism with a smile. Varipapa had something called class."[36] Reddy learned there were two Andys. Most knew the larger-than-life Andy "The Great" Varipapa. Fewer knew the humble father, husband, and friend.

He was self-deprecating when he knew it could draw a smile. In 1974, Chuck Pezzano asked Andy how he felt when introduced as a fine instructor. Andy replied, "Sure I am. I once wanted to prove how easy it was to teach a woman how to bowl.

I worked a month straight with a girl, and when I unveiled her at an exhibition, she got nervous and rolled a 13." He added, "And I'm the guy who said that Don Carter would have to change his style before he could make it and that Dick Weber would have to fatten up his wrists."[37]

Newspapers not only promoted Andy's performances but recapped them too. Stories often included match scores and the occasional misleading headline. On March 3, 1935, Andy won five of six games against local opponents at Glen Lyon Alleys in Wilkes-Barre, Pennsylvania, outscoring them 1,329 to 1,140. But the headline in the *Times Leader* blared, "Varipapa Loses to Tarutis."[38] True, Jack Tarutis beat Andy 220–177 in their first game, but Andy took the next two, 228–203 and 237–198, and won the series 642–621.[39]

Earlier that day, Andy gave an exhibition at the Sacred Heart school alleys before heading to Glen Lyon. He rolled three games and lost all of them, leaving at least one spectator, "J.A.M., a Bowling Reader," unimpressed. Their letter to the sports editor of the *Evening News* said that Andy "certainly is a trick shot artist, but I was somewhat disappointed with his regular bowling." J.A.M. went to extoll the virtues of a local star who "made all of Varipapa's split shots with one ball" after Andy departed.[40] Journalists and fans were tough to please in Wilkes-Barre!

Andy's appearance in suburban Pittsburgh on March 9 was typical of his grueling schedule. He performed in three different centers, and as always, he challenged the locals to some bowling. Andy won two of three matches at Capital Alleys in Homestead at 3 p.m., eight of nine at Casino Alleys in Wilkinsburg at 7:30 p.m., and all four at Iroquois Alleys in the East End at 10 p.m.

Over 10 hours, Andy bowled 25 games and averaged 210 on alleys he had never seen before.[41] His loss at Homestead was to future ABC Hall of Famer Walter Ward, in town with the Cleveland Waldorf Lagers for another tournament. But at Casino Alleys, Andy made a hometown hero of Chuck Edge, who rolled just 183 but was forever known for defeating the Great Varipapa during his 1935 exhibition.

Beating Andy in a match, even in a single game, was often the defining moment in a bowler's career. In 2008, Robert Ripple died in Rapid City, South Dakota, aged 96. Mr. Ripple lived a long and productive life. A decorated World War II veteran, he returned from duty and became an active entrepreneur in Rapid City. Bob owned two bars, a Buick dealership, and a ladies' clothing store. He was married to the same woman for 56 years and was a director of the Aberdeen Chamber of Commerce and the South Dakota Automobile Dealers Association. Bob was also quite a bowler. His obituary mentioned that he rolled the first 300 game in South Dakota in 1939 and won the Rocky Mountain all-events title in 1934.[42]

But two impressive bowling facts were left out of the obituary: Bob's induction into the Rapid City Bowling Association Hall of Fame in 1982 and his then–South Dakota state record 776 three-game series in 1939.[43] And while those very significant bowling achievements were ignored, this was not: "In 1939, Bob defeated World Champion, Andy Varipapa, 247–236, in a match game at Casino Alleys."[44]

Ignore that Andy was not World Champion, and the year was off by one, but sure enough, the October 17, 1938, edition of the *Rapid City Journal* reported Bob's victory.[45] Ripple's bowling career was defined not as a hall of famer or state record holder but as the guy who beat Andy Varipapa. Dozens, if not hundreds, of those who had the good fortune to defeat Andy had their victory memorialized in their obituaries.

He was getting by on his appearances, but the Great Depression took its toll on tournament bowling. In 1929, the ABC Championships in Chicago attracted 9,888 singles entries and paid $107,790 in prizes. By the 1933 edition in Peoria, Illinois, entries dwindled to 4,687, and the event paid only $60,665.[46] Frank Dwyer stopped running his $1,000 individual tournaments, and Louis Petersen canceled the Petersen Classic after Mort Lindsey's win in 1934. The ABCs in Syracuse was the only tournament that Andy bowled in 1935. He shot a solid 1,834 in all-events, good enough for a small check but well outside the top 10.[47]

His 1935 ABC performance made news in other ways. In the team event, he joined the Grand Websters, a local Syracuse team. His pedestrian 563 series made headlines, but not for the right reasons. One read, "Varipapa Is Disappointing."[48] When he returned for the doubles and singles events a week later, it was not his performance but his partner that was noteworthy. His partner was "millionaire St. Louis sportsman" J.D. Wooster Lambert, an heir to the Listerine mouthwash fortune.[49] Andy bowled well—634 in doubles and 637 in singles—but Lambert gave him little help, adding just 513 to their 1,147 doubles total.[50]

Wooster Lambert was rich. Upon turning 21, Lambert inherited $800,000 (more than $25 million in 2023 dollars) and immediately became "the wealthiest and shyest of all the eligible bachelors in St. Louis."[51] His wealth and willingness to spend it on bowling impacted the sport for years. His team of the 1910s to 1930s, the Wooster Lamberts (yes, he named the team after himself), journeyed to tournaments in a Pullman car accompanied by personal valets.[52]

Lambert was ahead of his time with the idea of a sponsored travel team. In the mid-1930s, Breweries such as Stroh's, Falstaff's, and Budweiser began hiring the nation's best bowlers to tour the country on their behalf.[53] Referred to as the "beer teams," some powerhouse teams were not sponsored by breweries. Heil Products (a heavy machinery manufacturer) from Milwaukee and Hermann's Undertakers (no description needed) from St. Louis were two of the most successful.

Considering all the turmoil, Andy had a successful 1934–35 season. But the BPAA ban limited his work. Cirillo was unable to book anything west of Pittsburgh. The BPAA still ruled the Midwest with an iron hand, and proprietors feared what Schueneman and Petersen might do if they booked Andy. After Cirillo fell ill in May, he and Andy agreed to end their partnership.

That left Andy with no manager as the 1935–36 season approached, and he desperately needed appearances to make ends meet. So, he swallowed his pride, set aside his differences with Petersen and Schueneman, and signed on for the BPAA promotional tour. They booked his appearances, paid expenses, and provided him with a car: a black Lafayette coupe with a giant bowling pin graphic on each door.[54]

The BPAA roster expanded to 10 bowlers for the 1935–36 season. Marino, Stein, Bodis, Miller, and Warmbier returned; Jim Murgie did not. Andy, Ray Nolen, Ned Day, Harry Ledene, Jr., and Mary Jane Hubert joined.[55] The seven men on the tour were among the 10 finest bowlers in the country (Joe Falcaro, Mort Lindsey, and Nelson Burton, Sr., filled out a mythical top-10 list). But Ledene, Hubert, and Warmbier may have been the most popular attractions. Each brought something to the table that none of the veteran stars could match.

The diverse group of bowlers covered all bases. Warmbier and Hubert catered to women, Hubert and Ledene (both 14) to kids, but the other men, while great bowlers, were not entertainers like Andy. Only Ned Day, after he won the world championship in 1937, became as famous as Andy. Andy's personality and ability to command an audience made his performances memorable, and he embarked on the new season with renewed enthusiasm.

Nine

Andy Comes to Town

Andy and Alice climbed into the "BPAA mobile" in early October and headed west. Alice's sister Lottie stayed behind to mind the children. Newspaper stories and advertisements tracked their progress across the nation: Illinois, Wisconsin, Nebraska, Colorado, New Mexico, and Arizona. By early November, they arrived in Los Angeles. Then up to San Francisco, Stockton, and Fresno, followed by several stops in Texas.

Fans packed the alleys wherever he appeared. At a show at Tavener Alleys in Fort Worth, more than 1,000 fans showed up.[1] The fire marshal must have cringed: imagine 1,000 people packing a 10-lane bowling center. Andy did it all: great bowler, trick shot artist, and showman. He was fond of saying he was "bowling's most incredible one-man show."[2]

Before heading back to Brooklyn, Andy stopped in Dallas to bowl a 10-game match against Nelson Burton, Sr., on December 19. The hectic tour left little time for competitive matches, but Andy wanted to test himself against the best bowler not part of the BPAA tour. Andy beat Burton at Hap Morse Lanes, 2,268 to 2,196, firing a 278 in the final game to hold off the hard-charging Burton.[3] The pair tangled again two years later in a memorable 80-game home-and-home test.

Driving home from Dallas, disaster struck. Andy lost control of the Lafayette on a slick mountain road, spun several times, and bounced off both guard rails before coming to a stop. Fortunately, Andy and Alice were unharmed—a miracle in the days of no seat belts or airbags—but the car was a total loss.[4] As they arranged to get another car, some of Andy's long-simmering resentment towards the BPAA resurfaced.

While he agreed to join the tour, he felt underpaid and underappreciated. But he needed the money and benefits the tour offered, so he held his tongue. Staying silent did not come easy for Andy, and when the BPAA informed him they had no plans to replace the car, everything blew up again. Heated phone calls, insults, threats, you name it.[5] When the BPAA tour resumed in January, Andy was not part of it, and Schueneman once again reminded BPAA members that Andy was no longer welcome in their alleys.

Andy's spring 1936 schedule was a lot different than fall 1935. Instead of Chicago, Los Angeles, San Francisco, and Dallas, it was Elmira, Scranton, Binghamton, and Pottstown. And rather than performing six of seven days, it was more like three of seven. In May, he ran into Bill "Whitey" Munn of Elizabeth, New Jersey. Munn was looking for work, and Andy needed a new manager. They crossed paths at local events for several years, and while Munn had little experience as a promoter, he was outgoing and personable. He was a great bowler, eventually earning induction to the Union County Bowling Hall of Fame. And while he did not always outbowl his opponents, he could outlast them.

Munn's forte was bowling long matches. Really, really, long matches. His first was against Philadelphia's Frank Serpico in 1941. Their 100-game match was not unusual, but bowling it in just two days was. They first agreed to bowl a 200-game match *in a single day*; a harebrained idea likely fueled by several alcoholic beverages.[6] After coming to their senses, they agreed to roll 50 games at Serpico's Quaker City Lanes and another 50 at Newark Recreation the following week. It was no contest. Munn beat Serpico by more than 2,000 pins.[7]

After his victory, he declared himself the "World's Marathon Champion." There was no such title; he just made it up. Anyone who disputed Munn's claim was welcome to challenge him. Terms were a minimum side bet of $1,000 over no less than 100 games. Over the next three years, some of the best bowlers in the East tried: Ray Shultz, Fred Voelpel, Joe Krupa, and Serpico (for a second time).[8] Munn beat them all. Taking a page from the Falcaro playbook, he forever billed himself the "Undefeated Marathon Match Game Champion."[9] But unlike Falcaro, Munn's claim made sense because, after 1944, no one challenged him again. When Munn died in 1965, the Marathon Match Game Champion title died with him.[10]

Munn became Andy's manager when the 1936–37 season began and was a tremendous help.[11] Andy focused on performing rather than scheduling and promoting appearances. Besides his regular stops in the Northeast, Munn secured dates in Ohio, Kentucky, and Indiana. But he could not make any headway in Chicago, Detroit, and Milwaukee due to the BPAA ban. As the season ended, Munn told Andy that he did not care much for life on the road. Andy understood his desire to be closer to his family, so when the season ended, they parted ways.

In May 1937, Andy and Nelson Burton, Sr., agreed to an 80-game home-and-home match.[12] They met in a 10-game match in Dallas in December 1935 and may have discussed a rematch at the 1937 ABC Championships in New York. Andy respected Burton and believed a victory would boost his reputation. With all his barnstorming, Andy had not bowled a match like this in years. His status was still as a fancy bowler rather than a competitor. At times, he must have thought his first name was not Andy but "Noted Trick Shot Artist." He resented that reputation but could shake it by winning a big match against a top player.

Since Andy no longer had a manager, bowling promoter and ABC president Al Lattin and Capitol Alleys (formerly Dwyer's) owner Lew Markus negotiated terms on his behalf. As they drew up a letter to Burton, Andy took to the lanes at Capitol to pass the time. Without warming up, he threw 20 strikes in a row. Andy always preferred bowling on freshly resurfaced lanes, but Jimmy Smith, now Capitol's resident bowling instructor, had other ideas.[13] He watched and remarked that Andy would beat Burton by 1,000 pins if the lanes were not resurfaced.[14]

Andy agreed and instructed Lattin and Markus to say nothing about resurfacing the lanes. However, Markus said he received a phone call three days later and was told Burton was not competing without resurfaced lanes.[15] Andy was unconcerned; he figured the lanes would be the same for both and agreed to a resurfacing immediately before each leg of the home-and-home match.

The match began at Capitol on May 24. Each player put up $1,000 and split the gate 50–50. Upon arrival, Burton inquired about the resurfacing. Andy told him that per their agreement, the lanes were resurfaced three days earlier, and no one had bowled on them since. When Andy asked what was happening in Dallas, Burton replied, "My alleys have already been resurfaced."[16] Andy protested, but Lattin told him it was too late to fix things.

The match proceeded as planned, and Andy overcame an early deficit to take a 197-pin lead after 40 games in New York, averaging 212.6 to Burton's 207.7.[17] He drove to Dallas with Alice and Capitol manager George Newman for the match's second half, knowing he needed to bowl great on Burton's home lanes to win.

Andy arrived three days before the match and got some disturbing news. After speaking privately with Burton, Andy discovered that Lattin and Markus demanded the alley resurfacing, not Burton. It looked increasingly like Andy's backers were conspiring against him. Even more startling was that Al Lattin—apparently the shenanigans' mastermind—was the ABC president! Lattin and Markus figured that the few hundred bucks they might lose backing him would be peanuts compared to what they might win betting against him.

Andy asked local ABC officials to inspect the lanes. While the lanes themselves were acceptable, the pin decks were not. Andy said, "Underneath where the pins lay, the floor was shaped like a crescent moon facing the 7-pin. I don't know how they got that way."[18] After repairs, the lanes passed inspection, and the match resumed on June 4. But by then, Lattin and Markus took off for California, leaving Andy alone with Alice, Newman, and hundreds of Burton fans.[19] So much for loyalty.

Andy was furious. Their leaving before he started bowling was the last straw and confirmed his worst fears. It reminded Andy why he wanted to be a baseball player rather than a bowler. Match bowling was a nasty business. It was not as if Andy was not above a bit of trickery, but his methods were subtle. Andy told Carmen Salvino about a match in New York held to determine the city's "best Italian bowler."[20]

Salvino did not recall his opponent's name; it might have been Barney or Phil Spinella, Tony Sparando, or any number of great Italian bowlers. "It's a 20-game match, and Andy is losing at the halfway point," said Salvino. "But Andy noticed that when the other guy began his approach, he pressed his legs against the bench behind the lane. He took long strides and needed to use all the approach."[21]

Salvino continued, "So Andy begins to nudge the bench back ever so slightly after each frame. But the guy still starts his approach with his legs pressed against the bench. After a while, he's starting a foot further back. Now his timing is off because his steps are too long. He can't figure out what's happening until he looks down and sees the dust mark from where the bench started. He starts swearing at Andy in Italian when he realizes what he did. He lost his composure, and Andy won the match."[22]

Burton was confident and wanted to raise the stakes. He needed to pick up only five pins a game in his own house to win. Andy bet $350 of the $1,000 side bet himself, but not knowing what the lane conditions might be, he passed on Burton's offer.[23] Maybe Andy bowled better angry because he took it out on Burton. Andy won all four of the 10-game blocks in Dallas, including the final one by 346 pins, capping off a decisive 1,036-pin victory.[24] He out-averaged Burton 221.7 to 200.5 in his own house! Andy later said, "That was a milestone for me, because Burton was the most feared-match game bowler in the country."[25] Asked if he thought Burton was in on the lane resurfacing chicanery, Andy replied, "No, I don't think so. Burton was a gentleman."[26]

Andy was pleased with his win but still wondered what to do professionally. He was shut out of all BPAA houses except those in the Northeast and did not have a manager. Alice kept begging him to find a stable source of income that did not require him to be away 10 months a year. Andy was almost 50; she wanted him to settle down and buy a local bowling center. But at the time, he may not have had enough cash to do so. Moreover, Andy enjoyed spreading the gospel of bowling across the nation. He was good at what he did and wanted to continue.

That summer, he met with Max Grossman, a friend from when Andy was managing Lawler's. Grossman spent much time in Lawler's billiard room, having been once a top player, traveling secretary of the National Billiard Association, and billiard hall owner. Unlike Cirillo and Munn, Grossman was an experienced promoter and manager, having managed five-time world pocket billiards champion Erwin Rudolph for many years. Grossman was aggressive and a go-getter.

But Grossman's services came at a price. He insisted on a 40 percent share of Andy's income, far more than Cirillo or Munn commanded. Alice was skeptical, but let's face it, she wanted Andy off the road altogether. Grossman had some innovative ideas, and Andy wanted to try him out.[27] He figured 60 percent of something was better than 100 percent of nothing. And the way things were going, it was harder and harder for him to run "Andy Varipapa Incorporated" alone. So, in June 1937, Andy hired Max Grossman as his manager. It might have been the most intelligent business decision he ever made.

Grossman immediately raised Andy's fee to $100, but after applying his slick sales skills, he convinced proprietors they were getting a bargain.[28] Andy enjoyed enormous success with Grossman at the helm. He was booked solid from September through May, and Max always figured out how to get him back to Brooklyn for the holidays.

However, the greater Detroit region presented a problem. A BPAA stronghold, Andy was still a *persona non grata*. In 1938, he had an engagement scheduled at Jim Keating's Alleys in Ferndale, Michigan. A few days before, under pressure from the BPAA, Keating sent a telegram to Andy and canceled. Andy returned the message and said, "I have a contract to appear in your establishment, and I'm coming."[29]

Andy's persistence paid off. Keating honored his agreement and introduced Andy to *Detroit News* sportswriter John Walter. A year later, Andy made 60 appearances in Detroit. In 1940, Walter convinced the higher-ups at the *Detroit News* to sponsor Andy's first bowling school. Schools sponsored by the *Chicago Tribune* and *Los Angeles Examiner* followed. The 1942 Detroit school drew 58,000 students, and even more attended the Chicago edition.[30] This instructional model began a shift away from Andy challenging local hot-shots and more teaching during his appearances.

Grossman helped Andy in other ways. On January 15, the *Brooklyn Daily Eagle* published the first of a series of eight instructional columns "written" by Andy.[31] The articles targeted beginners: the need for bowling shoes and a professionally fitted ball, how to release the ball correctly, the importance of spares, etc. The articles provided Andy with increased publicity and may have encouraged some non-bowlers to try the sport. The series was consistent with his transition to more teaching and

> **MR. OPERATOR:**
> Increase Your Business! With Personal Appearance of
> # ANDY VARIPAPA
> *The Greatest Bowler of All Times and Master of the Lanes!*
>
> **HAS ROLLED 49 "300" GAMES**
>
> World's Most Sensational Bowler and Fancy Trick Shot Artist. Star of MGM Screen Plays "Strikes and Spares" and "Set 'Em Up." Write Now for Dates and sure-fire ticket sale plan that is packing 'em in—everywhere—and building up open play!
>
> MAX GROSSMAN, *Manager*
>
> 743 Macon Street   Columbus, Ohio

Max Grossman ran ads in bowling publications to drum up business for Andy, like this one from the *National Bowlers Journal and Billiard Revue* (now *Bowlers Journal International*) around 1940 (courtesy *Dr. Jake's Bowling History Blog*).

less entertaining. In 1947, after his first BPAA All-Star championship, the series was expanded and repackaged as the nationally syndicated "Improve Your Bowling by Andy Varipapa."[32]

Andy spent nine months of the year on the road. "He'd pack two or three balls in his car and be off in September to do exhibitions," said his son, Frank. "He'd be back at Christmas then off again until June."[33] A good athlete, Frank did not bowl much as a youngster, although he became a very accomplished bowler years later. While at Richmond Hill High School, he played baseball alongside future Yankee great Phil Rizzuto. After he enrolled at the prep school Adelphi Academy in Bay Ridge, he played with someone who became more famous than The Scooter.

His Adelphi roommate was Bay Ridge native Kevin Connors, who, like Frank, lettered in football, basketball, and baseball. Frank was a good athlete, but Connors was exceptional. His rare abilities made him one of only 13 athletes to play in the National Basketball Association and Major League Baseball.[34]

In 1951, after the Chicago Cubs demoted him to their Los Angeles Angels farm team, Connors began acting in the off-season and found his tough-exterior, soft-interior persona was in demand. Acting was far more lucrative than playing in the Pacific Coast League, so after the 1952 season, he retired from baseball and became a full-time actor.[35] Using his baseball nickname, Chuck Connors became a star, best known for his role as Lucas McCain in the television series *The Rifleman*.

Accepted to the engineering program at the University of Illinois, Frank needed to be in Champaign to start classes in September 1938. Frank rarely traveled with Andy, and he never forgot one time he did. While on vacation in Minnesota, Max Grossman booked several appearances in the Land of 10,000 Lakes in September. The scheduling allowed for a father-son road trip: Andy would drop Frank off and continue to Minnesota for his performances.[36] The trip did not go exactly as planned.

Near Dayton, Ohio, Andy lost control of his Ford sedan on a damp road at dusk. The car banked off both guard rails, rolled through a drainage ditch, and finally skidded to a halt on its side. The trunk flew open, and bowling balls rolled aimlessly on an adjacent cornfield. Finding humor in almost any situation, Andy commented that the car crash was "wonderful." "Why wonderful?" exclaimed Frank. Andy replied, "This is the first time in my career that I've had five balls in play."[37]

Andy on the *Set 'Em Up* set, Culver City, California, 1939. Notice Andy using a two-finger grip, just his thumb and middle finger in the ball (MGM photograph; Varipapa family collection).

They exited the car out of the door facing up, and other than some minor bumps and bruises, both emerged unharmed.

The car was damaged and not drivable. They walked to a distant farmhouse where the owner welcomed them in and allowed Andy to use the phone to call home. When the phone rang at the Varipapa home, Alice assumed they had made good time and had already arrived in Champaign. Lorraine, sitting at the kitchen table, described the conversation:

> **ANDY:** "Frank is all right and so am I."
> **ALICE:** "What do you mean, all right? What happened?"
> **ANDY:** "Just a little accident. We are both fine, but the car got some damage."
> **ALICE:** "Are you sure you are both fine? And just how much damage is there?"
> **ANDY:** "Well, we turned over into a ditch, and the car is completely wrecked."
> **ALICE:** "Oh no! You're not hiding anything from me? Frank's not hurt?"[38]

Ah, mama Varipapa was worried about her boy Frank. His first time away from home, and Andy damn near killed him. Frank took the phone and reassured his mother he was all right. The next day Alice went to the bank and wired money to Andy. He bought a new car, retrieved the bowling balls, and headed to Champaign. Frank arrived in time for classes, and Andy made it to Minneapolis for his first scheduled appearance.

Ned Day (left) and Andy on the *Set 'Em Up* set, Culver City, California, 1939. The arm-in-arm shot did not appear in the film but was the basis for the movie's poster (MGM photograph; Varipapa family collection).

Nine. Andy Comes to Town

Andy wrecked two cars in less than three years. When it came to Andy, everyone agreed on a few things: he was a great bowler, honest, and a terrible driver. For someone who drove hundreds of thousands of miles in his life, it was a minor miracle that Andy never hurt himself or anyone else. In later years, he always drove a big Cadillac and did so until his early 90s. His grandson Andy Ruffolo said that when anyone honked their horn at him—presumably because he was driving too slow or had just cut them off—Andy said, "You see that! They recognize me!"[39]

Andy was busy touring but took time out for two important matches. In April, he defeated ABC Hall of Famer Frank Benkovic in 30 games in Milwaukee. He agreed to take on Benkovic at his home alleys, the Antler's Hotel Lanes, and even allowed him to select his favorite pair of lanes.[40] Benkovic twice soundly defeated Joe Falcaro on lanes 15 and 16, so that is where the match was held. Andy held a slim three-pin lead after the first two 10-game blocks. Benkovic came out firing in the final block on April 3. He opened a 129-pin lead with just six games to go, but Andy dug deep and rallied for an 82-pin victory.[41]

His other big match was against Eddie Heineman in June, an 80-game home-and-home at Empire Alleys in Brooklyn and Heineman's in Hempstead. Billed as the "Eastern Match Game Championship," the winner was in line to challenge the current world's champion, Ned Day. It was no contest. Andy jumped out to an early lead and annihilated Heineman by 1,724 pins.[42]

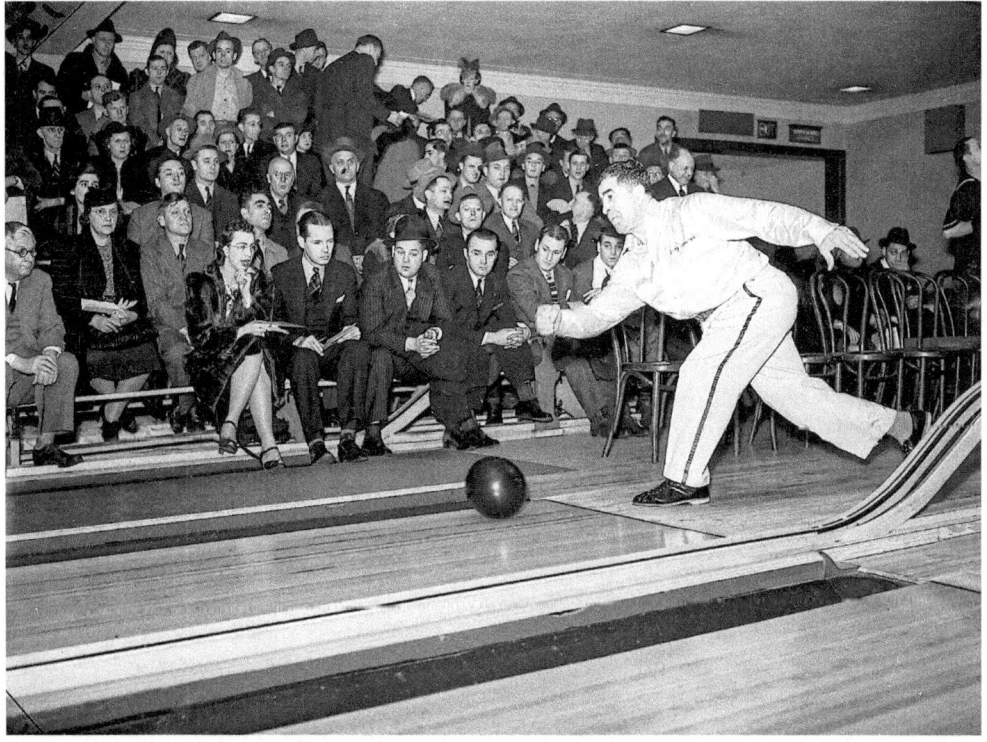

Andy during a doubles match at Club Bob-Lo lanes in Detroit, February 15, 1941. He and Joe Norris collected $1,000, defeating Ned Day and Nelson Burton, Sr. Notice the bleachers so close to the lanes and the fans' formal attire (*Detroit News* photograph; Walter P. Reuther Library, Archives of Labor and Urban Affairs, Wayne State University).

Unfortunately for Andy, Day had little interest in defending his crown against Andy or anyone else. MGM signed Day to appear in the new Pete Smith short film, *Set 'Em Up*. Day was handsome and cut a dashing figure, and unlike most top bowlers, he was always perfectly coiffed and nattily attired. Nelson Burton, Jr., recalled, "Ned was impeccable. Silk gabardine slacks, custom shirts, the works. He was something else."[43]

Smith knew Day was pleasant, good-looking, and an outstanding bowler but not a showman like Andy. Then again, who was? When Smith found out Andy was traveling to Los Angeles in the summer of 1939, he asked if he would like to be in the movie. Andy initially declined, telling Smith he preferred to work alone (Andy was becoming a diva already). Smith persisted, and after Brunswick executives pressured Andy—and offered him more money—he agreed to appear in the film.[44]

Smith filmed *Set 'Em Up* on lanes installed inside a massive tent on the MGM lot, like *Strikes and Spares*. But early in the shoot, Andy and Day complained that the lanes were not in good condition, which was odd since they were brand new and carefully maintained by Brunswick personnel. Unbeknownst to everyone, employees snuck into the tent at night, and their bowling damaged the soft shellac surface. Having a pair of bowling lanes on the premises was too tempting. After Brunswick resurfaced the lanes, MGM management posted signs warning the staff that late-night bowling was a firable offense.[45]

Varipapa and Day did not appear together. Day gave his equipment suggestions and instructional tips, followed by Andy's trick shot performance. It is not as if Varipapa and Day were enemies; Andy respected Day, and by all accounts, the feeling was mutual. They posed for a publicity photograph, arm in arm, rolling balls at the foul line. Although Day signed on to the film first, the opening credits read: "Set 'Em Up with Andy Varipapa and Ned Day."[46] One wonders if Andy demanded top billing before agreeing to appear.

Andy and Day shared billing again in 1942's *Better Bowling*, another Grantland Rice *Sportlights* series installment. The plot was like *Set 'Em Up*, in which Day instructed for several minutes, followed by Andy's tricks. Director Jack Eaton added a comedy skit at the end, starring comedian F. Chase Taylor playing his alter-ego Colonel Stoopnagle.[47] The scene was corny and not particularly funny; it lacked Pete Smith's sharp wit. Of Andy's four short films that still exist, *Better Bowling* is the least interesting.

Over the next 10 years, only Andy was as popular and successful a bowler as Day. While filming *Set 'Em Up*, Day met silent film star and bowling enthusiast Harold Lloyd. They later partnered with Hank Marino and opened Llo-Da-Mar Bowl in Santa Monica, California, which became *the* place to bowl if you were among the Hollywood elite.[48] Coca-Cola, Gillette razor blades, Havoline motor oil, Jockey underwear, and Wheaties featured the stylish Day as their spokesperson.[49]

Andy and Day spent much time together on the lanes during the late 1930s and 1940s, most notably as *Detroit News* Bowling School co-leaders. But they met in a serious match only once. Before leaving town after their 1941 school, Andy and Detroit's favorite son Joe Norris beat Day and Nelson Burton by just 27 pins at Club Bob-Lo Lanes.[50]

Day became one of bowling's all-time greats. *Bowlers Journal* ranked him as the fifth greatest bowler of the 20th century, one spot behind Marino and one spot ahead of Andy.[51] While in Hollywood, Day was careful not to give Andy any indication that he was willing to put his title on the line against him, or anyone for that matter. Day did not defend his title for more than three years.

Bowling lacked something that most other sports had figured out. There was nothing like the World Series, Masters Tournament, Wimbledon, or a World Cup in bowling. Who was the best bowler in the world? The answer depended on who you asked. Andy said he was, but so did Day, Falcaro, Marino, and many others. Members of the bowling community were still frustrated with the method of deciding the world champion, but a change was in the offing.

Ten

Who's the Champ?

Competition, by definition, is an integral part of sports. Fans, coaches, the media, administrators, and players constantly try to answer a simple question: *Who is the best?* Champions are relatively easy to determine, at least in American team sports.[1] A league sets a schedule; teams play each other in the regular season, some percentage advance to the playoffs, and one emerges as champion.

Individual sports each have systems to determine champions. In auto racing, NASCAR and Formula 1 drivers compete for season-long driver championships. Professional golf and tennis tours use a point system to determine yearly champions, but greatness also hinges on performance in major championships.[2] Tennis uses a ranking system to determine the best player at any moment in time. But rankings are decided by algorithms, viewed by distrust by those who cannot fathom that a computer determines who is "number one." Regardless of the system used, there will be controversy about whoever is crowned champion, ranked number one, or otherwise considered "the best."

Boxing has a unique system of deciding champions. Think about it: there is no such thing as a professional boxing tournament. Young fighters rely on managers and promoters to schedule bouts and, if successful, earn the opportunity to compete against more accomplished boxers. At the highest levels of boxing, an alphabet soup of national and international governing bodies ranks the contenders, sanctions bouts, and awards championship belts.[3]

It is no secret that the history of championship boxing has been riddled with controversy. Unscrupulous promoters, corrupt referees and judges, fighters tanking bouts, fighters not getting a chance, fighters getting too many chances, and titles awarded and stripped for no good reason. Name the administrative irregularity, and it probably has occurred in boxing.

Bowling champions were once determined using a system like boxing. In 1906, Jimmy Smith defeated Johnny "The Little Wizard" Voorhies in a best-of-11 match at the Superba Bowling Parlors in Brooklyn to become bowling's first world champion.[4] A referee, a foul judge, and an official scorer supervised play. Reserved tickets were $2 ($65.95 in 2023 dollars), and general admission was $1. Bowling was so popular at the time that *The World* characterized the crowd of 500 as "disappointing."[5]

The financial terms of the match were typical: Superba proprietor Charles Ebbets (yes, *that* Charles Ebbets, owner of the Brooklyn Dodgers) kept half of the gate. The players split the other half, with 60 percent going to the winner and 40 percent to the loser. The players had an additional side bet of $250.[6] Between the gate and the side bet, Smith netted approximately $475 ($16,051 in 2023 dollars), while Voorhies lost about $100 ($3,379 in 2023 dollars).[7]

After the win, Smith said, "I don't think anybody will find fault with my claim to the championship. I will be open to meet all comers under fair conditions."[8] Smith was, by consensus, the world champion. Over the next 15 years, he defended his title dozens of times against challengers from all over the country. No governing body organized and monitored the matches, but everyone *knew* that Smith was the champion.[9]

Smith occasionally lost matches during his reign, but not every match was considered a "title bout." In 1921, Jimmy Blouin of Blue Island, Illinois, defeated Smith by more than 300 pins in a 60-game match. Afterward, some wondered if Blouin ought to be considered the world champion.[10]

In 1922, Chicago bowling promoter Louis Petersen organized a tournament that would determine, once and for all, the world champion of bowling. Christened the "World Classic," Petersen invited 24 bowlers to compete on four lanes installed on the floor of the Chicago Coliseum. A new scoring system, the "Louis P. Petersen System" ("Petersen Points"), determined the winner. His system rewarded bowlers for both total pinfall and match victories.[11]

The World Classic was an endurance test. Bowlers rolled 115 games over 15 days, but that was still not enough to determine the world champion. The winner needed to defeat the second-, third-, and fourth-place finishers in subsequent 60-game matches to claim the crown.[12] On February 24, Jimmy Blouin, whose earlier defeat of Smith was the impetus for staging the World Classic, won the $1200 ($21,723 in 2023 dollars) prize and a $400 gold medal. He averaged almost 207 and collected 547.14 Petersen Points.[13]

To claim the title, Blouin still had to win three more matches. After disposing of Phil Wolf and Mort Lindsey, only one bowler stood between Blouin and the world title, and it was none other than Jimmy Smith. Bensinger's Randolph Recreation in Chicago hosted the match, where a crowd that "spilled out into the streets" watched the action.[14] Blouin, the hometown favorite, rallied from behind and took the lead in the 57th game. When it was over, Blouin defeated Smith 278.00 to 273.54 points. He won 31 games, lost 28, and tied one.[15] The pinfall difference was a mere 23 pins, but Blouin won the title comfortably because his better match play record earned him significantly more Petersen Points.

And, of course, since this is bowling, a match of such titanic proportions was not without controversy. Some suspected the pinboys who bet on Blouin of placing sticky powder in Smith's fingerholes during the final 10-game block. By the end of the match, Smith's fingers were raw and bleeding, but he never complained or accused the pinboys of treachery.[16] This incident led to the practice of requiring pin boys to wear white gloves, one of the stipulations in Andy's 1930 doubles match with Falcaro against Murgie and Reilly.

The World Classic was a success. Jimmy Blouin's performance on the lanes, rather than acclamation, made him a champion. Petersen's scoring system, while convoluted, met with general approval because it rewarded both wins and high scores.[17] However, one organization was unhappy with the whole affair, and that was ABC.

Concerned that the World Classic might make their annual championships less relevant, they reminded everyone of the ABC rule that placed a $25 limit on entry fees (the World Classic charged a $100 entry fee). ABC leadership made it clear that anyone entering future iterations of the World Classic risked a suspension and thus be ineligible to bowl in the ABC Championships.[18] The threat worked, and the World Classic became a one-and-done affair.

Ironically, Petersen himself did not expect the Classic to become an annual event. He never believed anyone could win three straight post-tournament matches and claim the title. Petersen underestimated Jimmy Blouin's greatness. He defeated all challengers until 1926, when Frank Kartheiser challenged him to a $5,000 championship match. Blouin declined, citing failing health, and retired at 39, having never lost a prearranged match.[19]

For the next few years, no one held the title for more than 14 months. The crown passed from Kartheiser to Charley Daw, Adolph Carlson, and Joe Scribner. In December 1929, Joe Falcaro defeated Scribner by 129 pins over 60 games to claim the title. And like all things Falcaro, controversy soon followed. Champions typically defended their title at least a couple of times per year. Falcaro took almost two years to grant Scribner a 60-game rematch, but when he did, he soundly defeated him by 993 pins.[20] Falcaro rebuffed all challengers, including his doubles partner Andy, smugly telling them to "go get a reputation first."[21]

Falcaro made dodging contenders an art form. He agreed to matches in principle, then backed out when the terms (venue, length, side bet, etc.) were not to his liking. Or he got sick. Or his kids got sick. Or he had too much work managing his lanes. Falcaro said he would bowl anyone, anytime, anywhere, for any stakes, but rarely did. He ignored the barbs of challengers and media alike, including Milwaukee bowling writer Billy Sixty. He taunted Falcaro in his syndicated bowling column: "Little Joe Falcaro, world match bowling king, sits back and idly twiddles his thumbs while American's alley aces howl loudly for his scalp."[22]

In 1932, the newly formed BPAA informed Falcaro that while they recognized him as the world champion, they arranged a national elimination tournament to identify a challenger. Always classy, Falcaro replied, "Who the hell are you bums? Falcaro the Great arranges his own matches."[23]

The BPAA ignored Chesty Joe and went ahead and arranged the Eastern Match Game Championship. The survivors of eight city championships met in January 1933 and, over three weeks, in nine cities, bowled 128 games to decide a champion. Andy won the Brooklyn championship and entered the Eastern as the odds-on favorite to win, which, if he did, set up a much-anticipated clash with Falcaro for his title.

But it was not Andy or other stars like Barney Spinella or Chester Arnhorst who won; it was Joe Miller. Like many top bowlers of the day, Miller was an immigrant and a former pinboy. Born Josef Obuszkiewicz in Poland in 1900, he became Joe Miller because his teachers could not spell his name correctly.[24] A top bowler in Buffalo but little-known outside the city, Miller built a comfortable 446-pin lead after 72 games, but Andy whittled it down to just 143 pins going into the final eight-game block.[25] In White Plains on February 5, Andy made a charge. He averaged 232 for the first five games, cutting Miller's lead to only 66 pins. But Miller responded by blasting games of 265, 224, and 278 and won the title going away.[26]

Falcaro, unnerved by the BPAA's threat to strip his title, agreed to the matchup with Miller. The showdown would start on Friday, March 31, in the neutral site of Philadelphia. But as Victor Kalman once wrote in *Sports Illustrated*, Falcaro lived his life "like an accident looking for a place to happen."[27] This time, the place was Queens, and the accident involved a convicted felon and a gun.

On March 30, Falcaro lay in a hospital bed. He was shot three times by Frank Mazzola, recently paroled from prison after serving a five-year term for the killing of Bronx labor leader Ben Bonfanti. At the time of the shooting, Falcaro rented a room in the home of Mazzola's estranged wife.

Mazzola became upset when his 10-year-old son told him that Falcaro had become "friendly" with Mrs. Mazzola.[28] He admitted to police that he shot Falcaro as revenge for the "theft of his wife's affections" but had acted in self-defense.[29] The shooting made headlines across the nation. It occurred in broad daylight on the front lawn of the Mazzola residence in Astoria. Hundreds of children (including Mazzola's son) returning from their lunch break at a nearby school witnessed the attack.

Even Mazzola's capture was spectacular. Al Johnson, a former amateur heavyweight boxer, saw the shooting and, after a brief chase, tackled and held Mazzola until police arrived. While early news reports suggested that Falcaro's bowling career might be over, he recovered and returned to the lanes a few months later. He refused to press charges, and Mazzola eventually pled guilty to a lesser gun possession charge.[30]

Plans were already in place for the winner of the Miller-Falcaro match to meet the Chicago match play champion (who turned out to be Stewart Watson) in a title match in late April.[31] With Falcaro in the hospital, the BPAA declared his match with Miller a forfeit and his title vacant. They would recognize the winner of the Miller-Watson match as the new world champion. Miller won the 80-game match handily, by 1,169 pins, but Falcaro protested, claiming it was unfair to lose his title due to injury.[32] While others may have agreed with him in principle, this was Falcaro, and his claims garnered little sympathy. He never recognized Miller, or any of his successors, as champion.

Ever the self-promoter, Falcaro turned lemons into lemonade and forever billed himself the "Undefeated Match Game Champion." While correct, his claim was grossly misleading.[33] Miller lost his world championship to Otto Stein in May 1934 and faded into obscurity after losing a title match to Hank Marino in 1937. His competitive career was cut short by a series of heart attacks, but he gave lessons and clinics until his death at age 58.[34] Outside of Buffalo, where Miller was a Greater Buffalo ABC Hall of Fame charter member, he may be best known for being among the last great players who bowled in street shoes.[35]

Falcaro's rocky tenure as champion shed light on the problems with the boxing-style method of deciding a world champion. The process of arranging matches was ad hoc. There was no timetable for challenges, and years might go by without a championship match. There was no standard length of matches. Matches had to be scheduled home and home. It was all unsatisfying to bowlers, the media, and fans.

Of course, the ABC leadership still felt that their annual tournament's all-events champion was the most prestigious title in the sport. But they felt threatened. Otherwise, why put the kibosh on the World Classic? Deep down, ABC leadership must have known that with open entries, only three games per event, and nine games total, and without a match-play component, their tournament was not a legitimate test.

Andy received criticism throughout his career for never winning an ABC title. Contemporaries, including Charley Daw, Ned Day, Junie McMahon, Joe Norris, Joe Wilman, and Gil Zunker, won at least one eagle. Andy was consistent, usually shooting above 1,800 (a 200 average), but the closest he came to winning an all-events title was in 1947 when his 1,906 total trailed Junie McMahon by 59 pins.[36]

The media held lofty expectations for Andy. The 212th Coast Artillery Armory in midtown Manhattan hosted the 1937 ABCs, and fans hoped that their Brooklyn hero performed at his best. Unfortunately, in front of 3,500 partisan fans, Andy shot 148, 170, and 221 games in the team event for a 539 series, not even a 180 average.[37] The Associated Press reported Andy's scores as "mediocre."[38] Headline writers were brutal: "Andy Varipapa Disappointment in A.B.C. Play" and "Famed Stars Fail Before ABC Crowds."[39] One read, "Andy Fails."[40]

He came back and rolled 682 in the singles event, good enough for a top 10 finish, and after adding 620 in doubles, managed a respectable all-events total of 1841. His singles performance made headlines but in a much smaller font! Andy was headline material whether he bowled good, bad, or indifferent. Even later in his career, the media did not let up. In 1947, *Time* magazine commented that "Varipapa's confidence is unbruised by the fact that in 16 tries he has never won the A.B.C., biggest tourney of all ... [and] in Los Angeles last week.... Andy Varipapa again flunked his A.B.C.'s."[41] It wasn't that he bowled poorly—he finished sixth in the singles with 715—but for Andy's critics, only a win would suffice.

As early as 1934, when he had participated in only six ABC Championships, Andy downplayed the event: "I never do well in the A.B.C. ... so [it] means little to me."[42] His explanations sounded more like excuses: too many bowlers, too few games, not enough practice time. Any ABC member could enter, and tens of thousands did. Guys averaging 150 bowled alongside the stars. In 1937, Andy suggested splitting the tournament into two divisions for average bowlers and experts. That reduced the chance of a random bowler on a hot streak toppling one of the game's stars.[43]

The vast field, coupled with a short format (each event was only three games), made luck a more significant factor. Andy said, "For me personally, it will lack interest until they lengthen the series from three to more games."[44] Joe Falcaro agreed: "If a guy could roll 20 games in this tournament, us good men would finish at the top ... in nine games I can't prove anything. I might not even get warmed up in nine games."[45] Brunswick vice president Robert Kennedy, while giving butchers everywhere a backhanded compliment, added that "you seldom see a national star win at the A.B.C. The top prize is usually won by a big butcher from Milwaukee who happens to have a lucky streak."[46]

The ABC's short format gave bowlers little chance to experiment with the lanes. Andy noted that top bowlers "first must get the feel of an alley where we bowl. We have to try a few practice balls, just as a pitcher has to warm up before a game ... so some mediocre bowler comes along, has a good night, and shows us up."[47] Andy's negative self-talk may have been a self-fulfilling prophecy. Andy knew full well that the all-time greats—including Smith, Blouin, Lindsey, and Knox—overcame these so-called obstacles and won the all-events title. But in his mind, he purposely downplayed the importance of the ABCs. The built-in excuses reduced his disappointment when he did not win.

Ten. Who's the Champ?

In May 1935, Hank Marino defeated Otto Stein to claim the world championship. Marino, already an established star like Falcaro, rarely felt the need to defend his crown. He did so only once, in January 1937, when he defeated former champion Joe Miller by 486 pins over 120 games.[48] Growing impatient, the BPAA held elimination matches to determine a challenger and force Marino to defend his title. Ned Day won the eliminations, and he just happened to be Marino's protégé and teammate on the powerhouse Heil Products team.[49] Assuming the BPAA would award the title to Day, Marino retired rather than bowl against him.

But much like when the BPAA vacated Falcaro's title, they demanded that Day immediately bowl against the runner-up in the elimination tournament, Lowell Jackson of St. Louis.[50] Scheduled to begin in February, illness and injuries to Day, then scheduling problems, led to a series of postponements.[51] When they finally met in October, Day convincingly defeated Jackson by more than 1,000 pins and 60 Petersen points over the 120-game, four-city tilt.[52]

The bowling industry weathered the Great Depression and looked optimistically toward the 1940s. From 1929 to 1940, the number of bowling centers almost tripled (from 1,658 to 4,848), as did the number of league bowlers (220,000 to 683,000).[53] Bowling, like the nation, seemed to be turning the corner. Still, the method of deciding the world champion frustrated many in the bowling community.

Andy believed that the sport of bowling would never reach its potential without a professional championship tournament.[54] In a May 1940 interview, he conceded the difficulty of finding a suitable venue for such a tournament, specifically one able to accommodate thousands of spectators. If an appropriate facility were found, Andy described his vision for the event: "The way such a tournament should be run would be to have 10 or 12 of the best in the country roll a double round robin on four new alleys so that each bowler will bowl each of the others twice…. That would be as close to neutral conditions as could be achieved."[55]

When a reporter suggested holding the tournament on the same specially-installed lanes before or after the ABCs, Andy smiled and said, "The ABC wouldn't agree to that for it would detract from their tournament."[56] He believed that a professional bowling tournament—or better yet, a series of tournaments—would gain widespread appeal, like tours in golf and tennis. Twenty years before the PBA Tour held its first event, Andy's prescient comments demonstrated his innate marketing expertise.

Back home in Brooklyn, Alice pestered Andy for years about slowing down his pace of touring and finding another source of income. Andy finally gave in, either to get her off his back or because she was right. Probably a little of both. Lorraine recalled her father coming home one evening in late 1940 and announcing, "Alice, you may finally have your way."[57] He explained that Joe Spinella, owner of Albemarle Lanes on Flatbush Avenue, was considering opening another bowling center but needed a partner.[58] In the summer of 1941, Andy bought a one-half interest in the Kenmore Bowling Center, a 16-lane center on Church Avenue in Flatbush.

Located opposite the Flatbush Theater for the Performing Arts and less than a mile from Ebbets Field, Kenmore was the place for Brooklyn celebrities to bowl. Dodgers Pee Wee Reese, Jimmy Wasdell (who owned a bowling center in Cleveland), and Yankees Phil Rizzuto, and Red Ruffing were regulars. Alice enjoyed mingling with the ballplayers and entertainers appearing at the Arts Center, including avid bowlers Henny Youngman and Ben Blue.[59]

After 15 years in their home on MacDonough Avenue in Bushwick, Andy and Alice decided to move their family closer to Kenmore. It was important to be nearby because, with Andy on the road for almost all the bowling season, it was up to Alice and the kids to take care of Kenmore in his absence. Alice found a lovely ground-floor apartment on Avenue I, just a short trolley ride from the alleys.[60]

Alice was a fantastic cook. Andy liked bringing guests home to enjoy her cooking, but her lack of sports knowledge often led to unintended comedy. The Detroit Tigers were in town playing the Yankees, and Andy called Alice and told her he was bringing Dizzy Trout and Barney McCoskey home for dinner. She cried, "Trout! I don't know how to cook trout! And why are you bringing tigers home? Have you been drinking?"[61]

That same summer, Andy's one-time nemesis Louis Petersen, still Secretary of the BPAA, was creating a new tournament. It would determine once and for all who was the world's champion bowler, but also be the event that cemented Andy's legacy as not only a great entertainer but one of the best bowlers in the nation.

Eleven

A New Kind of Tournament

The BPAA considered running a national match play tournament since its founding in 1932, but the devil was in the details. The biggest obstacle was figuring out how to finance the event. BPAA leadership wanted to limit the number of entries, keep the entry fee reasonable, and create an attractive prize fund to entice the best players. And they needed to accomplish all those objectives and still have enough money left to cover operating expenses.

In an era without media rights fees, the only sources of revenue for sporting events were entry fees, gate receipts, and sponsorships. A tournament financed by entry fees alone was unsustainable, so the BPAA searched for external revenue sources. Holding an event in a typical 1940s bowling center limited attendance to just a few hundred spectators. The alternative was a large arena with thousands of seats, but that required the installation of at least a dozen lanes. Installing a pair of lanes in 1940 cost approximately $2,300, so a 12-lane installation cost about $14,000 ($290,000 in 2023 dollars).[1]

Sports marketing and sponsorships did not exist in 1941. There were no corporate title sponsors, VIP hospitality packages, facility naming rights, personal seat licenses, or "official" product placement. The "Capital One Orange Bowl" was still just the Orange Bowl, and Coca-Cola was not yet the "Official Soft Drink of NASCAR." But finding a sponsor was crucial because it was the only way the BPAA would meet its goals of a limited field coupled with low entry fees. If not, bowling supremacy would continue to be determined by the whims of the reigning champion, an unsatisfying situation for everyone involved.

On September 16, 1941, the *Chicago Tribune* unveiled plans for "The First Annual All-Star Tournament for the Individual Match Play Championship of the United States." Later known simply as the "All-Star," the event was scheduled for December 7 to 14 in Chicago.[2] The tournament chairman was BPAA Secretary Louis Petersen, organizer of the 1922 World Classic. The BPAA and *Chicago Tribune* Charities Inc. were presenting sponsors.

The All-Star was a new kind of bowling tournament designed to address many of the issues Andy raised in his 1940 interview. The field was limited to 60 invited players who would bowl 75 games over eight days. The entry fee was $25. The competition would be held on 10 brand-new alleys in the Chicago Coliseum, accommodating up to 6,000 spectators.[3]

The *Tribune* had experience sponsoring sporting events. Their famed sports editor, Arch Ward, created and marketed the Major League Baseball All-Star Game, the Chicago College All-Star Game, and the Golden Gloves boxing tournament.[4] With circulation exceeding 1,000,000 readers per day, the *Tribune* supplied uniformly positive coverage before, during, and after the event.[5]

Bowlers earned a spot in the field by winning one of 10 elimination tournaments or being chosen by a selection committee.[6] As the November 8 deadline approached, the *Tribune* published the name of every bowler who applied—stars and unknowns alike.

Few bowlers got headline treatment, but on November 9, a *Tribune* headline blared: "Andy Varipapa Enters 10 Pin All-Star Meet: Bowling's Number 1 Competitor Beats the Deadline."[7] In breathless tones, the article explained how Andy's entry reached the secretary of the BPAA only minutes before the midnight deadline.

The story illustrates the reverence in which the bowling community held Andy: "The star of stars, the man who combines outstanding ability with more color than is displayed by any other individual in the game."[8] His last-minute entry revealed Andy's flair for the dramatic. There was little doubt that Andy would enter and less doubt that he would be selected. But, by applying just before the deadline, he got his entry noticed by the *Tribune*.

Installation of the 10 tournament lanes commenced on November 13.[9] The tournament's integrity depended on quality installation and meticulous maintenance of the lanes. To the untrained eye, every bowling lane looks the same. It is 60 feet long and 42 inches wide. But every lane has hidden characteristics that can make an identically thrown ball react differently from one lane to the next.

Unlike a hole at your local golf course, where the sand and water eager to swallow up your next shot are in plain sight, hazards on a bowling lane are invisible. These hidden characteristics may create unfairness caused by "asymmetric information," e.g., one party possesses more information than another.[10] Bowlers who know the characteristics of a particular lane or bowling center can use that information to their advantage. Their opponents, without the same knowledge, compete at a disadvantage.

Modern bowling lanes receive a daily coating of oil (referred to as "oiling" or "dressing" the lanes). It must be applied to keep the lane surface from wearing out. Without lane oil, the friction from thousands of balls rolling down the lane would damage the surface in weeks. Beyond this practical function, oil can be used to influence scoring. The amount of oil used, and the specific places oil is applied across the width and length of the lane, will significantly affect how a ball reacts when thrown.[11]

Oil was not used to dress lanes in the 1940s, but lanes still needed protection. They were sealed with shellac (four or five fresh coats, once per month) and coated with a paste wax (applied by hand, usually daily). Knowing how the lane man applied the shellac and wax gave a skilled bowler an advantage over their opponents. These idiosyncrasies explained why bowlers were reluctant to accept anything other than a home-and-home challenge match. Knowing their home lanes' peculiarities and unique aspects gave players an advantage.

Choosing a neutral site for a match mitigates potential asymmetry. But after observing years of underhanded tricks, skeptical bowlers would still wonder if their opponent: (a) snuck into the center to practice before the match, (b) bribed the lane man to apply shellac and wax to the lanes in a particular manner, (c) asked the same lane man to make the approaches stickier or slipperier than usual, (d) bribed pinboys to kick over the occasional stubborn pin or put grease in their opponent's thumbhole, or (e) all of the above.

At the All-Star, ABC officials measured, tested, and approved the Coliseum lanes before competitors rolled a single ball. Louis Petersen and his staff monitored the lane waxing each night to ensure consistent and fair conditions. To the delight of the competitors, these steps helped eliminate the shenanigans that plagued challenge matches for years.

The BPAA and the *Tribune* could not have picked a more effective tournament director than Petersen. Besides running the only other tournament akin to the All-Star (the 1922 World Classic), he ran his eponymous Petersen Classic since 1921. The event had difficulties during the Great Depression, so much so that Petersen suspended the tournament after 1934 (won by Andy's trick-shot brethren Mort Lindsey).

The Petersen Classic resumed in 1938, and entries grew steadily: 128 in 1938, 224 in 1939, and 352 in 1940. In 1941, 800 bowlers entered, and Chicago's John Ryan took home the $4,100 ($84,611 in 2023 dollars) winner's check.[12] The Petersen became the second-largest tournament in the world, surpassed only by the ABC Championships.[13] No one doubted Petersen's ability to promote and run a tournament effectively.

On November 18, the 15-person selection committee met to finalize the All-Star's 60-man field. They had their work cut out for them. The committee received 143 entries; only 50 slots were available (10 were reserved for winners of the elimination tournaments). They had difficulty paring the field to just 60 bowlers. Petersen, not only the tournament chairman but also the selection committee chairman, made the executive decision to increase the field to 70 competitors and 10 alternates.[14]

Brunswick's crew completed lane construction on Tuesday, December 2. They applied the first of five coats of shellac, ensuring the lanes' readiness for the first squad on Sunday. The *Tribune* continued the drumbeat of positive news: "As the show draws closer, interest of bowling fans is shooting swiftly.... In short, the All-Star event isn't just a bowling tournament, but it's the show that bowlers and fans have wanted for years."[15]

The *Tribune* mentioned the arrival of each out-of-town star. With the tournament set to open, a bold headline across the front page of the Sunday sports section read, "All-Star Bowling Tourney Starts Today."[16] It was just above a full-length photo of reigning world champion Ned Day.

Andy was ready. He desperately wanted to show everyone he was more than just a trick-shot artist. His name was absent from the *Tribune*'s stories leading up to the tournament, besides his entry coming in at the last minute. Andy was 50, and most did not think he would be a factor. The tournament concluded with 55 games over the final four days, a grueling test even for younger men. Hank Marino (52 years old), Joe Falcaro (45), Barney Spinella (48), and Charley Daw (47) did not enter.[17] The only bowler in the field older than Andy appeared to be 52-year-old Mort Lindsey, already an ABC Hall of Fame member.

Everything was in place: reserved tickets were sold out, the lanes were certified by the ABC, and none of the top stars had withdrawn. C.B. Beukema's daily stories in the *Tribune* had whipped bowling fans into a frenzy. But in an unthinkable twist, the results of the first round of the All-Star did not make it to the front page of Monday's *Tribune*. Instead, this headline greeted readers: "U.S. and Japs at War: Bomb Hawaii, Philippines, Guam, Singapore."[18] Yes, the first day of the long-awaited BPAA All-Star was December 7, 1941. The same day that the Japanese bombed Pearl Harbor.

The inaugural All-Star began at noon CST on Sunday, December 7. Divided into seven squads of 10 bowlers, each rolled five games per day during the four days of qualifying. Every hour and 20 minutes, the next squad took the lanes. The first five groups bowled in the afternoon, ending about 6:30 p.m., and after a short break, the two remaining groups bowled, with a 10-game block of the Ned Day-Lowell Jackson championship match sandwiched in-between. The play ended each evening at about 12:25 a.m.

In a 50-year retrospect of the Pearl Harbor attack, *Chicago Tribune* columnist Mike Conklin wrote that news of the bombing first reached Chicago at 1:30 p.m. on December 7, coinciding with the kickoff of the Bears-Cardinals NFL game at Comiskey Park.[19] Several hundred spectators attended the afternoon blocks, and ABC Hall of Famer Joe Norris recalled, "One by one, people began leaving. We didn't know what was going on. Then they announced that the Japanese had attacked Pearl Harbor."[20]

But the tournament proceeded as planned. The next day, the *Tribune* sports pages did not reference the attack or impending war. Conklin noted that stories about the war began appearing in the sports pages two days later when Cleveland Indians star pitcher Bob Feller enlisted in the Navy. After the United States formally entered the war in Europe on December 11, war-related items appeared on the sports pages daily.[21]

The All-Star was unique for its 75-game length and the two-stage format. Everyone bowled a qualifying round, and the 11 bowlers with the highest scores advanced to the round-robin match play round. At the time, the highest aggregate score ("total wood") determined the winners of most tournaments and head-to-head matches. Some, like the Smith-Voorhies match in 1906, still used a straight match play format where only game wins mattered, typically in a best-of-11. Most tournaments used total wood, like the three-game ABC singles, the nine-game ABC all-events, and the eight-game Petersen Classic. But these tournaments were short compared to the 40, 60, and 80-game matches that decided the world champion.

To identify the best player, a long format is required. Imagine if professional golf tournaments were nine holes instead of 72, tennis matches best two out of three games instead of two out of three sets, or nine-ball billiards matches one rack instead of a race to seven. These formats gave weaker players a better chance of winning but may not identify the most deserving champion. A longer format allows players, regardless of the sport, to recover from one bad shot or one bad break.

In a two-stage bowling tournament, all contestants bowl a fixed number of games in a qualifying round. A pre-determined percentage of players advance to the next round while the rest are eliminated (or "cut"). Bowlers going to the next round face one of three formats. In a single-elimination knockout, players are seeded into a bracket and meet another bowler in a head-to-head match. A double-elimination knockout is the same as the single-elimination version, except players are not eliminated from competition until they have lost twice. Winners advance, and losers move to the losers' bracket.[22] Finally, there is the round-robin, where each contestant plays one or more matches against every other player. The All-Star adopted the round-robin format.

The first stage of the All-Star was a 20-game qualifying round. Competed over four consecutive days, the 11 players with the highest scores and the loser of the Day-Jackson match advanced to the round-robin stage. All other players were eliminated. Qualifying scores were erased ("dropping the wood") before the round-robin, so it did not matter if a player qualified first or 11th. The strategy was to finish among the top 11 ("make the cut") and advance to the next round.

And if this was not confusing enough, the All-Star used the same Petersen Point scoring system used in the 1922 World Classic. The unique benefit of the Petersen Point system is that it is a hybrid system that rewards high scores and match victories. In the All-Star, players earned points as follows: (1) one point for every 50 pins knocked down, (2) one point for each game won, and (3) one point should the player roll a higher five-game series against their opponent but won a fewer number of games.[23]

While the All-Star qualifying was going on, Ned Day battled challenger Lowell Jackson for the match-game championship. The match was a five-city affair, starting in Santa Monica, California, then moving to Indianapolis; West Allis, Wisconsin; St. Louis; and ending in Chicago. The choice of bowling centers gave Day an advantage before the match even started.

Day was the clear favorite; he held the title for four years and was considered the best bowler in the world. But he would bowl 60 of the 160 games in centers he literally owned! The Santa Monica match took place at Llo-Da-Mar Bowl, the center Day owned with Harold Lloyd and Hank Marino. And the match in West Allis was scheduled at Day's Recreation, lending a whole new meaning to the phrase *he walked around like he owned the place*.

The 160-game match began on November 7 in Santa Monica. Day jumped on Jackson quickly and left Llo-Da-Mar with a 28.92 Petersen Point lead.[24] By the time the match moved to Chicago for the final 40 games, Day had built an insurmountable 61.95-point lead.[25] Anticlimactic or not, Day and Jackson bowled 10 games each night, sandwiched between the other All-Star evening groups. Day coasted to a 61.25-point victory and, for the 160 games, averaged 203.10 to Jackson's 192.87.[26] Day took full advantage of his home centers, picking up 58.75 points during 60 games in Santa Monica and West Allis. For the other 100 games, he beat Jackson by just 2.50 points.

On the first day of the All-Star, Joe Sinke of Chicago led with 1,030 for five games. He was among only three players to break 1,000 (a 200 average) for the block.[27] Some of bowling's all-time greats struggled on the brand-new lanes: future ABC Hall of Famers Charley Daw, Nelson Burton, Sr., Connie Schwoegler, and Ed Kawolics failed to shoot 900 (a 180 average). Andy rolled a 923 (a 184 average) and sat in the middle of the pack, tied for 31st place.[28]

After three rounds, Andy's total after 15 games was 2,871, 45 pins out of the 11th-place cut line. He bowled well but was done in by a bad game each day: 146 on the first, 145 on the second, and 161 on the third. Only Johnny Crimmins and Joe Norris, both of Detroit, averaged over 200.[29] The field, comprised of the best bowlers in the United States, averaged just 188 on the brand-new Coliseum alleys.[30]

On the final day of qualifying, Andy bowled in the third group. Once again, he rolled one abysmal game, shooting just 156 in game three. He finished strong with games of 212 and 209 to post 1,022 for the block and a 20-game total of 3,893. After 15 games, Ray Newton sat in 11th place with 2,916, so the projected cut was 3,888.[31] Andy's score was likely to be close to the cut line.[32]

It behooves professional bowlers to be good at math. Bowling is a numbers game, and making quick calculations can be helpful. Knowing where one stands in a match or a tournament is useful. The knowledge also affects strategy: go all-out to convert a tough split, or make sure of one pin?[33] Others, however, say ignorance is bliss: bowl your best and add it up later; do not add pressure by knowing the exact score needed to win a game or a tournament.

Andy had to wait and sweat it out. The projected cut may have been a bit low because scores seemed to improve as the lanes broke in. On day four, 16 bowlers exceeded the 1,000 mark, while only 18 had done so in the first three days combined. Andy was in sixth place when he finished bowling, but 40 players remained to bowl their final 10-game block.

As the final group took the lanes, Andy was in 11th place. Things were looking grim. He would be eliminated if any of the 10 bowlers in the group beat his total. Joe Sinke, the leader after the first squad, entered the final round with a 2,964 and needed just 920 to make the finals. After starting with disappointing games of 172 and 171, Sinke got it together and fired 232 and 233 in games three and four, ending any further drama. He easily made the cut with 3,953.[34]

Andy missed advancing to the match play round by just six pins. Joe Wilman of Chicago, who went on to win the All-Star in 1944 and twice finish runner-up, took the final qualifying position with a 3,899 total. Whenever a bowler misses a cut by less than 10 pins, they usually dwell on a single bad break, a missed spare, or a split because just one shot may have made the difference. But Andy must have bemoaned rolling one dreadful game in each block. The *Tribune* noted Andy's performance in passing, lamenting that the round-robin "missed having one colorful bowler, Andy Varipapa of Brooklyn, who finished just six pins below Wilman."[35]

On December 14, Johnny Crimmins of Detroit won the All-Star. Fellow Detroiter Joe Norris took second, and Connie Schwoegler of Madison, Wisconsin, finished third. The Petersen Point system worked as designed—Crimmins had the best record (35–19–1) and the highest average (208.8)—and won the tournament with room to spare.[36] He earned the right to bowl Ned Day for his title. Immediately after the tournament ended, the *Tribune* and the BPAA announced they would sponsor the All-Star again in 1942.[37]

Reaction to the tournament was positive, with one notable exception. ABC Secretary Elmer Baumgarten went out of his way to criticize the All-Star. He was afraid, and rightly so, that the tournament would usurp the ABC Championships as the game's most important event. He commented that the tournament organizers "practically ruined the show."[38] Baumgarten objected to the Petersen system and the harsh scoring conditions, but the handwriting was on the wall. From now on, the All-Star was the most important bowling tournament of the year.

After returning to Brooklyn for the holidays, Andy set out for another year on the road, but there were more pressing matters this year. Like many athletes, Andy dedicated time to supporting the war effort. Nationally, he became a spokesperson for the Hale America campaign and entertained troops on military bases.[39] Other appearances supported the purchase of War Bonds, the USO, and the Women's Hospital Corps.[40]

Americans were in for a long, brutal war, coming on the heels of the deepest economic downturn the country had ever experienced. Just over two decades earlier, the United States entered World War I. The "War to End All Wars" lasted just 19 months. World War II lasted almost four years and took a far more significant toll on the nation.

Twelve

The War

President Roosevelt, as Woodrow Wilson did during World War I, insisted that professional athletes serve in the military. With Roosevelt's encouragement, Major League Baseball (MLB) and National Football League (NFL) games continued during the war. Teams stocked rosters with players who were too young, old, or otherwise ineligible to serve in the armed forces.[1] Over 500 MLB players served in the military, but most stayed stateside and played ball to entertain the troops. But many did see combat, including all-time greats Bob Feller (commander of a gun station on the battleship USS *Alabama*) and Warren Spahn (wounded at the Battle of the Bulge).[2]

While three former MLB players and at least 175 active minor league players were killed in action, not a single active player perished.[3] Unlike MLB players, most NFL players received no special treatment, and many saw combat. More than 600 served, and nine active players were killed.[4] Star bowlers Ned Day, Joe Wilman, and Tony Sparando served in the military, but no nationally known player was killed or seriously wounded in action.

The bowling industry potentially faced shortages of raw materials that might affect the manufacture of balls and shoes (rubber), pins (maple), and lane dressing (shellac). By 1943, technological changes eliminated most of these concerns. Existing inventory met the demand for bowling balls, manufacturers made bowling shoes using reclaimed rubber, a process to refinish bowling pins had been perfected, and bowling centers gradually switched from shellac to lacquer-based lane finishes.[5]

The industry's biggest problem was a shortage of pinboys. The absence of adult men and stricter underage employment enforcement left proprietors with few options. The BPAA suggested that the War Department employ prisoners of war and interned Japanese Americans as pinboys.[6] Fortunately, the government rejected the misguided proposal.

Female pinsetters were employed here and there, but they faced the misogynistic norms of the day. One male journalist was amazed at the idea: "Now they have girl pinboys. Of all things!"[7] He suggested that 17-year-old May—a "pert little blonde" sporting a "cute white blouse"—would "do well on tips, especially when setting for men."[8] Conversely, female bowlers would be "less appreciative of her services."[9] Unable to get enough people to set pins, bowling centers cut their hours.

Despite the war, Andy was busy in 1942. His exhibition schedule was less extensive due to gas rationing, but he spent a lot of time at his bowling schools in Detroit and Chicago. According to the sponsors, the *Detroit News* and the *Chicago Tribune*, almost 100,000 bowlers attended the schools.[10]

Back in Brooklyn, Andy had to admit Alice was right, buying into a bowling center was a good idea. The brisk business at Kenmore Lanes made up for some of his reduced exhibition revenue. His eldest daughter Connie was engaged, and his son Frank studied engineering at the University of Illinois. Youngest daughter Lorraine attended Packer Institute and showed interest in learning her father's trick shots.

The 1942 ABC Championships went as planned in Columbus, Ohio. The tournament attracted a record number of entries, more than double what competed in New York City five years earlier.[11] Andy bowled consistently as usual, compiling an 1,851 all-events total, keeping him close to the top of the 10-year average list.[12] But he failed to finish in the top 10 in any of the four events, and his all-events total was miles behind Stanley Moskal's winning score of 1,973.[13]

While the 1942 tournament was in progress, the ABC announced that the 1943 championships in Buffalo would go as planned but with a shorter duration and limited entries.[14] However, in November, the U.S. Office of Defense Transportation requested the ABC to cancel the tournament, citing transportation concerns.[15] The military usually gets the final say, especially during wartime. The ABCs did not return until 1946, when it drew another record number of entries.[16]

With the ABCs canceled, public attention focused squarely on the All-Star. With only 100 participants, travel restrictions would not be cause to cancel the All-Star, but there was still the nagging question of whether it was appropriate to hold such a tournament with the nation at war. Organizers employed a clever approach to show how holding the tournament supported the war effort and built morale.

If the All-Star continued at the Chicago Coliseum, there would be the annual cost of constructing, breaking down, and storing the lanes each year. Organizers deducted this amount from the prize fund, reducing the dollars available to entice the nation's best bowlers to participate. Tournament organizers sought a permanent site, and thanks to some quick thinking by Louis Petersen, one fell into their lap.

The Auditorium Theatre, once home to the Chicago Symphony Orchestra and the Chicago Opera Company, was in financial distress. Having expanded to include a hotel and an office building, the owners lost money each year and owed Cook County $1.15 million in property taxes.[17] The Auditorium and the surrounding buildings were unceremoniously closed on July 31. The neighboring Congress Hotel shut off power to the complex, citing unpaid bills.[18]

Soon after, the county began foreclosure proceedings, going as far as to auction off the buildings' contents. However, on August 31, 1942, Mayor Edward Kelly announced plans for the city to save the Auditorium. Chicago planned to take over the complex and convert it to a servicemen's center, providing rooms, meals, and recreation facilities for the expected 20,000 men attending radio schools at nearby hotels.[19]

On September 4, Louis Petersen announced the Auditorium Theatre as the site of the 1942 All-Star. Brunswick would install 12 lanes on the theater floor, and rather than break them down and store them, the lanes remained for use by servicemen year-round.[20] A $10 per lane assessment from all Chicago BPAA members raised the $25,000 needed to renovate the space and install the lanes.

The BPAA and the *Tribune* reinvested surplus funds into the facility, ensuring it remained free of charge to servicemen.[21] If there was any question about the appropriateness of having a bowling tournament during wartime, this arrangement ended any controversy. Petersen proved again that he was bowling's best promoter and most creative thinker.

Andy was busy in the months leading up to the All-Star. He stayed close to home in September to get the bowling season kicked off at Kenmore Lanes. Yankees Red Ruffing, Phil Rizzuto, and Gerry Priddy joined Andy for an exhibition benefiting the USO on September 21.[22] Andy went on the road a few days later, not to return until Christmas. As always, Max Grossman did a fantastic job keeping Andy booked solid, but for this one time, he wished he had a few days off.

Andy's oldest daughter Connie was engaged to Lieutenant Michael (Mike) Cornacchia, an officer in the Coast Artillery. They spoke of a summer wedding but never found a suitable date since Mike was on active duty. He finally got a three-day pass, and they scheduled their wedding for October 17.[23] Andy was already touring in Pennsylvania, and Alice called to see if he could get home for the wedding. He would be in Ohio on the weekend of October 17, not too far away, so she held out hope.

"I was home all summer. Why didn't they get married then?" asked Andy. "You know I can't cancel my commitments now. Too many things and places are involved. There is no way I can get back for the wedding."[24] Andy might have liked to walk Connie down the aisle but refused to miss a contracted performance. It exemplified his professional integrity, even when it caused personal pain.

Mike's father did not believe in wartime marriages, and he was not alone. Many thought that marriage should wait until after the war.[25] He never planned to attend a summer wedding and did not change his mind now. So, two Italian mothers stood alone at the wedding of their children at the Holy Rosary Roman Catholic Church in Stuyvesant Heights. Lorraine was the maid of honor, and Mike's brother Lawrence was the best man.[26] Alice made all the arrangements, including a small reception at the Hotel St. George in Brooklyn Heights. And despite all their differences, the guests included Joe and Adeline Falcaro.[27]

Andy spent late September and early October in Ohio. After stops in Lexington, Kentucky, for an exhibition, he spent the next three weeks touring the state of Indiana, appearing in Richmond, Muncie, Tipton, Indianapolis, and Lafayette. In November, Andy entertained troops at Chanute Airfield and the Great Lakes Naval Air Station.[28] He then settled into Chicago to start two weeks of bowling schools at various centers across the city before the All-Star on December 5. Andy entered the event confident if weary.

Organizers tweaked the tournament format to be more grueling than in 1941. A field of 100 players bowled five games per day for six days in the qualifying round while Ned Day and Johnny Crimmins finished their challenge match for Day's world title (which Day retained). The top 10 qualifiers joined Day and Crimmins in the match play round. The 12 finalists would bowl 24 games per day—four matches of six games each—until finally, after 102 games, a champion was crowned. Andy's qualifying rounds were steady. He was in eighth place after the first day, then never lower than sixth place after any round, finishing the qualifying in fifth place, a comfortable hundred pins inside the cut line.

The match-play round had serious star power. The top six qualifiers—Buddy Bomar, Connie Schwoegler, George Young, Frank Benkovic, Paul Krumske, and

Andy—became ABC Hall of Famers, as did Day and Crimmins.[29] Eight of the 12 finalists ranked among the greatest bowlers ever.

The match play round, however, was anticlimactic. The 25-year-old Schwoegler took the lead after the second block and ran away from the field, averaging 217.18 for the 72 games of match play. He outdistanced runner-up Benkovic (204.58) by more than 900 pins. Andy bowled well, finishing third, but no one challenged the "curly haired, blond giant of Madison, Wisconsin."[30] Schwoegler put on the most dominating performance in the 80-year BPAA All-Star/U.S. Open history.

Bowling the final 72 games in three days was a herculean task, especially for a 51-year-old. But the day after the tournament ended, he visited Sun Bowl lanes in East Chicago and gave lessons for three hours in the afternoon, followed by his trick shot exhibition at 11 p.m. He repeated this for the next week, wrapping up in Goshen, Indiana, on December 20 before driving back to Brooklyn for Christmas.[31] He had been on the road for two months and bowled for hours each day. But by mid–January 1943, he was off to Detroit for another installment of his bowling school, where over 56 days, he bowled 365 games in 39 different houses, averaging more than 209.[32]

Professional bowlers are used to bowling many games. When non-bowlers question whether bowling is a sport, my standard response is, *go bowl 10 games and let me know how you feel.* A bit unfair unless one is used to performing 175 lunges with the left leg carrying a 15-pound dumbbell (what a right-handed bowler does in 10 games). My point was that, like all athletes, bowlers are susceptible to repetitive motion injuries and must train specific body parts accordingly. Injured wrists, elbows, shoulders, and backs are commonplace, but the most widespread malady among bowlers is a sore thumb. Yes, sore thumbs.

Bowlers developed sore thumbs not long after balls had holes drilled in them. In their bowling tips columns, Jimmy Smith (1925), Joe Wilman (1960), and Dick Weber (1980) all wrote about the importance of thumb care.[33] Bowling's most infamous thumb belonged to the great Mark Roth. Over the years, journalists described his thumb as "grotesque," "ugly," "like it has passed through a meat slicer," and "as shredded as fresh hamburger meat."[34] Roth came to resent the media's fascination with his thumb: "Most of [the stories] were about my thumb, not a man behind the thumb."[35]

Modern bowlers benefit from improved technology that has reduced the incidence of sore thumbs. Bowlers have healthier thumbs today thanks to a more scientific approach to fitting bowling balls, computer-aided drill presses that more accurately duplicate grips, and protective tape (akin to KT Tape, placed on the thumb). But even with these improvements, keeping a perfect fit in the thumb can be a challenge. Changes in temperature, humidity, elevation, and diet can make a bowler's thumb shrink or swell from day to day or even hour to hour.

For his part, Andy never complained about a sore thumb or injuries of any kind until he was well into his 60s. But when it came to his thumb, he had a secret weapon. Andy always had three balls with him. Unlike modern bowlers who use different balls to combat varying lane conditions, his balls were identical, except each had a different-sized thumbhole. As his thumb swelled or shrunk, he changed balls accordingly and always had a perfect fit.[36] Just another example of Andy being ahead of his time.

The postponement of the 1943 ABCs had one positive effect. Bowlers were looking for tournaments to bowl in, and entrepreneurs obliged. The Petersen Classic attracted a record 832 entries in 1943.[37] Park Manor Recreation owner Dominick DeVito—to this day, the only three-time winner of the Petersen Classic—started his eight-game sweeper in Chicago, which ran concurrently with the Pete.

DeVito correctly assumed that many bowlers in town for the Petersen wanted to take a crack at another tournament with a big prize fund. Sixty-one-year-old Sarge Easter claimed the $1,000 first prize at the inaugural Dom DeVito Classic. In November 1943, Eddie Koepp of Cleveland pocketed the $1,500 first prize in another eight-game Chicago tournament, the Buddy Bomar Diamond Medal Classic.[38]

New York bowling impresario Bill Landgraf founded the Landgraf Classic, a four-game sweeper held at Bowlmor Recreation in Manhattan. Andy won the title in May, collecting the $500 first prize.[39] The Landgraf started modestly, a one-day event with a couple of hundred entries. In later years, it generated thousands of entries and lasted for several months. Offering as much as a $10,000 first prize, the Landgraf became a regular stop for the nation's best bowlers. Future winners included ABC Hall of Famers Steve Nagy, Lou Campi, Tony Sparando, Dick Weber, and Billy Welu.[40]

Andy returned to Flatbush in April after wrapping up his Detroit bowling school. He and Alice traveled to Pennsylvania to see Frank graduate with his engineering degree from Lafayette College on April 20.[41] Frank immediately enlisted and enrolled in Naval Training School in South Bend, Indiana, on the University of Notre Dame campus. Ensign Varipapa graduated in September and, after a few stops stateside, joined the 138th Naval Construction Battalion ("The Seabees") on the Aleutian Island of Attu. Frank used his engineering skills to design, build, and maintain runways, hangers, and barracks. After a promotion, Lieutenant Varipapa received an honorable discharge from the Navy in August 1946.[42]

Andy spent his summer tending to Kenmore Lanes, and due to travel restrictions, the *Chicago Tribune* suspended their fall 1943 bowling school. Andy traveled and performed less due to gas rationing, which left a lot of time to fill for someone used to being on the road so often. In early fall, he shared with Alice a conversation with Lou and Mary Geisler, owners of Hempstead Recreation. Andy told them if they ever put the center up for sale, Andy was interested in buying. The Geislers, also owners of Valley Stream Recreation, told Andy they appreciated his offer but had no interest in selling.[43]

Andy's revelation took Alice aback. She asked, "Do you really want to move to Long Island?" Andy replied, "If I can't travel for my exhibitions, I would prefer to be located where there is more activity among better bowlers."[44] She said "move" because Alice knew Andy did not want to be an hour's drive from his bowling center. He thought the six-mile commute from Bushwick to Kenmore in Flatbush was too far.

Leaving Brooklyn was something Andy had thought about for some time. Few top bowlers lived there anymore, and many Brooklyn residents with the financial resources to do so fled to the quieter suburbs of northern New Jersey or Long Island. Located on Front Street, just off Peninsula Boulevard, Hempstead Recreation was at the epicenter of the burgeoning Long Island bowling community. Top bowlers and proprietors who called Long Island home included Joe Falcaro, Eddie Heineman, Tony Kusky, Fred Voelpel, and George Young.

Andy preferred moving to Detroit, a bowling-crazed town he knew well after spending time there running his bowling school. His Detroit schools lasted for a month and drew more than 50,000 pupils, compared to the 4,000 that attended his *Nassau Daily Review-Star* six-day school at Heineman's in 1941.[45] He never had enough interest from newspapers or proprietors to run a bowling school in Brooklyn, once lamenting that while New York Mayor Fiorello LaGuardia goes to fires, Detroit Mayor Ed Jefferies goes to bowling alleys.[46]

But with all his and Alice's family in the East, moving to Detroit was unrealistic. Andy was confident that if he purchased a bowling center on Long Island, partner Joe Spinella would buy out his share at Kenmore. But Andy had more pressing matters: he needed to prepare for the 1943 All-Star.

Without the *Chicago Tribune* bowling school, he did not need to leave so early for the All-Star. In November, he faced George Young in an 80-game match. Young, just coming into his own as a bowler, took up the sport at 24 after moving to Long Island from Omega, Georgia.[47] He threw himself into the game and, by 1943, owned a six-lane center in Franklin Square. He also managed the brand-new Malverne Bowling Center and had a military job at Liberty Aircraft in Farmingdale.[48]

Young was the reigning Nassau County Champion, won the Outstanding Bowler Award at the Long Island Industrial Championships two years running, and finished ninth in the 1942 All-Star. In 1944, he moved to Detroit and continued his outstanding play, winning three ABC titles and two national doubles championships. He is a member of the ABC Hall of Fame, two state halls of fame (New York and Michigan), and two local halls of fame (Long Island and Detroit).

Tragically, Young died of lymphoma in 1959 at just 49 years of age. In 1962, the PBA created an award to honor the bowler with the highest average during their season. His reputation was such that even though he never bowled a PBA event, it was named George Young Memorial High Average Award.[49]

The match took place in eight houses over three weeks in 10-game blocks. It was a serious match with brand new, three-pound, six-ounce pins, freshly shellacked lanes waxed an hour before each match, pinboys wearing white gloves, and a $1500 purse. Fans paid 55 cents for tickets, and crowds as large as 300 greeted the bowlers at each stop.[50]

Andy jumped out to a 107-pin lead at his home lanes at Hempstead Recreation and never trailed. Young won only two of the eight blocks, and Andy coasted to a decisive 755-pin victory, averaging 207.29.[51] Fresh off this win over Young, coupled with his win at the Landgraf in May, Andy must have been confident that he could challenge for the All-Star title in December.

The organizers modified the All-Star format again for 1943 by expanding the field to 144 players and adding a stage. There were two cuts: one to 48 bowlers after the 24-game qualifying round and another to 13 after a 12-game semifinal round. Joining the survivors in the 16-man finals were current world champion Ned Day, 1941 champion Johnny Crimmins, and 1942 champion Connie Schwoegler. Four days of four-game round-robin matches determined the winner.[52] This 100-game format (24 qualifying, 12 semifinal, and 64 round-robin match play games) remained in place until 1962.[53]

Andy shot 4,940 for the first 24 games and sat in fifth place.[54] But this year, a 12-game semifinal block followed before determining the final 13 players who advanced to the match play finals. Andy bowled poorly the first six games of the semifinals, shooting just 1,112, dropping him to 13th place, right on the cut line. But after shooting a spectacular 1,131 for his first five games in the last semifinal block, his spot in the finals appeared secure. But disaster struck in the final game when Andy bowled just 159, giving him a 7,342 total. While he was in fifth place, there were still 24 bowlers left with a chance to pass him.

Andy watched as bowler after bowler passed him. Sitting in 12th place, Andy still had a chance going into the final squad, but Nelson Burton, Sr., and Bill Hargadon passed him, leaving Andy in 14th place, just three pins behind Adam Plunge of Chicago.[55] More annoying for Andy was that the foul judge called a foul—his foot went over the foul line, resulting in zero for that shot—on a ball that struck. Reports said he "put up a howl," but the foul call stood.[56] It is unclear when the foul occurred, but that 159 must have gnawed at him.

Andy missed the cut by just three pins. Eerily like 1941, when he missed by six. As the first man out of the finals, he was designated "alternate," meaning that if someone in the finals got injured, Andy would replace him and finish the tournament. Tournaments typically pay the alternate a nominal amount—at the All-Star, probably $25 or $50—to sit around for four days and see if someone got hurt. Andy declined; he made more at a single performance.[57]

While not as dominating as Connie Schwoegler's performance the year before, Ned Day comfortably won the All-Star over Paul Krumske, leading after each day of the finals to earn the $2000 first prize.[58] The win solidified Day's reputation as the world's best bowler. A week earlier, the National Bowling Writers Association (NBWA) named him Bowler of the Year, an honor he received again in 1944.[59]

Andy was back in Brooklyn for only a few days when he got a phone call from a distraught Lou Geisler. His wife Mary was killed when her car crashed into a tree near Hempstead Recreation.[60] Geisler told Andy that he and Mary decided if they ever chose to sell, it would be to Andy and Alice. Lou wanted to honor Mary's wishes, and if Andy was still interested, Lou stood ready to make a deal.

As expected, Joe Spinella bought out Andy's share of Kenmore, freeing up the cash required to close the purchase. *Newsday* announced Andy's purchase of Hempstead Recreation in January 1944.[61] Immediately renamed "Andy Varipapa's Hempstead Recreation," the 14-lane center became the "Home of the World's Most Sensational Bowler."[62]

The sale of Kenmore and the purchase of Hempstead Recreation also meant that the Varipapa family would be on the move. Andy and Alice lived in Brooklyn walk-ups their whole lives, so moving to Hempstead was going "to the country."[63] The first house they looked at had a lot of property, and Alice wondered who would take care of it all. "You certainly don't have the time," said Alice. "All I know is that grass is green, and roses are mostly red."[64]

"But Alice, look around. You can really breathe here," said Andy. "Now, Andrew, just when did we ever have trouble breathing before now?" replied Alice. "Can we just look around a little more?"[65] They finally settled on a two-story colonial on a manageable 50' × 100' lot at 78 Kernochan Avenue, a few blocks west of Hofstra University just south of Hempstead Turnpike.

It was an excellent location, just one mile from Hempstead Recreation. The home was also near the family's favorite beach, Point Lookout. The Varipapas often spent sweltering summer days at Brighton Beach in Brooklyn, which was convenient but crowded. Sometimes the family piled into Andy's car and headed to Point Lookout on the south shore of Nassau County, just east of Long Beach.[66] While much less crowded and cleaner than Brighton, it was a 30-mile drive, and with typical Sunday traffic, it took an hour or more to get there. Point Lookout was now 12 miles from home via Robert Moses's new Meadowbrook Parkway. Hempstead seemed like the perfect location for the Varipapas.

For the first time since the 1939–40 season, Andy was left off the *Bowlers Journal*'s All-American teams. In 1938, taking a cue from all-American teams selected in college football, editor Mort Luby, Sr., selected six bowlers to form an All-American team. Selection to those teams, especially to the first team, carried significant weight with ABC Hall of Fame voters.

Andy had never been a first-team selection, nor had anyone else residing east of Cleveland besides Tony Sparando in 1938. Andy earned a third team selection in 1939–40 and a second team in 1940–41, 1941–42, and 1942–43.[67] He garnered some respect but was not perceived in the same class as Ned Day, Joe Wilman, Buddy Bomar, and the other top players.

Announcements of exhibitions or tournaments always referred to Andy's trick shot rather than competitive abilities. Promoting a benefit at Bronxville Bowling Alleys in 1944, a news story noted that participants included "Joe Falcaro, world's match game titlist.… Andy Varipapa, trick-shot artist; Marty Cassio, former Metropolitan Champ; Chester Arnhorst, former State Champ; Barney Spinella, former American Bowling Congress titlist."[68]

After a year's hiatus, the *Chicago Tribune* resumed its annual bowling school in October and November. But Andy was not part of it. Ned Day, now the world match game champion for four out of the past seven years, led the school.[69] No one knows if the *Tribune* asked Andy to lead the school, and he declined, or if they decided it was time for a new face to take over. Unfortunately for Day, his reign as world champion ended before the school did.

Paul Krumske, as was his right as the 1943 All-Star runner-up, challenged Day for his title. Krumske took a 613-pin lead at the first 30 games at Bowling Lanes in Chicago, and although Day mounted a comeback at his home lanes in West Allis, Krumske won by 287 pins.[70] The Day-Krumske match was the last world championship challenge match. The BPAA announced that whoever won the 1944 All-Star would be the world champion, and no more challenge matches were permitted.

At the 1944 All-Star, Andy bowled well in the qualifying and semifinal rounds, overcoming a weak 1,117 in the third block. He qualified third with 7,250, 120 pins inside the cut line.[71] Andy started match play poorly, averaging just 199 on the first day and winning just 6 of 16 matches.[72] He languished near the bottom of the standings: 13th after the second day and 14th after the third. Andy bowled well on the final day, going 12-4 and averaging 209 to finish in 10th place, while 28-year-old Buddy Bomar coasted to victory.[73]

Ned Day was the king, but Bomar was nipping at his heels. Bomar already held the 1944 national doubles title and, in 1947, pulled off an unprecedented double. He won the regular Petersen Classic in January and a second in May in Buffalo. His 1947 earnings of $17,400 ($233,433 in 2023 dollars) likely stood as an inflation-adjusted single-season record until Therm Gibson won $75,000 ($750,026 in 2023 dollars) on *Phillies Jackpot Bowling* in 1961.[74] By 1947, Bomar usurped Day's crown.

The NBWA voted Bomar Bowler of the Year twice, and *Bowlers Journal* selected him to five All-American teams and named him 1940s Bowler of the Decade. Elected to the ABC Hall of Fame in 1966, *Bowlers Journal* ranked Bomar the 18th greatest bowler of the 20th century, ahead of better-known contemporaries Joe Falcaro, Therm Gibson, George Young, and Connie Schwoegler.[75]

In January 1945, Andy did not tour other than making local appearances on behalf of the Infantile Paralysis Fund (later, the March of Dimes). In February, he ventured to Chicago to bowl the Petersen and DeVito Classics. As usual, he bowled horribly in the Petersen (1,299 for eight games, including a 126 game).[76] Andy fared better in the DeVito, finishing ninth and earning $575.

Immediately following the Petersen, the Associated Press reported that Andy agreed to meet Buddy Bomar in a $2,000 home-and-home match in March.[77] Bomar was hot: after winning the 1944 All-Star, he finished third in the DeVito Classic and third in the Petersen doubles in early February. He was confident, too. The *Detroit Times* reported that of the $2,000 wagered by Bomar, $1,300 was his own money, a rarity when most bowlers had backers and put up only a fraction of the purse themselves.[78]

Andy averaged 219 for the first 27 games at Hempstead Recreation and built a modest 83-pin lead, but Bomar took over when the match moved to Chicago two weeks later.[79] Bomar erased Andy's lead in just two games in a performance aided by an abundance of asymmetric information. Bomar crushed him on his home lanes at Faetz Recreation, averaging 239 to Andy's 196 and winning the match by almost 1,100 pins.[80]

Andy sought revenge in May when he teamed with George Young and took on Bomar and partner Joe Norris in a 56-game home-and-home match. The side bet was $2,000 per man. Andy and George got off to a good start, taking an 843-pin lead after 28 games at Baldwin Modern on Long Island. The Baldwin lane man gave Bomar a taste of his own medicine. Bomar averaged but 171 for the first seven games.[81]

Before leaving for Detroit, Andy and Young completed the 27-week-long Nassau Bowling Association Individual Classic tournament, better known as the Long Island Championship. After 216 games, they ended the season tied for first place, necessitating a 30-game roll-off to decide the winner.[82] However, their roll-off had to wait until they returned after their match with Bomar and Norris.

The New Yorkers did not rest on their laurels, winning three of the four blocks at Palace Recreation in Detroit, including the final block, despite an opening 300 game by Norris. They won decisively by 974 pins. Andy and George averaged 214, Norris 209, and Bomar 203.[83] It must have been satisfying for Andy to get his $2,000 back!

Andy and Young squared off for the Long Island Individual Championship when they returned from Detroit. Down 30 pins going into the final game at Brown's Recreation in Valley Stream, Andy saw Young's lead grow to 41 pins by the fifth frame.[84] Andy's five straight strikes, coupled with Young's misses in the sixth and ninth frames, gave him a chance to put away the title in the 10th frame. He spared and struck for a 213 and won the 30-game match by just three pins.[85]

As the calendar turned to summer, the good news was that the war in Europe was over. The bad news was that war continued in the Pacific, with Frank stationed in the Aleutians. War raged for three more months until a new and relatively unknown president took unprecedented action to end the hostilities.

Thirteen

All-Star Andy

The summer of 1945 was a joyous yet bittersweet time for Americans. Hitler committed suicide on April 30, and a week later, the Germans surrendered, ending the hostilities in Europe. Victory in the Pacific followed in August after the United States unleashed two devastating nuclear weapons on Japan. Celebrations were raucous but tempered by the fact that the war left approximately 400,000 Americans dead.

Sports returned in full force: from 1945 to 1946, attendance increased by 71 percent in MLB and 48 percent in the NFL.[1] Demand for football was so great that a new league, the All-American Football Conference, commenced operations and drew almost 1.2 million fans, yielding an increase in overall professional football attendance of 130 percent.[2] All major golf and tennis tournaments in the United States and Europe resumed in 1946, as did the ABC Championships.

As the 1945 All-Star approached, Andy was 54 years old and not mentioned in any of the *Tribune* stories promoting the tournament. In 1941, his entry into the tournament made headlines. In 1945, he was an afterthought. What no one knew, and no one expected, was that Andy would dominate the All-Star over the next four years like no one before or since.

The 1945 All-Star included five players seeded into the match play finals: Buddy Bomar, Joe Wilman, Ned Day, Joe Sinke (the top four finishers in 1944), and Paul Krumske (the world champion before the 1944 tournament).[3] That left 11 spots for the top qualifiers. Andy started slowly and was in 29th place after the first 12 games. That pace was sufficient to advance to the semifinals but nowhere near enough to achieve a top-11 finish.[4] He bowled much better over the next two days and was in fourth place after 24 games.[5]

Andy bowled steadily during the 12-game semifinals and qualified fifth, easily advancing to the match-play finals. The finals included 12 future ABC Hall of Famers: Andy, Wilman, Day, Bomar, Krumske, Walter Ward, Steve Nagy, Therm Gibson, Nelson Burton, Sr., Frank Benkovic, Connie Schwoegler, and Fred Bujack.[6] In the All-Star, the cream always rose to the top. Andy, at 54, was by far the oldest bowler in the finals: only Ward (47) and George Vallos (46) were even in their 40s.

Andy bowled superbly on the first day of match play, averaging 220 and winning 10 of 16 games. Still, he trailed Joe Wilman, runner-up in 1944 and finalist in 1941. *Tribune* writer Charles Bartlett, who had little respect for Andy, described him as the "voluble and acrobatic ... veteran trick-shot practitioner."[7] By contrast, he described Wilman as "the confident and poised Berwyn campaigner" and Benkovic, sitting in third, as "the roving Milwaukee strike and spare professor."[8]

Wilman extended his lead on the second day, partly because although Andy bowled well, he did not win many games. Wilman led in pinfall by only 58 pins but posted a 25–7 win/loss record versus 17–15 for Andy, translating into a 7.08 Petersen point advantage.[9] Wilman maintained his seven-point lead through the next day's matches, and Andy was in a virtual tie with Therm Gibson for second place.

In Bartlett's accompanying *Tribune* story, he revealed just how little regard he had for Andy: "Still continuing to startle the most fulsome and enthusiastic audience ... [Varipapa] the man of a thousand grimaces and gestures, normally respected as a trick shot artist and a no boy as competitive bowlers go, is still maintaining the terrific pace with which he set out in the first match play matinee on Thursday."[10] Andy finished among the top 14 in the first four All-Stars, including a third-place finish in 1942. He possessed the third-highest 10-year ABC Championships average. But Bartlett still described him as "a no boy."

Andy had a chance to catch Wilman on the final day, but a poor start derailed his chances. He lost three out of four games in his first match to the unheralded George Vallos of Youngstown, Ohio, shooting a dismal 733 and falling another five points behind Wilman, who took three of four from Ned Day. Andy split with defending champion Buddy Bomar in the next block but fell to third place as Gibson passed him. Through the luck of scheduling, Andy bowled Wilman in the penultimate block. Even though he was trailing by more than 13 points, if he swept Wilman, he could pick up six or seven points and move into second place.[11]

The final block was a position round, where the first-place bowler met the second, the third met the fourth, and so on. If Andy bowled well enough to move into second place, he would meet Wilman face-to-face in the position round. Andy trounced Wilman 241–202 in the first game, but after Wilman came back with 237–186 and 203–188 victories, the tournament was all but over.[12]

Therm Gibson swept Wilman in the position round, but his lead was so large that it did not matter. Wilman compiled the best win-loss record (41.5–22.5), knocked down the most pins (a 209.95 average), and was thus a deserving champion. Andy fell behind Walter Ward after a dismal 151 in the first game of the position round but rebounded to fire 733 over the final three games (252, 244, and 237) to secure third place and a $500 prize.[13]

After returning to Hempstead for the holidays and tending to Hempstead Recreation, Andy embarked on his 1946 bowling season. He made a conscious effort to bowl more tournaments and matches and fewer trick-shot exhibitions, but the year did not get off to a rousing start. In January, Andy lost matches to rising star Marty Cassio of Rahway, New Jersey (by 121 pins in a 60-game match at Heineman's) and veteran Walter Ward (by a whopping 737 pins in a 40-game match at Khoury's Arcadian Recreation in Cleveland).[14]

Andy bowled poorly in the Petersen Classic in early February, scoring just 1,435 for eight games, more than 200 pins behind the winner, veteran Adolph (Swede) Carlson of Chicago.[15] In March, he finished second at the Wilmington Individual Bowling Sweepstakes, shooing 910 for four games but losing by a single pin to fellow New Yorker Tony Sparando.[16] In April, Andy teamed up with Sparando for a big doubles match at his home alleys, Hempstead Recreation, where they took on Wilman and James (Junie) McMahon.

These were tough opponents. Wilman was hot: in eight days in February, he won the Waibel Classic in St. Louis ($1,500) and the Anderson Classic in Moline, Illinois ($1,250).[17] Those 14 games earned him more than he did in the 100 needed to win the All-Star. Junie McMahon, a 34-year-old right-hander originally from Passaic, New Jersey, was best known for his outstanding performance in the 1940 ABCs. While he did not win an eagle, he finished in the top four in doubles, team, and all-events.[18]

Despite winning a $1,000 four-game sweeper in Playdium Lanes in St. Louis in February, he did not yet have a national reputation. McMahon participated in all five All-Stars but never advanced to the finals.[19] Over the next decade, bowling fans got to know the great Junie McMahon.

McMahon went on to win the 1947 ABC singles and all-events titles, the 1949 and 1951 All-Stars, and the 1953 *Newsday* Eastern Open. From 1949 to 1953, he was the best bowler in the world. He was named the BWAA Bowler of the Year in 1950, selected to five *Bowlers Journal* All-American teams, and inducted into the ABC Hall of Fame in 1955. *Bowlers Journal* ranked him the 12th greatest bowler of the 20th century.[20] McMahon's career ended tragically on January 9, 1959, when he collapsed in his dressing room after taping the first episode of *Phillies Jackpot Bowling* at T-Bowl in Wayne, New Jersey. He never bowled again, having suffered a stroke that left him partially paralyzed until he died in 1974.[21]

McMahon and Wilman earned Andy's respect, which was not an easy task. Andy threw compliments around like manhole covers when it came to other bowlers. He usually noted their deficiencies and ignored their strengths. USBC Hall of Fame coach Tom Kouros wrote, "One day, I brought up Junie McMahon's name, fully expecting the typical rebuff. Andy looked me straight in the eye and said, 'He could bowl.'"[22] Of Wilman, Andy said, "You've got to go out and beat the best in the country, and when you beat Wilman, that is language the bowling world can understand. They don't come any tougher than he."[23]

In what must have been considered an upset, Andy and Tony beat Wilman and McMahon handily by 399 pins. Andy led the way by averaging 210.0.[24] Nothing like a home-field advantage! A few weeks later, Andy and Tony traveled to Detroit for the first leg of a 42-game home-and-home match with Andy's friend George Young, teamed with Therm Gibson. In Detroit, the New Yorkers ran up a 274-pin lead, and when they returned to Heineman's for the second leg, they added another 441 pins for a decisive 715-pin victory. Sparando did the heavy lifting this time, averaging 206.6 in a match when no one else averaged over 200.[25]

Andy seemed to thrive in doubles matches. He rarely lost. When asked about his doubles prowess, he remarked, "All I know is when I get a new doubles partner he soon becomes world champion."[26] His doubles record contrasted with his distaste for five-man team bowling, where he never got used to the slower pace.

In April, Andy took a trip to Buffalo to bowl in the New York State Bowling Association (NYSBA) championships and the ABCs. He won the NYSBA all-events title with 1,917 and rolled a steady 1,883 at the ABCs.[27] Sadly, it was another year without coming close to an ABC title. His nemesis Wilman shot a record 2,054 to take his second all-events crown in the past five tournaments. But Andy's consistency was remarkable. He had gone into the 1946 ABCs with the third-highest 10-year average of 202.6, behind Johnny Crimmins (203.4) and Ned Day (203.1).[28] His 1,883 all-events total moved him past both Crimmins and Day, but Marty

Cassio overtook him after a strong 1946 performance, raising his average to 203.6, while Andy stood at 203.4.[29]

Considering the popularity of big-money sweepers, it was no surprise when Andy decided to run one at Hempstead Recreation. He borrowed an idea from Dom DeVito in Chicago, who ran his tournament simultaneously with the Petersen Classic. When Joe Falcaro held his annual sweepstakes at Peninsula Lanes, Andy ran his at Hempstead Recreation. Bowlers traveling from out of town welcomed another chance to earn some cash while on Long Island. Eddie Heineman got in the act, too, and hosted a six-game sweeper at his center right down the road from Hempstead Recreation. All three tournaments ran from May 24 through June 2, and *Newsday* bowling columnist Ed Buckley called the series the "Nassau Sweepstakes Carnival."[30]

Most of the country's top bowlers showed up, including all five All-Star champions: Crimmins, Schwoegler, Day, Bomar, and Wilman. Falcaro's eight-game sweeper featured a gigantic $5,000 ($76,102 in 2023 dollars) first prize, won by Charlie McDonough, an unheralded 23-year-old former GI from White Plains. Sarge Easter, Nelson Burton, Sr., and Crimmins finished in the top 10.[31]

ABC Hall of Famer Buzz Fazio won Andy's tournament. His 1,360 for six games was enough to pocket the $1,200 winner's check. National stars Joe Ostroski, Ed Kawolics, Chet Bukowski, and Joe Sinke posted top-10 finishes. Heineman did not get the turnout of the other two tournaments, and Eddie may have put the event's future in doubt when he proved a rude host. He shot 1,286 and won his own tournament.[32]

Andy's spent his summer out west with George Young. Salt Lake City in June, San Francisco, Fresno, and Los Angeles in July, and Tucson and St. Louis in August. They bowled matches and tournaments, and Andy did his trick-shot exhibitions. The most interesting tournament was a six-game sweeper held at Speedway Lanes in Tucson on August 4. Most of the entrants were local players. Besides Andy and George, Leo Rollick, Ernie Soest, and Sarge Easter were the only recognizable names entered.[33]

Proprietor John McKenzie advertised a guaranteed $1,000 prize for first place to promote the tournament. However, with only 96 entries, the only prize he could afford to pay was the first-place guarantee. Young shot 1,264 to claim the winner-take-all affair, and Andy finished second with 1,252.[34] However, Andy was not upset because, like many doubles teams, he and George split winnings 50–50. Andy quipped, "But the third place guy was sure sore."[35]

After returning from his trip, Andy rested for a few weeks and started the winter bowling season at Hempstead Recreation. In late October, he bowled a short 20-game home-and-home match with little-known Sam Vitola of Lyndhurst, New Jersey. Andy beat him handily while averaging 238.[36] In November, he took second place in a sweeper at Central Bowling Academy in Bethlehem, Pennsylvania, and then headed out to Chicago for the 1946 All-Star.[37]

Despite finishing third the year before, Andy's name once again was nowhere to be seen in the *Tribune*'s numerous promotional stories. A slight change in the format affected Andy: in 1944 and 1945, the top four bowlers from the previous All-Star, along with the champion from the year before, were seeded into the match-play finals. In 1945, tournament organizers decided to seed only the two most recent champions (Wilman and Bomar), leaving 14 spots in the finals for the other 142 contestants.[38] So Andy had to qualify like everyone else.

The tournament began on Sunday, November 30. Andy bowled well in the qualifying round, posting six-game blocks of 1,210, 1,245, 1,266, and 1,274. His 4,995 placed him third behind George Young and Joe Norris.[39] As good a form as he showed over the first 24 games, Andy did not bowl well in the semifinals. His first six-game block of 1,164 dropped him to eighth place, leaving him just 50 pins ahead of the 14th and final qualifying spot for the match play finals. Lurking just outside the cut line were a slew of seasoned veterans, including Paul Krumske, Chet Bukowski, Ned Day, Johnny Crimmins, and Tony Sparando.

Bowling in the first of the two semifinal squads, Andy's first three games of 168, 205, and 174 left him right on the cut line. He rebounded with games of 214 and 228, but after shooting a 188 in his final game, his 36-game total stood at 7,336. Based on the scores after 30 games, the projected cut was 7,331, so Andy was close. Fortunately, the scores drifted lower in the last squad, so it was not as close as expected. Andy qualified in ninth place, making the cut with 43 pins to spare.

Andy made it to the finals, but if he expected to contend, he needed to bowl much better than he did in the semifinals. He averaged 208 for his first 24 games of qualifying but just 195 in the 12-game semifinals. And there was Joe Wilman to contend with, sharp as ever, leading the field with a 212 average and looking like the odds-on favorite to defend his title. Andy led after the first round of match play on the strength of his 11–5 record. However, there was still cause for concern because Allie Brandt, Junie McMahon, Leo Rollick, Wilman, Walter Johnson (not *that* Walter Johnson), Adolph Carlson, and Lee Braymiller all knocked down more pins than Andy's 3,244.[40]

Andy scored much better on day two, shooting 3,397 for his 16 games, but was passed by Allie Brandt. A 44-year-old veteran from Lockport, New York, Brandt was noted for being a tiny man who rolled the highest three-game series on record. Brandt stood five foot four (or five foot one, depending on the source) and weighed just 125 pounds, described by the *Tribune* as "the greying mite from Lockport."[41] In 1939 he rolled his ABC-record 886 series, which stood for 50 years until Tom Jordan rolled an 899 in Union, New Jersey.[42] George Young was close behind in third place, with McMahon, Wilman, Norris, and Krumske all within striking distance of the lead.[43]

Andy bowled marvelously on Saturday night, averaging 222 and regaining the lead from Brandt by winning 11 of 16 games.[44] He entered the final day of the All-Star with a 1.5-point lead over Brandt and 4.6 over McMahon, who had charged into third place. Andy took the lanes on Sunday morning and won three out of four games in his opening match from Young, rolling a strong 895 series. At the same time, Brandt managed just 723 and dropped three of four against 26-year-old All-Star rookie Semo Stavich of Wheeling, West Virginia.

Meanwhile, McMahon swept Joe Sinke and moved into second place, four points behind Andy. Andy then met Wilman in the second block, who, despite all his excellent bowling during 1946, never contended for the title (he eventually finished in seventh place). Andy took three of four from Wilman, shooting another strong series of 848, and watched his lead grow to 4.5 points when McMahon split with Buddy Bomar. McMahon saw his chances disappear in the penultimate match when he dropped three of four from young Stavich.

By chance, Andy matched up with Brandt in the third block. Brandt mounted a charge, winning the first game 212–192, the second 179–160, and the third 246–244. A win in the fourth game could pull him to within a couple of points, but Andy buckled down and fired a 267. That won the game and gave him a crucial bonus point for having a higher series in a match when losing three of four games. Andy took a six-point lead heading into the final block, where he would meet Brandt again in the position round.[45]

Brunswick publicity photograph, 1946 (Brunswick Bowling Products LLC photograph; IBM-HOF collection).

Once again, Brant cut into Andy's lead. He won the first game 236–221 and the second 234–159. If Brandt won the next two games, there was a real chance he could claim the title. Brandt, playing the role of David to Andy's Goliath, had the momentum and a crowd of 2,500 behind him.

After being handed the lead when Brandt opened in the sixth frame, Andy doubled in the 9th and 10th frames to squeeze out a 205–202 victory. It provided him with an insurmountable four-point lead going into the final game.[46] Andy finished in style, shooting a 269 to Brandt's 168, finally winning that big title that eluded him all these years. In his victory statement, in true Varipapa style, he proclaimed, "This has been long overdue. It's about time the world's greatest bowler was also world champion."[47]

Andy's win meant much more than the $2,000 winner's check. Some estimated his win to be worth $50,000.[48] That may have been true if someone like Brandt won, but besides Ned Day, Andy already had more endorsement contracts than any other bowler. Nonetheless, his win substantially increased his earning potential.

An article in the *Tribune* two days after his win cryptically referred to him stopping by "the offices of a bowling supply concern" he was already under contract with to discuss "bigger digits on the document now that he has captured the national title."[49] Of course, the company was Brunswick, whose corporate offices were in Chicago and whom Andy had represented since 1934. Andy said, "A new agreement was reached," one in which Brunswick sponsored all his future appearances.[50]

Articles published after his victory noted his age as 52 or 53 despite being 55. Andy understated his age, typically by three years, in articles as early as 1934.[51] At that time, he did not mind being considered younger than he was, and it went on for years. In a 1948 *Collier's* profile, at age 57, Andy claimed to be 54.[52] But as he got older, he ensured that journalists got his age correct. In 1982 he told ABC Hall of Fame writer Dick Evans, "Make sure you make that 91½, because, at my age, that half-year is very important."[53]

The *Tribune*'s Bartlett, Andy's passive-aggressive critic, credited him for winning as the tournament's oldest competitor. Still, he reminded readers that it was Andy's "first major triumph in a competitive career dating back to 1928."[54] The AP wire story referred to him as a "veteran."[55] Other articles used more colorful language and described Andy as a "foxy grandpa," "a pudgy grey-haired ex-machinist," and a "squat, chunky, laughing hombre."[56]

Most articles were complimentary and referred to his fitness, regardless of whether he was chunky, pudgy, or what have you: "To be a successful bowler you have to stay in perfect shape," said Andy, "in the recent Chicago tournament…. I was the only contestant to finish without sore legs, sore arms, or some other unpleasant reminder."[57] Sports columnist Dan Daniel said Andy's victory "must be recognized as a singular feat in skill, stamina, condition, and persistence."[58]

While proclaiming Andy the "greatest all-around bowler of the day," Milwaukee bowling writer Billy Sixty noted that his extraordinary trick-shot prowess had long overshadowed his competitive talents.[59] Sixty was a rare bowling writer who was also an outstanding bowler. A sportswriter for the *Milwaukee Journal* for 60 years, he was a four-time Wisconsin Match Game champion and made the All-Star finals in 1944.[60] Elected to the ABC Hall of Fame for superior performance in 1961, Sixty's syndicated columns appeared in papers nationwide. Unlike Bartlett, Sixty

Andy, likely at Brunswick headquarters in Chicago, after his 1946 All-Star Victory. From left: Andy, Joe Norris, Ned Day, Joe Wilman, and Buddy Bomar (Brunswick Bowling Products LLC photograph; IBMHOF collection).

was an elite bowler and respected Andy's ability. Sixty never referred to Andy as just a trick-shot artist.

On December 31, Nassau County Bowling Proprietors Association members threw a dinner party to celebrate Andy's victory at Heineman's.[61] Andy reveled in the adulation because he finally confirmed what he knew in his heart: he was the world's best bowler. And now he had the title to prove it. If it were even possible, Andy would be more in demand come 1947 than ever before. Brunswick planned a nationwide tour as Andy traveled to and from Los Angeles for the 1947 ABC Championships. Would 1947 be the year he claimed that elusive eagle?

Fourteen

Back-to-Back

Andy expected his All-Star victory to change public perception of him. More of "Andy Varipapa, great bowler," and less of "Andy Varipapa, trick-shot artist." It would not happen overnight. Two weeks after Andy won the All-Star, Tait Cummins, the sports editor of the *Cedar Rapids Evening Gazette*, described Joe Wilman as "the best bowler the country has seen ... no trick shot artist like Andy Varipapa. Joe is a bowler's bowler."[1] Cummins noted Wilman's outstanding 10-year ABC Championships average of 202.8. He failed to mention that Andy's 203.4 average was even higher.[2] Respect would take time.

Andy proudly wore an embroidered National Match Game Champion shirt in his official Brunswick Staff of Champions portrait in 1947 (Brunswick Bowling Products LLC photograph; IBMHOF collection).

His win created new opportunities. In February, a syndicated series of 12 articles, "Better Bowling by Andy Varipapa," appeared in national newspapers. Based on an eight-part *Brooklyn Eagle* series from 1940, editors added installments directed at female bowlers and on etiquette.[3] His most ironic comment was in the etiquette column, where he advised bowlers to "not brag about your accomplishments. If you are good, others will tell you."[4] Place that in the *do as I say, not as I do* file. The most significant opportunity was that Brunswick scheduled and promoted his appearances. Andy always represented Brunswick, but his itinerary expanded to parts of the country he had never been to.

Andy skipped the annual Chicago and St. Louis sweepers in February because Brunswick had him booked solid from March through October. He usually took the summers off, but not this year. Frank put his engineering career on hold and managed Hempstead Recreation with Lorraine's help while Andy and Alice took to the road. Their first destination was the ABC Championships in Los Angeles, noteworthy because the ABC had never held their tournament west of Kansas City.

Along the way, Andy performed exhibitions in Indiana, Oklahoma, and New Mexico and bowled in two big-money tournaments in Utah. At the Ritz Classic in Salt Lake City, his 1,611 eight-game set was enough for a top-25 finish but well behind champion Bill Flesch's 1,779.[5] He partnered with Los Angeles star Jack Quinn for a second-place finish at the Ogden Doubles Classic behind Cleveland's Joe Kissoff and Eddie Koepp.[6]

Andy arrived in Los Angeles for the ABCs on April 15. His Brunswick Mineralite team included veterans Bill Hansly, Felix Gelhausen, and Val Werner. They were well-known in the tri-state area, but none ever had a national reputation. But the fifth member of the Mineralites was Brooklyn's 30-year-old Graz Castellano, one of the top bowlers in the East. He toured with Joe Falcaro at 16 and won a boatload of local tournaments, but his best bowling was yet to come. Castellano won the prestigious *Newsday* Eastern Open in 1948, 1950, and 1954 and stood as the only three-time winner until Johnny Petraglia won his fourth in 1982.

He became the answer to a bowling trivia question after shooting a 300-game in the Eastern Classic League on October 4, 1953. WATV-13 cameras broadcast the action at Newark Recreation that night, and Castellano became the first to roll a perfect game on live television.[7] As the owner of three bowling supply houses in New York, he did not spend as much time traveling as some of his contemporaries, so he did not bowl as often as other top players. Castellano died of a heart attack at just 47 in 1964 and was posthumously inducted into the ABC Hall of Fame in 1976.[8]

The Mineralites took the lanes at the National Guard Armory on Thursday, April 17, alongside stars Nelson Burton, Sr., Joe Norris, and Mort Lindsey.[9] They got off to a dreadful start, shooting 888 in the first game. Andy was the main culprit, shooting a miserable 140. Maybe there was something to his assertion that he needed time to warm up and study the lanes. The team rebounded with 1,040 in game two, but Andy managed just 170. In game three, everyone got hot. Andy fired a 246, and the Mineralites' big 1,095 game gave them 3,023 total and the lead. Gelhausen led the way with a 684. Castellano and Werner shot 617, Andy 556, and Hansly 549.[10] They led, but the tournament had three weeks remaining. More than 1,500 teams had a crack at topping the Mineralites' score.

Andy bowled better the next day. Solid games of 236, 238, and 241 for a 715 series in singles moved him into second place. Andy rolled 635 and Castellano 636 in doubles, and their 1271 total was good enough for a sixth-place tie. Andy's 1909 all-events and 715 in singles were career highs for Andy, but his 140 game haunted him because the Mineralites' score did not hold up.[11] On April 27, the Eddie and Earl Linsz Five of Cleveland rolled 3,032, nine pins more than the Mineralites. For Fred Drury, Sam Pantelione, Charles Whiteman, Steve Piscalko, and Ted Miller, the 1947 ABC Championships was their 15 minutes of bowling fame.[12] None ever won another eagle, nor are Greater Cleveland Bowling Hall of Fame members.

The Mineralites finished second and earned $1,800. Andy finished sixth in singles, tied ninth in doubles, and 14th in all-events.[13] He took home more than $900 but no eagle. All four finishes represented his highest in ABC Championship play,

Brunswick Mineralites, second place finishers at ABC Championships, National Guard Armory, Los Angeles, April 17, 1947. From left: Graz Castellano, Bill Hansly, Felix Gelhausen, Andy, Val Werner. Captions handwritten by Andy (photographer unknown; Varipapa family collection).

and Andy never again broke 1800 in all-events. Missing the title by just nine pins—with his 140 in the first game—must have eaten at him for a while. His excellent showing did move him past Marty Cassio to the front of the coveted 10-year ABC average list at 204.72. Wilman was second at 203.87, while Cassio slipped to third at 203.58.[14]

Andy and Alice's West Coast travels were just getting started. Andy bowled in four big-money sweepers in the last two weeks of April and did not bowl particularly well in any of them. He made some headlines at the Airway Classic in Los Angeles. After the first seven games of the eight-game tournament, he knocked down just 1375 pins and trailed leader Tony Sparando by more than 200 pins. Andy fired a 300 in his final game, and while it was not enough to win the tournament, he earned a few bucks and thrilled the crowd.[15] He performed a few exhibitions on the coast between San Francisco and Los Angeles before returning to Hollywood to meet an old friend.

Pete Smith was ready to do another movie with Andy. *Bowling Tricks* featured nine minutes of Andy performing trick shots. No comedy sketches, bowling instruction, or sharing billing with Ned Day. Dave O'Brien, a regular collaborator of Smith's, directed. Best remembered for a role in the cult classic *Reefer Madness*, O'Brien directed movies for Smith under the pseudonym David Barclay.[16]

When Andy and Alice arrived in California and firmed up their schedule with Smith, Alice called their youngest daughter Lorraine to see if she wanted to join them for a spell. Lorraine could watch the filming of *Bowling Tricks* and then travel with them to Las Vegas and Salt Lake City. She flew out on a Lockheed Constellation, a state-of-the-art 40-seat airplane. Eleven hours after leaving Idlewild Airport in Queens, Andy and Alice met her at the airport in Los Angeles. Lorraine was star-stuck as the Varipapas dined with Hollywood celebrities at the best restaurants in the city.[17]

Due to a work stoppage, Smith could not film *Bowling Tricks* in a tent on the MGM lot as he did with *Strikes and Spares* and *Set 'Em Up*. He shot the film at a bowling center, the Pan Pacific Bowling Lanes on Beverly Boulevard, part of the sprawling Pan Pacific Village, an ambitious entertainment center anchored by the Pan Pacific Auditorium. The concept of a multi-use facility like Pan Pacific Village was ahead of its time. It housed the auditorium, a theater, a 14,000-seat indoor arena, restaurants, shops, and the Pan Pacific alleys.[18]

Smith was often asked if Andy's shots in *Strikes and Spares* and *Set 'Em Up* were enhanced using trick photography. Smith addressed those doubts right up front in *Bowling Tricks*. Immediately after the opening credits, a still shot of a signed and notarized affidavit appeared: "Pete Smith being first duly sworn, deposes and says: All bowling trick shots by Andy Varipapa depicted in this picture are real and authentic and were actually executed as they appear in this film. No camera tricks have been employed."[19] With that out of the way, the movie began.

Andy performed variations of shots from his previous movies. He made his 7-pin by pushing the ball with his foot, but he lied on the approach this time. After the pin fell, Andy folded his hands and put his head down as if to nap. When obstacles were required, glass hurricane lamps replaced pins. Smith's voice-over conveys Mama Varipapa's dismay with her prized possessions placed in harm's way. Andy did not always convert the complex shots in one take, and Lorraine recalled broken glass all over the lanes.[20] The film's crescendo was a new and more spectacular version of the flying dutchman.

Andy introduced his original flying dutchman in *Strikes and Spares*. He increased the degree of difficulty in *Set 'Em Up* and *Better Bowling* by adding more pins and spanning an additional lane. In *Bowling Tricks*, Andy upped the ante again. The latest three-lane version included the 7-pin on the left, the 10-pin on the right, and a full rack in the center. Less than a ball width apart, two pins sat on the center lane about 10 feet before the pin deck. He needed to split those two pins, convert the pins on the adjacent lanes, while the ball continued and struck on the center lane.

It was a tough shot. Andy's margin for error 45 feet down the lane was a half-inch, and the ball needed to carry enough momentum to knock down 10 pins. There is no record of how many takes were needed—Smith included one miss in the film for dramatic effect—but of course, Andy made the shot. It took a bowler with Andy's powerful hook to split the pins and retain enough energy to strike. After he made the shot, Andy flashed a big smile and gave the "OK" sign as the film faded to black.[21] More than two decades later, he rated this final version of the Flying dutchman as his most difficult trick shot.[22]

Lorraine accompanied her parents to Las Vegas and Utah and flew home in late May. Andy and Alice remained on the road the entire summer, visiting the Pacific

Fourteen. Back-to-Back

Clowning around at Pan Pacific Bowling Lanes in Los Angeles during the filming of *Bowling Tricks*, 1947. From left: Andy, Pete Smith, Brunswick staffer Catherine Fellmeth, and Davey O'Brien (MGM photograph; Varipapa family collection).

Northwest but spending most of their time in California. Andy performed daily exhibitions but found time to bowl a few serious matches.

Andy won them all except one. The winner of the 6th annual San Francisco Bowling Writers tournament, Milan Zlokovich, earned the right to bowl Andy in a 27-game match at Downtown Bowl. Like Graz Castellano, Zlokovich owned a chain of pro shops, which required his constant attention. He was an outstanding bowler but did not travel enough to gain a nationwide reputation. Andy rolled into town talking trash. The day before the match, he said, "Even your best bowlers out here are heavers, not bowlers. None of them ever took the time to learn the game properly."[23]

Zlokovich led the whole way, but Andy closed within striking distance heading into the last game. Zlokovich held him off by just 14 pins, marking in the 10th frame of the final game to seal his win. He averaged 195.6; Andy 195.2.[24] *San Francisco Examiner* bowling columnist Bob Buchman clapped back at Andy's "heavers" comment. "San Francisco's bowling lanes hold no respect for the eastern boys with the astronomical averages," wrote Buchman. Due to the west coast's more demanding lane conditions, he added that Andy should expect to "kiss from ten to fifteen pins of his average goodbye."[25] Fifty years after the founding of the ABC, the East/West divide was still a thing.

Time profiled Andy in their May 5, 1947, issue. While the title of the article was "The Greatest," the first line of the story referred to "Andy ('The Greek') Varipapa."[26] Many believed Andy to be of Greek heritage with his olive complexion and his roots in Carfizzi, populated by many residents of Albanian origin. The article prompted a telegram from Andy, which *Time* published, caps and all:

> STORY ON ME IN MAY FIFTH ISSUE CONTAINS BAD TYPOGRAPHICAL ERROR. YOU REFER TO ME AS ANDY ("THE GREEK") VARIPAPA. YOU EVIDENTLY MEANT ANDY ("THE GREAT") VARIPAPA FOR NONE IS GREATER THAN ANDY ("THE GREAT") VARIPAPA. ALSO YOU DEPRIVE THE ITALIAN PEOPLE OF A GREAT ATHLETE WHEN YOU CALL ME A GREEK.
> ANDY ("THE GREAT") VARIPAPA[27]

The editors replied, "Chalk up one Brooklyn strike for Bowler Varipapa."[28]

In June, *Bowlers Journal* selected Andy as a 1946–47 All-American. Andy joined Joe Norris, Allie Brandt, Junie McMahon, Hank Lauman, and Ed Kawolics on the first team.[29] While *Bowlers Journal* stated that "the editors" made the selections, everyone knew the choices belonged to editor Mort Luby, Sr. But the bowling community held him in such high regard that few had problems with it. *Bowlers Journal* did not select a bowler of the year, but Luby's selection of Andy as "captain" signified that he thought Andy had the best season.

Members of the NBWA thought differently. In their Bowler of the Year award balloting, Buddy Bomar came out on top with 843 votes, Joe Wilman second with 742, and Andy was third with 621.[30] Curiously, neither Bomar nor Wilman made the *Bowlers Journal*'s first team.

Award voting is subjective and can provoke controversy. Some writers, like Howard Millard of the *Decatur* (IL) *Herald*, thought Andy was "given the business" by the bowling writers.[31] Others, like Art McMahon of the Passaic *Herald News*, favored Junie McMahon (no relation) and did not think much of Andy: "Varipapa, aside from his Pete Smith movie shorts, his usual assortment of 300 games and his consistent pinning with Brunswick, has nothing spectacular to recommend him."[32] Other than he was the reigning All-Star champion, of course.

Some writers stirred the pot and claimed regional bias. Ed Maurer of the Nyack, New York *Journal-News* pointed out that the Midwest has more bowling writers than elsewhere. He said those writers "may be able to out-vote us when it comes to naming 'Bowler of the Year.' ... [Andy's win at the All-Star] must have been a bitter pill for those western keglers to take but we love it."[33] After reading that, Omaha sportswriter Robert Phipps ranked that sentiment as his "best laugh of last week" and exclaimed, "Those poor little orphan chillun in New York."[34] No one was ambivalent about Andy Varipapa. Some loved him, others hated him, but everyone paid attention to him.

Andy and Alice gradually worked their way back home. Their final stop was in Houston for the annual BPAA Match Game Doubles Championship. Andy's partner was 42-year-old Lou Campi of Dumont, New Jersey. Campi had an unassuming presence and unorthodox delivery. Bowling historian J.R. Schmidt described him as "a little guy with glasses and a soft smile who looked like a sawed-off Clark Kent."[35]

An Italian immigrant like Andy, Campi played bocce before he began bowling. Right-handed bocce players extend their right foot when tossing the ball, the opposite of what tenpin bowlers do. When Campi learned to bowl, he never changed his style, and despite his awkward appearance on the lanes, "Wrong Foot" could bowl. Years later, he became the answer to a trivia question when he won the first-ever PBA tournament, the 1959 Empire State Open in Albany.

Therm Gibson and George Young were defending champions, but the powerhouse team of Buddy Bomar and Ned Day were the favorites. The tournament's two-stage format was like the All-Star. Forty-eight teams bowled 32 games of qualifying, with the top seven joining Gibson and Young in the round-robin match play finals. Andy and Lou hung around the top five most of the qualifying and bowled well enough to claim the seventh and final qualifying spot. As expected, Bomar and Day led the qualifying. Many familiar faces were in the finals, including Joe Wilman, Joe Norris, Connie Schwoegler, and Nelson Burton, Sr.[36]

After dropping the wood from qualifying, the 32-game match play began on November 1. Petersen points decided the champion. Wilman and his partner Russ Creamer led after 16 games, but Andy and Lou took a slim lead after 24 games.[37] Andy rolled a tournament-high 911 four-game set in the penultimate block, extending their lead. Andy and Lou held off Bomar and Day, who made a run but fell short by less than 100 pins and three Petersen points.[38]

It was a hard-fought, low-scoring tournament. Andy and Lou averaged 202.57, and only 161 pins separated the top four teams.[39] Andy now had the distinction of simultaneously holding the BPAA individual and doubles match game crowns. He was in good company: only Bomar, Day, and Wilman had done so previously.[40]

Andy and Alice arrived in Hempstead just in time for the birth of their first grandchild. On November 20, Lorraine came home and found Andy reading the paper at the kitchen table, looking nervous. He waited for a call from Alice at the hospital with Connie and her husband, Mike. The newspaper was plastered with photographs of Queen Elizabeth and her new husband, Prince Philip; they were married the day before. Lorraine remembers the tension was so great they drank some cherry brandy, very out of character for a man who rarely drank.

Finally, the phone rang to announce that Alice Cornacchia had arrived, a happy and healthy baby.[41] Andy would defend his All-Star title as a grandfather! And there was something else for Andy to be proud of as he prepared for the 1947 All-Star. His son Frank would join him, having advanced through the New York qualifying tournament.

The 1947 BPAA All-Star moved to the Madison Street Armory. Shortly after the war ended, the military decommissioned the Servicemen's Center. Roosevelt College purchased the Auditorium Hotel and Theater complex from the city in 1946, and remodeling began in early 1947.[42] The field swelled to 168 bowlers, and Andy and 1945 champion Joe Wilman were seeded into the match-play finals.[43]

Andy may have been confident heading to Chicago, but he tamped down expectations of back-to-back titles: "Don't expect too much. It would be a miracle to repeat in the tournament."[44] During the qualifying round, Andy and Wilman rolled a 36-game match for a side purse of $750 (winner received $500, loser $250). Wilman ran over Andy and everyone else, for that matter. His 7,821 total was 235 ahead of the qualifying leader, unheralded Charley Johnson, Jr., from Bayonne, New Jersey. Andy's 7,418 would have placed him 10th among the qualifiers.[45] He was bowling well but had to pick up the pace to retain his title.

The finalists included the usual suspects alongside some not-so-familiar names. Buddy Bomar, Steve Nagy, Tony Sparando, and Walter Ward were there, but so were Johnson, Chuck O'Donnell, Stan Slomenski, and Frank Haynes.[46] Andy jumped out to a quick lead on the first day of match play. He averaged just 200.7 on a low-scoring day—only Andy, Sparando, and Nagy averaged over 200—but Andy posted a stellar 14–2 won/loss record. Wilman averaged 217.3 during his 36-game tune-up against Andy but mustered only a 196.5 average and sat in seventh place.[47]

Friday was a different story. Wilman averaged 218 and took a 0.35 Petersen point lead on Andy.[48] After Saturday's action, Wilman still led, but only by 0.09 Petersen points! Tony Sparando was in third place, more than 10 points behind, so it looked like a two-man race heading into the final 16 games on Sunday.[49]

Andy and Wilman had entirely different personalities on the lanes. Andy celebrated his strikes, clicked his heels, and interacted with the crowd. The unemotional Wilman kept to himself and chewed gum incessantly.[50] And as a Chicago native, he had the crowd on his side. Fanes jeered Andy when he missed a 10-pin, and after a fortuitous strike, someone in the audience cried, "you're lucky, Andy."[51]

Heading into the final four-game position round match, Wilman held a one-point lead. He stretched his lead by beating Andy in the first two games, 241–225 and 202–190. Andy now trailed by almost four points. He rallied in game three, firing 257 to Wilman's 183.[52] Incredibly, after 63 games of match play, Wilman had knocked down exactly four more pins than Andy. Wilman won 40½ of 63 games; Andy won 39½. The winner of the final game would win the crown and become the first two-time winner of the All-Star.

The finish was something out of a Hollywood movie.[53] The All-Star came down to the 10th frame of the 100th game. Andy finished the game first. After rolling a strike in the ninth frame, he needed one more in the 10th to clinch the title. But his ball wandered high on the headpin; fortunately, he left a makeable spare, which he converted. Andy threw a strike on his fill ball and finished with a 236, but left the door open for Wilman, who needed a double to win.

Andy described Wilman's shot to Lorraine: "He rolled a beautiful ball that seemed destined for a strike, but the ten-pin trembled and remained standing. That was costly for Joe but a tremendous break for me."[54] Wilman's 215 left him 17 pins behind Andy. They finished with identical 40½–23½ won-loss records.

Andy embraced Wilman, then took a moment to deal with the crowd. Sixty-five years before Pete Weber uttered his infamous line, "Who do you think you are? I am!" Andy stood before the packed house and bellowed, "Who said I wasn't a man? I'm a man, huh. I'm a man!"[55] He found his son Frank, pale and out of breath, who said, "Dad, I don't think I could go through that again." Andy replied, "Boy, to win this championship, I sure could!"[56]

Andy was the match game champion for the second year in a row. In the 82-year history of the All-Star and the U.S. Open, only Don Carter, Dick Weber, and Dave Husted went back-to-back.[57] Bowlers such as Earl Anthony, Mark Roth, Walter Ray Williams, Jr., Jason Belmonte, and Pete Weber—who won a record five U.S. Opens—never matched Andy's accomplishment. From this point forward, anyone who did not respect Andy's bowling ability did so at their own risk.

Fifteen

Respect

The Hempstead Chamber of Commerce proclaimed December 29, 1947, "Andy Varipapa Day." Executives from Brunswick and MGM were on hand to see Andy receive his All-Star trophy at the Hempstead Theater.[1] On February 21, the Nassau Bowling Proprietors threw Andy a testimonial gala at the famed Garden City Hotel. The dinner was of such magnitude that WGBB 1240 radio in Freeport broadcast the event live.[2] The keynote speaker was Andy's vanquished foe, the always gracious Joe Wilman, who came in from Chicago to attend.[3]

Andy was riding high. He was now, without question, the most famous bowler in the country. *Bowling Tricks* opened nationwide on January 10 and kept his name in the newspapers all year. He also began acquiring endorsement deals from companies outside the bowling industry, something few bowlers ever do. He endorsed bowling-related products since 1934, most notably Brunswick bowling balls, but endorsed bowling shoes, shirts, and socks.[4]

When it came to non-bowling products, only Andy, Ned Day, and Joe Falcaro broke through. Andy appeared in advertisements for Goodyear tires, Pennzoil Motor Oil, Pepsi-Cola, Fitch Hair Tonic, Beech-Nut Gum, Gold Bond Acoustical Products, and Teacher's Scotch. Day was a spokesperson for Coca-Cola, Havoline Motor Oil, Jockey Underwear, and Gillette Razor Blades. They both appeared in ads for Equitable Life Insurance, part of a series of pen and ink drawings by Robert Riger. Falcaro did ads for Munsingwear Underwear, Fleishman's Yeast Tablets, and Seagram's Whiskey.

All of Andy's contemporaries did beer ads—Andy himself appeared on behalf of Rheingold and Schafer. Beer and bowling were complements from the days of alleys being part of saloons, as were cigarettes. Andy's rivals Day, Joe Norris, Joe Wilman, Buddy Bomar, and Connie Schwoegler appeared in ads for Camels, Reynolds Tobacco's best-selling brand in the 1940s and 1950s. It is unclear if Andy chose not to participate on principle (he never smoked) or if Reynolds believed him too old for their target demographic.

In 1948, Andy led bowling schools in St. Louis, Cincinnati, Dayton, Columbus, Akron, Chattanooga, and Newport, Kentucky. The schools usually ran three in three-hour blocks, one each in the afternoon and evening, with Andy performing trick shots after the evening session. Lessons were free, although in some cities, bowlers had to pay for their games. Some centers charged admission of 50 or 75 cents for Andy's trick shot performance. Marketing was guaranteed because each school was co-sponsored by a local newspaper. The bowling school model slowly replaced the tip/match/trick-shot format his performances usually followed.

Publicity poster for Bowling Tricks, 1948. Andy no longer shared billing with anyone (MGM image).

Andy bowled the February sweepers in Chicago and St. Louis and did not cash as usual. Besides his 1943 win at the Landgraf, Andy was consistently unsuccessful in these six- and eight-game tests. After a string of high-profile winners at the Petersen, unknown Emil Wansa, a 29-year-old maintenance man from Lincoln Park, Michigan, walked away with the $5,100 ($64,600 in 2023 dollars) first prize. Buddy Bomar made a valiant effort to win three straight Petersen's but fell 17 pins short. He took home $3000 for finishing in second place.[5]

Andy's performance at the ABCs in Detroit was disappointing after so much success in 1947. Andy's all-events total of 1,747 was his lowest score ever, and the Mineralites team totaled just 2,781. He rolled with Lou Campi in the doubles, but neither broke 600.[6] The fact that he cashed in all four events was of little consolation. The headline writers were at it again: "Varipapa Fails in A.B.C. Tourney," "Varipapa Fails to Roll a 600," and "Varipapa Blows Chance in ABC."[7] It did not help matters that his rival Ned Day fired 1,979 in all-events and captured his first eagle.[8]

Joe Falcaro, probably miffed that Andy was getting all the publicity, decided he needed some attention. In April, he publicly challenged Andy to a 60-game neutral-site match for $5,000 ($63,300 in 2023 dollars).[9] Joe still used the "Undefeated Match Game Champion" title and figured with Andy's popularity at its height, this was the time to cash in. With so much history between them, a match with Andy would generate big crowds and lots of cash.

Andy was still on tour in Ohio, but Frank told *Newsday* his father accepted Falcaro's offer, and they could work out the details when he returned to Long Island.[10] In early May, Falcaro traveled to Philadelphia, won the Quaker City Classic ($1,000), and took second in the Crescent Individual Sweepstakes ($450). Further emboldened and flush with cash, he announced he wanted to bowl *anyone* for $5,000.[11]

On June 1, Andy laid out his terms for the match: four mutually agreeable bowling centers, each with freshly polished lanes, three-pound six-ounce pins, and a side bet of $2,000 to $5,000. Oh, and Andy wanted 60 percent of the net gate receipts (knowing Falcaro would bristle at that suggestion). If the four-house plan were not to Falcaro's liking, Andy agreed to bowl 40 games at Hempstead Recreation and 40 at Falcaro's center in Lawrence. Andy said the match would be on once Falcaro handed over a certified check for his portion of the side bet to *Newsday* sports editor Bob Zellner.[12] Not surprisingly, Falcaro never delivered a check or countered Andy's proposal.

Their attempts to schedule a match became an on-again, off-again soap opera, and *Newsday* bowling writer Dick Clemente often found himself in the middle of it. After a tournament at Heineman's in June 1949, the match came up again, and insults flew. Some were good-natured, others were not. Each proposed a site they knew the other would reject. Falcaro stuffed a wad of hundred dollar bills in Clemente's hands, saying, "Let him [Andy] put up the same amount, and we will bowl right here at Heineman's."[13] Unsure if he had ever had that much money in his pocket before, Clemente quickly turned the cash over to Heineman's manager Ray Van Cott for safekeeping.

Andy wanted to bowl at Sheridan Academy in Mineola, but Falcaro refused. After the commotion, Clemente wrote, "The long-awaited Varipapa-Falcaro match is stalemated for the umpteenth time … both are doing overpatient bowling fans a great injustice by failing to come to terms on a site."[14] Falcaro died in 1951 without meeting Andy in a meaningful one-on-one match since their epic 1932 clash.

Because of his travel schedule, Andy missed the first edition of a brand-new tournament. In March, *Newsday* announced plans to hold the first "Long Island Open Bowling Championship." It was Dick Clemente's brainchild and borrowed heavily from the All-Star. It had a newspaper sponsor, a lengthy two-stage format, and used the Petersen point system. The host was Heineman's in Hempstead, with 32 lanes, the largest center on Long Island.[15] A few years later, Heineman's was renamed Mid–Isle Lanes and stood on Peninsula Boulevard near exit 19 of the Southern State Parkway until it closed in the early 1990s. A self-storage facility now occupies the site.

Graz Castellano won the title, holding off youngster Sis Mantovani in the final position round.[16] But Mantovani had his moment in the sun earlier in the tournament, rolling a 300 game during match play on May 27. And poor Frank—already used to standing in his father's formidable shadow—was again upstaged. A half-hour after Mantovani's perfecto, Frank rolled a 298 after his final ball hit light and left the 5–7 combination.[17] Even with a 298, he was not the lead story, but he later rolled a certified 300 game at Baldwin Modern in 1951.[18] Frank finished in seventh place, just 0.11 Petersen points behind Joe Falcaro.[19] Andy must have been rooting hard for Frank to get the better of Joe, just this one time.

After a slow start, the Long Island Open gained traction and became one of the premier tournaments in the country. Following a rule change that allowed anyone to enter, regardless of residence, the "*Newsday* Eastern Open" did become the "All-Star of the East." Future winners included some of bowling's all-time greats, such as Junie McMahon, Dick Weber, Johnny Petraglia, and Mark Roth. And in a marketing coup that the *Chicago Tribune* never achieved with the All-Star, New Yorkers referred to the tournament simply as "The *Newsday*." The paper dropped its sponsorship in 1983, and the tournament ceased operations after the 1986 event.

Andy turned 57 in March, and his thoughts began to turn to his family. He was already a grandfather, and Lorraine and Frank would soon marry and want to start their own families. Frank managed Hempstead Recreation with help from Lorraine and Alice and did an excellent job, but the bowling alley life was not the greatest environment. Many late nights and weekends, coming home smelling like a smokestack, dealing with customers who drank too much.

Here was Frank, with an engineering degree from Lafayette, running a bowling alley. But even if he wanted to start his engineering career, he would not let his father down and leave Hempstead Recreation. And as much as he loved owning a bowling center, Andy and Alice were not getting any younger. Andy began considering how it affected his family.

Lorraine was becoming one of the area's top female bowlers, but other than the WIBC Championships, competition for women was scarce in the 1940s. And besides Floretta McCutcheon, no woman made a living as a bowling professional. Lorraine's serious bowling days would end soon; in April, she got engaged to Fordham University pharmacy student Bob Ruffolo. They married the following summer after he earned his degree.[20] And this time, Andy would be present at his daughter's wedding.

Andy was named a first-team *Bowlers Journal* All-American for the second consecutive year.[21] In August, he received an even more significant honor when the NBWA named Andy their Bowler of the Year. The vote was closer than it should have been. He held both the singles and doubles match game titles; Andy should have won

Andy watching Lorraine at Hempstead Recreation, 1946 (Brunswick Bowling LLC photograph; Varipapa family collection).

in a landslide. Andy received 26 of 70 first-place votes and 406 in all. Wilman was second with 362, followed by Day (361), Bomar (358), and Paul Krumske (350).

Maybe the Midwest bias among voters was real: Day hailed from the Milwaukee suburbs, and the rest lived in Chicago. Or maybe he never shook the "trick shot" label. The opening line of the Associated Press story announcing the NBWA award read, "Andy Varipapa, Hempstead N.Y., trick-shot artist, was named 'bowler of the year.'"[22] Or, just maybe, writers had a tough time accepting that a 57-year-old grandfather was the best bowler in the world.

Leading up to the All-Star, Andy ran bowling schools in Akron and Chattanooga. He headed to Chicago in early December and joined Frank, who qualified again this year, along with his best-man-to-be, Tony Kusky. Unlike prior years when Wilman, Day, and Bomar got top billing, most *Tribune* stories promoting the 1948 All-Star included Andy's name.

Even their advertising department got into the act. One advertisement ran with a bold headline, "Where's Andy?" After tricking readers into thinking that Andy did not enter the All-Star, smaller type read, "You mean Andy Varipapa? He'll be in Chicago from December 11 thru 19."[23] Andy and Wilman earned seeds into the 16-man final and competed for a $750 side pot during the 36-game qualifying session.[24]

Frank and Tony were eliminated after the 24-game qualifying round as neither beat the cut score of 4,744.[25] Andy's 4,712 would not have made the cut either, which was cause for concern. He bowled much better in the semi-finals, tossing six-game blocks of 1,265 and 1,283, but far behind the scores turned in by Steve Nagy (1,393), Bill Flesch (1,364), and Buddy Bomar (1,359).[26] And, like 1947, Wilman beat him in their side match, this time by 126 pins.

As always, bowling royalty abounded in the final. Ed Kawolics, Sarge Easter, Joe Norris, Johnny Crimmins, and Connie Schwoegler joined Andy, Wilman, Nagy, Flesch, and Bomar in the finals. Andy was bowling just OK, and with five former All-Star champions in the field, he needed to pick up the pace.

Andy got off to a good start, ending the first day in second place behind Cleveland's Steve Nagy. He might have led had he not lost three out of four games to Ebber "Sarge" Easter.[27] Maybe Andy was thrown off because he was in the odd position of bowling someone older than him. And not just a year or two older—Easter was 65!

Easter burst on the bowling scene at 60 when he won the Marino and DeVito Classics in 1943.[28] Even more remarkable, he only began bowling seriously in 1940 while stationed as an ROTC instructor at the University of Wisconsin in Madison. He wandered into nearby Schwoegler's Lanes, where Tony Schwoegler and his son Connie taught Easter the game's finer points.[29] When he retired from the service after World War II (rising to the rank of, believe it or not, sergeant), he devoted all his energies to bowling and became one of the game's best. He bowled his last 300 game in 1955, aged 72.[30]

Andy took the lead after 32 games. The possibility of a three-peat was alive, and Charles Bartlett could not believe it: "Bowling's Ol' Man River is rolling again! That would be venerable Andrew Varipapa, the Hempstead, N.Y., proprietor who last night made his move."[31] (It may have been the first time Bartlett did not refer to Andy as a trick-shot artist.) Andy bowled great, averaging 210.19, but Nagy and Schwoegler knocked down more pins. Andy led on the strength of his better won-loss record. On day three, Nagy and Schwoegler passed him. Now seven points out of the lead, he needed to chip away at Nagy's lead quickly when the competition began on Sunday.[32]

It was not to be. Out of the running for the title, Joe Wilman met Andy in the first match. Wilman won three out of four games, allowing Nagy to open an 11-point lead on Andy. With only 12 games remaining, Andy's hopes were slim. He made up ground by beating Joe Norris and young Stan Slomenski of Newark but entered the position round in third place.

To win, Andy required several things to happen. He had to beat his opponent Bill Flesch soundly and hope that Nagy and Schwoegler split their match while bowling poorly. Andy held up his part of the bargain, winning three of four from Flesch and shooing an 871 series, but Schwoegler did not cooperate. He finished like a champion, sweeping Nagy with 226, 236, 234, and 243 games for a spectacular 939 series. Nagy bowled just 770, and Andy went around him to claim second place.[33]

Andy completed the most extraordinary four-year run in the history of the BPAA All-Star. He finished third, first, first, and second. He won almost 60 percent (153 of 256) of his games against the greatest bowlers in the world and averaged 210.41. Only Don Carter from 1951 to 1954 (fourth-, first-, first-, and third-place finishes) and Dick Weber from 1961 to 1964 (second, first, first, and fourth place) came close to repeating Andy's four-year run. And most significantly, except for Sarge Easter, he did so against bowlers far younger than he was.

Each tournament required him to bowl 100 games. Andy was 56 when he won his second All-Star. At 57, John Handegard was four months older than Andy when he won the 1995 PBA Northwest Classic.[34] While taking nothing away from Handegard's accomplishment, the Northwest Classic is not exactly the BPAA All-Star. Andy's back-to-back titles, aged 55 and 56, remain a unique feat in the annals of sports history.

After returning to Hempstead for the holidays, Andy decided it was time to leave the bowling alley business. On Christmas Eve, *Newsday* reported that he closed a deal to sell Hempstead Recreation to Tony and Walt Kusky.[35] Andy raised the possibility with Tony in Chicago during the All-Star. After talking it over with his family (they already owned Oceanside Recreation), Tony visited Alice at Hempstead and told her the Kuskys were interested. When Andy returned from the All-Star, he met with the Kusky brothers and closed the deal in 10 minutes.

Andy said he had "too many commitments to give the place my personal attention."[36] But there was another unspoken and more important reason for selling. Frank and Lorraine, now free from their responsibilities at Hempstead Recreation, could plan their personal and professional lives accordingly.

Andy ran his Detroit school as usual in January and then headed to Chicago for another poor showing in the Petersen. He shot just 1,365, and Charles Bartlett took immense pleasure in pointing out that Frank trounced him with 1,467.[37] An important date in Philadelphia loomed in early February, where Andy and Lou Campi would defend their match game doubles crown at Glenwood Recreation. Seeded into the match-play finals as defending champions, several strong teams joined them, including Steve Nagy and Walter Ward, Joe Norris and Joe Wilman, and Buddy Bomar and Ned Day.[38]

Andy and Lou took the lead after the first block, which included a four-game sweep of Bomar and Day.[39] But as the matches progressed, a relatively unknown duo from Newark emerged from the pack. After the seventh round, Johnny Dayon and Stan Slomenski held a one-point lead over Andy and Lou. With Norris and Wilman far behind in third place, this was a two-team race with four games remaining.

After splitting the first two games, Andy and Lou won the third, 456–401, on the strength of Campi's big 255 game. Now separated by less than a point, the winner of the final game would claim the title. But it was no contest; Campi rolled 166, Andy 177, and the Newark pair's modest 383 was plenty to win the title. It was a massive upset for two up-and-comers like Dayon and Slomenski to beat the defending champions.[40]

Andy no longer held the singles or doubles match game titles, but as he approached his 60th birthday, he was busier than ever. Bowling was poised to become the nation's most popular participation sport, and Andy was its most recognizable figure. And it would all happen at an age when most folks were looking to wind down, rather than ramp up, their careers.

Sixteen

Traveling Man

After wrapping up the doubles tournament in February 1949 and bowling the Chicago and St. Louis sweepers, Andy headed south to cities he had never visited: Miami, Tampa, and New Orleans.[1] Visiting new markets was one advantage of his deal with Brunswick. Andy stopped home for a brief rest on March 26 before a series of performances at the "Sports and Vacation Show" at the Milwaukee Auditorium.

Andy bowled twice daily on specially-built lanes next to log rollers, ski jumpers, canoe tilters, diving sea lions, fly-casters, swimsuit models, and Larry Griswold, "The Aqua Fool."[2] He appeared on April 2 and 3, took three days off (Wisconsin native Connie Schwoegler took his place), and returned to perform on April 7, 8, 9, and 10.[3] And what did Andy do on those three days? Drove to Atlantic City and bowled in the ABC Championships.

Like in 1948, he cashed in each event for a small amount, but his results disappointed. Andy rolled 562 in the team event, 569 in the doubles (son Frank added 537 for a 1,106 total), and 626 in the singles.[4] He totaled a respectable 1,767 in all-events, a good score considering that during 60 frames of singles and doubles, he left 17 10-pins.[5] He never exceeded that total in the ABC Championships.

He returned to Hempstead on April 11, not to rest but to do laundry and pack. For the first time since arriving in New York in 1903, he and Alice left the 48 contiguous states and embarked on a three-week exhibition tour of Hawaii. Andy visited 15 centers in Oahu, Hawaii, and Maui during his stay, taking only three days off. Massive crowds greeted Andy at every stop, many reasoning (correctly) that this might be his only visit to the Islands.

At his first exhibition at Kapiolani Lanes in Honolulu, 800 fans packed into the center under the watchful eye of Honolulu Fire Department inspectors. They counted the house to ensure the crowd did not exceed the legal capacity.[6] At the Honolulu Bowling Center, 700 fans surrounded the lanes, 300 watched through windows, and another 200 were turned away.[7] Andy rolled 44 games in Hawaii and averaged a modest 185.6.[8] Maybe the lovely scenery and beaches distracted him.

After a brief stop in San Francisco, Andy and Alice returned home on May 11. Although Andy did not travel again until September, the Varipapa's had a busy summer. Frank wed Dottie Marshall on May 15, and Lorraine married Bob Ruffolo on June 12. The San Su San in Mineola, next door to the Sheridan Academy on Jericho Turnpike, hosted both receptions. Andy and Alice were now officially empty nesters. Soon after, they sold their house on Kernochan Avenue and moved 3 miles southwest to Madison Avenue in West Hempstead. Their new home was less than half a mile from Frank and Dottie's house on Guildford Court.

Andy and Alice got the traditional welcome at Honolulu Airport on April 12, 1949 (United Air Lines photograph; Varipapa family collection).

Free from his responsibilities at Hempstead Recreation, Frank began his engineering career at Grumman Aircraft. He was a stalwart on Grumman's company bowling team, which competed against other company teams throughout the season. The most significant team event of all was the Long Island Industrial Bowling Tournament. Founded in 1942 to boost the wartime morale of employees, 16 of Long Island's most prominent companies competed annually for the Jake Swirbul Trophy.

May 15, 1949, at the San Su San in Mineola, New York, the wedding of Frank Varipapa and Dottie Marshall. From left: Andy, Alice, Dottie, Frank, Madeline and Frederick Marshall (photographer unknown; Varipapa family collection).

Defense contractors Grumman, Liberty Aircraft, and Republic Aviation dominated the tournament's early years, winning 19 of the first 20 Swirbul trophies.[9] *Newsday*, Doubleday, and Long Island Lighting also fielded teams. Held each spring at Heineman's (later Mid–Isle Lanes), Frank led Grumman to championships in 1951 and 1952. In 1951, he won the Outstanding Bowler Award, shooting a record 2,535 for 12 games, breaking the mark held by Andy's good friend George Young.[10]

As winter approached, Andy focused once again on the All-Star. After two years at the Madison Street Armory, the 1949 All-Star moved to the Northwest Armory on Kedzie Avenue. A women's match game championship was held concurrently with the men for the first time. Apart from local, state, and national WIBC championships, women's tournaments were rare. Since 1946, the Greater Cincinnati Bowling Council had conducted a match-game championship for women, and the Chicago Bowling Proprietors Association started its own in October.[11] This national tournament was the natural extension of those local events.

The BPAA extended invitations to 48 bowlers, including top finishers in the Chicago and Cincinnati tournaments and high-average bowlers nationwide. Brunswick installed four additional lanes so the women could compete alongside the men. The women's version was shorter than the men's, only 48 games, with 12 bowlers advancing to the final match-play round.[12]

June 12, 1949, at the San Su San in Mineola, New York, the wedding of Lorraine Varipapa and Bob Ruffolo. From left: Andy, Alice, Bob, Lorraine, Mae and Joseph Ruffolo (photographer unknown, Varipapa family collection).

Andy and Connie Schwoegler earned seeds in the final round as the two most recent champions. In the traditional side match during qualifying, Andy defeated Schwoegler 7,350 to 7,220. Andy's score would have been good enough to qualify third, and he was peaking at the right time. His final six-game block of 1,300 beat all 48 semi-finalists except Buddy Bomar, who nipped Andy by a pin.[13]

Unfortunately, his momentum did not carry over into the finals, and after day one, Andy was in 15th place, ahead of the only bowler older than him, Sarge Easter.[14] He bowled much better on the second day, winning 10 of 16 games and moving to eighth place. But that is where Andy finished, just behind Schwoegler. The 1949 All-Star belonged to Junie McMahon, who comfortably won the crown.[15]

On December 8, Marion Ladewig, a "small brunette housewife from Grand Rapids," averaged 201.1 over 24 games to claim the women's All-Star crown.[16] Only runner-up Catherine Burling of Cincinnati, at 191.7, averaged more than 186. Ladewig's win started a 15-year run of unprecedented dominance. Before retiring in 1964, she won eight All-Stars, two WIBC all-events titles, and five Women's World Invitational tournaments. The NBWA named her Bowler of the Year a record nine times.[17]

In 1951, Ladewig won the all-events at the local (Grand Rapids), state (Michigan), and national WIBC championships. The feat is so rare there is no evidence that anyone has duplicated it. (So much for Andy's theory that nine-game tournaments are all luck.) *Bowling Digest* ranked her the fourth most influential bowler in history. A *Miami Herald* poll of 20 bowling writers named her the top woman bowler of the 20th century, and *Bowlers Journal* named her the seventh greatest bowler of the 20th century.[18] The only other woman on the list was Floretta McCutcheon at 25th.

After the All-Star, Andy returned to Hempstead to celebrate the holidays with his family. Then it was off to Detroit for his bowling schools and Chicago for the Petersen and DeVito sweepers. He rolled 1,486 and 1,538, respectively, more than 175 pins off the lead in each event.[19] After a stop in Omaha, including an appearance at Boys Town on February 9, he picked up Alice in Hempstead and returned to Florida.[20] It was a combined tour and vacation, including stops in Fort Lauderdale, West Palm Beach, and Miami. On his way back north, they made their way to Louisville, the site of the 1950 BPAA National Doubles Championships, where Andy teamed with Connie Schwoegler.

No longer a match-play event, the tournament was a 20-game total wood competition. Sarge Easter and Ed Lubanski won the title. They were an unusual pairing in that Easter was the oldest competitor at 66, and Lubanski, at 21, likely the youngest. Easter could have been Lubanski's grandfather. However, there was no denying the results because they were the only team to average over 200. Andy and Schwoegler finished second, 116 pins behind, followed by Bomar and Day in third.[21]

Lubanski is best known for rolling back-to-back 300 games on a local Miami television station on June 22, 1959.[22] Like Johnny Vander Meer's back-to-back no-hitters, someone may tie Lubanski's mark, but it will take a 900 series to break it. An unfortunate incident as a minor leaguer in the St. Louis Brown's organization ended his promising baseball career.[23] After compiling a 50–18 record over three seasons, the 19-year-old met with the general manager of the Muskogee Reds to express dissatisfaction with his $278-a-month salary. After considering the request, he pointed a pistol at Lubanski's head and remarked, "We make the decisions around here, not the players."[24] After carefully weighing his options, Lubanski withdrew his request, returned to Detroit to focus on bowling, and became the national doubles champion less than two years later.

In May, Andy suffered through his worst ABC Championship ever. His 592 in the team event started with a 235 game, and he failed to break 190 after that. He added 503 in the doubles and 531 in the singles, for an all-events total of 1,626.[25] His only cash was in the team event where his Brunswick Red Crowns of Cleveland earned a few bucks with their 2,674 (low to cash was 2,633).[26] He spent June at home in Hempstead, and on July 4, Andy left to visit several of his favorite West Coast alleys for a few weeks of exhibitions and tournaments.

Unfortunately, Andy slipped in the shower after arriving in Oakland and fractured two ribs.[27] He taped them up before rolling four games at Albany Bowl, winning them all and shooting 921, cracked ribs and all.[28] Andy drove to Modesto to toss three games in the team event at the Peach Bowling Tournament. He shot 651 for three games and gutted out his trick-shot exhibition but was in tremendous pain. Andy skipped the singles and doubles events, canceled his remaining appearances, and returned home to rest.[29] When he arrived in Hempstead, he met Dottie and Frank's daughter Susan, born on July 11. Andy was now a grandpa twice!

His broken ribs were Andy's first severe injury since he broke his leg in 1919.

Given his attention to fitness, it must have shocked him that the injury prevented him from bowling. The decision to cancel his tour was not made lightly; remember, this man missed his daughter's wedding because of scheduled performances. He returned to action a month later at the opening of Somerset Recreation in North Plainfield, New Jersey, where he shot just 539 (including a 145) for three games and performed some trick shots.[30] It was doubtful he was yet 100 percent.

Andy was fully recovered by September. As runners-up in the national doubles, he and Connie Schwoegler exercised their right to challenge Ed Lubanski and Sarge Easter for their crown. Andy and Schwoegler jumped out a 331-pin lead after the first 24 games at Schwoegler's Lanes in Madison, but Lubanski and Easter turned the tables in Detroit.[31] The lanes at State Fair Recreation were friendly to the home team, who retained their title by 285 pins.[32]

At the 1950 All-Star, Andy was in 11th place after 24 games of qualifying. But he faltered in the semifinals and missed the cut by 59 pins.[33] For the first time since 1943, Andy did not reach the match-play round of the All-Star. The winner was 21-year-old Dick Hoover of Cleveland, becoming the first bowler to win the All-Star in their first appearance (excluding 1941, when it was everyone's first appearance).[34]

Andy was one of the most outstanding performers of the All-Star's first 10 years. His two victories tied Connie Schwoegler; (his seven finals trailed only Schwoegler

From left: Connie Schwoegler, Andy, Ed Lubanski, and Sarge Easter at State Fair Recreation in Detroit, September 24, 1950 (*Detroit News* photograph; Walter P. Reuther Library, Archives of Labor and Urban Affairs, Wayne State University).

Andy posing behind a Brunswick B-10 semi-automatic pinsetter filled with Brunswick Red Crown pins circa 1950. Andy came a long way from his days as a pinboy in Brooklyn (Brunswick Bowling Products LLC photograph; IBMHOF collection).

and Buddy Bomar's eight) among those who participated in each tournament, he compiled an average of 205.41, second only to Wilman's 205.71.[35] It was hard to choose amongst those four as the greatest All-Star bowler of the first 10 years. When the BPAA began recognizing All-Star performance with their "Award of Merit" in 1961, Andy was the third recipient, after Junie McMahon and Wilman.[36]

Andy began 1951 with good news; he signed with Brunswick for another year of appearances. At the 1951 ABC Championships in St. Paul, he posted a 1,763 all-events total.[37] His performance was far better than in 1950 but still nowhere near Tony Lindemann's winning score of 2,005. After leaving Minnesota, he appeared in Iowa for the first time, and 500 fans greeted him at Lee's Lanes in Mason City.[38]

When Andy was in Iowa, the ABC announced the Hall of Fame voting results. When Elmer Baumgarten announced the inaugural class of 11 members in 1941, he said the ABC planned to add members yearly. World War II changed things; the 1951 vote was the first in 10 years. The sole criterion for induction, as it was in 1941, was the nominee's performance in a minimum of 15 ABC Championship appearances. Andy bowled only 12 ABC Championships before 1941, so this was the first time he was eligible for induction.

Andy was among 24 nominees in 1951. Thirty-eight voters cast votes for up to four bowlers, and anyone receiving 75 percent of the vote earned induction (the same criteria as the Baseball Hall of Fame). Andy received 15 votes, and only Joe Wilman, with 29 votes, was elected. Ned Day received 22 votes, Jimmy Blouin 19, and Joe Norris 13; no one else received more than six.[39] The early years of any hall of fame are tricky because there are many worthy candidates. Of the 20 players receiving votes, 17 eventually earned induction. Andy and the others had to wait their turn.[40]

In May, 68 NBWA members voted to determine the "Bowler of the Half-Century." Hank Marino won an almost unanimous decision, receiving 995 out of 1020 possible votes.[41] Marino received at least 43 of the 68 first-place votes, and maybe more, depending on where he ranked among voters who did not have him first.[42] Jimmy Smith was second with 888 votes, followed by Jimmy Blouin (842), Ned Day (803), Andy (736), and Joe Wilman (730).[43] Joe Falcaro finished 13th. Andy fared better in this poll because, unlike the ABC Hall of Fame vote, voters considered all the nominees' accomplishments, not just their ABC Championships record.

In 1951, the ABC debuted a new event near the end of the ABC Championships in St. Paul. Originally called the "ABC Clinics and Exhibitions," it featured 32 participants. Eight were national stars Dick Hoover, Junie McMahon, Sarge Easter, Ned Day, Lee Jouglard, Joe Wilman, Buddy Bomar, and Andy.[44] The other 24 were survivors of eliminations held across the state of Minnesota. Bowling a 30- or 40-game total-pin tournament gave the locals little chance, so the ABC used a double-elimination format (see Chapter 11). There was no qualifying round. Bowlers were seeded into a 32-man bracket with three locals and one national star in each pod of four bowlers. National stars could not meet until the round of eight.

While the tournament was a crapshoot compared to the 100-game grind of the All-Star, it had the excitement of March Madness. Given the short format, upsets were commonplace. Andy was eliminated after losing his first two matches to locals Sig Bye (539–511) and George Harrison (571–539).[45] Next to depart was Buddy Bomar, followed by Ned Day and Junie McMahon.

Despite the format, two seeded stars met in the finals. All-Star runner-up Lee Jouglard came out of the losers' bracket to defeat Joe Wilman twice and claim the $500 first prize.[46] Even before the event ended, the media changed the tournament name to the "ABC Double Elimination Championship" and, shortly after that, the "ABC Masters."[47] That name stuck, and the annual event became one of professional bowling's major championships.

May of 1951 marked another milestone for the Varipapa family. Frank embarked on a business venture that transformed his professional life. In late 1950, he accompanied Andy on a cocktail cruise sponsored by the Nassau-Suffolk Bowling Proprietors Association (NSBPA). They met Stan Lewis, a former Brunswick salesperson, who recently opened a pro shop, Bowl Mart, on Nassau Boulevard in West Hempstead.[48]

Lewis was a pioneer in the bowling pro shop industry. The concept of a stand-alone pro shop selling custom-fit bowling balls, shoes, bags, and accessories was new. Sporting goods, department, hardware, and even jewelry stores sold bowling balls, often by salespeople who knew little or nothing about the sport.[49]

Until the 1930s, all bowling balls had just two holes. Bowlers grabbed a ball using their thumb and middle finger and tossed it. Besides weight (men used the maximum allowable 16 pounds, women and children less), a ball was a ball. The placement and size of the holes were of little concern. In 1933, Sully Bates patented the three-holed "Bates Grip," which added the ring finger for stability.[50] By the late 1940s, most bowlers switched to the three-hole grip. And once Connie Schwoegler succeeded with his fingertip grip (where fingers are inserted only to the first joint rather than the second), fitting and drilling a custom-fit bowling ball became more complicated than ever.[51]

The rush to deliver custom-fit bowling balls led to the development of gauges, jigs, and measuring tools to make the job quicker and more accurate. While primitive by today's standards, these devices allowed the ball driller to customize the holes' size, spacing (span), and angle (pitch) for a perfect fit. Robert "Doc" Hinkley, a pro shop owner from La Brea, California, is often credited with popularizing the concept of a custom-fit ball. In 1940, he said, "You can't walk comfortably unless shoes fit. How can you expect to bowl well unless your ball fits your hand?"[52] Billing himself as "The Doctor of Bowling," Hinkley turned Hinkley Bowling Supply into the first modern pro shop.[53]

On the NSBPA cruise, Lewis told Andy and Frank that he wanted to expand Bowl Mart but needed additional capital. The timing was perfect: after selling Hempstead Recreation in 1949, Andy was looking for a brick-and-mortar investment in the bowling industry. And although Frank enjoyed his work at Grumman, he assumed that Bowl Mart was merely a side hustle to supplement his income. Frank negotiated a 50/50 partnership with Lewis that lasted 25 years and revolutionized the pro shop business.

On May 9, 1951, Bowl Mart moved to a larger store on Jericho Turnpike in Mineola, a half-mile from Sheridan Bowl.[54] Andy supplied the cash (which Frank paid back in a few years) and served as the public face of Bowl Mart. The business was a rousing success, and in 1952, Frank left Grumman to devote all his time to Bowl Mart. The business remained in the Varipapa family until after Frank died in 1988.

The Department of Defense invited Andy to a special event in August. To build morale among troops stationed in Europe, Andy joined Joe Norris and pool champion Willie Mosconi on a two-week tour of more than 700 lanes installed at Western European military bases. ABC Secretary Frank Baker (who recently replaced the retired Elmer Baumgartner) and Brunswick European head Jim Whitaker accompanied the stars.[55] Scheduled to depart for Nuremberg on August 24, the group assembled at Westover Air Force Base in Massachusetts. Delayed for two days due to a paperwork issue, a local reporter found Andy and interviewed him for a local radio station.

One of the topics of discussion was the missing papers. Norris recalled Andy saying, "We're going overseas to entertain the troops, that is if we ever get there. I don't know how they operate, and these generals don't seem to know what they're doing. I wonder how we won the war."[56] Less than an hour after the interview aired, the papers magically appeared, and the group was on their way. It may have all been a coincidence, but Andy gleefully reminded his companions of the benefits of traveling with the Great Varipapa.[57] After performing in Nuremberg, the troupe appeared in several other German cities and at Wheelus Air Force Base in Tripoli, Libya.[58]

While in Berlin, Andy bought souvenirs for his family—Norris believed it was at least a thousand dollars' worth—but neglected to save the receipts.[59] Norris needled him that he could not get the items through customs. Predictably, Andy announced that "Varipapa would not have absolutely no problem at all" because

Sixteen. Traveling Man

Berlin, 1951. From left: Andy, unidentified serviceman, Willie Mosconi, Frank Baker. Andy looked pensive, maybe worried about the small plane he was about to board or the need to wear a parachute. Or both (photographer unknown; Varipapa family collection).

"Varipapa never has any difficulty doing anything."[60] Some in the group bet that he could not. The chirping continued until they arrived at Frankfurt airport.

They should have known better. When the entourage arrived at customs, the others pushed Andy to the front to get a bird's-eye view of the proceedings. As the customs agent began to unzip his suitcase, he looked up and said, "Andy! How are you? I saw your show, and it was just great."[61] Norris said the agent took Andy off to meet his supervisors, where he stayed for 25 minutes. When he returned, the agent escorted Andy through without glancing at his bag and whisked the Brunswick party to their waiting airplane.[62]

Andy returned home to some sad news. Joe Falcaro, suffering from heart trouble for the past three years, died of pneumonia on September 6.[63] For all their years of trading insults and high-stakes matches that never materialized, Andy and Joe remained friends. Andy visited Joe frequently when he was ill.[64] Both were master showmen: they concocted their public feud to create publicity. A Varipapa-Falcaro match would have been the Ali-Frazier bout of its day. But when it came down to it, they both had too much to lose in a head-to-head match.

Falcaro's obituary appeared in newspapers coast to coast. Those who knew him best mentioned his compulsive gambling, cocky attitude, and brusque personality.[65] But they also noted how much he did to promote the game. *Newsday*'s Ed Comerford wrote, "He was the most colorful bowler the sport has ever, or will ever, known. He loved to grab headlines and be the center of attraction at gatherings. He was boisterous and loquacious, yet even his foes couldn't stay mad at him ... the sport has lost a great man."[66]

Andy toured the Midwest in the fall, making stops in Kentucky, Ohio, and Indiana before heading to Chicago for the 1951 All-Star. He missed the semi-final cut by five pins, shooting 4,698 for 24 games.[67] But even if he made that cut, he would have been hard-pressed to pick up the 300 pins needed to advance to the finals. Junie McMahon marched to his second All-Star title, and 1951 marked the finals debut of the player who dominated the tournament over the next decade, Don Carter of St. Louis.[68]

Andy spent his spring in the Midwest, doing a lot of inconsistent bowling. He experienced another lousy year at the Chicago sweepers but managed a third-place finish at the BPAA doubles elimination tournament in Buffalo. Teamed with young Bill Lillard, they finished less than 100 pins behind winners McMahon and Ed Brosius.[69] The 24-year-old Lillard was just starting his career that was known for outstanding bowling and longevity. In 68 ABC/USBC Championship appearances, Lillard knocked down a record 124,087 pins (a 196 average) before retiring from competition in 2015 at 87.[70]

The 1952 Hall of Fame vote, announced during the ABC Championships in April, disappointed Andy. Ned Day received 27 of 36 votes and earned election; Andy finished third with 15 votes, just behind Joe Norris, who garnered 16.[71] The 75 percent hurdle was a high bar. It is hard to believe that any voter thought Day unworthy of the Hall of Fame, and he barely made it. There were so many quality candidates. An encouraging note was that the ABC told voters to consider "other accomplishments" (besides ABC Championship performance) when evaluating nominees.[72] This minor change was good news for Andy.

At about the same time, Andy became a published author with the release of *Andy Varipapa's Quick Way to Better Bowling*, a 74-page soft-bound volume edited by Tom McLaughlin.[73] The book was little more than a compilation of Andy's instructional columns. It included a 10-page section on duckpin bowling by National Duckpin Congress Hall of Famer Nick Tronsky.

However, books took a back seat to an emerging technology when it came to bowling and just about everything else. Few knew it then, but the widespread adoption of television provided the platform for bowling to reach a wider audience than ever before. Stars became household names and set the stage for the bowling boom of the late 1950s.

Seventeen

Television

While Andy continued to tour the country on Brunswick's behalf, his days as a movie star were over. Double features, newsreels, and short films fell out of favor due to the increasing popularity of television. When Andy won his first All-Star in 1946, there were 18 television stations and 44,000 television sets in the United States. Six years later, when he finished second at the Masters, there were 225 stations and 24.3 million sets.[1] By the decade's end, 86 percent of American households had televisions.[2] The rapid growth in viewership required broadcasters to find popular content that was cheap to produce. Bowling delivered both.

It is hard to imagine today, but in the 1950s, sports teams and leagues did not rush to televise their games. The problem was two-fold. First, team owners did not correctly estimate the value of media rights. Whatever broadcasters paid for the rights to televise their events was not enough. Second, conventional wisdom was that fewer fans would attend a televised game. If the added revenue from media rights did not offset decreases in gate revenue, profits decreased. Therefore, in the short run, televising home games made little sense.

What team owners failed to understand was in the long run, television viewers who liked what they saw might become ticket buyers. Watching a game on the primitive black-and-white sets of the 1950s encouraged fans to get out and see games in person. Once the owners figured that out, the rush was on to televise games and benefit from multi-million (and later multi-billion) dollar media contracts.

By contrast, televising bowling had little downside, even in the short run. Broadcasts generated excitement and created valuable publicity for the host center and the industry. From the networks' perspective, indoor sports like bowling, boxing, and wrestling were easier to film than outdoor sports. Only one or two cameras were needed, and there were no worries about inclement weather.[3]

Bowling was first televised in 1947 from the Capitol Alleys in Manhattan (formerly Dwyer's, where Andy was an instructor in the early 1930s). The one-hour show featured matchups between local stars Tony Sparando, Marty Cassio, Mickey Michaels, and Ann Sabolowski. The competition ended early, so Joe Falcaro performed trick shots and gave host Win Elliot some tips to fill the time.[4] Broadcast on WCBS, the show aired within a 50-mile radius of Times Square and reached fewer than 100,000 homes. However, the limited audience flooded the station with positive phone calls.[5] The show was a hit, but bowling did not return to the air until the end of 1948.

On Saturday, December 18, 1948, WGN in Chicago planned to televise two hours of the third block of the BPAA All-Star finals. It would have been great exposure for Andy; he led the tournament after two blocks and received extensive coverage. Unfortunately, the day before the broadcast, producers discovered lighting in the Madison Street Armory was woefully inadequate.[6] The primitive cameras of the day were not as sensitive to light as modern ones, so WGN executives canceled the broadcast rather than broadcasting a dim picture.

The following year at the Northwest Armory, the lighting and cameras improved because WGN and WBKB televised portions of the 1949 All-Star. Brunswick and Pabst Blue Ribbon sponsored the broadcast, starting a partnership between broadcasters, bowling equipment manufacturers, and breweries that continues to this day.[7]

Al Cirillo—Andy's manager during the 1934–35 season—saw televised bowling differently. He believed a television show, rather than tournament coverage, was easier to produce and more profitable. Producers controlled lighting, sound, and the environment. Cirillo produced and hosted *Bowling Headliners,* television's first weekly bowling show, which premiered on ABC in December 1948. Viewers in New York, Philadelphia, Baltimore, and Washington, D.C.—the location of two-thirds of America's televisions—watched top bowlers compete in head-to-head matches during a one-hour show.[8]

Cirillo added well-known guest announcers (including the famed boxing announcer Don Dunphy), fashion models, and occasional celebrity contestants, making *Bowling Headliners* more than just competition between great bowlers. The show received positive press from *Variety, TeleVision Guide,* and the *Bowlers Journal* and consistently drew higher ratings than boxing, wrestling, and roller derby.[9]

Despite Cirillo's involvement, Andy never appeared on *Bowling Headliners.* Many top stars did compete, including Tony Sparando, Lou Campi, Graz Castellano, and Joe Wilman. Andy's busy travel schedule may have precluded it. The fledgling DuMont network picked up the show's second season in 1949, and the show continued to be successful. However, DuMont faced financial difficulties in 1950 and canceled *Bowling Headliners* in April.[10] While short-lived, *Bowling Headliners* served as a template for future bowling shows.

Andy first appeared on television in 1950. In October 1949, WXYZ-TV in Detroit premiered a weekly bowling show, *Make It and Take It,* broadcast live from State Fair Recreation. On January 30, 1950, Andy partnered with Ned Day—both in Detroit for their annual bowling school—and trounced local stars Hank Nosakowksi and Eddie Briskie 426–364.[11] The show's format allowed the winners to return the following week to defend their title (a "King of the Hill" format), but Andy and Day had already left the city. Andy did not appear again on television for several years.

The second edition of the ABC's special invitational tournament began on June 1, 1952. Now known simply as the ABC Masters, Andy's name was still popular enough to earn an invitation. But he had not contended in the All-Star, or any other significant tournament, in almost three years. None of the Masters' preview articles mentioned him as one of the favorites, and at 61, few expected Andy to be a factor.

The ABC expanded the 1952 Masters field to 64 bowlers: 31 survivors of Wisconsin eliminations, 21 state all-event champions, and 12 national stars.[12] The format was still double elimination, but matches were now four games each. Andy breezed through his first two matches and won two tougher ones, which set up a match with Junie McMahon in the winner's bracket semifinals.[13]

Despite Andy's pedigree, McMahon was a clear favorite. The world's best bowler averaged 220 for his first 12 games at the Masters and fresh off a thrilling 903–886 victory over Ned Day.[14] The other winner's bracket semifinal match appeared lopsided, with soon-to-be ABC all-events champion Steve Nagy taking on little-known Willard Taylor of Charleston, West Virginia. The fans and the press were salivating over a potential McMahon-Nagy matchup.

The underdogs did not cooperate. Both matches went down to the wire. Andy defeated McMahon 864–850, closing the match with five consecutive strikes in his final game 246. Taylor's 10th-frame spare in his final game was enough to squeak by Nagy 762–761.[15] In the winner's bracket final, Andy dispatched Taylor to the loser's bracket by a 776–751 count.[16]

In the final loser's bracket match, McMahon met Taylor for the right to bowl Andy for the title. Andy was confident, knowing whoever emerged had to beat him twice to claim the crown. At 61, he must have known this might be his last chance to claim a major title. Although Andy already beat McMahon and Taylor, Andy was surely rooting for Taylor rather than his highly decorated opponent. Sure enough, with Andy watching, Taylor crushed McMahon 908–751.[17] Things were falling into place for Andy to take home the Masters crown.

The match had a David vs. Goliath feel to it. Taylor was a 34-year-old chemical engineer at Union Carbide who had taken up bowling just seven years before. He averaged a modest 194 in his weekly league.[18] Before the 1952 Masters, his national tournament experience consisted of three BPAA All-Stars in which he never advanced beyond the qualifying round. However, Taylor had two things going for him. First, he already beat three all-time greats in Joe Wilman, Nagy, and McMahon. Second, and most importantly, he had nothing to lose. Nobody expected him to win.

Taylor built a significant lead after two games, and the outcome was never really in doubt, as Taylor won 834–792. The second match was even less tense. Andy lost the first game by 62 pins, 224 to 162, and proceeded to roll his worst four-game series of the Masters, a meek 702. Taylor's 756 was more than enough to claim the title.[19] Andy must have been bitterly disappointed, but he was not a sore loser. He knew he did not have his best stuff, so when the match ended, Andy turned to the crowd and said, "Every bowler has his day. I have just had mine."[20] They roared, and with that, Andy left the Milwaukee Arena with the $500 second-place prize but with regrets about what might have been.

To his credit, Taylor did what he needed to do to win. In his one-pin victory over Nagy, he needed to cover a 4-pin in the 10th frame to win, and recalled, "That thing looked like a toothpick as I got set for my next shot."[21] He made the spare, won the match, and with it, a big boost of confidence. The fact that Andy bowled poorly helped, too: "I didn't think I would crack, and I felt sure Varipapa would be at his very best ... but he was throwing the ball all over the alley and I won easily."[22] In 1954, Taylor made another improbable run at an ABC Masters title, coming out of the loser's bracket to finish second. That performance made his win in 1952 less fluky in the opinion of fans and media.

Andy's disappointment faded when he returned to Hempstead. He was now a grandfather of four and enjoyed his schoolteacher's schedule. Andy worked hard from September through June and had his summers off. Frank qualified for the finals of the *Newsday* Eastern Open, eventually finishing fifth, and Andy was at Baldwin Modern Lanes rooting him on.[23] After a summer spent at home in Hempstead and on the beach at Point Lookout, Andy hit the road in late September for numerous appearances in the Midwest.

In March 1953, Lou Marks announced the creation of the Eastern All-Star Classic League, which met each Sunday evening at Newark Recreation. Structured like other "majors" or "classic" leagues, the Eastern All-Star added a new wrinkle: WATV-Newark would televise the final game of each week's action.[24]

The league gained publicity when G. Krueger Brewing Company signed Andy to captain their team and paid him $15,000 ($172,700 in 2023 dollars) for 50 yearly promotional appearances.[25] Andy insisted on paying Marks a 10 percent commission for brokering the deal. Junie McMahon, Marty Cassio, Graz Castellano, Tony Sparando, Eddie Botten, Frank Serpico, and Lou Campi signed up. Sponsors included Marcal Paper Products, Ronson Lighters, and Mennen.[26]

However, Andy's deal with Krueger hit a snag. Someone at Krueger dropped the ball, unaware of an obscure New Jersey Alcohol Beverage Commission regulation that capped the amount of money a company spent on promotion in licensed premises. And that included bowling alleys. The $15,000 was way over the limit, but Krueger prepared to pay Andy in full since he had signed a contract. After hearing the news, Andy told the Krueger brass, "I don't want something for nothing. I didn't earn the $15,000."[27]

Andy settled for a $5,000 buyout, gave Marks $500, and canceled the deal. Few knew about the settlement until Marks disclosed the facts in his *Palm Beach Post* bowling column in 1984, shortly after Andy died. "How many men would have done what Andy did?" wrote Marks. "It indicates the great sense of fairness, the honesty, and the integrity that made up the character of Andy Varipapa."[28]

The league was a success. It did not hurt when Castellano rolled the first-ever televised 300 game on the second telecast.[29] The Eastern All-Star Classic became must-see TV in the Northeast. Andy bowled the first week of the season but very little after. On most Sunday nights, he performed out of town. He did not return for the league's second season, which folded in 1957 after losing its television deal.[30]

Many bowling television shows aired in the 1950s, including *National Bowling Champions*, *Bowling Stars*, *All-Star Bowling*, and *Top Star Bowling*. But the most popular and longest-lived was *Championship Bowling*. Each show featured two bowlers in a three-game head-to-head match, with the winner returning the following week. In the inaugural 1954–55 season, 26 matches were filmed in Chicago over the summer and aired weekly throughout the bowling season.[31]

Andy did not appear in the first season but was a regular after that. During the series, which ran through 1965, Andy tangled with the top stars in the game, including Steve Nagy, Joe Wilman, Buddy Bomar, Bill Lillard, Ray Bluth, Buzz Fazio, and Therm Gibson. He never won more than one match in a row, so he did not get much airtime. (In 1955, Bill Lillard won eight straight matches and stayed on *Championship Bowling* for two months. Andy was one of his victims.)[32] While his best competitive days were behind him, Andy remained in the public consciousness by touring 150 days per year for Brunswick.

On August 20, 1955, Andy performed before his largest audience ever at Crosley Field in Cincinnati as part of the "Bowler's Night" promotion before the Reds-St.

Louis Cardinals game. The 1955 Reds were a lousy team on the field and at the box office. They finished fifth in the National League with a 75–79 record. Average attendance was just 9,009; only the Pittsburgh Pirates and Washington Senators drew fewer fans. (The Milwaukee Braves led the majors with 26,050.)[33]

Andy performed his trick shots on a lane installed between home plate and third base. Paid attendance on Bowler's Night was 16,856, representing the Red's seventh-best day at the box office all season.[34] The *Cincinnati Enquirer* reported a total crowd (paid and unpaid) of 25,030.[35] Just two days prior, the Reds hosted the Cubs before 1,257 paying fans.[36]

Bowling outdoors was challenging. Players usually do not deal with wind, heat, and humidity, but if they must, the results can be disastrous. The PBA held outdoor events in 1999 and 2001 without incident, but they were lucky that the weather cooperated. On June 27, 2012, the USBC held the stepladder finals of the Women's U.S. Open on the streets of downtown Reno. It was a unique promotional idea, with the lanes installed directly underneath the "Biggest Little City in the World" arch. A big crowd assembled, live music played, fireworks went off, and the competition began at dusk.[37] And then everything went wrong.

Players first dealt with the setting sun's glare. Then 24 mph gusts blew dust, dirt, and sand all over the approaches and lanes. The footing was treacherous, and debris stuck to the lane oil, rendering the lanes virtually unplayable.[38] USBC Hall of Famer Kelly Kulick's 170 in the championship match was enough to win. Organizers planned a showcase for women's bowling; instead, the 2012 Women's U.S. Open became a cautionary tale of the hazards of bowling outdoors. Five outstanding bowlers rolled eight games and averaged a measly 162.[39]

The wind was not an issue at Crosley Field, but it was a typical August day in Cincinnati: 92 degrees and high humidity.[40] Warm temperatures make lane surfaces softer (balls will hook more), and high humidity makes thumbholes sticky. But Andy was undeterred. After a brief warmup, he performed several trick shots, including a nod to *Bowling Tricks* using hurricane lamps as obstacles. He made all his shots in one take. Not a single lamp broke. Asked years later if he was nervous, an 83-year-old Andy replied, "Varipapa never gets nervous. He's too busy."[41] After his performance, workers dismantled the modular lane, and the Reds-Cardinals game began on time.

The size of the crowd grew as time passed. A few months later, the *Plainfield (NJ) Courier-News* reported "30,000 paid fans" in attendance (and the Reds' opponents were the Brooklyn Dodgers).[42] In a 1968 interview, Andy recalled a crowd of 34,000 fans (never mind that the capacity of Crosley Field was 29,980).[43] In 1974, it was back down to 30,000, but up to 34,000 in 1982.[44] Safe to say that paid attendance that night was about double the Red's season average. Whatever the Reds paid Andy to appear, it was worth it. And it was the largest crowd ever to watch bowling.

Andy returned to Cincinnati in November to instruct at his *Times-Star*–sponsored bowling school. Always candid, he served up straightforward opinions to students. One young lady threw a gutter ball and asked, "What's wrong with me?" Andy responded, "You can't bowl."[45] But unlike his appearance at Crosley Field, this visit did not end triumphantly. On November 10, he returned to his hotel room after dinner to rest before his evening session. Andy remembers sitting down; when he woke up, he was at Jewish Hospital. The sportscaster Jimmy Powers reported that he was "seriously ill" in a Cincinnati hospital, and the Associated Press reported that Andy was hospitalized with an unspecified stomach ailment.[46]

Alice was not feeling well, so Frank flew to Cincinnati to be with his father. Frank hardly recognized Andy. He asked the doctor, "Is he dead?"[47] The doctor explained that Andy's skin was yellow due to severe jaundice from gallstones. Once Andy was strong enough to travel, Frank took him back to New York for further treatment.

About two months later, on January 9, 1956, Dr. Robert DeNicola removed Andy's gallbladder and several gallstones from his bile duct at North Shore Hospital in Manhasset.[48] Today, this surgery is routine. Performed arthroscopically, patients typically spend at most one night in the hospital. The procedure was not so simple in 1956. Andy's surgery took more than three hours and he spent 10 days in the hospital recuperating.

The illness shook Andy. Before the gallbladder attack, he did not recall being sick a day in his life.[49] Besides a handful of appearances canceled due to broken ribs, he had never missed a performance due to injury or illness. Andy prided himself on being "punctual, reliable, and ready."[50] His life on the road was a grind: driving tens of thousands of miles a year, sleeping on all sorts of hotel beds, and eating questionable restaurant food for months. He admitted that his single-mindedness did not allow time to worry about his health: "I had a lot to do and a great deal to accomplish, and I forged ahead with this purpose to guide me. I gave little thought to the gift of good health. I took that for granted."[51]

Andy benefited from good genes. While his father died at 33, his mother Concetta lived to 98. "I can't tell you why I am this way. Some people got it, and some people don't … who can explain it? I don't know."[52] Given his attention to health, the entire episode made him consider his mortality for the first time: "I have never been afraid or blind to the realities of life, but my well-being had never been attacked before," he said. "It took me a little time to adjust to the new development."[53]

Besides bowling, Andy did not exercise. He did not run, lift weights, or do calisthenics. Cross-fit aficionados may scoff, but bowling several hours daily provided all the physical activity he needed. Andy was solidly built and strong at five feet, six inches and 185 pounds. He extolled the health benefits of bowling his entire life. In 1971 he said, "The exercise you get while bowling and having fun conditions your legs, trims the waistline and hips, and overall strengthens the back and the legs."[54] While few argue that bowling is optimal for weight reduction, it beats sitting in a chair.

Andy watched what he ate. His granddaughter Susan recalled that he took a bite or two of dessert and pushed the rest away.[55] Andy's grandson Andy II remembered a birthday party where Andy dissected his slice of cake like a surgeon, carefully removing the icing and eating just the cake.[56] He lived by a simple motto: "Moderation in everything."[57]

He never smoked or drank alcoholic beverages except for the occasional beer on a scorching summer day or a glass of wine with dinner. When he drank beer, Andy preferred Gablinger's Light Beer.[58] While "pale in color and undoubtedly pale in taste," the world's first low-calorie beer made sense for health-conscious consumers like Andy.[59]

In his 70s and 80s, long after his competitive career ended, Andy indulged in the occasional scotch on the rocks. He told servers, "Make it a Cutty Sark and nothing else!"[60] This was from a man who endorsed Teacher's Scotch in the early 1960s.

Andy's physical condition was the topic of a 1957 article in *Scope Weekly*, a magazine published by Upjohn Pharmaceuticals, which targeted doctors, pharmacists, and other health professionals. Its mission was to discuss breakthroughs in medical research, diagnoses, and treatments, but most of all, to promote Upjohn's prescription drugs.[61] Dr. DeNicola was amazed at the 65-year-old's overall health: "Observations prior to and after surgery indicated to me that, physiologically, Andy was in the 35-year-age classification."[62] He added that Andy's blood pressure, reflexes, and pulse rate were those of a much younger man.

Andy's self-discipline served him well during his recovery. Dr. DeNicola noted that Andy followed his post-operative instructions carefully and "reacted exactly like the great athlete he is. Long years of constant adherence to rigid self-disciple and his overwhelming desire to excel in sports were evident in his recuperative behavior."[63] Andy was more succinct: "I am just too busy to talk about getting old."[64]

Andy returned to the lanes mid–March and was well enough to travel to Rochester for the ABC Championships in May. He totaled a modest 1,689 in all-events, but given what he had been through, Andy was glad to be back bowling.[65] But while recuperating, Andy learned he was again passed over for the ABC Hall of Fame. He finished second in the 1954 and 1955 voting, and with no new bowlers on the ballot, it was a foregone conclusion that 1956 would be his year. Andy got the most votes (37) but fell short of the 75 percent required to earn induction.[66]

In the wake of the snub, several bowling writers came to Andy's defense, none more so than his friend and former teammate Chuck Pezzano. He wrote, "Many bowlers are surprised that Andy isn't already a member," and "the Hall of Fame voting requirements are too tough when to date such a great figure as Andy Varipapa still hasn't been elected."[67]

Publicly, Andy never complained but must have wondered what the problem was. Midwestern bias? Still just a trick-shot artist? The world's most famous bowler, and someone who spent their entire life promoting the sport, was not in the Hall of Fame. The situation created such an uproar that ABC leadership modified the voting procedure for 1957. They reduced the nominees from 24 to 14, and if no one received 75 percent of the vote, a runoff would be held among the top three vote-getters. The system would ensure at least one inductee each year.[68]

In February 1957, Andy finally got the call telling him he was the newest member of the ABC Hall of Fame. But even with the voting changes, his election was not a landslide. He needed 47 votes on 62 ballots; he got 48.[69] Sure, Andy was thrilled but could not resist a dig at the voters who shunned him. He told *Newsday*, "It's wonderful. I'm very, very pleased. It is certainly a big honor—and I guess it's better late than never."[70]

He put his induction into perspective: "Everything has come to me late in life. I guess I'm a late comer. I didn't really move into top-notch league competition until I was in my late 30s … so you see, everything happens to me late."[71] Andy was not bitter; it was not in his makeup. He shed tears of joy during his induction ceremony at the 1957 ABC Championships in Fort Worth. He relished being a Hall of Famer so

ABC Hall of Fame induction ceremony, April 9, 1957, at the Will Rogers Civic Center, Fort Worth, Texas. Andy, facing the camera in tears, is congratulated by (from left) Joe Wilman (obscured), Ned Day, Adolph Carlson, Hank Marino, Harry Steers, Mort Lindsey, Joe Norris, and Herb Lange (USBC photograph, IBMHOF collection).

much that he did not miss an annual ABC Hall of Fame induction ceremony until 1984, shortly before he died.

By 1959, Andy was still making 150 personal appearances a year. He was 68 but had no plans to retire from touring and promoting the sport he loved. Asked when he might retire, Andy said, "I hope never. I won't do it as long as I can roll a ball and talk. When a man retires, he's had it."[72] But the bowling industry was growing faster than ever. Two bowling centers opened each day, and the newly formed PBA took the sport to heights even Andy had never dreamed of. It was too late for Andy to benefit from the PBA, but he still had enough maple moxie to thrill a national television audience before the decade was out.

Right: Andy's Hall of Fame shirt is on display at the International Bowling Museum and Hall of Fame in Arlington, Texas (IBMHOF photograph, IBMHOF collection).

Eighteen

Boom, Jackpot, and Heartache

Technological change is often the catalyst for rapid industry growth. Bowling was no different. What was once a pipe dream—a machine that set pins automatically without the need for pinboys—became a reality in the 1950s. The idea for an automatic pinsetter dates to 1911 but was not commercially available until 1952.[1] Events during those 40 years illustrate the benefits of risk-taking and the costs of not adapting to a changing environment.[2]

Brunswick's failure to join the pinsetter revolution cost them their virtual monopoly in the bowling equipment business. American Machine and Foundry (AMF), a company with no experience manufacturing bowling equipment, embraced the automatic pinsetter. By the 1960s, AMF was Brunswick's equal in the bowling business.

In 1946, AMF demonstrated an automatic pinsetter at the ABC Championships in Buffalo. The prototype was almost eight feet tall and weighed more than two tons. It was noisy, slow, and frequently broke down. But proprietors were smitten; the thought of jettisoning pinboys was too good to be true. AMF took orders for thousands of pinsetters, but perfecting the technology proved challenging.

It took six years, but AMF finally installed the first mass-produced models at Brooklyn's Farragut Pool Lanes in 1952.[3] Brunswick executives were stunned. They scrambled to build their own pinsetter and began installing them in 1956, but by then, AMF had a 10,000-unit head start.[4] Rather than adopt AMF's business model in which proprietors leased their machines, Brunswick sold them for $7,700 with 10 percent down and eight years to pay.[5] By 1960, 90 percent of the nation's 10,000 bowling centers utilized pinsetters.[6]

The automatic pinsetter revolutionized the bowling business. Beyond the obvious advantages—automatic pinsetters did not drink, fight, curse, or call in sick—automation allowed bowling anytime, anywhere. Bowling centers opened in the suburbs and promoted daytime leagues. Women took up the game in droves.[7] Automation also meant that capital replaced labor as the proprietor's essential resource. Instead of 20 or 25 unskilled pinboys, a 50-lane house needed 50 machines and just one skilled mechanic to maintain the house.

Consumers expected new bowling centers to be luxurious and offer the latest amenities. Opened in 1955, Tony Vogel spent $1.5 million ($16.8 million in 2023 dollars) to build The Bolero in Clifton, New Jersey. The center featured 50 lanes, a cocktail lounge, and a restaurant "worthy of a Miami Beach hotel" in its 150,000-square-foot space.[8] Victor Kalman wrote in *Sports Illustrated*: "Almost overnight, bowling has been transformed from a small-time operation run by individuals into big business."[9]

Ted Drake's 1959 caricature of Andy. Sports fans see Chicago artist Drake's work daily: he composed the University of Notre Dame leprechaun and the Chicago Bulls (NBA) logo (Brunswick Bowling Products, LLC image; Varipapa family collection).

Brunswick publicity photograph, circa 1959 (Brunswick Bowling Products LLC photograph; IBMHOF collection).

    Andy welcomed the changes. A former pinboy himself, he knew all too well how proprietors were at the mercy of their pinboys. No pinboys, no bowling, no revenue. After listening to an alley owner complain about his cranky pinboys, Andy walked away, muttering, "And they call me temperamental. Some of these pinboys make me look like 'Mister Humility.'"[10]

    He noted how mechanization changed the atmosphere of bowling alleys. Andy credited automatic pinsetters for transforming centers into "clean, comfortable, and attractive places to bowl ... equivalent to a country club for the working man's family—pop, mom, grandpop, and the youngsters."[11] Andy paid tribute to his fellow pinboys but bid them, "So long, farewell, and AMEN."[12]

The automatic pinsetter fueled the bowling boom from 1958 to 1962. In the 1957–58 season, 3.5 million Americans bowled leagues in 7,458 centers. At the beginning of the 1961–62 season, those numbers swelled to 6.5 million bowlers in 11,163 centers.[13] During those four years, an average of two bowling centers opened daily. Each had automatic pinsetters; most had luxurious bars, restaurants, nurseries, and ample parking. Nurseries! Once dirty, dank, and smoky dens of debauchery just 50 years earlier, modern bowling centers offered family-friendly entertainment.

Bowling was riding an unprecedented wave of popularity. More people were bowling than ever before. New Jersey became the first state to recognize bowling as an interscholastic sport in 1958.[14] The PBA held its first tournament in 1959, and the National Bowling League began operation in 10 cities in 1961. Chicago aired seven television shows dedicated to bowling; New York had four. Television devoted more hours to bowling than any other sport.[15] *Championship Bowling* was named Billboard's "Number One TV Sports Series" three years running.[16]

In this bowling-crazed environment, NBC premiered *Phillies Jackpot Bowling* on January 9, 1959. (Phillies was the most popular brand of the show's sponsor, Bayuk Cigars.)[17] While network television might not have needed another bowling show, *Phillies Jackpot Bowling* differentiated itself by eschewing the 10-frame format.

Two professionals threw nine balls each, and the bowler with the most strikes won $1,000. Spares were meaningless. A bowler throwing six consecutive strikes hit the jackpot, which started at $5,000 and increased by $1,000 each week it went unclaimed.[18] The show used a king-of-the-hill format, so winning bowlers stayed on the show until they lost a match. Losers earned a $250 consolation prize.

It was fitting that Don Carter, regarded as the world's best bowler, hit the first jackpot. He won four matches and an $8,000 jackpot, earning $12,250 ($127,704 in 2023 dollars) for little more than an hour's work.[19] Not only was Carter the best bowler in 1959, but maybe the greatest to put on a pair of bowling shoes. He won the All-Star four times, the World's Invitational five times, and was named BWAA Bowler of the Year six times.[20]

Bowler's Journal ranked Carter the greatest bowler of the 20th century.[21] In 1964, his $1 million endorsement deal with Ebonite was the first seven-figure contract for any professional athlete.[22] The 10-year deal paid him $100,000 ($973,664 in 2023 dollars) yearly when baseball's highest-paid player, Willie Mays, earned $105,000.[23]

Despite his name recognition, producers were apprehensive about booking Andy on *Phillies Jackpot Bowling*. One producer told Chuck Pezzano, "He's an old man, we want a good show with somebody who has a chance to win big money. Can't we get Don Carter back?"[24] Maybe so he did not look too much like his opponent's grandfather, producers pitted Andy against 51-year-old Buzz Fazio of St. Louis on April 17, 1959.

Animated like Andy, Fazio would drop to his knees and pray for strikes. With Andy clicking his heels, the duo made for entertaining viewing. Media historian Nick Hirshon noted another factor in their popularity: "The five-foot-six Fazio and the near-septuagenarian Varipapa were relatable to viewers unused to seeing people of their height and age playing professional sports."[25]

Bowling remained the sport for the everyman even after moving in front of bright television lights. Tall or short, fat or skinny, young or old, the pins did not care. You did not need to be exceptionally big and strong. Your family did not need to belong to a private country club. Almost everyone had the potential to become a good bowler, and Andy and Buzz proved it.

Filmed at T-Bowl in Wayne, New Jersey, just 20 miles west of Manhattan, Andy was the hometown favorite. He did not disappoint. He threw five perfect strikes and needed the sixth to win the $8,000 jackpot. Andy received some good fortune on the sixth shot because his ball crossed over to the left side of the headpin but still struck.[26] Andy threw the next three strikes for good measure and pocketed another $1,000 for defeating Fazio.

Andy took over the show after his victory. He commandeered the microphone from host Bud Palmer and delivered a lengthy monologue with other matches still to be played. He said the check was "more money than I've seen in a long time; used to have to bowl all year for this kind of money. Sure can use it!"[27] Chuck Pezzano said the incident almost cost Palmer his job.[28]

When order was restored, he lost his next match to Ralph Engan of Yonkers, but his $9,250 payday ($96,430 in 2023 dollars) was his largest ever. At 68, Andy still made headlines and drew eyeballs. The producers' concerns proved unfounded. More than four million viewers tuned in to watch, the show's largest audience to date.[29]

For the next year, *Phillies Jackpot Bowling* enjoyed continued popularity. Viewership routinely exceeded five million.[30] One of the most popular contestants was Frankie Clause, a 47-year-old former schoolteacher from Old Forge, Pennsylvania. On February 12, 1960, he hit the $25,000 jackpot and took home $33,000 ($338,209 in 2023 dollars), several times a history teacher's annual salary.[31]

Ironically, Clause's rise to bowling fame began after defeating Andy in a 1937 match. It was not one of Andy's casual one- or two-game exhibition matches: they rolled 20 games in two different bowling alleys with $1,000 at stake. Clause's 102-pin victory gave him the confidence to quit his teaching job and make bowling his profession.[32]

One of Clause's victims during his four-week run was J. Wilbert Sims of Chicago. Sims won the 1959 Illinois state singles title, which qualified him for the 1960 BPAA All-Star in Omaha. He acquitted himself nicely, averaging 204.9 and placing 30th out of 240 entrants.[33] None of this was remarkable, but for the fact Sims was Black. For all of bowling's inclusiveness regarding social class and income, people of color were unwelcome for many years.

The ABC's original 1895 charter specifically excluded non-whites and women.[34] The WIBC's original 1916 charter included similar language regarding non-whites. Only in 1950, when an Illinois judge fined ABC leaders $2,500 each and threatened to revoke their state association's charter, did bowling's governing bodies end their racially exclusionary practices.[35]

Sims was the first Black bowler to compete in the All-Star and presumably the first to bowl on television. Profiled in *Jet* and *Ebony*, Sims, along with Don Scott, were the first Black members of the PBA.[36] The PBA never excluded non-whites, and Scott said that his peers were supportive and he encountered little racism during his days on tour.[37] Several Black players have appeared in the television finals of PBA

Andy posing with Milton Berle (left) and Peter Lawford during the taping of *Phillies Jackpot Bowling* at Hollywood Legion Lanes in 1960. This is *not* the show when Andy hit the $8,000 jackpot—that was in Wayne, New Jersey, in 1959 (NBC photograph, IBMHOF collection).

tournaments, including Sims, who made two finals in 1962. But among more than 350 PBA titlists, George Branham III (five titles between 1986 and 1996) and Gary Faulkner, Jr., (one title in 2015) remain the PBA's only Black champions.[38]

Andy returned to *Phillies Jackpot Bowling* in 1960 and won three matches (one against Sims) before being defeated by Earl Johnson.[39] He never came close to hitting the jackpot, which reached $55,000 after being unclaimed for months. The jackpot grew to $75,000 in a few weeks when Detroit's Therm Gibson threw six strikes and won it. At $764,787 in 2023 dollars, it remains bowling's largest inflation-adjusted payday, including the megabuck tournaments of the 1980s.[40]

Unfortunately, the days of *Phillies Jackpot Bowling* were numbered. The show moved to Hollywood and rebranded *Phillies Jackpot Bowling with Milton Berle*. Unfortunately, the updated version was more showbiz schtick than bowling. Despite the big money, bowling fans were bored. Berle took the job to fulfill his contractual obligations to the network, and it showed. Ratings plummeted, and NBC canceled the show in the summer of 1961.[41]

Business at Bowl Mart, the pro shop Frank Varipapa and Stan Lewis owned, was growing. It was now a chain, operating 11 locations in four states and selling more Brunswick products than any other pro shop in the United States.[42] The owners and managers of Bowl Mart locations included names familiar to Long Island bowlers, including Roy Ryan (Babylon), Warren Mathias (Rockville Centre), Jerry Messina (Roslyn), John Peterford (Franklin Square), and Charlie Kraus (Babylon). Frank commented at a 1960 Christmas party at Stan Lewis's home, "Do all these people really work for me?"[43]

By 1965, Bowl Mart closed or divested all locations except the flagship store in Mineola. When Stan accepted a position with the Bowling Corporation of America in 1976, he sold his share of the business to Frank.[44] Bowl Mart remained wholly owned by the Varipapa family until 1990.

In 1958, sports agent Eddie Elias interviewed Don Carter and Dick Hoover on a local television show, *Akron Tonight*. During the interview, they expressed disappointment that there was no organization for bowlers like the Professional Golfers Association.[45] A couple of months later, Elias met with 17 of the nation's top bowlers in a hotel room in Mountainside, New Jersey, and outlined his plan for a national bowling tour. In May, during the ABC Masters, Elias collected $50 from 33 charter members and founded the PBA.[46] Andy and Frank joined the following January and were two of the first 100 members of the PBA.

In May 1959, the PBA held its first tournament, the Empire State Open. Andy's old doubles partner Lou Campi won the title, holding off Ed Lubanski and Dick Weber.[47] Weber won the other two events in 1959 and dominated the first three years of the PBA. Of the first 23 tournaments, Weber won 10. Only Don Carter won more than one. In 1961, he won seven of 13 events, a Tiger Woods–like single-season win rate never equaled on the PBA Tour. Weber won 30 PBA titles, and his record of four All-Star/U.S. Open victories was surpassed only by his son Pete, who won five. *Bowlers Journal* ranked Weber the second greatest bowler of the 20th century.[48]

Despite all his accomplishments on the lanes, Weber had a more significant impact off them. In 2001, *Bowling Digest* named him the most influential bowler in history (Joe Norris ranked second and Andy third).[49] *Miami Herald* bowling writer Dick Evans updated the ranking in 2009 to include bowlers and non-bowlers. Eddie Elias was first, and Weber was the highest-ranked bowler at fifth.[50]

What Arnold Palmer did for golf, Weber did for bowling. He was bowling's first television star and like Palmer, was friendly, humble, and kind.[51] The former postal worker signed every autograph, kissed every baby, and did every interview asked of him. Andy must have been jealous of some of his stunts: Weber bowled a game in a

PROFESSIONAL BOWLERS' ASSOCIATION

9 OVERWOOD RD.
AKRON 13, OHIO
TE 6-5568

OFFICERS

Don Carter
President
4226 Calvert St.
St. Louis, Missouri

George Young
First Vice-President
18579 Edinburgh St.
Detroit, Michigan

Steve Nagy
Second Vice-President
2756 Boling Broke St.
Birmingham, Michigan

Bill Welu
Secretary
2301 Locke Lane
Houston 19, Texas

Eddie Elias
*Executive Director
Treasurer and
Legal Counsel*
9 Overwood Rd.
Akron 13, Ohio

TOURNAMENT CHAIRMAN
Morris Cramer
1 Old Hickory Dr.
Albany, New York

PUBLICITY DIRECTOR
Bruce Koch
94 Holloway Rd.
Rochester, New York

EXECUTIVE MEMBERS

Buddy Bomar
5036 Broadway
Chicago, Illinois

Allie Brandt
P. O. Box 303
Lockport, New York

Frank Clauss
156 Drakes Lane
Old Forge, Pennsylvania

Eugene "Red" Elkins
1889 Orange Grove Dr.
San Jose, California

Frank Esposito
Route 17
Paramus, New Jersey

Basil "Buzz" Fazio
23707 Petersburg St.
East Detroit, Michigan

John Fazzio
P. O. Box 8094
New Orleans, Louisiana

Lou Franz
Thermal Lanes
Louisville, Kentucky

Therm Gibson
17378 Painview
Detroit, Michigan

Jerome "Whitey" Harris
4226 Calvert St.
St. Louis, Missouri

John Klares
1545 Superior Ave.
Cleveland 15, Ohio

Joe Kristoff
529 Des Plaines Ave.
Forest Park, Illinois

Marvin Lowry
1919 Fifth Ave. North
Birmingham, Alabama

Ed Mady
2011 Goodrich Ave.
St. Paul, Minnesota

Chuck Pezzano
The Morning Call
Patterson, New Jersey

January 31, 1959

Mr. Andy Varipapa
461 Madison Avenue
W. Hempstead, New York

Dear Andy:

Welcome to our organization. The Executive Board voted unanimously to make you one of us.

You were sponsored by one of our most respected members, Frank Esposito, and we are happy that you have seen fit to make application and are pleased to accept you.

Enclosed you will find a publicity questionnaire which you will fill out and return as soon as possible. Also enclosed is an insurance card which we must have filled out and returned at once.

Again allow me to congratulate you on becoming a member of our Association and enclosed is your membership card.

Sincerely,

Eddie

Eddie Elias
Executive Director

EE:rgs

Enclosures

Andy's PBA acceptance letter from executive director Eddie Elias (Varipapa family collection).

cargo plane at 35,000 feet. He rolled a game on Miami Beach. In the 1990s, a whole new audience of fans discovered Weber when he became a frequent guest on the *Late Show with David Letterman*, knocking over ketchup bottles and lava lamps outside the Ed Sullivan Theater.[52]

Weber died suddenly in 2005 at age 75. Like Andy, he was active and vibrant in his 70s, so his death was a shock. Johnny Petraglia commented, "When you say we have lost one of the giants of the sport, that's not true. We lost *the* giant. There is no one else."[53] Bowling writer Joan Taylor paid tribute to Weber by recalling her first interview with him in the mid-1970s.

Flustered upon meeting one of her idols, she stumbled over her words until blurting out, "I'm sorry, Mr. Weber." He quickly replied, "Mr. Weber is my father. Call me Dick. And I know how you feel, when I first came out on tour, I was in awe of people like Ray Bluth, Don Carter, and Billy Welu."[54] Now at ease, Taylor wrote her story, and she and Weber became lifelong friends. Everyone fortunate enough to meet Dick Weber remembered his quiet grace.

The All-Star, the ABC Masters, and its success on television proved that bowling was a spectator sport. As far back as 1940, Andy claimed that a series of professional bowling tournaments could be as popular as those in golf and tennis.[55] He did his best to support the PBA in its early years. Andy participated in all three events in 1959 and two more in 1960 with little success. Finding complete results for these early tournaments is challenging, but the *Bristol* (PA) *Courier-Times* published all game scores at the 1960 Fairlanes Open. Examining those scores reveals why Andy struggled.

At the Fairlanes Open, all 140 entrants rolled 16 games of qualifying over two days. Andy finished in 129th place with a two-day total of 2,870 (179.4 average). He was 342 pins off the cut line (32nd place, a 200.8 average) and 602 pins behind leader Dick Hoover (217.0 average).[56] In the first eight-game block, he started well with games of 178, 204, 203, 202, and 214, a 200.2 average, almost good enough to make the cut. But his last three games of the block were 152, 167, and 129.[57] The next day, he closed with games of 161 and 148.[58] At 69 years of age, Andy was getting tired at the end of a long day bowling. For someone who referred to himself as the "Iron Man," it must have been difficult for him to consider his bowling mortality.

With so many new bowling centers opening, Andy was busy. He was in Louisiana in late July when he canceled several of his appearances to be with Alice, who was hospitalized with a "serious illness."[59] She recovered, and Andy headed for appearances in Missouri, Iowa, and Illinois in mid-August. But on August 20, he slipped on a flight of stairs at the Branding Iron restaurant in Kansas City—ironically to attend a dinner in his honor—and spent the night in the hospital.[60] A sprained knee forced the cancellation of several appearances and his withdrawal from the BPAA Doubles tournament in Chicago.[61] He returned to the lanes on September 17 at the grand opening of the Bowl-O-Mat in Newark.[62]

Unfortunately, Alice's health continued to deteriorate. Andy made several local appearances in September and October but did not venture far from home. Alice died on October 26, aged 64, but other than a note by bowling columnist Carl Reich of the *San Francisco Examiner*, Alice's passing was not in the news.[63] No obituary or death notice appeared in any local newspaper. Andy's granddaughter Susan recalled him sitting at his kitchen table, writing hundreds of thank you cards for those who attended services or sent mass cards.

Just before Alice's death, Andy's daughter Lorraine wrote to George W. Jones of Harper and Brothers to gauge their interest in Andy's biography. She had been working on the book for about a year. Jones asked Lorraine to forward her half-completed manuscript. Although the content was entertaining and timely (smack in the

The Ruffolo home in Wantagh, New York, 1960. Seated (from left) Andy Ruffolo, Lorraine Ruffolo, Joe Ruffolo, Robert Ruffolo, Jr., Alice, Andy, Connie Cornacchia, and Dottie Varipapa. Standing (from left) Bob Ruffolo, Michael Cornacchia, Mike Cornacchia, Frank Varipapa, Andy Varipapa II, and Susan Varipapa (photograph by Alice DeForest; Varipapa family collection).

middle of the bowling boom), the original draft's eight chapters were rough and disorganized.[64]

Lorraine admitted she was not a writer. In her August 11 letter to Jones, she wrote, "I certainly do not possess the essential requirements of a literary writer but I do have the knowledge and heart for this story."[65] Jones wrote back two weeks later and told Lorraine, "It is a long way from being a publishable book ... certainly, the warmth of feeling in the Varipapa family circle comes through. This is nothing for Harper's, but it is possible that you may find another outlet for your material."[66] Undeterred, she contacted Andy's friend Dick Clemente of *Newsday*, who suggested that although the market was full of instructional books, such a book was an easy sell.

Jones agreed. "The book which you have now decided to write sounds as if it ought to have a wider sales appeal than the manuscript you just showed us," wrote Jones. "Mr. Varipapa's instructions for better bowling, is what we would particularly like to see."[67] Lorraine corresponded with *Detroit News* writer John Walter, who helped Andy set up his first bowling school in 1938 to get his ideas on the book. He wrote, "Any instructional book on bowling moves these days."[68]

Unfortunately, at that point, Lorraine's shelved her project. There were two reasons. First, she was disappointed that Harper had little interest in Andy's biography. Most of Andy's bowling tips were already in the public domain via *Andy Varipapa's Quick Way to Better Bowling* and dozens of syndicated newspaper articles. He was known as the outspoken and gregarious trick-shot artist, but few knew the honest and caring family man that Lorraine and her family knew.

The second reason is that the Ruffolo family moved, which diverted Lorraine's attention from the book. After Alice died, the family agreed that Andy was better off living with one of his children. He enjoyed being around people, especially his family, and already spent one-third of his adult life traveling alone. Andy did not need to come home to an empty house, especially soon after Alice's passing.

In the summer of 1961, Andy sold his house in Hempstead, the Ruffolos sold their house in Wantagh, and they purchased a larger house together in Plainview, in eastern Nassau County. The basement, set up like a hotel room, was Andy's. He enjoyed the privacy and could come and go as he pleased. He did not travel as extensively as he used to, but he was still on the road for more than 100 days annually.[69]

The basement included a pool table, the site of epic battles between Andy and his son-in-law Bob Like most great athletes, Andy was competitive at everything he did. Be it bowling, pool, or tiddlywinks, Andy wanted to win. Matches often ended in arguments, usually over minor rules interpretations, with each swearing they would never play with the other again. But in a week or two, all was forgiven, and the two returned to the table until the next disagreement erupted.[70]

After bowling a handful of PBA tournaments in 1961, Andy entered early 1962 events in Akron and Winston-Salem (he missed the cut in both) before heading to the Birmingham Open in March. Arriving early after missing the cut in Winston-Salem, Andy told Clyde Bolton of the *Birmingham News*, "The Professional Bowling Association [sic] is the best thing that ever happened to be bowling and to the better bowlers. Now some young bowlers have a chance to be somebody."[71] And, of course, he could not resist a bit of self-promotion. When asked why bowling had grown so fast, he cited women's participation, automatic pinsetters, fancy new bowling centers ... and himself.[72]

While practicing at Bowl Lo-Mac Lanes, Andy noticed a group of fans gathering behind him. Carter and Weber were the big stars on tour, but the Varipapa name was still gold. He chatted with them, signed autographs, and posed for pictures while he continued to practice. When a perfect pocket hit left the 10-pin standing, he turned and said, "That's why I have this premature gray."[73] He still was bowling's greatest showman.

But at age 71, Andy's participation in PBA tournaments was ceremonial. And he knew it. In Winston-Salem, he said his visit was "to see bowling grow in this area because I have many friends here."[74] In Birmingham, he entered "to be congenial and to see the boys."[75] Not surprisingly, he missed the cut. He bowled the PBA event in Memphis the following week (another missed cut) before heading to Cincinnati for a few appearances before the next PBA stop in Houston.

However, his poor driving caught up with him in Carrollton, Kentucky. His car jumped a ravine, banked off a utility pole, and slid down a 30-foot embankment. But once again, good fortune prevailed. Although complaining of only a sore back, Andy refused medical attention, procured a new car, and forged ahead to Cincinnati.[76]

At the Houston Open, he was near the bottom of the standings for the third straight week. The car accident may have accelerated matters, but Andy realized he could not measure up with the younger, stronger bowlers. He decided, right then and there, to retire from competition. Andy would no longer take a precious spot away from an up-and-coming professional trying to get their career off the ground.

Andy continued to support the PBA by appearing at tournaments to sign autographs and perform trick shots. His retirement was passive: no announcement, press conference, or victory tour. Just a quiet drive back to Plainview. But he did not retire from bowling—far from it. While his competitive days were behind him, Andy continued to spread bowling's gospel into his 90s.

Nineteen

No Slowing Down

The bowling boom that began in 1958 went bust just a few years later. Very few bowling centers opened, and league participation plateaued. As the market became saturated, many proprietors walked away from highly leveraged operations. By 1962, the numerous defaults left Brunswick saddled with $359 million ($3.6 billion in 2023 dollars) in debt.[1] The company survived because it had diversified into industries such as school furniture, watercraft, medical supplies, and outboard motors.[2]

Bowl Mart, which had grown to 11 locations in 1961, also scaled back. By 1965, Bowl Mart had divested all locations except Mineola, Rockville Centre, and Williamsport, Pennsylvania.[3] But despite the slowdown in the growth of recreational bowling, professional bowling flourished as a spectator sport. Bolstered by increased television coverage with high ratings, professional bowlers cashed in.

In 1963, Harry Smith earned about $75,000 ($732,257 in 2023 dollars) between prize money, endorsements, and his salary for being the house professional at Johnny Unitas' Colt Lanes in Baltimore.[4] Don Carter signed his million-dollar ($973,664 per year in 2023 dollars) endorsement deal with Ebonite in 1964. In 1965, Billy Hardwick pocketed $25,000 ($236,312 in 2023 dollars) by winning the Firestone Tournament of Champions, while golfer Jack Nicklaus earned just $20,000 for winning the Masters the very next day.[5]

Andy was never bitter about the financial success of modern professionals. He admitted to earning as much as $30,000 annually, a comfortable living in post-war America.[6] That was probably in 1948 or 1949, after his two All-Star wins, more than $375,000 in 2023 dollars. In 1981, New York sportscaster Len Berman and hockey legend Phil Esposito interviewed Andy at Bowl Mart for their local WCBS-TV show, *Sportspeople*. Berman asked Andy if he wished he were still in his prime during the big-money days of the 1960s and 1970s. Andy replied, "No, not really. My life has made me a millionaire—not with money, but with friends."[7] Proud to have blazed the trail for young professionals, he fancied himself as their "granddaddy."[8]

Andy noted the changes to the sport brought on by the switch from shellac- to lacquer-based lane finishes. He watched a match alongside Tony Kusky during the 1963 PBA National Championship at Garden City Bowl. It featured Don Johnson and Billy Hardwick, two of the game's brightest young stars. Like Don Carter and Dick Weber, they threw the ball very straight.

Andy prided himself on his ability to throw a powerful hook ball. He remarked, "Look at these kids. Neither one of them throws a big hook but they know how to get the pins down. Maybe after all these years I'm going to have to change my style."[9] For his part, Kusky commented on the money: "A guy, if he's good enough, can concentrate on bowling alone and not have to worry about making a living and bowling on the side like we did."[10]

Changes in the scoring environment, rather than the changes in financial rewards, sometimes upset Andy. As discussed in Chapter 11, the methods and quality of lane maintenance procedures influence scoring.[11] In 1964, Andy blamed changing lane conditions on why it was harder and harder for a 73-year-old to keep up with the younger players. Lanes hooked more than in previous decades, so top bowlers needed to throw the ball faster to hold the pocket. "Conditions today have made the game for the young," he said. "Today the bowler just throws the ball and the alley does most of the work."[12]

Andy maintained that lanes were not more challenging in his prime but simply different. When lacquer finishes started to replace shellac after World War II, Andy praised the new "mineralistic" finishes. He said that shellac "gives you fake scores. Constant friction caused when rolling the ball in the general direction of the pocket wears out shellac and makes grooves in the alleys. It creates a path for the ball to go in by itself."[13]

During his first visit to Miami in 1949, he learned why no one averaged 200 in South Florida. "Man, these alleys in Florida are really flat," he said. "I haven't found one grooved alley since I've been down here."[14] Without a groove to the pocket, how else could he and Falcaro have averaged over 250 with hard rubber balls in their epic 1932 showdown?

Bowlers have debated lane conditions since the days of Jimmy Smith and Count Gengler. The most significant controversies erupted when lane dressings changed from shellac to lacquer (the mid–1940s) and later from lacquer to polyurethane (the late 1970s). Technologies changed, and bowling techniques had to follow. Jimmy Smith's style would be ineffective today, as would those of Andy, Ned Day, Don Carter, Dick Weber, and Earl Anthony. Each change required more ball speed and increased "rev rates" to knock down pins and spelled trouble for older competitors.

Athletes take care of themselves better than ever before. They have an improved understanding of training, nutrition, rest, sleep, etc. Tom Brady at 45, Dara Torres at 41, and LeBron James at 38, excelled at their respective sports. Bowlers, too, are fitter than ever before. Professional bowlers of the 1960s and 1970s were known for all-night drinking bouts, staking out all-you-can-eat buffets, and smoking on the lanes. Although you can spot the occasional unathletic-looking player at a PBA event, most modern professionals understand staying in shape helps their game. But while today's bowlers are better athletes, many are convinced that no one will repeat Andy's mid–50s accomplishments.

Norm Duke is one of them. He, like Andy, was successful in his mid–50s. He won back-to-back PBA titles in 2019, just a few weeks before his 55th birthday. At the 2022 USBC Masters, Norm Duke was in the same situation as Andy was in 1952. Duke marched through the winner's bracket as the only undefeated player.[15] If he won one more game, he could pull off an incredible double: at age 58, Duke would become the oldest player to win a PBA event while already being the youngest to do so (he won the Cleveland Open in 1983 at age 18). Jeff Richgels commented that if Duke won, he might join the discussion as the greatest bowler ever.[16] But it was not to be. Anthony Simonsen of Las Vegas, who happened to be the second-youngest player to win a PBA title, struck on his first ball in the 10th frame to defeat Duke 219–216.[17]

Despite his near-win and still formidable skills, Duke retired a few months later. "It was not like I was not competitive," said Duke. "Over the last five to eight years, I was never once satisfied with my performance. Then I realized I was comparing myself to a young, more vibrant man."[18] He felt unable to compete week-to-week in this new high-revolution, high-ball-speed environment. Duke was grateful to compete as long as he did but understood that "there is no beating Father Time."[19] As for anyone repeating what Andy did at 56, he is skeptical: "The man won the All-Star twice in a row, 100 games, the most grueling event in the world. I don't think that is possible now. There was no power game back then. You could be dominant with your touch and accuracy because the pins didn't know your age. It was a little less taxing. No, it was a lot less taxing. If you are going to try and do what Jason Belmonte does for 100 games, no one is doing that today at 58 years old. Nowadays, the pins know exactly how old you are."[20]

One can only imagine what Andy might think about today's scoring environment. At one time, a 300 game was an infrequent occurrence. When a bowler managed to throw the first nine strikes in a row, the entire bowling center fell quiet. Everyone stopped bowling and gathered to watch the presumptive hero's 10th frame. Each strike generated a louder cheer, and the applause was deafening if the bowler threw the 12th strike and completed a perfect game.

In the 1940s, 300 games occurred once in every 533,000 games. In the 1960s, that ratio was roughly the same, one in every 550,000 games. But by the 2000–01 season, that ratio dropped to once in every 4,300 games.[21] The epidemic compelled the *New York Times* and the *Wall Street Journal* to investigate the issue.[22] In the 20 years since then, the pace has not slowed. During the 2020–21 season, the ratio was one 300 for every 3,100 games. Rolling a 300 game today is 175 times more likely than the 1960s.[23]

Andy claimed to have bowled 78 perfect games. The first was in 1927 in a match at Lawler's, and the last in 1956 while practicing for an appearance on *Championship Bowling*.[24] However, official USBC records credit Andy with only one 300 game, rolled in the Brooklyn Alley Owners' Tournament on January 5, 1931.[25] He rolled the rest in practice, exhibitions, challenge matches, or otherwise "unsanctioned" competition.

A "sanctioned" (now referred to as "certified") league or tournament implies that the equipment and lanes meet ABC specifications; thus, scores are considered official.[26] Until the late 1980s, a representative of the local bowling association (affiliated with the ABC or WIBC) visited the center after a 300 game to inspect the lanes, pins, and balls. If everything met specifications, the ABC awarded the bowler a gold ring commemorating their achievement.

But as 300 games became commonplace in the 1980s, the ABC was going broke handing out rings and could not keep up with the requests to inspect lanes. To save money, gold rings were replaced with siladium, a stainless-steel alloy used in high school and college class rings. By the late 1980s, the ABC no longer inspected lanes, and proprietors were on their honor to provide fair playing conditions.

Without oversight, proprietors figured that bowlers liked high scores better than low scores. Easier lane conditions and improved bowling ball technology resulted in a scoring explosion.[27] Higher scores made Andy's once record total of 78 perfect games irrelevant. Through the 2020–21 season, Andy Neuer of Lewisburg, Pennsylvania, rolled 267 certified 300 games.[28]

It is impossible to document each of Andy's 78 perfect games. Newspapers reported his first in 1927 and second in 1929. After that, record-keeping was spotty. His 300 games became so commonplace that newspapers failed to mention them. In 1947, in response to a skeptical reporter (he claimed 65 300s at the time), Andy said, "All of my perfect games are registered on the alleys I scored them."[29] That is probably true; any bowling center where Andy performed would be pleased to note something to the effect of *Andy Varipapa Rolled a 300 Game on These Alleys in 1934.*

While several of Andy's 300 games came in tournaments or matches, he rolled many in exhibitions and practice. In 2013, a writer attributed this quotation to Andy: "If I throw 12 strikes in a row over two games, in my mind, it is a 300 game."[30] The author used quotation marks as if he heard Andy say it (unlikely, he was dead for 30 years) or read it elsewhere. Did Andy ever say such a thing? No one can say for sure, but there are good reasons why many people think he did.

Dick Clemente often practiced with Andy at Hempstead Recreation in the 1950s and 1960s. He explained what it was like bowling with Andy: "When Andy was in town, you bowled his way—a lot of 'practice shots' that suddenly counted when he realized that he had seven consecutive strikes. Down on the scoresheet went the X's, and when Andy reeled off five more he had one of his 80-odd 300s. Such 'perfect' games became facetiously known as 'Varipapa 300s.'"[31] The same thing happened when he threw a few strikes in a row during an exhibition. Andy started counting, and if he rolled 12 in a row, it went in the books as another 300.

The phrase "Varipapa 300" has become part of the bowling lexicon. Some consider it a significant achievement. As recently as 2021, a Utah sportswriter noted that a local bowler's "outstanding resume includes four sanctioned 300 games, [and] four Andy Varipapa 300s."[32] That said, few bowlers consider a Varipapa 300 a legitimate feat.

While many of Andy's 78 perfect games were indeed "Varipapa 300s," this should not diminish his accomplishments. Of his first 10 documented 300s, rolled between 1927 and 1934, all were in matches or tournaments. None were "Varipapa 300s." Andy did not bowl in leagues after 1930, and besides his local, state, or national ABC championships, and the All-Star, he rarely bowled in certified events. Andy may have bowled more games in his lifetime than any human being, but Andy Neuer surely had more opportunities to bowl a certified 300 game than Andy Varipapa.

Andy continued to criticize soft lane conditions until he died. When asked about Glenn Allison's famous 900 series, shot in 1982 when Andy was 91, he said, "I think it's ridiculous because they condition lanes today with this oil that is so good that a bowler can consistently hit the pocket."[33] When he met Allison, he offered a passive-aggressive compliment: "It's not your fault you shot 900, but in all my years the best I could do was 857."[34] Allison, one of bowling's great gentlemen, replied, "Andy, if scoring conditions were as easy as they are now, you would have rolled six 300 games in a row."[35] As Carmen Salvino told me, "Andy was the only guy who could insult you and still get you to like him."[36]

On one occasion, Andy's candidness created controversy. In 1972, St. Louis Hall of Famer Ray Orf rolled games of 290–300–300, an 890 series that beat Allie Brandt's long-standing record of 886. However, the ABC refused to approve the series, ruling that the lane dressing did not meet specifications. Orf sued the ABC and settled out-of-court with the proviso that neither side would speak about the case.[37] Andy appeared on KMOX-TV in St. Louis to promote the National Bowling Council's (NBC) Fifty-Plus program. When asked about Orf's series, Andy said, "[ABC executive secretary] Mr. Baker told me he caught him (Orf) cheating on the lane dressing."[38]

Orf was upset, and rightly so. He said, "I have nothing against Andy. He's a nice old guy and I wouldn't want to cause him any trouble, but I can't have him going around the country saying things like that."[39] His reputation was at stake, and if Andy's statement were true, Baker violated the non-disclosure agreement. Orf contemplated legal action, but with legal expenses of $50 per hour, the cost of winning was too great. He had to settle for an apology from NBC president Rex Golobic: "We are at a total loss as to why Andy would say such a thing … it is our understanding that no responsibility was ever attributed to you when the American Bowling Congress did not accept your 890 series."[40]

The ABC was one of several bowling organizations bankrolling the NBC, so it was no surprise that Golobic threw Andy under the bus. It is easy to ignore the ramblings of an 81-year-old man, but Andy was not your average 81-year-old. Having been in the media spotlight for 40 years, he was well-versed in giving interviews and knew the seriousness of the word "cheating," Despite his aversion to the modern scoring environment, he had no reason to hold ill will towards Orf. And if nothing else, Andy was honest. It is unlikely that he just made up his conversation with Baker. No one will ever know if Frank Baker told Andy that Orf was cheating.

Andy's mother Concetta died on March 12, 1964, at age 96. She lived with Andy's stepsister Marie in Levittown. Concetta outlived four of her seven children and was survived by nine grandchildren and 23 great-grandchildren.[41] Less than a year later, Andy's brother Josh died on January 6, 1965, at 71. While only two years apart, they were not close. They lived under the same roof until Andy married and worked together for the railroad for several years. But at some point, they went their separate ways.

Andy never spoke of Josh except for a 1984 interview with Jim Dressel, who asked Andy about playing baseball under an assumed name (Andy Bell). Andy said it was common for people to use aliases, pointing out that his brother boxed under the name Josh Matthews.[42] None of Andy's grandchildren remember Josh being around, even at family gatherings.

Compared to his famous brother, Josh had a rough life. He married 17-year-old Filomena (Millie) Croce in 1920. Less than a year later, she gave birth to a daughter Elanor, who lived only six days. They did not have another child, and Millie died in 1953 at just 51. Josh worked as a billiard parlor manager, city inspector, and cab driver. His name appeared in the newspapers only twice. In 1930, his driver's license was suspended because he made a false statement (maybe on his cab driver's application), and in 1948, he was convicted and fined $50 for drunk driving.[43]

After Millie died, John LaSpina said Josh occasionally visited Maple Lanes in Brooklyn, where John's father gave him a hot meal and a few bucks.[44] Andy was appreciative, but it was apparent that he had no relationship with Josh. At some point, Josh changed the spelling of his last name to "Veripapa." He used it on his petition to naturalize, draft registration card, and in his mother's obituary. It is on his gravestone at St. Charles Cemetery in East Farmingdale, New York.[45] One wonders if changed his name to distance himself from his family.

In 1965, Andy toured Europe for six weeks on behalf of AMF. The tour was not covered by American newspapers—and not much by European papers either. Two stories appeared in England, and both made it a point to note that Andy was reputed to have earned more than $500,000 in prize money and exhibition fees.[46] In a way only the British press can do, Andy was described as "the only bowler in history to become a legend during his own lifetime."[47]

There is humorous raw footage of his visit to a bowling center in Wolverhampton. After he threw a couple of shots, ATV (Associated Television) presenter Reg Harcourt introduced himself. It took Andy some time to figure out that his name was Reg, not Rich.[48] One can only imagine the British fans' difficulty understanding Andy's Brooklyn-Italian accent.

After departing England, he visited Germany, Belgium, Denmark, Ireland, and his native Italy. It was his only visit to the country of his birth. Andy remarked, "It was like a collection of postcards coming to life and I found it one of the most fascinating experiences of my life."[49]

At the 1966 ABC Championships in Rochester, the Hall of Fame induction ceremony fell on Andy's birthday, March 31. After honoring new inductee Buddy Bomar, the ABC presented Andy with a 75th birthday cake. A local baker, who happened to

Andy's 75th birthday celebration, March 31, 1966. Buddy Bomar dotted Andy's nose with icing during the ABC Championships at the Rochester War Memorial Auditorium. Joining the celebration were (from left) Hank Marino, Allie Brandt, Billy Sixty, and Joe Norris (USBC photograph; IBMHOF collection).

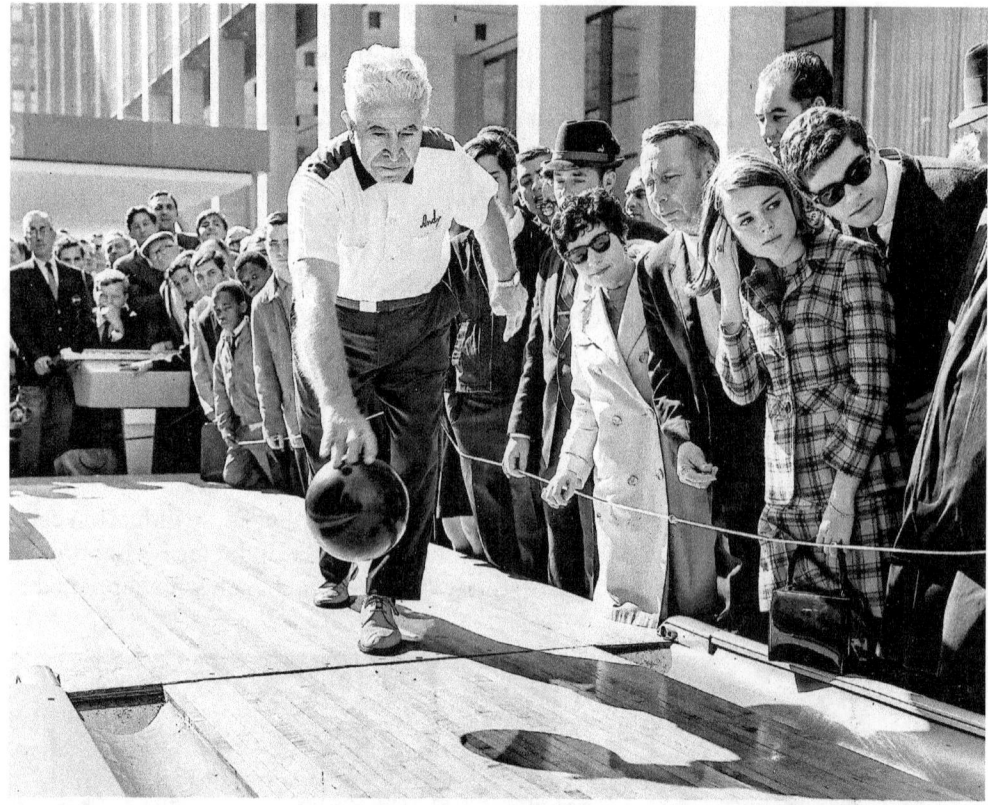

Andy performed trick shots on a specially built lane outside Madison Square Garden on October 23, 1968 (AMF photograph; Varipapa family collection; courtesy Bowlero Corporation).

be a bowler, whipped up a treat that would make the "Cake Boss," Buddy Valastro, envious. Andy and his fellow Hall of Famers enjoyed a lane, ball, and pins made of chocolate and cake.[50]

On October 23, 1968, AMF installed a regulation lane outside the Madison Square Garden Bowling Center entrance at Seventh Avenue and 32nd Street in Manhattan. Unlike the 2012 Women's U.S. Open, the weather cooperated. Dick Weber defeated Dave Davis in a two-game match, 393–343, and then Andy took to the lanes and performed his trick shots. Wire services carried pictures of 77-year-old Andy bowling with fans peering just inches from the lanes. Part of New York City's "Bowling Week" celebration, Chuck Pezzano wrote how the event "drew a standing room only crowd. That's all there was, standing room."[51]

Shortly after his inauguration, President Richard Nixon reorganized the President's Council on Physical Fitness and Sports. Nixon inherited a group of high-ranking bureaucrats and a few star athletes, but he believed practitioners should dominate the Council. But besides Chairman Jim Lovell (the command pilot of Apollo 13 and the world's most experienced astronaut), the rest were accomplished yet little-known physicians, physical education experts, and business leaders.[52]

Nixon created the Advisory Conference on Physical Fitness and Sports in October 1970 to boost the star power of the council. He appointed 50 famous athletes, including Hank Aaron, Joe DiMaggio, Arnold Palmer, Willie Shoemaker, Joe

Richard and Pat Nixon greet Andy on February 19, 1971, at a White House reception for Advisory Conference on Physical Fitness members (photograph by George G.H. Ortiz for International News Service; IBMHOF collection).

Frazier, Billie Jean King, and Peggy Fleming. Listed among these sports legends was "Andy Varipapa, professional bowler."[53] He was the first bowler ever associated with the Council and, at 79, the oldest member.

Nixon and his wife Pat were avid bowlers. Supporters of President Truman financed the installation of two lanes in the White House in 1947, but they were later moved to the Executive Office Building next door. Nixon did not want to leave the White House to bowl, so he had a single lane installed in the basement.[54] At the reception recognizing new members, Andy was typically candid. "When I shook hands with the President, I could see that he didn't have the calluses like I have. That means he doesn't get out on the lanes three or four times a week," said Andy. "I told President Nixon that if he wanted to become a really good bowler, he'd have to practice more."[55]

Andy made some speaking appearances shortly after being appointed to the council, but being overshadowed by the likes of DiMaggio and Palmer was not Andy's cup of tea. Not long after his appointment to the advisory council, he became the spokesperson for the National Bowling Council's (NBC) "Fifty-Plus Program."[56] At 80, it seemed appropriate that Andy was the face of a program designed to encourage bowling among senior citizens.

The NBC sent Andy all over the country to promote the A-B-Cs of bowling: "A" for activity, "B" for better health, and "C" for companionship. He became the face of the program and with good reason. Andy's name was more familiar to anyone over 50 than any active PBA star other than possibly Dick Weber. At an appearance in Hartford, Connecticut, one retiree said, "What a day, open bowling, free shoes, every old-timer's idol—Andy Varipapa—showing us how to bowl and a free buffet."[57]

One of Andy's stops on the Fifty-Plus tour was in New York to appear on the syndicated television show *What's My Line?* The show was likely taped on October 7, 1971, and the International Bowling Museum and Hall of Fame (IBMHOF) has a copy of the segment in their video archives.[58] Andy signed in as "Mister X," and none of the panelists (Gene Rayburn, Florence Henderson, Henry Morgan, and Arlene Francis) recognized him by sight.[59] Morgan thought Andy was the physical culturist and bodybuilder Charles Atlas. The panelists did not figure out Andy's profession (the point of the show) after their 10 allotted questions.

Like Andy, Atlas (born Angelo Siciliano) was born in Italy, immigrated to the United States as a child, sported a shock of white hair, and at 79, was just a year younger than Andy. Andy must have been flattered to be taken for Atlas because even at age 79, Atlas was in outstanding condition and often photographed shirtless. He played the role of the "World's Most Perfectly Developed Man" until he died in 1972.[60]

In 1969, Andy announced that he was bowling left-handed. Andy was ambidextrous anyway, evidenced by the fact that he batted left-handed when playing baseball. He bowled well enough left-handed to convert the 7–10 split by throwing a ball with each hand. Even at 78, retired from competition for years, his switch made headlines coast to coast. Asked why he changed, he initially claimed it was due to a painful left knee (the long-term effects of his 1919 broken leg) and to gain additional ball speed.[61]

Later, he was coy about the reason for the switch. He denied any physical problem: "An injury? Hell no. I'm strong as a bull. Here, feel my muscle. I just decided to change to lefty when I was 78 to make things interesting."[62] Later, he said, "I roll the ball a little better left-handed."[63] Finally, after a stretch in 1971 when southpaws won four consecutive PBA tournaments, he said, "I've seen so many left-handers winning on TV that I thought I'd better get with it."[64]

Andy did not recall a good left-handed bowler when he was in his prime, and with good reason. Since right-handers comprise 90 percent of the population, lane dressing applied to the right side of any bowling lane wears out faster than the left. On lanes coated with shellac, right-handers benefited from broken-in lanes by wearing a groove that led directly to the pocket. Natural left-handers learned to bowl right-handed because there was no chance for them to be competitive otherwise. The slick conditions on the left side of the lane were too demanding.

However, as the technology of dressing lanes changed, lefties benefited from smoother lane conditions on lanes finished with lacquer (and later polyurethane). Andy explained, "Because the left-hand side of the lane received a good deal less traffic, it is easier for left-handers to be more consistent rolling the ball into the 1–2 pocket."[65] Lacquer surfaces allowed left-handed pioneers such as Roy Lown and Bill Allen to break through and win multiple PBA titles. Their success paved the way for the next wave of left-handed stars like Dave Davis, Johnny Petraglia, and Earl Anthony.[66]

Andy used this ball when bowling left-handed. He modified the ring fingerhole to grip the ball with his left hand. If he wanted to throw a ball right-handed, he inserted a slug, returning it to its original drilling. Notice the logo above the fingers, "Andy Varipapa Champion" (photograph by the author; courtesy Mineola Trophy and Awards).

After a few months of practice, Andy was averaging in the 180s.[67] While he never seriously considered returning to competition as a lefty, he did have a little fun with the thought. As a past champion, he was invited to the 1971 U.S. Open, despite having been retired for nine years. His letter to PBA executive secretary Joe Antonora was classic Andy:

Dear Joe,

I wish to thank you for the invitation to compete in the U.S. Open at St. Paul. I regret that I have to decline at this time. I am presently bowling left-handed and in serious training. My progress is most encouraging ... in fact, I have reason to feel that in a year or so I will be ready for top-notch competition. I wish to serve notice to the big boys that the Great Varipapa is on his way back to the battlefield as a left-hander. That should give them something to worry about.

As ever, Andy Varipapa[68]

By 1976, Lorraine and Bob Ruffolo decided to downsize from their big home in Plainview. They relocated to Stony Brook, 25 miles further east, and Andy moved to Huntington Bay to live with his oldest daughter Connie and her family. Huntington

Bay is a quiet community on the north shore of Long Island, where stately mansions sit side by side with modest ranches and capes. For Andy, it was ideally located just a few miles from his favorite bowling center, Century Lanes, which became his home away from home for the rest of his life.

Twenty

Century Lanes

Andy enjoyed teaching bowling as much as performing trick shots. Over the years, between his appearances, schools, books, and newspaper articles, Andy's lessons reached millions of bowlers. He believed in his cause, often saying, "The biggest problem confronting the bowler is the lack of proper instruction."[1]

Like everything else, Andy had strong opinions about instruction, declaring, "There is only one way to bowl—the right way."[2] Some instructors maligned Andy's techniques, but often he was ahead of his time. He encouraged bowlers to use a four-step approach in the 1930s when most took three. "I was criticized for being persistent, insisting that everyone take four steps," he told *Bowlers Journal* in 1968. "Now, everyone takes four steps."[3] Andy was also an early adopter of the three-finger grip when two-fingers were the norm.[4]

Andy's most radical advice was that bowlers should use lighter balls. In 1972, he said, "The only problem [women] have—and men, too—is that they are using bowling balls that are too heavy, and they can't get a proper backswing."[5] Conventional wisdom was that a heavy ball knocked down more pins, so most adults used the maximum-allowable 16-pound ball. Andy never took a physics class but understood that the ball's velocity was part of the pin-pounding equation. Today, few professionals use 16-pound balls.[6]

His instructions for beginners were simple. Get a ball that fits, focus on your footwork, do not try to overpower the lanes, and develop a smooth rhythm to your approach. He also stressed the need for practice. Belying the book's title (*A Quick Way to Better Bowling*), the first page of Andy's 1952 instructional book read, "Don't look for a magic formula for quick success because there isn't any easy way to the top. If and when you succeed at the game, you will find that it was because you were observant, willing to take advice, and willing to put in sufficient time at practice."[7]

Andy made 20 to 30 appearances per year in 1976, far less than the hundred or more he made just a few years earlier. His lighter travel schedule left a lot of free time for someone not used to sitting still. The Cornacchia home on Huntington Bay Road was just two miles from Century's Huntington Lanes on Wall Street. Century Lanes (as it was known to locals) became Andy's retreat for the rest of his life. Andy was the honorary mayor of Century Lanes, if not the entire town of Huntington.

When it opened on September 3, 1959, Century Lanes was the most modern and luxurious bowling center on Long Island. Built for an estimated $1,500,000 ($15,637,000 in 2023 dollars), Yankees Yogi Berra, Hank Bauer, Moose Skowron, and Phil Rizzuto appeared on opening night. Yankee announcer Mel Allen served as master of ceremonies, and Ned Day rolled the ceremonial first ball.[8] The 50-lane center featured Brunswick pinsetters, underground ball returns, a nursery, a full-service pro shop, and the Sportsman's Restaurant and Lounge.

Century Theaters, a publicly traded entertainment company, owned Century Lanes. They also owned Century's Shore Theatre right next door. Corporate ownership of bowling centers was unusual in 1959; sole proprietorships and partnerships were the norm. The culture was evident in Century's managerial structure. Most centers had one manager (often the owner), but Century had a general manager, a bowling manager, a tournament coordinator, and a maître d'hôtel.[9]

Andy gave lessons to those who asked and many who did not. Andy never missed an opportunity to help someone improve. "I just can't resist making it easier for somebody who doesn't know what he's doing," he said. "And I can't ever keep my big mouth shut."[10] He added, "I don't like to see people bowling any old way.... I can usually take somebody by the hand and make a good bowler out of them if they have the physical attributes."[11]

A 1972 *Newsday* profile described a typical Andy Varipapa lesson. After watching two strong and athletic young men throw ball after ball in the gutter, Andy walked over to help them out. He introduced himself by saying, "Let me show you something. The way you are approaching the foul line, you might get yourselves killed."[12] Pins fell quickly once Andy straightened them out, and they enjoyed bowling a bit more for at least one day. The two had no idea they had just received a lesson from one of the greatest bowlers who ever lived.

I was the recipient of one of Andy's unsolicited lessons. In December 1979, I visited Century Lanes with two friends from Sheridan Bowl to prepare for the upcoming Long Island Masters tournament. Never having bowled at Century before, we were unaware that the best way to play the lanes was with an outside line (near the gutter). We struggled for about 20 minutes using an inside line and grew frustrated that strikes were hard to come by.

Right on cue, an elderly gentleman strode purposely toward us. It was the great Varipapa, 88 years old, all five foot six inches of him. My friend Gerry Carmody previously met Andy through his father, Dick Carmody, the long-time bowling and harness racing columnist for the *Long Island Press*, *Newark Star-Leger*, and *Newsday*. After exchanging pleasantries, it was my turn to bowl, and I did not come close to striking. The ball either ended up high on the headpin and left a split or sailed past the headpin on the right.

Without hesitation, Andy offered his analysis. "Hey, kid, you throw that ball good, but you're stupid," he said. "Move out closer to the gutter and throw it harder." I took his advice, and as if by magic, the ball reacted appropriately and rolled into the pocket and struck. My friends made the same move on the lanes, and suddenly we were lined up. After throwing a couple more good shots, I said, "Thank you, Mr. Varipapa," he replied, "You're welcome. Call me Andy." He then marched to a different pair of lanes to assist another group of bowlers.

Andy's suggestions didn't help us much come tournament time. We were young and inexperienced, and it showed. None of us advanced past the qualifying round. Gerry and I bowled together for several years, and Andy's blunt criticism resurfaced occasionally. If one of us thought the other was not playing the lanes correctly, we said, *hey, kid, you throw that ball good, but you're stupid*. The impromptu lesson was the only time I met Andy. Our encounter lasted less than 10 minutes but was unforgettable.

Andy visited Century almost every day in the late 1970s and early 1980s. Sam Zurich ran the pro shop at Century Lanes and recalled, "When Andy strolled into the center, it was like a ray of sunshine came through the door. He talked to everyone, gave bowling tips, and then bowled for a while."[13]

Jim Lizzo worked at Century's front desk. One of his duties was to be on the lookout for Andy. Andy was pushing 90, and his already sketchy driving skills were worse than ever. "I would see him pull into the parking lot in his huge Cadillac. He reclined his seat so far that all you saw was the top of his head," said Lizzo. "He always tried to get a spot close to the door, which often meant playing bumper cars. Andy popped the trunk, I grabbed his bowling ball, and five minutes later, he'd be holding court at the snack bar."[14]

Andy took young bowlers like Zurich and Lizzo under his wing. A talented young professional, Zurich vividly recalls Andy accompanying him to one of his first PBA regional tournaments: "I was bowling professionally, which already had me awe-struck. Then, on top of that, Andy is standing behind me, helping me out. It was a remarkable experience."[15]

Andy's sheer presence gave Zurich confidence. "Andy had such a love for the game. I saw a proudness in him, a feeling which stayed with me throughout my career," recalled Zurich. "That's something I will never forget about Andy. He glowed from his love of the game; if you were around him, you glowed too. He was one-of-a-kind."[16]

Zurich became a successful professional. He won twice on the PBA Tour, once on the PBA50 (senior) Tour, and added a once-record 38 PBA Regional Tour titles.[17] But years earlier, Andy coached a slim left-hander who became one of the PBA's all-time greats. In 1960, Bill Petraglia arranged a 30-minute lesson with Andy for his 13-year-old son, Johnny. The Petraglias lived in the Bensonhurst section of Brooklyn, and without a car, the journey to Long Island took more than an hour.[18]

Young Johnny Petraglia delivered the ball with a stiff right leg (his sliding leg) and approached the foul line with a 20-board (20-inch) drift from right to left.[19] Given these flaws in his game, Bill Petraglia unwittingly picked the perfect instructor for his son. Two of Andy's fundamental principles were to (1) bend the sliding knee sufficiently to facilitate a smooth release of the ball and (2) walk straight to the foul line without "zigzagging, lurching, or turning from one side to the other."[20]

Andy watched Johnny throw a few warm-up shots and started the lesson:

ANDY: "So, you want to be a good bowler?"
JOHNNY: "Yes, Andy, that's why I'm here."
ANDY: "Good, then you will do exactly what I tell you to do, no questions."
JOHNNY: "Of course."
ANDY: "OK. The next shot you throw, after you let the ball go, I want you to bend down until your left knee touches the lane and then get back up like you are genuflecting in church."[21]

Johnny threw a couple of shots with his left knee touching the lane. Andy said, "You just keep doing that. I'll be back in 20 minutes." Johnny continued, but his right leg became more tired and sore with each successive shot. The only way to get his left leg to touch the lane was to make a deep knee bend with his right. Not wanting to disappoint Andy, he gritted his teeth and pressed on.

After what felt like an eternity, Andy returned. He announced, "Good, now you have knee bend. Next week, if you are still doing this, we will go to the second step. If not, you will do this again for a half hour."[22] Johnny practiced the deep knee bend all week, and when he returned a week later, Andy approved of his progress.

In his second lesson, Andy taught Johnny how to walk straight to the foul line. Andy scotch taped two pencils in a V-shape, a little more than a shoe width apart, just before the foul line. Andy said, "All you have to do is slide between the pencils." Johnny took his usual starting position, allowing for his 20-board drift. Andy grabbed Johnny's shoulders and moved him 20 boards left, so he had to walk straight to the foul line.

Johnny protested: "But Andy, I drift." Andy replied, "I know. So don't drift. Because if you do, you will hit the pencil, slip, and fall on your ass." Johnny, still confused, asked, "OK, but how do I walk straight?" Andy replied, "You'll figure that out. You don't want to get hurt, do you? And don't forget the knee bend."[23]

Johnny slid about six feet before the foul line on his first try to avoid hitting the pencils. But with each successive shot, he slid closer to the foul line, and his approach became straighter. Johnny recalled Andy barking before each shot, "AND DON'T FORGET THE KNEE BEND!" By the end of the 30-minute lesson, Johnny walked straight to the foul line and avoided the pencils. In an hour of instruction, Andy fixed the two most significant flaws in Petraglia's game.

Years later, Petraglia understood what made Andy such an exceptional instructor. "He could get you to do something by just telling you what he wanted you to do. He didn't need a lot of words."[24] Consider Johnny's first lesson. Andy focused his pupil's attention on his *left* knee to teach him how to flex his *right* knee. Johnny developed his trademark deep knee bend without thinking about it. Such simplicity was the genius of Andy's instruction.

Subsequent lessons focused on ensuring Johnny's feet arrived at the foul line before the ball, keeping his elbow higher than his shoulder on the follow-through, and maintaining rhythm as he walked to the foul line. After his fifth and final lesson, Andy told Johnny, "You're 13. You have the fundamentals of a good approach now. You will get bigger and stronger, and if you keep working, you will get better and better. I'll look at you in a couple of years, and then we can discuss the other side of the foul line, how to play the lanes."[25]

As Andy predicted, Petraglia got better and better and better. By age 15, he was averaging over 200. In 1966, at age 19, Johnny won the first of his 14 PBA titles. Ranked the 16th greatest player in PBA history (as of 2008), Petraglia is one of nine players to win bowling's triple crown (U.S. Open, PBA World Championship, and PBA Tournament of Champions) and the only bowler to win PBA national titles in six decades.[26]

Petraglia's career almost ended before it got started. A week after his 1966 win, his draft notice arrived. In Viet Nam, he drove a truck for the 71st Battalion, which saw heavy combat during the Tet Offensive. "We were guarding a post east of Saigon and were pinned down for four days. Some of my buddies got shot, but nothing happened to me. I was lucky," said Petraglia.[27] He returned to the United States in July 1968, 37 pounds lighter, and his wartime experience burned on his mind.[28]

"It's kind of a double-edged sword," he said. "You want to remember it so others won't have to go through it. On the other hand, you try and put it behind you so that you can get on with your life."[29] Shortly after his return, he visited wounded soldiers with athletes, including Johnny Unitas, Brooks Robinson, and Jesse Owens.[30] He continues to support veterans today, most notably as the Bowlers to Veterans Link (BVL) spokesperson. Since 1942, the BVL has raised more than $57 million to fund recreation programs that address the emotional and physical needs of veterans and active-duty military.[31]

One of Petraglia's great regrets involved Andy. At the 1978 Long Island Open, Petraglia threw the first 11 strikes in his match against Mark Roth. With one more strike, Petraglia would win $10,000 and a new automobile for rolling a televised perfect game. Andy, 87 at the time, was seated in the front row. Unfortunately, Johnny's 12th ball went through the face and left the 2 and 4 pins for a 298 game. He told ABC announcer Chris Schenkel immediately after the match, "Boy, couldn't have thrown it any worse. I did everything wrong. I was too fast. I pulled the ball. It was just a bad shot. I choked."[32]

Petraglia was disappointed, not only for missing out on 10 grand and a car. He recalled, "When I'm getting up to throw that last shot, Andy is sitting three feet behind me, watching the last shot. And then I threw it through the nose for 298. I choked on the twelfth shot in front of my coach. It was just horrible."[33] In 1994, he got his televised 300 at the PBA National Championship in Toledo. He flashed back to the scene 16 years earlier, and lamented, "Andy already passed away. I couldn't make it up to him."[34]

Andy turned 90 on March 31, 1981. While Garden City Bowl hosted the PBA Long Island Open, the Nassau Bowling Proprietors Association held a dinner in his honor at the nearby Wheatley Hills Golf Club. *Newsday* sports editor Bob Zellner commented, "34 years ago we held a dinner to honor 'old man' Varipapa for his feat of winning the All-Star at age 55. I guess we'll never stop having dinners for him."[35] Long Island proprietor John LaSpina, Andy's good friend from Maple Lanes in Brooklyn, made sure all the stars came out. Earl Anthony, Dick Weber, Carmen Salvino, and many other bowling A-listers were in attendance.

Salvino spoke of the time Andy upstaged Ed Sullivan at Madison Square Garden. "Andy grabs the microphone out of Sullivan's hand and says to the crowd of 20,000, 'I'm the greatest,'" said Salvino. "The crowd yelled and screamed, and Sullivan just stood there, not knowing what to do."[36] Salvino closed by saying, "Andy, I hope we're around for your 100th birthday." Andy rose, scanned the crowd, and remarked, "We should be; everybody here looks pretty healthy."[37]

Even superstars were in awe of Andy. The great Earl Anthony, already the winner of a record 36 PBA titles, asked Andy to sign his program. Andy obliged and wrote, "To Earl, keep bowling. You'll be good someday." Anthony could only laugh and said, "He's the best. The greatest."[38]

In 1980, ABC premiered *That's Incredible!*, an hour-long variety show in the tradition of *You Asked for It* and *Ripley's Believe It or Not*. Andy was no stranger to the genre; he displayed his trick shots on *You Asked for It* in 1954.[39] Andy appeared on *That's Incredible!* on September 21, 1981. The show's theme was the extraordinary skills of the young and the old. Other segments included Henri Lamothe, a 77-year-old diving into 11 inches of water from 40 feet, and nine-year-old, 46-pound Tammy Stafford, lifting 400 pounds.[40] Andy, age 90, performed his trick shots for a new, younger audience, the vast majority of whom had never seen his movie shorts.

Segments on *That's Incredible!* contained two distinct parts: footage of the performer's feats followed by an interview in front of a live studio audience. Producers filmed Andy's trick shots at Century Lanes on a quiet weekday morning in the summer of 1981. Jim Lizzo recalled that the film crew knew little about bowling. "They had no idea what they were getting into," said Lizzo. "Andy, with his Italian accent, talked with the producer, who then ran around asking, 'What did say? What did he say?'"[41]

Before attempting his trick shots, Andy needed to place oil on the lanes strategically. "Setting up the lanes took more time than the producer accounted for," said Lizzo. "She wanted to start filming and wondered aloud what this little 90-year-old man was doing out on the lanes with a big squeegee."[42]

As Andy prepared the lanes, Lizzo remembered the producer becoming

Andy (left) with Earl Anthony at Andy's 90th birthday party at the Wheatley Hills Golf Club, East Williston, New York, April 1, 1981 (photographer unknown; Varipapa family collection).

increasingly impatient. But once he had the lanes set up, things moved along rapidly. "The actual takes went very quickly, and the producer was surprised at how fast Andy worked," recalled Lizzo. "Andy said, 'You want this shot? OK. How about his one? OK.' He knew what he was doing. The filming was over by early afternoon."[43] Lizzo remembered Andy missing only one shot and making the rest on the first take. After the miss, Andy said, "The wind was blowing."[44]

In September, Andy's grandson Joe Ruffolo accompanied him to Los Angeles to tape the studio segment of *That's Incredible*. Ruffolo recalled the trip for several reasons, mainly because it was his first time on an airplane. "We stayed at a hotel on Hollywood Boulevard where everyone treated Pop like royalty. For a 23- or 24-year-old kid, it was all fascinating," said Ruffolo. "When we arrived, Pop was exhausted and went straight to bed. I decided to go for a walk and check out Hollywood for myself. The bellman stopped me and said, 'Be careful out there; the Boulevard can get dangerous at night. By the way, where are you from?' When I said New York, he laughed and said, 'All right, you'll be fine.'"[45]

Ruffolo accompanied Andy to the studio the next day. Producers discussed how the taping worked and asked Andy several questions. That evening, stars Cathy Lee

Crosby, John Davidson, and Fran Tarkington hosted a dinner for the show's guests at the studio. They enjoyed a barbeque at a long banquet table and got to know each other. "The hosts were very inquisitive," recalled Ruffolo. "I don't think any of them knew much about my grandfather, but they were genuinely interested in learning about his life. They were most impressed by the fact that he was still bowling and performing at 90."[46]

As with most video productions, everyone spent a lot of time waiting around. When it finally was time to shoot Andy's segment, Cathy Lee Crosby interviewed him. Ruffolo clearly remembered one of her questions and Andy's answer. "She asked something like, 'What keeps you going at your age?'" said Ruffolo. "My grandfather responded with a line he repeated a million times: 'Keep practicing. If you don't succeed in the first 50 or 60 years, keep at it. Something is bound to happen.'"[47]

The September 21, 1981, episode of *That's Incredible!* drew a 17.6 Nielsen rating and was the 14th highest-rated television program of the week. (The same week, hit shows *M*A*S*H* and *Dallas* drew 18.8 and 17.3 ratings, respectively.)[48] An estimated 14 million households tuned in, and although Nielsen did not calculate actual viewership until 1988, at least 18 million Americans watched the show.[49] It was the biggest audience Andy had ever performed in front of. Unfortunately, while some episodes of *That's Incredible!* survive on YouTube and the Internet Archive, Andy's is not among them. Joe and his brother Andy recall watching the broadcast, as does Andy II, but no one has a copy.

Andy's name was mentioned on the CBS hit show *M*A*S*H* a few months later. In an episode aired on January 18, 1982, Corporal Maxwell Klinger (played by Jamie Farr) says to Colonel Sherman Potter (Harry Morgan), "What a day for us! I haven't been this excited since Andy Varipapa came to Toledo for a trick bowling exhibition." Potter looks up and says, "You met Andy Varipapa?" Klinger replied, "Met him? He gave me an autographed copy of his biography, *Life Is a 7–10 Split*."[50]

After returning from Los Angeles, Andy continued to visit Century Lanes regularly. Jim Lizzo cherished the time he got to spend with Andy. "I'm still amazed. Jeff [Jim's identical twin] and I were enamored with him," said Lizzo. "We took his word as gospel when others said, 'he's just a crazy old man.'"[51] He recalled how Andy was ahead of the curve regarding bowling intelligence. "Andy was talking about [lane] topography and oil patterns when no one else was," said Lizzo. "He was incredibly insightful about the game."[52]

Andy offered Lizzo a job at Bowl Mart in Mineola, but Jim declined because it was too far from his home in Huntington. Ironically, for the past 18 years, Jim has owned the Bowler's Touch Pro Shop, located inside Bowlero Mineola (formerly Sheridan Bowl), less than a half-mile east of where Bowl Mart once stood.

"I still talk about Andy. He comes up in so many conversations," explained Lizzo. "Sometimes when I'm giving a lesson, I will say, 'I used to know this guy Andy, and this is what he would suggest.' He had a significant impact on my life."[53] Lizzo might be best known on Long Island for what a mathematician described as a once-every-10-million-year event. In 1995, he and his twin brother Jeff bowled 300 in the same league game, a feat worthy of a front-page story in *Newsday*.[54]

He received innumerable honors and awards during his career, but in late 1981, his long-time sponsor Brunswick gave Andy a special honor during their annual World Open bowling tournament. The event also allowed the bowling community to thank Andy for his many contributions to the game he loved.

Twenty-One

A Lasting Honor

Although he spent much of his life on the road, family was important to Andy. He never missed an opportunity to talk about how successful his grandchildren were, that they all went to college and were pharmacists, attorneys, and teachers.[1] His children and grandchildren, in turn, were proud of Andy and felt blessed to have him as a father and grandfather. In 1982, Frank said, "He was our father, and this was his job. My mother ran a pretty tight ship, and my father made a good living. And when he was home he spent a great deal of time with us…. I couldn't think how anyone could be a better father."[2]

Lorraine added, "We knew that he was famous and that in order to do what he had to do he had to travel. But we always knew we were first in his thoughts, wherever he was. It wasn't always easy, but it was our way of life."[3] Whether it was the holidays, or the summer, when Andy was home, he was home. As a great-grandfather, Andy enjoyed having young children around once again, and when asked to support youth bowling, Andy never said no.

In 1971, Long Island proprietor Fred Ridolf founded the "Andy Varipapa Stars of Future" tournament. Junior bowlers teamed up with PBA players in a professional-amateur (pro-am) competition before the annual PBA Long Island Open at Garden City Bowl. Sponsored by the Long Island Lighting Company, juniors got to bowl with their heroes for free while competing for trophies.[4] It was an event that became near and dear to Andy's heart: "I like to work with the youngsters. When I see a prospect, I ask him if he likes to bowl. Then I tell him, 'You got to learn how.'"[5]

Andy never just lent his name to an event. He got involved. In 1975, he was the honorary chairman of the 15th annual Cerebral Palsy Hi-Pin Tournament at Yonkers Bowl. He promoted the event for weeks by visiting local bowling centers, then appeared at the tournament to perform trick shots, sign autographs, and pose for pictures.[6] Andy did the same with the Stars of the Future tournament. He walked up and down the lanes helping the youngsters, handed out trophies, and gave a brief (or not-so-brief) speech.[7] By 1981, entries swelled to more than 1,000, the largest junior pro-am tournament on the PBA Tour.[8]

John LaSpina saw firsthand Andy's loyalty and how he gave back to the game. "I lived in Long Beach, and he was always helping Flo Housman [manager of Long Beach Bowl] with something. She supported the AHRC, and I watched him doing trick shots for special needs children. That's what formed my love and respect for him."[9] LaSpina has also given back as a proprietor, serving as Board Chair of the BVL for 20 years and raising millions for veterans.

In 1977, Brunswick announced plans for a new tournament, the "Great and the Greatest Doubles Championship." Hosted by the Showboat Hotel Lanes in Las Vegas, the event paired a current PBA player ("great") with an all-time great ("greatest"). A BWAA vote determined the 10 "greatest" competitors, while the "great" included the top 10 on the current PBA points list.[10] Brunswick added four additional players to each group (which amounted to sponsor's invitations) to round out the 14-team field.

Fittingly, Don Carter led the "greatest" voting and received 219 of 222 possible votes, followed by Ray Bluth (185 votes), Buzz Fazio (180), and Andy (159). At 86, Andy was by far the oldest vote-getter. Joe Norris and Buzz Fazio, each 70, were the next oldest.[11] Considering he had not bowled a tournament in 16 years and had not won one in almost 30, Andy was honored to finish fourth in the voting.

But by the time of the event, he would be 87 and knew he could not compete with the likes of Carter (52 years old), Bluth (50), Bob Strampe (47), and Bill Lillard (51). Andy declined the invitation and wrote to Brunswick, "Though I still bowl, I have not competed professionally in years. Therefore I feel it is only right and proper that I give another the opportunity to participate."[12]

Although he did not bowl, Brunswick included Andy in the Great and the Greatest. In May, he and ABC Hall of Fame president Sam Weinstein picked the teams. Andy drew names from a hat in New York, while Weinstein did the same in Chicago.[13] The random pairings made for at least one odd matchup. At 48, Dick Weber was still active and successful on tour, having just won the 1977 PBA King Louie Open. His partner Bob Strampe, 47, retired from the tour years earlier.[14] On their team, the "great" was older than the "greatest." Weber and Strampe entered as one of the favorites, along with the teams of Marshall Holman and Bill Lillard, Mark Roth and Don Ellis, and Carmen Salvino and Dick Hoover.

Andy traveled to Las Vegas in September with his son Frank. At the pre-tournament banquet, he visited with old friends, including rivals Buddy Bomar and Joe Norris, doubles partner Bill Lillard, and protégés Carmen Salvino and Johnny Petraglia. Earl Anthony and Tom Hennessey led the qualifying, but the fourth-seeded team of Tommy Hudson and 60-year-old Joe Joseph won three matches to claim the $14,000 first prize.[15]

Hudson was one of the best players on tour, a seven-time titlist, and runner-up to Mark Roth for 1977 BWAA Bowler of the Year. Joseph, on the other hand, had not bowled competitively since 1971.[16] He seemed surprised as anyone that his team won. "I never thought we had a chance," explained Joseph. "My partner was super. He never complained … and when we won chills ran up my spine. We had the perfect partnership."[17]

The Great and the Greatest was an enormous success. It was not an official PBA event, but nobody cared. Standing-room-only crowds packed the Showboat; fans who never saw Carter, Bomar, and Norris bowl in person had their chance.[18] The older players were grateful for the chance to compete, and the young bowlers got to team up with their idols.

Bomar said, "This is the best thing that has ever happened to bowling. I'm so excited by the competition that I plan to join my first bowling league in 10 years."[19] Fiery 23-year-old Marshall Holman, already well on his way to a hall-of-fame career, said, "I watched these guys on TV when I was a kid. Because of that and their records, I had respect for them. That respect tripled when I bowled with and against them."[20]

Brunswick added a women's event in 1979. Marion Ladewig (naturally) was the leading vote-getter but declined to compete on her doctor's advice.[21] Budding 21-year-old superstar Donna Adamek partnered with Dotty Fothergill to claim the victory, while Mark Roth teamed with Don Ellis to win the men's crown.[22] The success of the Great and the Greatest led directly to the founding of the PBA Senior (PBA50) Tour in 1981.

In the first event at Don Carter's All-Star Lanes in Harvey, Louisiana, Bill Beach defeated Bill Lillard 200–191 in the final to claim the $9,000 first prize.[23] Still active on the regular tour at 51, Beach was one of the youngest participants. When 73-year-old Buzz Fazio saw him checking in, Fazio shouted, "Get the hell out of here—you're too young!"[24] Among the finalists was none other than 61-year-old Frank Varipapa, who finished in 18th place.[25]

Brunswick capitalized on the popularity of bowling nostalgia and incorporated it into their flagship event, the Brunswick World Open. Held in the Chicago suburbs since 1971, the World Open was usually the final event of the PBA Tour season. It was the "World" Open because Brunswick invited several international players to compete with the PBA's best.[26] Renamed the Brunswick Memorial World Open in 1979, the tournament honored a bowling legend each year. The first honoree was the greatest bowler of the first half of the 20th century, Hank Marino.[27] Unable to secure a suitable television deal, the PBA did not hold the World Open in 1980, but the event returned to the schedule in November 1981.[28]

In October, Brunswick announced that the 1981 honoree was Andy Varipapa. Never mind that the term "memorial" did not apply to Andy—he was very much alive and well—Brunswick realized it was high time to honor the 91-year-old legend. Andy II accompanied him to Chicago for the November tournament, but Andy insisted they first stop in Milwaukee to visit an old friend.

ABC Hall of Fame bowler and writer Billy Sixty was in failing health, suffering from Parkinson's disease. Andy II recalls how Sixty's face lit up when he realized who had come for a visit. "I saw Billy come alive when he saw Pop," said Andy II.[29] They reminisced about good times but also how many friends they had already lost, far younger they were: George Young at 49 in 1959, Graz Castellano at 47 in 1964, Steve Nagy at 53 in 1966, Joe Wilman at 63 in 1969, Ned Day at 60 in 1971, and Junie McMahon at 62 in 1974. Despite his health problems, Sixty hung on until November 1983, when he died at age 83.

Andy greeted the participants at the banquet on the eve of the tournament. Few were alive when Andy last raised a trophy. He reveled in the adoration and stole the show with his after-dinner speech. "I was called Mr. Brunswick long ago, so I guess this makes me Mr. Brunswick of all time," said Andy. "Go ahead and applaud!" In closing, he commented, "This honor just proves that if you live long enough, they finally catch up with you. God bless you and keep 'em rolling."[30]

Steve Martin, a 23-year-old from Kingsport, Tennessee, defeated Wayne Webb 243–191 to claim his fifth PBA title. He was built like a young Andy, compact and powerful at five feet, six inches and 175 pounds. "The Tennessee Twister" also threw a big hook like Andy.[31] A quiet Southerner, Martin was better known for his performance on the lanes than his loquaciousness. When he accepted the trophy from Andy, he looked at him and said simply, "Mr. Varipapa, you're a wonderful man."[32]

Martin's kind words were an apt tribute. It was as if he spoke on behalf of every PBA member. Had Andy not blazed a trail a half-century earlier, pro bowling would have looked quite different in 1981. "He did more for the game than any person, was a great competitor, and the finest advertisement I ever saw for the game," said Allie Brandt, the man Andy outlasted to win the 1946 All-Star. "Anybody who ever said he wasn't a terrific bowler had to be a bit jealous."[33] The outpouring of love at the World Open was a great big thank you to who many consider bowling's first professional.

But the "iron man" was now in his 90s. He continued to make appearances, albeit on a reduced schedule. He was the face of the Andy Varipapa Stars of the Future competition, and newspapers and bowling publications profiled him regularly. Age factored into Andy's popularity. "When you reach the age of 90 in this country, you seem to take on some majestic qualities you never had before," commented Chuck Pezzano. "Just check your daily newspaper. Seldom does a week go by without the local nonagenarian being queried about life, love, and the most delicate military and political situations."[34]

Senior citizens were now the target market for Andy's performances. One significant difference from his shows 40 years earlier was that they started at 9:30 a.m. rather than 9:30 p.m.[35] He still retained his sharp wit, as the hosts of an event in Darien, Connecticut, found out. When presented with a rocking chair as a gift, Andy growled, "Thank you, but that chair is not for me. That's for old people."[36]

Andy made it a point to attend the ABC Hall of Fame induction ceremonies. He recalled the emotion of his induction ceremony in 1957 and wanted to be on hand to welcome new inductees, like Marino, Day, and Norris were there for him. Of course, he loved the attention, signing autographs, posing for photos, and basking in the adulation he so rightfully deserved. During the introductions, standing ovations were reserved for Andy and Dick Weber, the game's two greatest ambassadors.

Andy II accompanied Andy to several Hall of Fame ceremonies. The 1982 ceremony in Baltimore was memorable. "Like Joe DiMaggio at Yankees old-timers' day, they always introduced Andy last," said Andy II. "When Pop came out, the applause and the cheering, it was like nothing I ever heard. All the Hall-of-Famers got a warm welcome, but it was different for Pop. Like on the PGA Tour, there were birdies, and then there were Tiger Woods' birdies. The sound was unique."[37]

In early 1983, *Newsday* reported that Andy's beloved Century Lanes planned to close its doors in June. Despite being one of the most successful bowling centers on Long Island, boasting more than 4,000 league bowlers, the owners RKO Century contracted to sell the building to Waldbaum's Supermarkets. Andy joined the chorus of those denouncing the sale. "Bowlers have been enjoying themselves there for 20 years," he said. "Now their home is being taken away."[38] But when the story broke, the sale appeared to be a done deal. Waldbaum's senior vice president of real estate Adam Malinsky said the contract was "signed, sealed, and delivered."[39]

One ray of hope remained. The Suffolk County Industrial Development Agency (IDA) initially recommended allowing Waldbaum's to float $6.7 million in tax-free bonds to finance the deal. This recommendation was controversial because the government typically issues tax-free bonds to pay for public goods such as schools, highways, and firehouses. Not the construction of a privately-owned supermarket.[40]

Without the tax-free provision, Waldbaum's financing costs would increase by at least $1.5 million, and many believed that might be enough to scuttle the deal.

At a June public hearing, numerous speakers encouraged the IDA to rescind its recommendation. Andy said, "We should keep it as a bowling center because it is a monument to the Town of Huntington."[41] Andy's grandson Michael Cornacchia focused on the corporate-welfare aspect of the tax-free bonds, adding: "Government should not play a part in destroying that institution."[42] Century Lanes' supporters had reason to be optimistic. Waldbaum's Malinsky commented, "If we don't get the financing, what it means is that the store will be built in Massachusetts, not here."[43]

The public outcry led the IDA to change their recommendation, and county executive Peter Colahan concurred. Supporters of Century Lanes saved Suffolk County taxpayers roughly $1.5 million in forgone tax revenue, but it was too little, too late. When Colahan announced the change, workers were already removing pinsetters and lanes from the building.[44] Despite pronouncements to the contrary, Waldbaum's was committed to buying Century, tax-free financing or not.

Professional sports teams have used this strategy for years: *Give us tax breaks, or we will go elsewhere.* Malinsky's threat was designed to extract additional profits for Waldbaum's at taxpayer expense. If more communities acted like the residents of Huntington, taxpayers would be all the better.[45] Waldbaum's opened in December and remains a supermarket today, operating as a Stop-and-Shop, owned by the Dutch conglomerate Ahold Delhaize.

Andy was lost without Century Lanes to occupy his time. Hospitalized with pneumonia in December, Andy II believed it was a turning point. "After that, he didn't bowl much, if at all. He was 92, and it took a lot out of him."[46] Century Bowlers Limited, a group of former Century Lanes regulars, threw Andy a 93rd birthday party at the local Elks Lodge.[47] It may not have been the fanciest affair Andy had ever attended, but it was the most heartfelt. Still, not getting out and bowling took its toll. Granddaughter Susan Varipapa said, "It was as if he lost his reason to live. I believe he died of a broken heart."[48] Johnny Petraglia concurred: "He got tired and just died when he didn't have any place to go."[49]

Andy's final public appearance was in June 1984, at the National Bowling Hall of Fame and Museum (now the IBMHOF) dedication in St. Louis. For seven years, the ABC, WIBC, BPPA, Brunswick, and AMF worked to create a shrine worthy of bowling's rich history. The original bowling hall of fame outgrew its home in the Milwaukee suburb of Greendale, at the headquarters of the ABC and WIBC.

As many as 31 cities expressed interest in hosting the new hall, from bowling hotbeds Detroit, Milwaukee, and St. Louis to cities without a bowling pedigree, such as Colorado Springs, Nashville, San Diego, and Tampa.[50] St. Louis won due to its rich bowling history and a prime location near Busch Stadium and the Gateway Arch. In the early 1980s, the area attracted more than 3.2 million visitors yearly, foot traffic that finalists Akron and Toledo could not match.[51]

Building the Hall took less than a year, but it took six to raise the necessary funds. In 1980, the ABC Hall of Fame board president Chuck O'Donnell asked that members donate to the museum fund campaign. The two oldest members were among the first to respond: Bill Doehrman, 91, and Andy, 88. Andy matched Doehrman's $500 donation and included a note with his check: "I am enclosing a copy of my bowling accomplishments. No museum should be without them."⁵²

Frank accompanied Andy to St. Louis. Andy needed a cane, a sight that shocked his friends. They assumed that like all larger-than-life characters, Andy was invincible. Cal Whitmore noted, "His eyes were still clear and his wit fairly sparkling, but his body was failing."⁵³

Jim Dressel, editor of the *Bowlers Journal*, recalled speaking with Andy in St. Louis. "It was the renewal of an old friendship. He greets me, 'Hey Dressel, good to see you again.'"⁵⁴ Andy befriended many bowling writers, including Mort Luby, Sr., Mort Luby, Jr., Billy Sixty, John Walter, Chuck Pezzano, and Dick Clemente, but his relationship with Dressel was special. "Andy was an early idol of mine. In the late 1960s, Norm Edelman asked me to accompany Andy on an exhibition tour of the Northeast, and I jumped at the chance," said Dressel. "We spent a lot of time together."

Andy respected Dressel's tell-it-like-it-is attitude and was likely why they got on so well. Fellow bowling writer Jeff Richgels commented, "I never saw Jim in fear of offending anyone. He called 'em as he saw 'em. A journalist and columnist can receive no greater praise."⁵⁵ For Dressel's part, he respected those qualities in Andy. "He was the same type of guy. Andy would say anything to anybody. His calling card was his honesty," said Dressel. "It was always done with the best of intentions. He brought out the best in others."⁵⁶

Candid shot of Andy at the dedication of the National Bowling Hall of Fame and Museum in St. Louis, June 1984. It was his final public appearance (IBMHOF photograph, IBMHOF collection).

Dressel never considered Andy's mortality until he saw him that June morning. "Andy made the observation, 'When you get to be 90, something goes out of you.' I took a closer look at him and told myself, 'This guy will not be around forever,'" said Dressel. "But he was a friend for life; what little of it might have been left. Unfortunately, I was right. I never saw Andy again."⁵⁷

Andy spent most of his final days at the Cornacchia home in Huntington Bay. "He didn't have heart disease; he didn't have cancer," recalled Andy II. "His health gradually declined, and at a certain point, we all realized what would happen." On August 25, 1984, Andy died in his sleep. The life of arguably the world's most famous bowler ended quietly, just as it began 93 years earlier in the Calabrian mountains. Fittingly, his last newspaper mention before his death referenced an audio exhibit at the Bowling Hall of Fame. When asked whom he feared during his years on the lanes, Andy replied, "Nobody."[58]

In death, Andy earned the respect that was sometimes missing when he was alive. His Associated Press obituary began, "Andy Varipapa, once recognized as the supreme bowler of his time, died Saturday of natural causes."[59] The story did not refer to his trick-shot proficiency. Instead, Andy was remembered as "a trailblazer and goodwill ambassador of his sport" and the winner of "back-to-back national championships ... at the unheard-of age of 57."[60]

In the months following Andy's death, journalists offered their thoughts on the man who may have done more for bowling than anyone:

MORT LUBY, JR.: "Maybe he wasn't the greatest bowler of all time but Andy did more to implant the image of the sport in the American consciousness than anybody in history.... He was the most accessible and entertaining subject I ever interviewed."[61]

CHUCK PEZZANO: "You can argue as to whether legends are born or made. There is no argument that Andy Varipapa was a living legend for more than half a century."[62]

LOU MARKS: "He was the sport's greatest ambassador, its first and only complete showman, the most famous bowler in the world, and probably the best of all time."[63]

CAL WHITMORE: "Anyone who ever met Varipapa always will remember that meeting. You just couldn't forget one who was so outstanding, both in his bowling and his brashness."[64]

JOE KRAJKOVICH: "He was an ambassador for the sport of bowling, the likes of which will never be seen again. He was brash, comical, a gentleman, a showman, and the consummate bowling promoter."[65]

DICK CARMODY: "From Presidents to starry-eyed youngsters who received their first bowing instruction from him, Varipapa had an influence on millions during his 93 years."[66]

USBC Hall of Fame coach Tom Kouros' tribute was the most poignant. Instead of the usual bowling tips, his monthly instructional column in the *Bowlers Journal* paid homage to his friend. Kouros met Andy in 1970, and they hit it off right away. That, according to Kouros, was because each knew their role. Andy talked, and Kouros listened.[67]

Listening was enough for Kouros because Andy always had something interesting to say. Kouros wrote that Andy was "a perfectionist, an idealist, and a sentimentalist. He cared about people—and above all, he was honest."[68] Kouros wanted his readers to know the Andy that he got to know. Many knew the larger-than-life "Great Varipapa," but few knew how Andy "encompassed empathy, compassion, pride in his family, appreciation for his many friendships and an abiding faith in his Creator."[69]

Kouros recalled visiting with Andy and Frank at the 1981 ABC Championships in Memphis. Andy was in rare form, holding court in the Sheraton hotel lobby, drawing from his never-ending cache of stories. After about four hours, Frank finally tapped out and said it was time for everyone to go to bed. As they all stood up to leave, Kouros grasped Andy's hand and said, "Before you go, Andy, I want you to know something. I love you. I really love you. His eyes looked into mine and they softened. Squeezing my hand, he winked and then whispered, 'Hey kid. I luva-u-too.'"[70]

Epilogue

Andy is buried next to Alice at the Cemetery of the Holy Rood in Westbury. He left three children, seven grandchildren, and five great-grandchildren (five more were born after his death, 10 in all). His son Frank might have taken his passing the hardest. Andy Varipapa II said, "I don't think my father ever got over losing Pop. He was his best friend."[1] Andy's daughters inherited their father's genes: Lorraine died in 2014 at age 90, and Connie in 2019, incredibly, at 100. Unfortunately, Frank died of complications from a brain tumor in 1988 at 69.

When he passed away, Frank was the sole owner of Bowl Mart. Stan Lewis sold his share of the business to Frank in 1976 when he accepted a position with the Bowling Corporation of America.[2] After Frank's death, Andy II managed Bowl Mart for a couple of years, but in 1990 the family decided to sell.

Bowl Mart has moved twice and is now known as Mineola Trophy & Awards. A drill press remains on site, but the company no longer sells bowling equipment. Tom Adams has owned the business for 23 years, now located across Jericho Turnpike from Mineola Bowlero (formerly Sheridan Bowl), where Jim Lizzo—who knew Andy from Century Lanes—has owned the Bowler's Touch Pro Shop for 18 years. In the early 1980s, Adams and Lizzo were members of the St. John's University bowling team, and I was their coach. It is, after all, a small world.

Ironically, the day before Andy's death, Long Island tournament promoter Jim Lustig mailed flyers announcing a new event, "The Andy Varipapa Match Game Championship." Lustig, co-promoter Ernie Petersen, and sponsor Richie Varone planned to honor "the 93-year-old living legend of bowling."[3] The flyers arrived after Andy died, so Lustig added "Memorial" to the tournament name and proceeded with the planned November event. Unfortunately, he did not attract enough entries to guarantee the advertised first prize of $7,500 and postponed the tournament. Finally, in March 1987, the first annual Andy Varipapa Memorial Match Game Championship ("The Varipapa") was held at Garden City Bowl. It was worth the wait.

Bowlers in the East were hankering for a big-time scratch tournament. The *Newsday* Eastern Open folded after the 1986 edition, and the PBA announced it was not returning to Long Island in 1987.[4] The Varipapa, part of the Jim Lustig Scratch Tournament Club series, excluded current touring professionals or anyone who won a PBA national tournament. The club was for amateur bowlers only, as much as anything can be "amateur" in bowling.[5] The guaranteed first prize of $10,000 attracted 801 entrants competing for a total purse of $75,600. In the final match, Barry Warshafsky of Chelmsford, Massachusetts, beat Mike Faliero of Buffalo 248–220.[6]

The Varipapa was instantly the biggest scratch tournament in the East. Amateurs could try the High Roller in Las Vegas for a shot at $200,000, but the entry fee was $1,000 and required winning 10 or 11 consecutive matches. At the ABC Championships, you needed to beat 50,000 other bowlers, including all the top professionals. At the Varipapa, $90 allowed you a chance to win 10 grand and re-enter if you bowled poorly.

The event grew steadily and, by 1991, attracted more than 1,000 entries. The first prize ballooned to $16,000 ($35,911 in 2023 dollars), and in 1994, it paid out a total of $157,158. Some of the biggest names in amateur bowling won the Varipapa, including Chris Viale (1989), Rudy "Revs" Kasimakis (1992), Patrick Allen (1994), Mike Neumann (1995), and Brian Boghosian (1997).[7]

Apart from a few "Andy Varipapa 300" references, Andy's name disappeared from the newspapers after the Varipapa folded in 1997. Veteran bowling writers occasionally mentioned Andy in their columns, but their ranks were dwindling. When bowling columnists retired, newspapers rarely replaced them. The days of weekly bowling columns by the likes of John Archibald (*St. Louis Post-Dispatch*), Dick Carmody (*Newsday*), Dick Evans (*Miami Herald*), Matt Fiorito (*Detroit Free Press*), Pearl Keller (*Yonkers Herald-Statesman*), and Chuck Pezzano (*Bergen Record*) were ending. It seemed like Andy's name might be relegated to history books, but trick shots got him back in the news.

In 2004, the PBA introduced the "PBA Skills Challenge," a 16-person single-elimination knockout tournament. The made-for-TV event was like a game of "horse" in basketball. The first player tried a shot, and if successful, their opponent needed to make it to avoid elimination. In the first few matches, players chose shots of the Dead Center Green or Count Gengler variety: convert the 5–7–8 pin combination, pick the 10-pin out of a full rack, or throw a shot without putting their fingers in the ball.[8]

Shots became more complex as the tournament progressed. Brian Himmler struck without seeing the pins, like Ned Day's shot in *Set 'Em Up*. Parker Bohn III paid tribute to Andy's tunnel shot from *Strikes and Spares* by rolling his ball through three chairs on the lane (with a nervous child sitting in each). After Bohn III struck, Himmler—who told Bohn III he was "crazy"—threw his shot through empty chairs. It was good that he did because his ball crashed into the second and third chairs and sent them flying.[9]

PBA and USBC Hall of Famer Chris Barnes defeated Bohn III in the final and pocketed the $20,000 first prize. In the preliminary rounds, Barnes converted the "flying eagle," his version of Andy's "flying dutchman" from *Strikes and Spares*.[10] The PBA discontinued the Skills Challenge after the 2009 edition. Barnes and Norm Duke (aided by his "towel shot") won two titles each.

But during all the years of the Skills Challenge, there is no evidence that announcers or players referenced the history of trick shots. Never a mention of Andy or Mort Lindsey, let alone Dead Center or the Count. That all changed in 2015 when the PBA, with a big assist from Wheaties, returned Andy squarely to the public eye 31 years after his death.

The PBA arranged a virtual competition to determine the best trick shot ever. Videos of the nominees appeared on their YouTube channel, which directed fans to the PBA's website to vote for the winner. The competition featured shots by Barnes,

Duke, Osku Palermaa, and Andy. Barnes' entry was the "flying eagle," and Duke's was the two-ball spinning spare shot, identical to Andy's from *Bowling Tricks*.[11] Palermaa, the powerful Finnish star and the first two-handed bowler to appear on a PBA telecast, performed a spectacular shot few could duplicate. Palermaa placed a chair halfway down the lane and threw his ball over the chair, on a fly, and struck.[12]

Andy's shot was from *Bowling Tricks*, and he called it the "Pawn Shop Special" because three balls were in play. He kicked one ball down the center of the lane at the 5-pin. While the ball rolled slowly, Andy converted the 7 and 10 pins by tossing a ball from each hand, his old "crisscross" shot, with all three balls simultaneously arriving on the pin deck.[13]

When the votes were tallied, Andy edged Barnes by a 51 to 49 percent margin.[14] While close, consider the context. In 2015, every voter knew Chris Barnes. He was one of the best bowlers in the world, having won 17 PBA titles (he now has 19) and three majors. On the other hand, Andy died in 1984, last bowled competitively in 1962, and his shot appeared on film in 1948, when few voters were even alive. Andy's win was a testament to his trick-shot skills.

Concurrent with the trick shot competition, Wheaties sponsored a team in the new "PBA League," an annual competition between five-man teams of PBA professionals. No stranger to sports marketing, Wheaties typically partnered with athletes such as Michael Jordan and Tiger Woods. Since no current bowler approached their Q-ratings, General Mills set out to find one who did. Chief Creative Officer Michael Fanuele said, "In researching the history of bowling, there was one guy above all else who exhibited the spirit of a champion that Wheaties has always admired and applauded."[15] That "one guy" was Andy.

The campaign included six 15-second television advertisements, each featuring a different shot from *Bowling Tricks*.[16] The narrator identified Andy as "Grandpa." Humorous missives criticizing millennial behavior replaced Pete Smith's voiceovers. When Andy rolls a ball through his legs for a strike, the narrator states, "Grandpa wasn't allergic to cats, or dust, or pollen. He was allergic to whiners. And losing."[17]

In another spot, the narrator commented, "Grandpa's cross-training included bowling, and his breakfast was cereal. Not a microwaved, five-dollar, turkey-bacon,

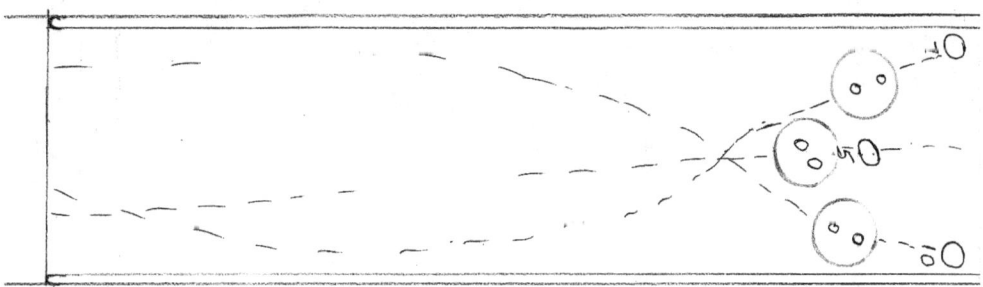

This I call the pawnshop. Using three balls one ball I kick and hits the 5 pin the left and right hits 7 and 10.

Andy's original diagram of the "Pawn Shop Special," winner of the PBA's Best Bowling Trick Shot Challenge in 2015. He performed the shot almost 70 years earlier in *Bowling Tricks* (Varipapa family collection).

egg-wrap frittata."[18] Each spot ended with the familiar tagline, "Wheaties, Breakfast of Champions."

The PBA trick shot competition, and the Wheaties commercials, kick-started a resurgence in Andy's popularity. A publisher reprinted his 1950 and 1952 instructional books. Full versions of his four short films appeared on YouTube. *Bowlers Journal International* editor Gianmarc Manzione wrote a five-page feature article,

The original, unretouched 1947 Brunswick Staff of Champions photograph of Andy was the basis for Louis Kudlik's painting (Brunswick Bowling Products LLC photograph; Varipapa family collection).

"Andy Varipapa: The Man We Refuse to Forget."[19] In 2017, the International Bowling Museum and Hall of Fame (IBMHOF) prepared a month-long exhibition dedicated to Andy. His family donated memorabilia to the IBMHOF, as did long-time friend John LaSpina.

Louis Kudlik's painting of Andy hung in Bowl Mart from 1980 to 1990. Since 2017 it has been on display at the IBMHOF. Notice that Kudlik removed one of the ball returns and the fluorescent lights and added a nicer-looking settee area (IBMHOF photograph, IBMHOF collection).

After retrieving several storage bins from the Cornacchia family home, LaSpina sent most of the contents to the IBMHOF. However, he kept some items that fill a display case at Maple Lanes Rockville Centre on Long Island, one of his five bowling centers. It is a shrine to the man who meant so much to LaSpina: "I cannot begin to tell you. Andy was like a second grandfather to me. I'd hug and kiss him every time I saw him." Andy remains in LaSpina's thoughts even today. "My parents are buried at Holy Rood, about 200 feet away from Andy. Every time I visit, I break off a flower and leave it on Andy's gravestone. I have this thing in my heart for him."[20]

The IBMHOF unveiled the Varipapa exhibit on March 27, 2018.[21] Andy's grandchildren and several of his great-grandchildren attended. One item on display was a large portrait of Andy, based on one of his Brunswick publicity photos from the late 1940s. In 1980, Susan Varipapa received a call from a woman in New Jersey who said she had a painting of Andy. At the time, none of the Varipapas knew of its existence. Louis Kudlik, a commercial artist from Scotch Plains, New Jersey, had painted it and tucked it away in his studio. The painting surfaced when Kudlik's daughter went through his belongings after he died in 1979.[22]

What possessed Kudlik to paint Andy is anyone's guess. Maybe he met Andy, saw one of his trick-shot exhibitions, or was just a bowler who admired him. In any event, Kudlik's daughter asked Susan if the Varipapas were interested in purchasing the painting. Frank and his wife Dottie picked up Susan and drove to Scotch Plains to see it themselves. Dutifully impressed, they discussed it with Andy and Frank's sisters, and the family decided to buy it.[23]

The Varipapas displayed the painting prominently at Bowl Mart until they sold the business in 1990. Andy II kept it in his home until he donated it to the IBMHOF in 2017.[24] Bowl Mart was filled with trophies and bowling equipment, but the painting of Andy was often the first thing customers saw. It was a conversation piece and a fitting tribute to the family patriarch.

Like most museums, the IBMHOF maintains a high-quality virtual presence. Its website features 22 exhibits in "The Vault," most covering a specific topic, such as "Celebrities Go Bowling," "Bowling and Accessibility," and "Brews and Bowling."[25] There are, however, two featuring individual bowlers. One is dedicated to Marion Ladewig, the greatest female bowler of the 20th century. The other belongs to Andy, including titles such as "Instructing the Troops," "Varipapa in the White House," and "There's Only One Varipapa."[26]

The last link is an apt description of Andy's legacy. Andy claimed to be the greatest bowler ever, but he was not. He was not even the greatest bowler of his era. (Ned Day was.) The question is, does that matter? The answer hinges on the definition of "greatness." Bo Burton bowled his first 300 at age 16, won 17 PBA and nine ABC titles, and was the *Professional Bowlers Tour* color analyst from 1975 to 1997. He is one of the most recognizable faces in the game and has watched the best bowlers in the world since he was a child.

"It's hard to identify the best player of all time. I can't definitively say any one player is a whole lot better than another because of the lane conditions, the balls, the amount of competition, and who oiled the lanes," said Burton. He recalled that his father (Nelson Burton, Sr.), Buddy Bomar, and Joe Norris agreed that "until Don Carter came along, Ned Day was the best player. Dick Weber told me that when Day entered a tournament, he and Carter skipped lunch just to watch him bowl."[27]

Burton stressed the challenge of comparing pre- and post–the PBA Tour players: "Different times. There weren't many tournaments, so bowlers didn't have a chance to develop their games. Andy and Ned bowled one tournament and then threw balls between their legs for six months," said Burton. "Bowlers like me had the chance to compete against the best players in the world, week, after week, after week. It made me a better player. Andy was a unique talent. The trick shots that he did, nobody else could do. I admired that. He was the greatest showman bowling has ever had. His naysayers? They were probably guys that he beat. After you whip enough guys, they don't like you."[28]

In 1969, Andy befriended Larry Lichstein, a young left-hander from Windsor Locks, Connecticut. Lichstein joined the PBA in 1968, was named PBA Rookie of the Year, and by 1971 captured a PBA title, two ABC titles, and the Landgraf Classic. Despite his early success, he sought a job with a steadier income than a touring professional. In 1974, he became the PBA's Director of Player Services and held the position until 1996.[29] Like Burton, Lichstein watched the best bowlers in the world up close for decades.

"The first time I saw Andy in person was on November 8, 1966, at New Park Lanes in West Hartford. The second time was at the 1969 PBA National Championship, and Andy watched me bowl all week," recalled Lichstein. "You've got to understand; I'm 20 years old, and Andy Varipapa is watching and talking to me. This guy I watched on TV when I was eight years old."[30]

After their first meeting, Lichstein and Andy met for breakfast or lunch whenever Andy came to Garden City Bowl to watch the PBA Long Island Open. "We became good friends, and I picked his brain. I'd ask him about his diet, how he practiced, and what traveling around the country was like," recalled Lichstein. "He was *the* first touring professional. Andy played an important role in my life. I idolized him. I loved him."[31]

Like many others, Lichstein considers Andy a unique figure in bowling history. "This guy was from another world. Consider what he did and how he did it. As good as Bomar was, as good as Day was, I'm sure they would say there was nobody like Andy Varipapa," said Lichstein. "Andy commanded an audience like a maestro. He sold you the game of bowling and then did things on the lanes nobody dreamed of doing. No one dared to kick a ball down the lane or throw a ball through showgirls' legs."[32]

"Andy believed God blessed him with talent and spent his entire career returning the favor," said Lichstein. He also reflected on Andy's accomplishments in the context of his times: "Andy came over here on a boat without an education and figured everything out himself. He became famous without the Internet, cell phones, or social media. There will never be anyone ever close to him. It will never happen. He was a remarkable man."[33]

Norm Duke summed up Andy's greatness by paralleling his competitive and trick-shot skills. "I'll put it in perspective after all I've learned about this about this amazing man," said Duke. "For him to be known today for his trick shots rather than his regular bowling ability, well, that tells you a lot. His trick shots are his legacy. And that trumps all his incredible bowling accomplishments? Let me tell you, that man must have been some trick-ball player!"[34]

Andy Varipapa was bowling's first superstar. He was the best trick-shot artist who ever picked up a bowling ball and was one of the game's toughest competitors. More importantly, his excellence on the lanes was surpassed by how he lived off them. He was a devoted husband, father, and grandfather and endeared himself to everyone he met.

Andy was proud of his family and their accomplishments: "I love to sit at the family table and be surrounded by doctors, lawyers, pharmacists, scientists, and teachers, and know that I had something to do with instilling the need for learning in them."[35] His good friend Joe Norris said, "Andy has a brashness and a charisma that opens doors and hearts. He's given all of us plenty of thrills, laughs, and some very good ideas on the subject of bowling, too."[36]

Besides his grandchildren, no living person knew Andy as long as Carmen Salvino. A charter member of the PBA, he met Andy as a teenager and developed a lifelong friendship. They were the first two bowlers enshrined in the National Italian American Sports Hall of Fame. Born and raised in Chicago, he is 90 and still resides in the Chicago area with Ginny, his wife of 67 years. To Salvino, Andy was one of a kind.

"No one ever made a mark on bowling like Andy. There were other great bowlers, and they were nice people off the lanes, but personality is where Varipapa has got them all," said Salvino. "He separated himself from everyone else because he had a warm way about him and knew how to put on a show. And that is why Varipapa's name will never die in the sport of bowling."[37]

Appendix I
Tournament Victories, Awards, and Honors

Tournament Victories

Orpheum Doubles (with Mike Tepedino), Brooklyn, 1924
Brooklyn Alley Owners Individual, 1928
Long Island Individual, 1928
Brooklyn Alley Owners Doubles (with Charley Ritter), 1929
Metropolitan Doubles (with John Giannone), 1931
Metropolitan All-Events, 1932, 1934, 1936
Thum's Individual Classic, New York, 1933
Metropolitan Singles, 1934
Grand Central, New York, 1934
Jimmy Smith, Syracuse, 1934, 1935
Landgraf Classic, New York, 1943
Long Island Individual Championship, 1945
Archer, New York, 1945
New York State Bowling Association All-Events, 1946
BPAA National Match Game (All-Star), 1946, 1947
BPAA National Match Game Doubles (with Lou Campi), 1947
Bowlodrome Singles Classic, Cleveland, 1949

Awards

NBWA Bowler of the Year, 1948
BPAA All-Star Award of Merit, 1963
Professional Bowlers Association Lifetime Achievement Award, 1966
Hickok Golden Link Award, 1976
BWAA John O. Martino Award, 1977
Metropolitan Bowling Writers Association Bill Landgraf Memorial Award, 1980
Bowlers Journal Person of the Century, 1988

Honors

Bowlers Journal First Team All-American, 1945–46, 1946–47, 1947–48, 1948–49
Bowlers Journal Second Team All-American, 1940–41, 1941–42, 1942–43
Bowlers Journal Third Team All-American, 1939–40
New York City Bowling Association Hall of Fame, 1951 (charter member)
NBWA 5th Greatest Bowler of the Half-Century, 1951
American Bowling Congress Hall of Fame, 1957

Eastern Long Island Bowling Association Hall of Fame, 1965
Bowling Magazine Pre-1950 All-Time First Team, 1970
President's Advisory Conference on Physical Fitness and Sports, 1971
National Italian American Sports Hall of Fame, 1980
Brunswick Memorial World Open Honoree, 1981
New York State Bowling Association Hall of Fame, 1982 (charter member)
Long Island Sports Hall of Fame, 1984 (charter member)
Bowlers Journal International 6th Greatest Bowler of the 20th Century, 1999
Bowling Magazine All-Century Team, 1999
Bowling Digest 3rd Most Influential Bowler in History, 2001
Bowling Coaches Hall of Fame, 2008 (charter member)

Appendix II
Glossary of Bowling Terms and Acronyms

This glossary includes terms and acronyms used in this book and is not exhaustive. For more comprehensive glossaries, see "Bowling Terms" at BolwersMart.com, "Glossary" at Bowling2U.com, or "Bowling Lingo" at PBA.com.

ABC: American Bowling Congress. Governed men's bowling in the United States from 1895 to 2004. See **USBC**.

AJBC: American Junior Bowling Congress. See **YABA**.

All-events: Nine-game total of **singles**, **doubles**, and **team** events at a **USBC** national, state, or local championship **tournament**.

Approach: The part of the **delivery** preceding the ball's **release** onto the lane. Also: The area before the **foul line**.

Automatic pinsetter: A machine that sets pins and returns balls to bowlers.

Backer: A person who financially supports a bowler in **challenge matches** or on the **PBA Tour**.

Ball return: Track which delivers balls from the **pit** to the **approach**.

Board: Longitudinally placed strips of wood or markings printed on **synthetic** lanes, 1 1/16 inches wide.

Bowling center: An establishment whose primary business is bowling. Also called alleys, lanes, and houses.

BPAA: Bowling Proprietors Association of America, an industry trade group of bowling center owners.

BWAA: Bowling Writers Association of America. See **NBWA** and **IBMA**.

Cash: To earn money in **tournament** play.

Certified: **League** or **tournament** play approved by the USBC. See **sanctioned**.

Challenge match: Head-to-head gambling competition. The primary form of individual competition before 1941.

Channel: One of two trough-shaped structures surrounding a lane to catch errant rolls. See **gutter**.

Conditioner: A synonym for lane **oil**.

Conventional grip: A ball grip in which fingers are inserted into the second knuckle from the fingertips. See **fingertip grip**.

Conversion: To make a **spare** or **split**.

Cut line: In a **multi-stage tournament**, the minimum score required to advance to the next stage. See **make the cut**, **miss the cut**.

Dead wood: Pins knocked down but remaining on the **pin deck** or in the **channel** after the first ball of a **frame**.

Delivery: The process of walking to the **foul line** and rolling a ball down the lane.

Doubles: **League** or **tournament** competition between two-player teams.

Dressing: A synonym for lane **oil**. Also, applying **oil** to the lane.

Drop the wood: When scores from prior rounds in a **multi-stage tournament** are disregarded.

Eagle: Nickname for an **ABC** or **USBC** Open Championships trophy.

Fill: The number of pins knocked down following a **spare** or two **strikes** in the 10th **frame**.

Fingertip grip: A ball grip in which fingers are inserted only into the first knuckle. See **conventional grip**.

Foul: When any portion of the bowler's body (typically the foot) touches beyond the **foul line** during or after the **delivery**. Results in a score of zero.

Foul line: Separates the **approach** from the lane. See **foul**.

Frame: One-tenth of a regulation bowling game. See **open**, **strike**, **spare**, **miss**.

Gutter: Common term for the **channel**.

Handicap: Pins added to a bowler's score to make for competitive matches between bowlers of various skill levels. See **sandbagging**, **scratch**.

Hook ball: A ball released with spin, so it moves right to left for a right-handed bowler, or left to right for a left-handed bowler, as it travels down the lane. See **straight ball**.

IBF: International Bowling Federation, governs bowling worldwide.

IBMA: International Bowling Media Association. Known as **NBWA** from 1934 to 1953 and **BWAA** from 1953 to 2006.

IBMHOF: International Bowling Museum and Hall of Fame.

Lacquer: Used to coat lanes from the mid-1940s until the mid-1970s. See **shellac**, **polyurethane**.

League: An organized group of teams that compete according to rules and a regular schedule.

Make the cut: To advance to the next stage of a **multi-stage tournament**. See **cut line**, **miss the cut**.

Mark: To make a **spare** or a **strike** in a **frame**. See **miss**, **open frame**.

Match play: Head-to-head tournament competition. Often the second stage of a **multi-stage tournament**. See **qualifying**, **stepladder finals**, **tournament**.

Miss: Failure to convert a **spare**. See **open frame**.

Miss the cut: The failure to advance to the next stage in a **multi-stage tournament**. See **cut line**, **make the cut**.

Multi-stage tournament: Competition with two or more rounds. After each round, some players advance (**make the cut**), and the rest are eliminated (**miss the cut**).

NBC: National Bowling Council. The **ABC**, **WIBC**, **BPAA**, and bowling equipment manufacturers (primarily **AMF** and Brunswick) funded the trade association from 1943 to 1996.

NBWA: National Bowling Writers Association. See **BWAA** and **IBMA**.

Oil: Substance applied to protect lane surfaces. Also known as **conditioner** and **dressing**.

Open frame: Failure to achieve a **strike** or a **spare** in a frame. See **miss**.

Open play: Unstructured practice or recreational sessions as distinguished from **league** or **tournament** play. Obsolete: Bowling without having to pay for games.

Pair of lanes: Two adjacent lanes sharing a common **ball return**.

PBA: Professional Bowlers Association.

Perfect game: Twelve consecutive **strikes** with a resulting score of **300**.

Petersen point system: A **tournament** scoring system designed to reward high scores and **match play** victories. Bowlers earn one point for every 50 pins knocked down and each win.

Pin deck: The area at the end of the lane where pins are set.

Pinboy: A person who set up pins, cleared **dead wood**, and returned balls to bowlers before the invention of the **automatic pinsetter**.

Pit: The depressed area behind the **pin deck** where pins and balls collect. Also: The entire area behind the pin deck.

Pocket: Where a bowler aims to impact the pins, between the 1 and 3 pins for right-handers or the 1 and 2 for left-handers.

Polyurethane: Used to coat lanes since the mid–1970s. See **lacquer, shellac**.

Position round: A **league** session or **tournament match play** round in which teams or individuals adjacent to each other in the standings bowl against each other (#1 ranked vs. #2 ranked; #3 vs. #4, etc.).

Pot games: Informal competition between three or more bowlers. Each participant contributes a pre-determined amount of money, and the bowler with the highest score collects the pot.

Pro shop: A business that sells custom-fitted bowling balls, bags, shoes, and accessories.

Qualifying: The initial stage of a **multi-stage tournament**. See **match play, stepladder**.

Release: The **delivery** stage in which the ball leaves the bowler's hand.

Sanctioned: Obsolete term for **certified**.

Sandbagging: Intentionally bowling poorly to obtain higher **handicap** in the future.

Scratch: A **league** or **tournament** conducted without **handicap**.

Series: Three games.

Settee area: The seating area behind the **approach**.

Shellac: Used to coat lanes until the mid–1940s. See **lacquer, polyurethane**.

Side bet: A wager between participants in a **challenge match** beyond earnings from gate receipts.

Singles: League or **tournament** competition among individuals.

Spare: Knocking down all 10 pins in two deliveries in a single **frame**.

Split: A **spare** attempt when two or more pins remain standing with a gap between them.

Stepladder: The final stage of some **multi-stage tournaments**. The lowest-ranked finalist bowls against the second-lowest ranked finalist, with the winner advancing to oppose the third-lowest ranked finalist and so forth, through a final match involving the highest-ranked finalist. See **match play, qualifying**.

Straight ball: A ball that travels a relatively direct path down the lane. See **hook ball**.

Strike: Knocking down all 10 pins with the first **delivery** of a **frame**.

Strike out: To roll consecutive **strikes** from a particular **frame** through the end of a game.

Sweeper: A single-stage, single-event **tournament**, usually between 3 and 10 games. The highest aggregate score wins. Example: Petersen Classic.

Synthetic: Describes **approaches**, lanes, or pins covered with, or constructed entirely of, man-made materials. See **wood lanes**.

Team: League or **tournament** competition between four- and five-player teams.

Tenpin bowling: The most popular form of bowling in the United States, differentiated from five-pin, nine-pin, candlepin, and duckpin bowling.

300: Maximum score in a single game. See **perfect game**.

Topography: Lane surface characteristics, usually referring to the extent to which lanes are not perfectly level.

Tournament: A competition among many bowlers.

Trios: League or **tournament** competition among three-player teams.

USBC: United States Bowling Congress. Governs **tenpin bowling** in the United States. Formed by a merger of the **ABC**, **WIBC**, and **YABA** in 2005.

WIBC: Women's International Bowling Congress. Governed women's bowling in the United States from 1916 through 2004. See **USBC**.

Wood lanes: Lanes and **approaches** constructed of wood. See **synthetic**.

YABA: Young American Bowling Alliance. Governed youth bowling in the United States from 1946 through 2004 (**AJBC** before 1982). See **USBC**.

Chapter Notes

Preface

1. *Strikes and Spares*, directed by Felix E. Feist (Culver City, CA: Metro-Goldwyn-Mayer, 1934), https://www.dailymotion.com/video/x32qqbp.
2. John Grasso and Eric R. Hartman, *Historical Dictionary of Bowling* (New York: Rowman & Littlefield, 2014), 304, EBSCOhost eBook Academic Collection.
3. Chuck Pezzano, "Andy Tells It Like It Was," *Bowlers Journal*, February 1971, 40.
4. Chuck Pezzano, "Varipapa: Master of the Trick Shot," *Record* (Hackensack, NJ), November 14, 2002, S-12.
5. Jack Altshul, "Andy Varipapa at 81: And How He Keeps Rolling Right Along," *Newsday* (Garden City, NY), March 31, 1972, 42.
6. Chuck Pezzano, "Andy Varipapa: The Italian Farmboy Who Became the American Trick-Shot Master," *Bowlers Journal*, December 1988, S5.
7. Johnny Petraglia, in discussion with the author, September 30, 2022.
8. Andy Varipapa II, "Andy Varipapa: Bowling's Legendary Champion Showman," last modified March 13, 2022, http://www.andyvaripapa.com.
9. Jim Dressel, in discussion with the author, May 1, 2023.
10. Bill Fay, "Bowling's Talking Machine," *Collier's*, April 10, 1948, 6, https://archive.org/details/colliers121aprspri/page/n87.
11. Altshul, "Andy Varipapa at 81," 42.
12. Herman Weiskopf, *The Perfect Game: The World of Bowling* (Englewood Cliffs, NJ: Prentice Hall, 1978), 64; Pezzano, "Andy Varipapa: The Italian Farmboy," S5.

Introduction

1. "Visited by a Tornado," *Paterson* [NJ] *Evening News*, July 15, 1895, 1.
2. Jay Levin, "Recalling the Tornado that Ravaged River Edge 121 Years Ago," Northjersey.com, July 12, 2016, https://www.northjersey.com/story/news/2016/07/12/recalling-the-tornado-that-ravaged-river-edge-121-years-ago/92739130/; National Weather Service, "Northeastern New Jersey Tornado Statistics," National Weather Service, National Oceanic and Atmospheric Administration, accessed November 7, 2022, https://www.weather.gov/okx/NewJerseyTors.
3. Unless otherwise noted, all census and public record data are from Ancestry, Ancestry: Family Tree, Genealogy & Family History Records, 2023, http://www.ancestry.com; Stephen P. Morse, One-Step Webpages, accessed October 29, 2022, https://stevemorse.org; or United States National Archives and Records Administration, Census Records, accessed April 23, 2023, https://www.archives.gov/research/census.
4. Curiously, Tallman Island is not an island at all. It is the northernmost point of College Point, Queens.
5. Richard Holt, "Amateurism and its Interpretation: The Social Origins of British Sport," *Innovation in Social Science Research* 5, no. 4 (1992): 21–22, http://doi.org/10.1080/13511610.1992.9968318.
6. In 2005, the ABC merged with the Women's International Bowling Congress (WIBC) and the American Junior Bowling Alliance (AJBA) to form the USBC. The new organization is an inclusive national governing body not restricted by gender or age.
7. Weiskopf, *The Perfect Game*, 22, 34.
8. Mort Luby, Jr., "Early Bowling Americana," *Bowlers Journal*, November 1983, 104.
9. Three balls per frame is still the norm for duckpin (popular in the Mid-Atlantic states) and candlepin (popular in New England) versions of bowling. Each uses a smaller, grapefruit-sized ball, and scores are much lower than in tenpin bowling. Top duckpin bowlers average over 140, candlepin bowlers 120.
10. Luby Jr., "Early Bowling Americana," 106.
11. Weiskopf, *The Perfect Game*, 35–36.
12. Frank G. Menke, "Bowling," in *The Encyclopedia of Sports*, 3rd rev. ed., ed. Roger L. Treat (New York: A.S. Barnes, 1963), 211, https://archive.org/details/encyclopediaofspmen00menk/.
13. Luby Jr., "Early Bowling Americana," 106.
14. Weiskopf, *The Perfect Game*, 37–42.
15. Stephen Jay Gould, "The Creation Myths of Cooperstown," *Natural History*, November 1989, https://www.naturalhistorymag.com/picks-from-the-past/02484/the-creation-myths-of-cooperstown.

16. J.R. Schmidt, *The Bowling Chronicles* (Jefferson, NC: McFarland, 2017), 124–130. In 1907, the rival National Bowling Association formed to govern bowling in the East. It disbanded and members rejoined the ABC in 1921.

17. The ABC did not adopt the 16-pound weight limit for balls until 1913.

18. Weiskopf, *The Perfect Game*, 40.

19. "Brill Heads the List," *Daily Inter Ocean* (Chicago), January 12, 1901, 8; Ian Webster, "Inflation Calculator," U.S. Official Inflation Data, Alioth Finance, last updated August 10, 2023, https://www.officialdata.org/. All inflation calculations were made using this widget. Conversions prior to 1913 are approximations because that is when the U.S. Bureau of Labor Statistics began compiling official inflation data.

20. Petersen Classic, *Louis P. Petersen Championship Bowling Classic Honor Roll* (Wauwatosa, WI: Petersen Classic, 2019), http://www.petersenclassic.com/wp-content/uploads/2019/05/PetersenHonorRoll2018.pdf.

21. Prior to the invention of the automatic pinsetter, pins were set and balls returned to the bowler by hand.

22. Mark Miller, ed., *The Bowlers' Encyclopedia* (Greendale, WI: American Bowling Congress, 1995), 220–221.

23. Miller, 223. Just like Holland's 17th century tulip mania, bowling's bubble burst as well, exemplified by Brunswick's stock price: $4.75 in 1957, $75 in 1961, $13 in 1962. See Rick Kogan, *Brunswick: The Story of an American Company from 1948 to 1985* (Skokie, IL: Brunswick, 1985), 97.

24. Petersen Classic, *Louis P. Petersen Championship*.

25. Nicholas Hirshon, "Bowling Headliners, 1948–1950: The Creation of a Spectator Sport in Television's Emergent Years," *The International Journal of the History of Sport* 37, no. 11 (2020): 964, https://doi.org/10.1080/09523367.2020.1835868.

26. Robert Boyle, "A Guy Named Smith is Striking it Rich," *Sports Illustrated*, November 25, 1963, 36, https://vault.si.com/vault/1963/11/25/a-guy-named-smith-is-striking-it-rich.

27. Associated Press, "Million Dollar Pact for Bowler Carter," *Des Moines Tribune*, February 17, 1964, 16.

28. Joe Jares, "The Poor Man's Tour Begins to Strike it Rich," *Sports Illustrated*, April 19, 1965, 112, https://vault.si.com/vault/1965/04/19/the-poor-mans-tour-begins-to-strike-it-rich.

29. Tom Leferink, "Bowling and TV a Successful Marriage," *Fort Worth Star-Telegram*, January 30, 1982, 2D.

30. Miller, *The Bowlers' Encyclopedia*, 220–221.

31. Barb Spencer, "Bowling the Number One Participation Sport," *Daily Journal* (Franklin, IN), August 18, 1977, 8; "Bowling Gets a National Boost," *Gettysburg [PA] Times*, November 14, 1985, 17.

32. Many people mentioned in this book are members of the ABC, WIBC, or USBC Halls of Fame. The ABC and WIBC maintained their own halls of fame until the organizations merged in 2005, when all ABC and WIBC hall of famers joined the USBC Hall of Fame. ABC/WIBC/USBC are used to denote the name existing when the player was inducted.

33. Carmen Salvino, in discussion with the author, October 11, 2022.

34. "Person of the Century: Andy's the Man." *Bowlers Journal*, December 1988, 78.

35. Pezzano, "Andy Varipapa: The Italian Farmboy," S5.

Chapter 1

1. Altshul, "Andy Varipapa at 81," 42.

2. Larry Carmody, "Still Bowling 'Em Over," *Newsday* (Melville, NY), April 7, 1981, 80.

3. Bob Cherin, "Varipapa the Magnificent," *Bowlers Journal*, December 1981, 59.

4. Thomas Brinkhoff, "Italy: Regions and Major Cities," City Population, last modified April 16, 2023, https://www.citypopulation.de/en/italy/cities/.

5. Brinkhoff, "Italy: Regions and Major Cities."

6. MateriaFutura, "Genealogy in Carfizzi," Italianside.com, 2023, https://www.italianside.com/calabria/crotone/carfizzi/genealogy; Urbistat, "Municipality of Carfizzi," Aminstat Italia, 2023, https://ugeo.urbistat.com/AdminStat/en/it/demografia/popolazione/carfizzi/101003/4.

7. John Walter, "Andy Varipapa: Great Star Backs Up 'Pop Off' Reputation with Top Alley Action," *Bowling Magazine*, June 1951, 6.

8. Matteo Gomellini and Gianni Toniolo, "The Industrialization of Italy, 1861–1971," in Kevin H. O'Rourke and Jefferey G. Williamson, eds., *The Spread of Modern Industry to the Periphery Since 1871* (New York: Oxford University Press, 2017), chapter 6, section 5, http://doi.org/10.1093/acprof:oso/9780198753643.001.0001.

9. Lorraine V. Ruffolo, "The Andy Varipapa Story: From Alleys to Lanes" (unpublished manuscript, 1990), P-1, Varipapa Family Papers, private collection.

10. Lucy Riall, *The Italian Risorgimento: State, Society, and National Unification* (New York: Routledge, 1994), 1–3, https://archive.org/details/italianrisorgime0000rial.

11. Martin Collier, *Italian Unification 1820–71* (London: Heinemann, 2003), 83, https://archive.org/details/italianunificati0000coll/.

12. Riall, *The Italian Risorgimento*, 74.

13. Frank J. Cavaioli, "Patterns of Italian Immigration to the United States," *The Catholic Social Science Review* 13 (2008): 220, https://doi.org/10.5840/cssr20081314.

14. Mario Pretelli, "Italian Americans, Education, and Italian Language: 1880–1921, *Quaderni d'italianistica* 38, no. 1 (2017): 62, https://doi.org/10.33137/q.i..v38i1.31143.

15. G.E. di Palma Castiglione, "Italian Immigration into the United States 1901–04," *American*

Journal of Sociology 11, no. 2 (1905): 185, 192, https://www.jstor.org/stable/2762660.

16. Altshul, "Andy Varipapa at 81," 42; "Varipapa at 81 Still Delights in Performing," *Indianapolis Star*, October 29, 1972, sec. 4, 12.

17. Rhoda Barkan, "Life is Just a Bowl of Tricks: And Andy Has Done Them All!" *Observer* (Northport, NY), April 6, 1978, 3.

18. The document confirmed Andy's birth name as "Andrea," not "Andrew."

19. "Varipapa at Fannie's," *Newsday* (Hempstead, NY), January 8, 1955, 25.

20. The most common reason for detaining passengers was that no one was at Ellis Island to pick them up.

21. Barkan, "Life is Just a Bowl," 3.

22. "St. Patrick's R.C. Church Ranks Among Strongest Parishes in the Diocese," *Standard Union* (Brooklyn, NY), June 20, 1909, 25.

23. "Work of the Church for Italians in Brooklyn," *Brooklyn Daily Eagle*, June 24, 1900, 6.

24. "Work of the Church," 6.

25. Pretelli, "Italian Americans, Education, and Italian Language," 63.

26. Pretelli, "Italian Americans, Education, and Italian Language," 62.

27. Pretelli, "Italian Americans, Education, and Italian Language," 70. New York City began offering enrichment classes for non–English-speaking students in 1910.

28. Michael Schuman, "History of Child Labor in the United States—Part 1: Little Children Working," *Monthly Labor Review*, January 2017, https://doi.org/10.21916/mlr.2017.1; Moses Stambler, "The Effect of Compulsory Education and Child Labor Laws on High School Attendance in New York City, 1898–1917," *History of Education Quarterly* 8, no. 2 (1968): 189–190, https://doi.org/10.2307/367352.

29. Altshul, "Andy Varipapa at 81," 42. Although "pinboy" reeks of gender bias, only males set pins until the 1930s. "Pinsetter" is the gender-neutral phrase but more commonly describes a machine that sets pins automatically.

30. Oscar Fraley, "Varipapa, 54, Stands at Top of Nation's Bowling Ladder," *Green Bay Press-Gazette*, April 7, 1949, 42.

31. Ruffolo, "The Andy Varipapa Story," P-1.

32. Steven Kurutz, "Strikes, Spares, and Bruised Shins," *New York Times*, May 24, 2014, BU7.

33. Ed Reiter, "Days of Pin Boys Are Gone but Memories Still Remain," *Asbury Park* [NJ] *Press*, May 22, 1976. B4.

34. "Pinboys Make a Strike: Turn Bowling Term to New Use and Worry A. C. Anson," *Chicago Tribune*, December 21, 1902, 3.

35. United States Department of Commerce and Labor, *Census of Manufactures: 1905, Earnings of Wage-Earners*, Bulletin 93 (Washington, D.C.: Government Printing Office, 1908), https://babel.hathitrust.org/cgi/pt?id=nnc1.cu56779232.

36. Grasso and Hartman, *Historical Dictionary of Bowling*, 71,117; "Joe Falcaro Dead; Champion Bowler," *New York Times*, September 9, 1951,

88; Dick Evans, "Bowling's Greatest Recall Days as Pin Boys," *Bowl Magazine*, September 29, 2000, http://www.ncausbca.org/bowlmag/archives/Evans000929.htm.

37. "Ladewig was 'Pinboy,'" *Bowling*, September 1966, 35.

38. Bobby Jones is missing from this list because he never turned professional. He did not need to make his living as a golfer, a luxury afforded to him by a wealthy upbringing. He learned the game as a member, rather than a caddie, at the East Lake Golf Club in Atlanta.

Chapter 2

1. William J. Granger, "Andy Varipapa, Bowling King, Wanted to be League Ballplayer," *Brooklyn Citizen*, May 22, 1935, 7.

2. "Ready for Eagle Cup," *Brooklyn Daily Eagle*, December 2, 1894, 4.

3. Bowling lanes are usually installed in pairs and share a common ball return.

4. *Brooklyn Daily Eagle*, various advertisements, September 30, 1906, bowling, 2–4.

5. "Bowlers Preparing for a Busy Season on Local Alleys," *Brooklyn Daily Eagle*, August 19, 1901, 12.

6. Sources cite various birth dates for Smith between 1882 and 1885. His World War II draft registration card and multiple U.S. and New York State Censuses confirm his birth date as September 19, 1882.

7. Harvey T. Woodruff, "Jimmy Smith, Considered the Best 'Money Bowler' in the United States," *Chicago Tribune*, December 14, 1913, sec. 3, 3. This article mentions "Ahlyers' Alleys," but there was no such place. Herman Ehler owned several bowling centers in Brooklyn, including the Subway Bowling Academy.

8. Schmidt, *The Bowling Chronicles*, 79.

9. "National Bowling League: New York Schedule," *Brooklyn Citizen*, April 5, 1904, 5. The circuit lasted only one season, as did the ill-fated second NBL, launched in 1961.

10. "Brooklyns Doing Well in Big Bowling League," *Brooklyn Citizen*, May 8, 1904, 5.

11. Schmidt, *The Bowling Chronicles*, 79–80. Chapter 10 describes the ad hoc nature of deciding bowling's "world champion" in the early 20th century.

12. Grasso and Hartman, *Historical Dictionary of Bowling*, 327.

13. Woodruff, "Jimmy Smith Considered the Best," sec. 3, 3.

14. Ed Hughes, "Sportrait of a Royal Pin-Crasher," *Brooklyn Daily Eagle*, December 7, 1936, 18.

15. John F. Hinteroff, "He Couldn't Make the Dodgers but Became 'King of Keglers,'" *St. Louis Globe-Democrat*, February 2, 1947, 5E.

16. Ruffolo, "The Andy Varipapa Story," P-2.

17. Brunswick, *The 1981 Brunswick Memorial*

World Open Honors Andy Varipapa, Bowling's Living Legend (Chicago: Brunswick, 1981), 2, https://andyvaripapa.com/2015/12/20/av-t/.

18. "Navy Yard Bowlers Bowl Well for Victory Medals," *Brooklyn Citizen*, November 12, 1918, sec. 2, 4.

19. Dan Daniel, "Varipapa 'Arrives' at 'Old Age' of 53, Reaps Rich Harvest," *Memphis Press-Scimitar*, December 19, 1946, 18. Ridgewood residents know that their town is in the borough of Queens and not Brooklyn.

20. Altshul, "Andy Varipapa at 81," 42.

21. Chuck Pezzano, "Andy Varipapa: Hero or Villain, He Astounded ... Affronted ... Entertained," *Bowling*, December 1982, 20.

22. John J. Archibald, "Andy Varipapa: Rolling at 85," *St. Louis Post-Dispatch*, October 26, 1976, 7J; Harry Missildine, "Twice Over Lightly," *Spokesman-Review* (Spokane), March 11, 1959, 17; Jack Patterson, "Varipapa: He's Still the Greatest," *Akron Beacon Journal*, January 14, 1968, B4.

23. Pindy Wagner, "Cole Recalls Beating Varipapa—As an Unknown," *Akron Beacon Journal*, March 25, 1952, 33.

24. Pindy Wagner, "League and Scholarship Memorials to Benny Cole," *Akron Beacon Journal*, April 12, 1954, 22.

25. Charles S. Small, "The Railway of the New York and Brooklyn Bridge," *The Railway and Locomotive Historical Society Bulletin* 97 (October 1957): 18, https://www.jstor.org/stable/43520182.

26. NEGenWeb Project, "Railroad Job Descriptions," Iron Roads—Making Tracks Across Nebraska, last updated July 31, 2021, http://www.usgennet.org/usa/ne/topic/railroads/job.html.

27. "The Greatest," *Time*, May 5, 1947, 79, https://time.com/vault/issue/1947-05-05/page/81/.

28. Walter, "Andy Varipapa: Great Star," 6.

29. "Amateur and Semi-Pro Baseball," *Brooklyn Daily Eagle*, April 26, 1914, sports, 6.

30. Granger, "Andy Varipapa, Bowling King," 7; Archibald, "Andy Varipapa," 7J.

31. Bill Van Fleet, "At 69, He's Still Hot Bowling Name," *Fort Worth Star-Telegram*, May 30, 1960, sec. 3, 15; Curt W. Nix, "Varipapa: The Best Ever," *New York Post*, December 3, 1983.

32. "Hill Twirls No-Hit Game for Glenmores," *Standard Union* (Brooklyn, NY), May 22, 1911, 11; "Ramblers Walk Off with a Double-Header," *Standard Union* (Brooklyn, NY), June 5, 1911, 13.

33. "Amateur and Semi-Professional Baseball," *Standard Union* (Brooklyn, NY), July 14, 1911, 9.

34. "Amateur and Semi-Professional Baseball," *Standard Union* (Brooklyn, NY), August 4, 1911, 9.

35. "Bay Ridge Athletics Win," *Brooklyn Citizen*, September 23, 1914, 4; "Unions Win, 6 to 5," *Brooklyn Citizen*, October 10, 1914, 5; "Amateur Baseball," *Standard Union* (Brooklyn, NY), April 23, 1915, 15; "Cornelias Win Great Game from Cresswoods," *Brooklyn Citizen*, June 4, 1915, 5; "Elmhurst Grays Beat Cornelias Again," *Brooklyn Daily Eagle*, September 6, 1915, 14; "Amateur Baseball," *Standard Union* (Brooklyn, NY), April 27, 1916, 11; "Wayne Club Wins Opener from Flatbush," *Brooklyn Citizen*, May 1, 1918, 8.

36. Ruffolo, "The Andy Varipapa Story," P-3; "2 Die, Many Hurt as Auto Transit Replaces Trolley," *Brooklyn Daily Eagle*, August 8, 1919, 1.

37. Archibald, "Andy Varipapa," 7J.

38. Ron Maly, "A Talking Machine," *Des Moines Tribune*, April 13, 1962, 15.

39. Archibald, "Andy Varipapa," 7J.

40. Mark Travers, "No, You Were Not Happier Way Back When. Here's Why," *Psychology Today* (blog), January 20, 2021, https://www.psychologytoday.com/us/blog/social-instincts/202101/no-you-were-not-happier-way-back-when-heres-why.

41. Kieran McLean, "Embellish the Details! Exaggerated Stories Can Cultivate Closeness," *Psychology Today* (blog), February 13, 2020, https://www.psychologytoday.com/us/articles/201912/embellish-the-details.

42. Lou E. Cohen, "Sports Chat: Varipapa Pin Official," *Brooklyn Eagle*, November 25, 1938, Home Talk, 6.

43. Fraley, "Varipapa, 54 Stands at Top," 42.

44. Victor Kalman, "All-Star Andy," *Sports Illustrated*, January 17, 1955, 58, https://vault.si.com/vault/1955/01/17/allstar-andy.

45. "Interview with Andy Varipapa," hosted by Frank Toal, *Speaking of Sports* (WCRO, Johnstown, PA, April 24, 1950), https://andyvaripapa.com/listen-to-andy-live-speaking-of-sports-with-andy-varipapa-april-24-1950/.

46. Pezzano, "Varipapa: Master of the Trick Shot," S-12.

47. Kalman, "All-Star Andy," 58; "Andy the Great Proves That He Is," *Life*, December 29, 1947, 63, https://books.google.com/books?id=8E0EAAAAMBAJ&pg=PA62; Charles Bartlett, "Varipapa Wins National Bowling Crown," *Chicago Tribune*, December 9, 1946, 37; "I'm a Man, Huh?" *Time*, December 22, 1947, 58, https://time.com/vault/issue/1947-12-22/page/60/.

Chapter 3

1. "The Thirties," *Prattfolio: The Magazine of Pratt Institute*, May 2012, 29, https://issuu.com/prattinstitute/docs/prattfolio-125th-anniversary-2012.

2. "A Sampling of Courses at Pratt Institute 1887–2012," *Prattfolio: The Magazine of Pratt Institute*, May 2012, 15, https://issuu.com/prattinstitute/docs/prattfolio-125th-anniversary-2012.

3. K.D. Kirkland, *America's Premier Gunmakers: Remington* (East Bridgewater, MA: World Publications Group, 2007), 42–44, https://archive.org/details/americaspremierg0000kirk_e7w9. The Bolshevik Revolution might have cost Remington $10 million because rifles and ammunition were manufactured but not paid for. The U.S. Army bought 600,000 rifles, cutting Remington's loss to less than $300,000.

Notes—Chapter 3

4. Kirkland, *America's Premier Gunmakers*, 44.

5. United States Department of Commerce, *1910 Census*, vol. 3 (Washington, D.C.: Government Printing Office, 1913), 208, https://www.census.gov/library/publications/1913/dec/vol-3-population.html.

6. "Remington Co. Plant Marvel of Efficiency and Modern Machines," *Bridgeport* [CT] *Evening Farmer*, January 4, 1916, 1; "Remington Co. Plans Working in New Jersey," *Bridgeport* [CT] *Evening Farmer*, November 27, 1915, 1.

7. Remington Arms—Union Metallic Cartridge, *A New Chapter in an Old Story* (New York: Remington Arms—Union Metallic Cartridge, 1912), 51–59, https://archive.org/details/cu31924016409660.

8. United States Department of Commerce, *1910 Census*, 144.

9. Christina A. Ziegler-McPherson, *Immigrants in Hoboken: One-Way Ticket, 1845–1985* (Charleston, SC: History Press, 2011), chap. 6, eBook.

10. Cecelia Bucki, "Dilution and Craft Tradition: Munitions Workers in Bridgeport, Connecticut, 1915–19," in *The New England Working Class and New Labor History*, eds. Herbert G. Gutman and Donald H. Bell (Urbana: University of Illinois Press, 1987), 138, https://archive.org/details/newenglandworkin0000unse_n8b1.

11. United States Department of Labor, "Union Scale of Wages and Hours of Labor May 15, 1917," *Bulletin of the United States Bureau of Labor Statistics* (Washington, D.C.: Government Printing Office, March 1919), https://fraser.stlouisfed.org/title/union-scale-wages-hours-labor-3912/union-scale-wages-hours-labor-may-15-1917-476870. Hoboken was not listed, so wage estimates were calculated using data from Newark, New Jersey.

12. United States Department of the Interior—National Park Service, "National Register of Historic Places Registration Form: Brooklyn Navy Yard Historic District," May 22, 2014, section 8, 30, https://npgallery.nps.gov/AssetDetail/314d2a7b-7525-4998-8a77-dd3b9dba7073.

13. Ruffolo, "The Andy Varipapa Story," P-3.

14. John R. Stobo, "Unions at the Brooklyn Navy Yard," *The Brooklyn Navy Yard: Civil Servants Building Warships*, last modified October 2005, http://www.columbia.edu/~jrs9/BNY-unions.html.

15. Jack Diamond, "In This Corner," *Courier-Post* (Camden, NJ), February 15, 1936, 20.

16. John R. Stobo, "Labor History Timeline for the Brooklyn Navy Yard," *The Brooklyn Navy Yard: Civil Servants Building Warships*, last modified June 2005, http://www.columbia.edu/~jrs9/BNY-Labor-Time-Line.html.

17. Ruffolo, "The Andy Varipapa Story," P-3.

18. "New Bowling Venture to be Opened Here," *Brooklyn Daily Times*, October 6, 1918, 6. The article noted that among other modern amenities, Rational was outfitted with a ladies' restroom.

19. The American System was originally known as the Western System. The Eastern System was brought to the United States by German immigrants in the mid-1800s.

20. Not to be confused with the modern definition of open play, which refers to games bowled that are not part of a league or tournament.

21. "Western Ideas Will Be Tried in Bowling Here," *Brooklyn Daily Times*, October 6, 1918, 6.

22. William J. Granger, "Americanizing Game of 10 Pins Here to be Watched Closely," *Brooklyn Citizen*, September 23, 1918, 5.

23. "No Orpheum Tourneys," *Brooklyn Daily Times*, October 5, 1919, 13.

24. William J. Granger, "Selling Bowling an Idea Lee Johns Brings from West," *Brooklyn Citizen*, September 21, 1918, 5.

25. "Western Ideas," 6.

26. Granger, "Americanizing Game of 10 Pins," 5.

27. The "No. 1" suffix appeared because the department fielded two teams. The captain of the Machine Shop teams must have felt Andy was among the best five bowlers in the department, since bowled on the No. 1 team.

28. "Navy Yard Bowlers Bowl Well for Victory Medals," *Brooklyn Citizen*, November 12, 1918, sec. 2, 4.

29. "Beacon Blanks Bunker Hill in Odd Fellow Tourney," *Brooklyn Daily Times*, December 10, 1918, 6.

30. William J. Granger, "Only One Game Now Separates Leading Navy Yard Teams," *Brooklyn Citizen*, December 31, 1918, 5.

31. Most modern bowling leagues use complex point systems to determine standings. They award points for winning a game, the highest game of the night, and highest total pinfall (total wood). Many award "match points" when an individual bowler beats their opponent (e.g., the leadoff bowler on team A beats the leadoff bowler on Team B, team A is awarded one point).

32. "Alley Owners and Bowlers Profit by Working in Unison," *Brooklyn Daily Times*, October 13, 1917, 10. A handicap provides weaker bowlers with additional pins so they can better compete with stronger players. An unintended consequence of a handicap system is that it can encourage sandbagging (intentionally bowling poorly to obtain higher handicap in the future). Complex point systems (see the previous note) are designed to discourage sandbagging.

33. "Navy Yard Metal Trade: Final Standing," *Brooklyn Citizen*, April 15, 1919, 5.

34. "Champions Navy Yard Bowling League," *Brooklyn Citizen*, May 6, 1919, 9.

35. "Morse Dry Dock Pin Knights Whitewash Navy Yard Bowlers," *Brooklyn Daily Times*, April 7, 1919, 8.

36. "Navy Yard League," *Brooklyn Citizen*, December 30, 1919, 4.

37. "Navy Yard League," *Brooklyn Citizen*, January 27, 1920, 5; "Navy Yard League," *Brooklyn Citizen*, February 3, 1920, 5.

38. Author's calculation from various issues of

the *Brooklyn Daily Eagle*, *Brooklyn Citizen*, and *Brooklyn Daily Times*.

39. "Navy Yard Layoff Begins; 300 to Be Let Go by Monday," *Brooklyn Daily Eagle*, June 18, 1921, 22; "Navy Yard May Be Closed Down," *Brooklyn Citizen*, July 24, 1921, 1.

Chapter 4

1. Pat Armijo, "82-Year-Old Trick Bowler Visits City," *Albuquerque Journal*, October 27, 1971, E-8.
2. Walter, "Andy Varipapa: Great Star," 7–8.
3. Walter, "Andy Varipapa: Great Star," 7; Pat Rorre, "Amazing Andy Varipapa," *National Bowlers Journal and Recreation Age*, June 1937, 20; Lorraine V. Ruffolo, "From Calabria to Hollywood" (unpublished manuscript, 1960), 2–4, Varipapa Family Papers, private collection.
4. "Tepedino Bowls Perfect Score," *Standard Union* (Brooklyn, NY), December 1, 1915, 10.
5. "Bowling Notes," *Brooklyn Citizen*, May 1, 1925, 8; "Bowlers in the Orpheum to Get Their Prizes To-Night," *Brooklyn Citizen*, May 19, 1925, 8.
6. Vincent Adams, "Pin Champ Varipapa All-Arounder in Sports," *Daily News* (New York), March 5, 1947, 14B.
7. "Frank Brill the Champion," *Chicago Tribune*, January 12, 1901, 6.
8. "Grand Averages of Championship Bowlers," *Chicago Tribune*, January 13, 1901, 19.
9. Brooklyn bowlers were included in the New York totals and those from Bellville, Illinois, in the St. Louis total.
10. "Grand Averages of Championship Bowlers," 19.
11. Miller, *The Bowlers' Encyclopedia*, 32–33.
12. "Star Bowlers to Roll Elk Outfit," *Rochester Democrat and Chronicle*, March 29, 1925, 48.
13. "Five-Man Scores," *Buffalo Evening Times*, March 28, 1925, 9.
14. "Official Prize List, A.B.C. Five-Man, Shows Buffalo Bowlers Fared Very Well," *Buffalo Courier*, April 8, 1925, 10. "Cash" means to win money in a tournament, because only a certain proportion of contestants (typically 10 to 33 percent) earn money.
15. "Jimmy Smith in Brave Start for National Bowling Honors," *Buffalo Express*, March 29, 1925, sec. 7, 9.
16. "Leading Prize Winners in A.B.C. Tournament," *Buffalo Evening Times*, April 8, 1925, 14.
17. "Jimmy Smith in Brave Start," sec. 7, 9; "Buffalo Does Well in Two-Man Prizes," *Buffalo Evening News*, April 9, 1925, 12.
18. Pezzano, "Andy Tells It Like It Was," 39.
19. Prize sharing arrangements were commonplace. Sometimes, teammates split winnings equally, or the winner kept half and shared the rest with the team. Team sponsors occasionally took a cut of the winnings if they subsidized bowlers' travel expenses.

20. Lineups are irrelevant at ABCs because teams are not bowling head to head. Still, most teams recognize their best player and place them in the anchor position.
21. "Orpheums Get into the Money at A.B.C. Event," *Brooklyn Daily Eagle*, April 1, 1926, 4A.
22. "Phil Spinella Rolls 670 Score in Toledo," *Brooklyn Daily Eagle*, April 2, 1926, 2A.
23. "Jim Lawler in the Navy; His Brother in Class 1A," *Brooklyn Citizen*, May 16, 1918, 5.
24. "Lucke Wins Bowling Match at Lawler's," *Standard Union* (Brooklyn, NY), October 25, 1926, 9.
25. "Leo C. Lucke, 59, Bowling Star," *Brooklyn Eagle*, March 17, 1943, 15.
26. "Lawler Brothers Win," *Brooklyn Citizen*, November 4, 1926, 8; "Orpheum Bowlers Win the Return Series from Lawler Bros.' Stars," *Brooklyn Citizen*, November 9, 1926, 8.
27. "Andy Varipapa Bowls Perfect Score of 300," *Brooklyn Daily Eagle*, March 29, 1927, A-3.
28. "Varipapa Leads Lawler Team to Victory at Pins," *Brooklyn Daily Eagle*, November 15, 1927, A-4; "Andy Varipapa High Scorer in Alley Owners Tourney," *Brooklyn Daily Times*, December 20, 1927, 2A; "Varipapa in Great Form," *Brooklyn Citizen*, January 18, 1928, 8.
29. "Gotham Bowlers Take Boro Title," *Brooklyn Daily Times*, February 14, 1928, 2A.
30. "Luft Beats Varipapa," *Brooklyn Daily Times*, January 17, 1928, 2A.
31. "Brooklyn Alley Owners' Individual Tournament Standings," *Brooklyn Daily Times*, May 5, 1928, 2A. Averages in a match play tournaments can be deceiving. A bowler that falls so far behind that they cannot win a game may use the remaining frames to experiment with a different ball or a different line to the pocket. It is the appropriate strategy since margin of victory and total pinfall do not matter.
32. "Varipapa Pin Champion," *Brooklyn Daily Times*, June 23, 1928, 10.
33. "Lawler Bowlers Easily Best Ally Owners Team," *Brooklyn Daily Times*, February 6, 1929, 2A.
34. "Lawler Bowlers Easily Best," 2A.
35. "Lawler Takes Bowling Crown," *Brooklyn Daily Times*, May 17, 1929, 2A.
36. "Bay Ridge Team Brooklyn Alley Owners' Titlist," *Brooklyn Daily Times*, January 3, 1930, 2A.
37. "Brooklyn Alley Owners Championship Bowling League," *Brooklyn Daily Times*, October 13, 1930, 13.
38. Bob Neiman, "Floretta McCutcheon: Bowling Started Out as Her Therapy," *Bowlers Journal*, December 1988, S64.
39. Janet Woolum, "Floretta Doty McCutcheon," in *Outstanding Women Athletes: Who They Are and How They Influenced Sports in America* (Phoenix: Oryx Press, 1992), 151, http://archive.org/details/outstandingwomen00wool.
40. Neiman, "Floretta McCutcheon," S64. Woolum and Neiman reported Smith's final score

as 697. News wire stories reported Smith's score as 687. See "Bowling Champion Drubbed by Woman," *Lincoln* [NE] *Star*, December 19, 1927, 10.

41. Woolum, "Floretta Doty McCutcheon," 151.

42. Before 1960, the Brunswick Corporation was officially the Brunswick-Balke-Collender Company.

43. "World's Champion Woman Bowler to Appear Here," *Minneapolis Journal*, December 28, 1930, sports, 4.

44. "Woman Rolls High Scores," *Morning Call* (Paterson, NJ), April 21, 1930, 20.

45. Woolum, "Floretta Doty McCutcheon," 151.

46. Neiman, "Floretta McCutcheon," S64.

47. "Bowling League Is Organized Here," *Decatur* [IL] *Review*, January 4, 1911, 5.

48. Pearl Keller, "A Final Tribute to Andy Varipapa," *Herald Statesman* (Yonkers, NY), November 24, 1984, D-6.

Chapter 5

1. Stanley Frank, "The Falcaro Strikes Again," *Saturday Evening Post*, March 2, 1946, 38.

2. "Joe Falcaro, for Second Time, Wins the Dwyer with 1,850 Total," *Brooklyn Citizen*, December 6, 1927, 8.

3. "From Pin-Boy to King-Pin of Bowling," *Evansville* [IN] *Press*, March 16, 1930, 43.

4. Frank, "The Falcaro Strikes Again," 36.

5. Frank, "The Falcaro Strikes Again," 36.

6. Frank, "The Falcaro Strikes Again," 37.

7. Robert Lewis Taylor, "Man with a Thumb," *New Yorker*, March 28, 1941, 26.

8. Frank, "The Falcaro Strikes Again," 38.

9. Taylor, "Man with a Thumb," 31.

10. "Smith Defeated by Falcaro in Bowling Match," *Chicago Tribune*, October 30, 1924, 17; "Falcaro Defeats Smith by 28 Pins," *New York Times*, December 17, 1928, 31; "Falcaro Tops Smith," *New York Times*, December 9, 1929, 38.

11. "From Pin-Boy to King-Pin," 43.

12. "Joe Falcaro Dead," 88.

13. Victor Kalman, "Falcaro the Great," *Sports Illustrated*, September 13, 1954, 76, https://vault.si.com/vault/1954/09/13/falcaro-the-great.

14. Kalman, "Falcaro the Great," 76.

15. "Cap Anson's Team Wins the Bowling Championship," *Pittsburgh Post*, February 13, 1904, 10. Anson owned bowling alleys in Chicago, and was a good bowler himself. His team won the 1904 ABC championship in Cleveland.

16. "Bowl for Lucke Fund," *Brooklyn Citizen*, December 24, 1928, 8.

17. "Bowl for Lucke Fund," 8.

18. Grasso and Hartman, *Historical Dictionary of Bowling*, 330.

19. Lou E. Cohen, "Varipapa Meets Falcaro in Pin Duel Tomorrow," *Brooklyn Eagle*, June 26, 1941, 14.

20. Bergman & Trucks, "Bowling: Falcaro-Varipapa of NY vs. Reilly-Murgie of Phila.," advertisement, *Evening Courier* (Camden, NJ), November 28, 1930, 28.

21. Maly, "A Talking Machine," 15.

22. Fred Kirsch, "For the Record," *Record* (Hackensack, NJ), February 27, 1973, B-8.

23. Will Grimsley, "The Minnesota Fats of Bowling is 90," *Shreveport* [LA] *Journal*, April 6, 1981, 5C.

24. "Falcaro and Partner Take Bowling Lead," *Philadelphia Inquirer*, November 23, 1930, S9.

25. "Varipapa and Falcaro Now Have a Lead of 1,732," *Brooklyn Citizen*, November 24, 1930, 8.

26. "Murgie and Reilly Upset New Yorkers," *Philadelphia Inquirer*, November 29, 1930, 18.

27. "New York Bowlers Win Intercity Match," *New York Times*, November 30, 1930, 8S.

28. "New York Bowlers Win," 8S.

29. Punch Walker, "Punch's Bowling Comment," *Binghamton* [NY] *Press*, December 22, 1930, 25; "Bowling Scores," *Brooklyn Daily Times*, November 25, 1930, 2A.

30. Kirsch, "For the Record," B-8.

31. Chuck Pezzano, "The Birth, Rebirth of Andy Varipapa," *Bowling*, July 1976, 30.

32. Maly, "A Talking Machine," 15.

33. Robert S. McElvaine, *The Great Depression: America, 1929–1941* (New York: Times Books, 1993), 46–49, https://archive.org/details/greatdepressiona00mcel/; Harold Bierman, Jr., "The 1929 Stock Market Crash," EH.net Encyclopedia, March 26, 2008, https://eh.net/encyclopedia/the-1929-stock-market-crash/.

34. Peter Temin, "Lessons for the Present from the Great Depression," *American Economic Review* 66, no. 2 (1976): 40, https://www.jstor.org/stable/1817196.

35. Temin, "Lessons for the Present from the Great Depression," 42; Michael D. Bordo, Christopher Erceg, and Charles L. Evans, "Money, Sticky Wages, and the Great Depression," *American Economic Review* 90, no. 5 (2000): 1447, http://doi.org/10.1257/aer.90.5.1447.

36. David C. Wheelock, "The Great Depression: An Overview," Federal Reserve Bank of St. Louis, accessed December 11, 2022, https://www.stlouisfed.org/~/media/files/pdfs/great-depression/the-great-depression-wheelock-overview.pdf; United States Bureau of Economic Analysis, "Gross Domestic Product," Resources: Learning Center, April 26, 2022, https://www.bea.gov/resources/learning-center/what-to-know-gdp.

37. Miller, *The Bowlers' Encyclopedia*, 220–221.

38. Miller, *The Bowlers' Encyclopedia*, 222.

39. United States Census Bureau, "Introduction to NAICS," North American Industry Classification System, December 19, 2022, https://www.census.gov/naics/. Bowling centers are included in the "Service-Producing" class, "Leisure and Hospitality" super sector, "Arts, Entertainment, and Recreation" sector, "Amusement, Gambling, and Recreation" industry, and "Other Amusement and Recreation Industries" subcategory. The

subcategory also includes recreation and fitness centers, golf courses, skiing facilities, and marinas.

40. United States Department of Commerce, *Bicentennial Edition: Historical Statistics of the United States, Colonial Times to 1970* (Washington, D.C.: U.S. Government Printing Office, 1975), 319, 404, https://www.census.gov/library/publications/1975/compendia/hist_stats_colonial-1970.html.

41. United States Department of Commerce.

42. Punch Walker, "Bowling Comment by 'Punch,'" *Binghamton [NY] Press*, February 28, 1931, 14; "Varipapa, Falcaro Win," *Bergen Evening Record* (Hackensack, NJ), December 29, 1932, 17; "Strikes, Spares, and Splits," *Paterson [NJ] Evening News*, March 15, 1932, 18; "Falcaro and Varipapa in Pin Victory," *Rochester Democrat and Chronicle*, March 21, 1932, 17; "Varipapa and Falcaro Beat Benkovic, Daw," *Rochester Democrat and Chronicle*, May 3, 1932, 17.

43. Al Del Greco, "At Random in Sportdom," *Bergen Evening Record* (Hackensack, NJ), January 19, 1932, 18.

44. International News Service, "Rolls 1,652 for Six Games," *Des Moines Tribune*, January 18, 1932, 3A.

45. Robert Ripley, "Believe It or Not—By Ripley," *Akron Beacon Journal*, March 10, 1933, 20.

46. "Varipapa Defeats Schultz in Match," *Buffalo Times*, April 11, 1932, 7; George R. Loveys, "The Sports Periscope," *Post-Star* (Glens Falls, NY), April 14, 1932, 11.

47. "Joe Falcaro Wins from Andy Varipapa, Loser Rolls a 300," *Brooklyn Citizen*, April 26, 1932, 6.

48. Frank, "The Falcaro Strikes Again," 35.

49. "Andy Varipapa Bowls Today on City Alleys," *Morning News* (Wilmington, DE), April 27, 1932, 10.

50. "A.B.C. Doubles Champions Booked in Big Match Here," *Rochester Democrat and Chronicle*, April 19, 1932, 15; "Expects Crowd at Bowling Match," *Rochester Democrat and Chronicle*, April 24, 1932, 3C; "Varipapa and Falcaro Beat," 17.

51. "Falcaro, Varipapa, Bowl Here May 1," *Buffalo Times*, April 23, 1932, 10.

52. George R. Loveys, "The Sports Periscope," *Post-Star* (Glens Falls, NY), September 28, 1932, 9.

53. Bob Stedler, "Karpe's Comment," *Buffalo Evening News*, October 11, 1932, 21.

54. "Three Tied for Lead as Thum's Pin Classic Ends," *Bayonne [NJ] Times*, June 20, 1932, 8.

Chapter 6

1. Kirsch, "For the Record," B-8.
2. Ed Reiter, "Andy Varipapa Had More than Tricks up His Sleeve," *Asbury Park [NJ] Press*, October 21, 1978, B7.
3. Kirsch, "For the Record," B-8.
4. Reiter, "Andy Varipapa Had More," B7.

5. Tim Harris, *Players: 250 Men, Women and Animals Who Created Modern Sport* (London: Yellow Jersey, 2009), 382, http://archive.org/details/players250menwom0000harr.

6. Harris, 382.

7. S. Carlisle Martin, "Charlie Peterson, Cue Wiz, Goes Mrs. Belmont One Better; Wants to Encourage Wizesses," *St. Louis Post-Dispatch*, October 24, 1909, part 4, 18.

8. Rorre, "Amazing Andy Varipapa," 20.

9. World Pool-Billiard Association—Artistic Pool Division, "Sports History," World Pool-Billiard Association—Official Website of the Artistic Pool Division, 2017, https://www.wpa-apd.org/sports-history.

10. "Garry Green Dies in Rochester Hospital," *Evening Record* (Hackensack, NJ), February 8, 1915, 1.

11. "A $200 Bowling Game," *Passaic [NJ] Daily News*, December 11, 1893, 1.

12. "A Ringer," *Buffalo Commercial*, June 11, 1901, 6.

13. "Garry Green," *Buffalo Commercial*, October 30, 1902, 4.

14. "American Notes," *Pittsburgh Press*, November 20, 1904, 47.

15. Club Bowling Alleys, "Dead Center Green Champion Bowler of the World," advertisement, *Daily Republican* (Monongahela, PA), January 26, 1911, 4.

16. "Two Days Bowling Tournament," *New Castle [PA] Daily Herald*, June 12, 1907, 3.

17. "No Others in the Class of Jimmy Smith," *Rochester Democrat and Chronicle*, April 15, 1913, 21.

18. "Bowling Shark Gave Exhibition," *Coshocton [OH] Daily Times*, February 26, 1913, 8.

19. "No Money Left, Dies in County Hospital," *Rochester Democrat and Chronicle*, February 9, 1915, 17.

20. Schmidt, *The Bowling Chronicles*, 5–6.

21. Victor Kalman, "Not Dead Yet," *Sports Illustrated*, November 1, 1954, 75, https://vault.si.com/vault/1954/11/01/not-dead-yet.

22. International Jewish Sports Hall of Fame, "Elected Members: Mort Lindsey," International Jewish Sports Hall of Fame, 2023, http://www.jewishsports.net/BioPages/MortimerLindsey.htm. Barry Asher, Marshall Holman, Mark Roth, and Sylvia Wene are other bowlers enshrined for superior performance.

23. Associated Press, "Top Money to Draskovich in Bowlers Sweepstakes," *Monroe [LA] News-Star*, June 16, 1952, 9. Some sources incorrectly stated that Lindsey won the 1952 *Bowlers Journal* tournament.

24. Schmidt, *The Bowling Chronicles*, 6; "Mort Lindsey," USBC Hall of Fame, accessed January 24, 2023, https://bowl.com/usbc-hall-of-fame/hall-of-famers/mort-lindsey.

25. Schmidt, 193.

26. Ed Maurer, "Down the Alley," *Journal-News* (Nyack, NY), November 22, 1958, 10.

27. Mort. Luby, Jr., "A Legend to Count On," *Bowlers Journal*, December 1988, 113.

28. Luby Jr., "A Legend to Count On," 113.

29. Luby Jr., "A Legend to Count On," 113.

30. "Mort Lindsey Gives Great Exhibition of Bowling at Michelin Community House," *Daily Home News* (New Brunswick, NJ), June 24, 1921, 18.

31. "Mort Lindsay has Great Record," *Monrovia* [CA] *Daily News*, July 14, 1928, 8. Journalists often misspelled Lindsey's name, as they did with Johnny Voorheis. Andy was not immune, either. There are hundreds of newspaper articles, some with bold headlines, about the great "Veripapa," "Varapapa," or "Verapapa." See, for example, "Many to See Andy Veripapa, Famed Bowler, in Exhibition Here," *Elwood* [IN] *Call-Leader*, October 4, 1937, 6.

32. *Weatherproof*, featuring Mort Lindsey (New York: Pathé Exchange, 1927); "Reviews of New Short Subjects: Weatherproof," *Film Daily*, April 10, 1927, 7, https://lantern.mediahist.org/catalog/filmdaily3940newy_0835

33. "Exploit-O-Grams: Weatherproof— Rice Sportlight," *Film Daily*, March 27, 1927, 15, https://lantern.mediahist.org/catalog/filmdaily3940newy_0709; Pathe Exchange, "Weatherproof: Motion Picture Copyright Descriptions Collection. Class M, 1912–1977," January 13, 1927, https://www.loc.gov/item/s1229m03736/.

34. *Undercover*, featuring Mort Lindsey (New York: Pathé Exchange, 1931); "Reviews of Sound Shorts: Undercover," *Film Daily*, January 25, 1931, 12, https://lantern.mediahist.org/catalog/filmdailyvolume555newy_0222; "Short Subjects: Under Cover," *Motion Picture Review*, March 1931, 7, https://lantern.mediahist.org/catalog/motionpicturerev00wome_0_0029.

35. Reiter, "Andy Varipapa Had More," B7.

36. Less-than perfect lane maintenance helped Andy. Not always perfectly flat, worn wooden lanes tended to slope towards the center and made the double hook possible. See Ted Thompson, "Kegel's Revolutionary Slope Graphs," White Papers & Articles—Kegel, Built for Bowling, February 10, 2012, https://www.kegel.net/articles/kegels-revolutionary-slope-graphs.

37. Al Demaree, "Varipapa's Tricks Outdo Gengler's," *Daily Argus Leader* (Sioux Falls, SD), February 14, 1935, 11.

38. Parker Bohn III, in discussion with the author, February 7, 2023.

39. Jonni Falk, "Keansburg's Crover: Living Bowling Legend," *Sunday Register* (Shrewsbury, NJ), July 17, 1977, C3.

40. Perth Amboy Recreation, "Bowling Match Extraordinary," advertisement, *Plainfield* [NJ] *Courier-News*, April 25, 1931, 16.

41. Falk, "Keansburg's Crover," C3.

42. Reiter, "Andy Varipapa Had More," B7.

43. Wes Bogle, "Jim Crover, 82, Dies," *Sunday Home News* (New Brunswick, NJ), November 1, 1981, B9.

44. *Sport Slants No. 5*, hosted by Ted Husing (New York: Vitaphone, 1932).

45. "Reviews of Sound Shorts: Ted Husing in 'Sport Slants' (No. 5)," *Film Daily*, February 7, 1932, 11, https://lantern.mediahist.org/catalog/filmdailyvolume55859newy_0311.

46. "Super Pinmen Sport Slants Local Theater," *Pottsville* [PA] *Evening Republican*, February 4, 1932, 11.

47. "Varipapa, Trick Shot Star Performs Before 600 Fans," *Daily Argus* (Mount Vernon, NY), March 25, 1932, 24.

48. Orlo Robertson, "Champion U.S. Trick Shot Bowler Makes Difficult Ones Look Easy," *South Bend Tribune*, December 25, 1932, sports, 3.

49. Bohn III, discussion.

50. Bob Learn, Jr., *Stories from the Hall of Fame: Bowling*, aired on the History Channel, November 6, 2002, 3:08 to 3:20, https://www.youtube.com/watch?v=cZMBy2xXXKs.

51. Norm Duke, in discussion with the author, February 11, 2023.

52. Nelson Burton, Jr., in discussion with the author, June 6, 2023.

53. "Duke 300 Game Towel Shot," YouTube video, February 15, 2011, https://www.youtube.com/watch?v=EO11nTLqenI.

54. Duke, discussion.

55. Pezzano, "Varipapa: Master of the Trick Shot," S-12.

56. Tom Rossman, in discussion with the author, February 15, 2023.

57. Rossman, discussion.

58. Fay, "Bowling's Talking Machine," 6.

59. Fay, "Bowling's Talking Machine," 6.

Chapter 7

1. Richard Butsch, "American Movie Audiences of the 1930s," *International Labor and Working-Class History* 59 (2001): 107, https://www.jstor.org/stable/27672712.

2. Richard Ward, "Extra Added Attractions: The Short Subjects of MGM, Warner Brothers and Universal," *Media History* 9, no. 3 (2003): 221, https://doi.org/10.1080/1368880032000145542. One thousand feet of 35 mm film fit on one reel and ran approximately 11 minutes.

3. Rob King, "The Art of Diddling: Slapstick, Science, and Antimodernism in the Films of Charley Bowers," in *Funny Pictures: Animation and Comedy in Studio-Era Hollywood*, eds. Daniel Goldmark and Charlie Keli (Berkeley: University of California Press, 2011), 196. ProQuest eBook Central.

4. Legal Information Institute, "Tying Arrangement," Cornell Law School Legal Information Institute, accessed January 28, 2023, https://www.law.cornell.edu/wex/tying_arrangement. A tying arrangement conditions the sale of one product on purchasing another and is illegal when it restricts competition.

5. Ward, "Extra Added Attractions," 222; United States Department of Justice, "The Paramount

Decrees," United States Department of Justice, Antitrust Division, last updated August 7, 2020, https://www.justice.gov/atr/paramount-decree-review. This 1948 Supreme Court decision ended many of the studios' anti-competitive practices.

6. Ward, "Extra Added Attractions," 238; Advanced Title Search," IMDb, 2023, https://www.imdb.com/search/title/. Author's estimate calculated based on IMDb search engine.

7. Douglas W. Churchill, "Pete Smith—Invisible Star of the Screen," *Oakland Tribune*, January 6, 1935, sec. 2, 14; Richard Goldstone, "Pete Smith: A Decided Specialty," *Los Angeles Times*, January 28, 1979, calendar, 3.

8. Goldstone, "Pete Smith," 3.

9. John L. Scott, "Pete Smith Completes 20 Long Short Years," *Los Angeles Times*, March 11, 1951, part IV, 1.

10. Bob Thomas, "Shorts Maker Celebrates 20th Year," *Progress-Bulletin* (Pomona, CA), February 19, 1951, 13.

11. Academy of Motion Picture Arts and Sciences, "1953 (26th) Academy Awards—Honorary Award," Academy Awards Acceptance Speech Database, 2019, http://aaspeechesdb.oscars.org/link/026-27/.

12. *The Super Skittler*, featuring Mort Lindsey (London: British Pathé, 1934), https://www.britishpathe.com/asset/189394/.

13. Ruffolo, "The Andy Varipapa Story," 1–1.

14. Andy Varipapa with Mort Luby, Jr., "A Star That Will Always Sparkle," *Bowlers Journal*, October 1984, 56.

15. Ruffolo, "The Andy Varipapa Story," 1–2.

16. "Entries For Pin Classic Closes," *Bergen Evening Record* (Hackensack, NJ), May 2, 1934, 21.

17. "Three Tied for Lead as Thum's Pin Classic Ends," *Bayonne* [NJ] *Times*, June 20, 1932, 8.

"Varipapa Triumphs in Pin Roll-Off," *Bayonne* [NJ] *Times*, July 6, 1933, 10.

18. "Varipapa Alone in Tourney Play," *Bergen Evening Record* (Hackensack, NJ), May 28, 1934, 28.

19. "Eddie Botten Defeats DeVito," *Morning Call* (Paterson, NJ), June 25, 1935, 21.

20. Ruffolo, "The Andy Varipapa Story," 1–3.

21. Lorraine V. Ruffolo, "Chapter 1" (unpublished manuscript, 1960), 1–4, Varipapa Family Papers, private collection.

22. Ruffolo, "Chapter 1," 1–5.]

23. "World Champion Bowler Coming to Lynwood," *Lynwood* [CA] *Tribune*, June 1, 1934, 1.

24. "Pete Smith Over-Worked," *The Hollywood Reporter*, June 4, 1934, 2, https://lantern.mediahist.org/catalog/hollywoodreporte1821holl_1378.

25. Ruffolo, "Chapter 1," 1–5.

26. Ruffolo, "Chapter 1," 1–6

27. Ruffolo, "Chapter 1," 1–6.

28. Ruffolo, "Chapter 1," 1–6.

29. Photos of the tunnel shot indicate that the centerline of each pin is set 20 to 22 boards apart. A wooden bowling lane is made up of 40 1 1/16 inch boards, so counting boards means counting inches. The radius of a pin is 2 3/8 inches, so the gap between each pin is about 15 1/4 to 17 1/4 inches.

30. The first showgirl had her left foot on the fifth board her right foot on the 35th board. Allowing for the width of her feet, the gap is roughly 24 inches. Her feet were also spread further apart then her shoulders, another clue to the distance.

31. A ball is approximately 8 5/8 inches in diameter and a pin 4 3/4 inches. The ball just needs to touch the pin to convert a single-pin spare, so the target area is 8 5/8 + 4 3/4 ≈ 13 3/8 inches.

32. "Vet Comedian of 500 Films Now a Private," *Afro-American* (Baltimore), April 6, 1943, 8, https://books.google.com/books?id=VGBGAAAAIBAJ.

33. "Ray Turner (1895–1981)," IMDb, 2023, https://www.imdb.com/name/nm0877813/.

34. *Strikes and Spares*, 6:30 to 7:15.

35. "Personals," *Columbus* [NE] *Telegram*, June 18, 1934, 5. Andy was sighted in Omaha on June 16.

36. Pete Smith, letter to Andy Varipapa, July 12, 1934, Varipapa Family Papers, private collection.

37. Orpheum Theater, "Orpheum: Where the Big Pictures Play," advertisement, *Wisconsin State Journal* (Madison), October 7, 1934, 13.

38. Strand Theater, "Attention Bowlers," advertisement, *Oshkosh* [WI] *Northwestern*, October 25, 1934, 15.

39. ABC-affiliated state and local bowling associations coordinate grass-roots promotional activities.

40. Meder Recreation, "Bowlers: Don't Fail to See Andy Varipapa, The World's Most Sensational Bowler, Featured in Strikes and Spares," advertisement, *Mansfield* [OH] *News-Journal*, December 12, 1934, 16.

41. Sheboygan Bowling Association, "Bowlers Attention!" advertisement, *Sheboygan* [WI] *Press*, November 23, 1934, 14.

42. Blaney's Bowling Alley, "Can You Bowl a Perfect Spare Game or Make 5 Strikes in a Row?" advertisement, *Progress-Bulletin* (Pomona, CA), November 1, 1934, 10. Both are difficult feats for anyone averaging less than 190.

43. "Bowlers Rush to Enter Meet," *Atlanta Constitution*, November 8, 1934, 11.

44. "Short Showmanship," *Motion Picture Herald*, July 7, 1934, 47, https://lantern.mediahist.org/catalog/motionpictureher116unse_0177. As a publicist, Smith tended to exaggerate: Combined ABC and WIBC membership in 1934 was 216,000, not 6,000,000.

45. "Short Showmanship," 47.

46. Academy of Motion Picture Arts and Sciences, "The 7th Academy Awards—1935," Oscars® Ceremonies, 2022, https://www.oscars.org/oscars/ceremonies/1935. There were three short film categories (Cartoon, Comedy, and Novelty), each with three nominees.

47. Paramount Theater, "Strikes and Spares—Andy Varipapa," advertisement, *Post-Register* (Idaho Falls, ID), January 16, 1935, 8.

48. Ruffolo, "From Calabria to Hollywood," 2–8.

Chapter 8

1. Ruffolo, "The Andy Varipapa Story," 3–1.
2. Ruffolo, "The Andy Varipapa Story," 3–1.
3. Ruffolo, "The Andy Varipapa Story," 3–1.
4. Louis Petersen, letter to Andy Varipapa, October 22, 1934, Varipapa Family Papers, private collection.
5. Petersen, letter.
6. Leo A. Schueneman, letter to Andy Varipapa, October 23, 1934, Varipapa Family Papers, private collection.
7. Schueneman.
8. Schueneman, letter.
9. Schueneman, letter.
10. George Govlick, "Sports Previews and Reviews," *Plainfield* [NJ] *Courier-News*, May 4, 1959, 22.
11. "Sport Shorts," *Montreal River Miner* (Hurley, WI), November 16, 1934, 4.
12. "Henchen Hall Gets First Look at Varipapa," *Rochester Democrat and Chronicle*, January 28, 1935, 14.
13. "'Elmer's First Bowling Lesson' at Eagle's Grill Tonight," *Standard-Sentinel* (Hazelton, PA), November 10, 1937, 14.
14. Hirshon, "Bowling Headliners," 15.
15. "Varipapa Will Be Busy Man, To Show on Eight Alleys," *Rochester Democrat and Chronicle*, January 27, 1935, 4C.
16. W.W. Edgar, "Hitting the Headpin," *Detroit Free Press*, December 17, 1939, sports, 2.
17. Hinteroff, "He Couldn't Make the Dodgers," E1.
18. Byron Schoeman, "The Fabulous Varipapa," *National Bowlers Journal and Billiard Revues*, July 1959, 8.
19. Andy Varipapa with Lorraine V. Ruffolo, "Match Game Record" (unpublished manuscript, 1960), M-1, Varipapa Family Papers, private collection.
20. "Bowling: Handy Andy," *Newsweek*, December 23, 1946, 78, http://archive.org/details/sim_newsweek-us_1946-12-23_28_26.
21. Varipapa with Luby Jr., "A Star That Will Always Sparkle," 57.
22. Ritter Collett, "The Journal of Sports," *Dayton Journal*, May 20, 1948, 15.
23. Cherin, "Varipapa the Magnificent," 57.
24. Alvin Rosensweet, "Andy Varipapa Says He's World's Most Sensational Bowler—And Then Proves It," *Dayton Herald*, March 12, 1937, 36.
25. Rosensweet, "Andy Varipapa Says He's World's Most Sensational Bowler," 36.
26. Andy Varipapa with Lorraine V. Ruffolo, "Introduction" (unpublished manuscript, 1960), 9, Varipapa Family Papers, private collection; Walter, "Andy Varipapa: Great Star," 26.
27. Varipapa with Ruffolo, "Introduction," 10–11.
28. Walter, "Andy Varipapa: Great Star," 26.
29. Ron Maly, "Trick Grip Points to Bowling Success," *Des Moines Register*, August 13, 1997, 1D.
30. Don Carter, perhaps the greatest bowler of all time, tucked his pinkie.
31. Maly, "Trick Grip Points to Bowling Success," 5D.
32. Dave Burgin, "Dick Weber Bowls 'Em Over," *Shreveport* [LA] *Journal*, November 1, 1966, 11.
33. Burgin, "Dick Weber Bowls 'Em Over," 11.
34. Altshul, "Andy Varipapa at 81," 42.
35. Ed Reddy, "A Bowling Great, Varipapa Gave Lots Back to Game," *Syracuse Post-Standard*, August 29, 1984, C-3.
36. Reddy, "A Bowling Great," C-3.
37. Chuck Pezzano, "At 83, Varipapa Sparkles as Instructor, Fitness Expert," *Sporting News*, June 22, 1974, 55.
38. "Varipapa Loses to Tarutis," *Times Leader* (Wilkes-Barre, PA), March 4, 1934, 17.
39. "Varipapa Loses to Tarutis," 17.
40. "Willy's Letter Box," *Evening News* (Wilkes-Barre, PA), March 5, 1935, 12.
41. "Bowling Ace Scores Wins," *Pittsburgh Sun-Telegraph*, March 10, 1935, part 2, 2.
42. "Robert L. Ripple," *Rapid City* [SD[*Journal*, September 16, 2008, C2.
43. Kacky Ertl, "Ripple Is Back," *Rapid City* [SD] *Journal*, October 4, 1981, 19.
44. "Robert L. Ripple," C2.
45. "Varipapa in Final Pin Show Tonight," *Rapid City* [SD] *Journal*, October 17, 1938, 5.
46. Miller, *The Bowlers' Encyclopedia*, 34–35.
47. United States Bowling Congress, "Andy Varipapa Open Championship History" (unpublished data, March 3, 2023), PDF file.
48. Associated Press, "Varipapa is Disappointing," *Dayton Daily News*, March 29, 1935, 32.
49. Associated Press, "Andy Varipapa to Roll Tonight," *Elmira* [NY] *Star-Gazette*, March 28, 1935, 23.
50. "Budweisers Bowl Into Third Place in A.B.C.," *St. Louis Globe-Democrat*, April 8, 1935, 11A.
51. "6-Year-Old Boy is Made Wealthy by Clopton Will," *St. Louis Post-Dispatch*, November 24, 1911, 1; "Wealthy Jason Chases the Gold Fleece of Some 'Zippy' Music," *Ogden* [UT] *Standard*, October 25, 1913, 17.
52. Louis La Coss, "A Champion Bowler Carries On," *St. Louis Globe-Democrat*, June 21, 1931, sec. 2, 4.
53. J.R. Schmidt, "Famous Teams," *Dr. Jake's Bowling History Blog*, last modified August 10, 2023, https://bowlinghistory.wordpress.com/category/famous-teams/.
54. Lorraine V. Ruffolo, "Andy Varipapa Biography" (unpublished manuscript, 1960), 3–4, Varipapa Family Papers, private collection.
55. "Ten Bowling Stars Will Tour Country," *Rochester Democrat and Chronicle*, October 6, 1935, 5C.

Chapter 9

1. "Varipapa Shows Bowling Tricks; May Return," *Fort Worth Star-Telegram*, December 18, 1935, 19.

2. Weiskopf, *The Perfect Game*, 64.
3. Jack Ledden, "Seen and Heard in the Sport Realm," *South Bend Tribune*, February 13, 1936, sec. 2, 4.
4. Ruffolo, "Andy Varipapa Biography," 3–5.
5. Ruffolo, "Andy Varipapa Biography," 3–5.
6. Gene F. Hampson, "Thru Sportsland," *Plainfield* [NJ] *Courier-News*, February 18, 1941, 14.
7. "Munn Averages 217.27 in Beating Serpico," *Plainfield* [NJ] *Courier-News*, March 25, 1941, 15.
8. John Walter, "Rivals Pay Dearly," *Detroit News*, June 15, 1943.
9. "Public Grand Opening Set at Star Bowling Tonight," *Plainfield* [NJ] *Courier-News*, May 3, 1960, 23.
10. Lou Marks, *The Bowling Experience* (Boynton Beach, FL: Goldmark, 1987), 130.
11. Ruffolo, "Andy Varipapa Biography," 3–5.
12. "Burton and Varipapa Sign for 80-Game Bowling Match," *St. Louis Post-Dispatch*, May 14, 1937, 3C.
13. In 1937, resurfacing wood lanes meant sanding to the bare wood, applying three to five coats of shellac, and waxing by hand. Freshly resurfaced lanes were tougher to score on than worn ones.
14. Lorraine V. Ruffolo, "Nelson Burton Sr., vs. Andy Varipapa" (unpublished manuscript, 1960), 1, Varipapa Family Papers, private collection.
15. Ruffolo, "Nelson Burton Sr., vs. Andy Varipapa" 2.
16. Ruffolo, "Nelson Burton Sr., vs. Andy Varipapa" 2.
17. Associated Press, "Varipapa Takes 197-Pin Lead," *St. Louis Globe-Democrat*, May 28, 1937, 13A.
18. Cherin, "Varipapa the Magnificent," 59.
19. Ruffolo, "Nelson Burton Sr., vs. Andy Varipapa," 3.
20. Salvino, discussion.
21. Salvino, discussion.
22. Salvino, discussion.
23. Ruffolo, "Nelson Burton Sr., vs. Andy Varipapa," 3; Andy Varipapa, letter to Mort Luby Sr., September 1941, Varipapa Family Papers, private collection.
24. Associated Press, "Varipapa Finishes Match Far Ahead," *Fort Worth Star-Telegram*, June 8, 1937, 17.
25. Archibald, "Andy Varipapa: Rolling at 85," 7J.
26. Cherin, "Varipapa the Magnificent," 59.
27. Ruffolo, "The Andy Varipapa Story," 3–7.
28. Ruffolo, "The Andy Varipapa Story," 4–1.
29. Andy Varipapa with Lorraine V. Ruffolo, "Detroit Bowling Clinic" (unpublished manuscript, 1960), 14, Varipapa Family Papers, private collection.
30. C.H. Beukema, "School Opens Tomorrow for Chicago Bowlers," *Chicago Tribune*, March 1, 1942, part 2, 5.
31. Andy Varipapa, "Equipment Essentials of Bowling," *Brooklyn Daily Eagle*, January 15, 1938, 11.
32. Andy Varipapa, "Improve Your Bowling," *Morning Call* (Paterson, NJ), February 12, 1947, 22.
33. Carmody, "Still Bowling 'Em Over," 80.
34. Tim Zieroth, "Baseball and Basketball Players," Baseball Almanac, 2023, https://www.baseball-almanac.com/legendary/baseball_and_basketball_players.shtml. Others to play both sports at the highest level include Dick Groat, Dave DeBusschere, and Danny Ainge.
35. Charlie Bevis, "Chuck Connors," Society for American Baseball Research, accessed March 16, 2023, https://sabr.org/bioproj/person/chuck-connors/.
36. Ruffolo, "Andy Varipapa Biography," 4–1.
37. Varipapa with Luby Jr., "A Star That Will Always Sparkle," 57.
38. Ruffolo, "Andy Varipapa Biography," 4–3.
39. Andy Ruffolo, in discussion with the author, March 8, 2023.
40. Lorraine V. Ruffolo, "Frank Benkovic vs. Andy Varipapa" (unpublished manuscript, 1960), 6–7, private collection.
41. Associated Press, "Varipapa Wins from Benkovic in Match," *St. Louis Post-Dispatch*, April 4, 1938, 3B.
42. "Varipapa Takes Eastern Match Game Pin Title," *Nassau Daily Review-Star* (Freeport, NY), July 1, 1938, 13.
43. Burton Jr., discussion.
44. Lorraine V. Ruffolo, "Set 'Em Up" (unpublished manuscript, 1960), 1, Varipapa Family Papers, private collection.
45. Jimmie Fidler, "Touring in Filmland," *San Pedro* [CA] *News-Pilot*, August 24, 1939, 4.
46. *Set 'Em Up*, directed by Felix E. Feist (Culver City, CA: Metro-Goldwyn-Mayer), 0:07 to 0:12, https://www.youtube.com/watch?v=PUx5wKwo9Xc.
47. *Better Bowling*, directed by Jack Eaton (Hollywood: Paramount, 1942), https://www.youtube.com/watch?v=UPV5drhy8Co.
48. Annette D'Agostino Lloyd, *Harold Lloyd: Magic in a Pair of Horn-Rimmed Glasses* (Albany, GA: BearManor Media, 2016), 308. Lloyd was an avid bowler and used his notoriety to promote the sport.
49. Grasso and Hartman, *Historical Dictionary of Bowling*, 119.
50. "Norris Leads Blazing Finish," *Detroit Free Press*, February 17, 1941, 13.
51. Grasso and Hartman, *Historical Dictionary of Bowling*, 327.

Chapter 10

1. In other parts of the world, it is not always so simple. In global football (soccer), teams routinely play in multiple competitions simultaneously. For example, in the U.K., Premier League football clubs compete for the league title, the Football Association Cup, and the UEFA Champions League championship all at the same time.

2. Male golfers compete in four majors: The Masters, PGA Championship, U.S. Open, and Open Championship (formerly the British Open). Female golfers have five majors, and men's and women's tennis each have four. Performance in major championships is more crucial in defining a player's greatness winning a season-long point title.

3. ESPN Enterprises, "Boxing Champions List," *ESPN.com*, last modified July 25, 2023, https://www.espn.com/boxing/story/_/id/12370125/boxing-champions-list. The World Boxing Organization (WBO), the International Boxing Federation (IBF), the World Boxing Association (WBA), and the World Boxing Council (WBC) recognize boxing champions. As of July 2023, among 17 weight classes, only Carlos Alvarez (super middleweight), Jermell Charlo (junior middleweight), and Devin Haney (lightweight) are undisputed champions, recognized by all four governing bodies.

4. Schmidt, *The Bowling Chronicles*, 79–81; J.R. Schmidt, "Little Wizard Voorhies Deserves Place in History," *Bowlers Journal International*, February 2021, 24. In the early 20th century, a best-of-11 match game format was standard. Beginning with Smith's match with Louis Franz of Cleveland in 1909, matches stretched to 30 games or more and were decided by total pins rather than the number of games won.

5. "Smith Defeats Voorhies in Big Bowling Match," *The World* (New York), March 14, 1906, 11.

6. "Voorheis Will Go in Confident of Victory," *Brooklyn Citizen*, March 13, 1906, 5. Journalists had no idea how to spell Voorhies' name. He was referred to as "Voorheis," "Voorhees," "Voorhis," and "Voorhes." See J.R. Schmidt, "A Johnny Voorhies Bibliography," *Dr. Jake's Bowling History Blog*, February 11, 2021, https://bowlinghistory.wordpress.com/2021/02/11/a-johnny-voorhies-bibliography/.

7. "Voorheis Will Go in Confident," 5

8. "Jimmy Smith Defeats Voorheis in Nine Games," *Brooklyn Citizen*, March 14, 1906, 5.

9. Schmidt, *The Bowling Chronicles*, 24.

10. Schmidt, *The Bowling Chronicles*, 25.

11. "Entries Picked for Pin Classic Here Feb. 9–25," *Chicago Tribune*, January 29, 1922, A1.

12. Jim Dressel, "Jimmy Blouin: A Match Play Bowler Supreme, the 'Blue Island Bomber' Retired His Crown Undefeated," *Bowlers Journal*, December 1988, S88–S89.

13. "Bowling Tournament Ends: Blouin Wins First Place in National Classic," *Capital Times* (Madison, WI), February 25, 1922, 9.

14. Kevin Bourke, "Jimmy Smith: The Name No One Will Ever Forget," *Bowlers Journal*, December 1988, S90.

15. "Blouin Remains Monarch of Pins in Narrow Win," *Chicago Tribune*, December 20, 2022, 25.

16. Bourke, "Jimmy Smith," S90.

17. United Press International, "Bowling Tourneys May Be Scored by Points, Experts Say," *Port Huron* [MI] *Times Herald*, March 19, 1922, 11.

18. Mark Collar, "Louie Petersen: Scoring Points Both Inside and Outside the System," *Bowlers Journal*, December 1988, S86.

19. Weiskopf, *The Perfect Game*, 48, 58.

20. J.R. Schmidt, "Match Game Championship (Individual)," *Dr. Jake's Bowling History Blog*, January 1, 2009, https://bowlinghistory.wordpress.com/2009/01/01/match-game-championship-individual/.

21. Schmidt, *The Bowling Chronicles*, 225.

22. Billy Sixty, "Bowling Match Champion Rivals Silent Art Shires for Modesty," *Decatur* [IL] *Herald*, January 4, 1931, 11.

23. Kalman, "Falcaro the Great," 76.

24. Harold X. George, "Who Is Josef Obuszkiewicz?" *Evening Independent* (Massillon, OH), May 12, 1933, 14.

25. Associated Press, "Joe Miller Advances in Bowling Tournament," *Philadelphia Inquirer*, January 29, 1933, 23.

26. "Miller Is Kingpin of East's Bowlers," *Buffalo Evening News*, February 7, 1933, 22.

27. Kalman, "Falcaro the Great," 76.

28. Associated Press, "Falcaro Shot, Will Recover; Appeared Here," *Elmira* [NY] *Star-Gazette*, March 31, 1933, 18.

29. "Hearing Put Off in Shooting of Bowling Champ," *Daily News* (New York), April 16, 1933, B3.

30. "Mazzola Jailed," *Brooklyn Daily Eagle*, June 24, 1933, 4; Schmidt, *The Bowling Chronicles*, 225–226.

31. "Match Bowling Title Series Opens April 28," *Chicago Tribune*, March 28, 1933, 20.

32. "Miller Wins U.S. Match Game Bowling Title," *Chicago Tribune*, May 2, 1933, 23.

33. Schmidt, *The Bowling Chronicles*, 226.

34. "Bowling Champion Joe Miller Dies at 58; Held World Title," *Buffalo Evening News*, March 6, 1958, 47.

35. George, "Who Is Josef Obuszkiewicz?" 14.

36. Gene F. Hampson, "Sports Slants," *Plainfield* [NJ] *Courier News*, February 10, 1948, 14; Miller, *The Bowlers' Encyclopedia*, 38.

37. Associated Press, "Champ Braddock Rolls 298 in A.B.C.—But It's for 3 Games," *Indianapolis News*, April 1, 1937, 20.

38. Associated Press, "Champ Braddock Rolls 298 in A.B.C.," 20.

39. Associated Press, "Andy Varipapa Disappointment in A.B.C. Play," *Daily Home News* (New Brunswick, NJ), April 1, 1937, 21; Associated Press, "Famed Stars Fail Before ABC Crowds," *Herald-Press* (St. Joseph, MI), April 1, 1937, 13.

40. "Andy Fails," *Akron Beacon Journal*, April 1, 1937, 38.

41. Walter Johns, "The Greatest," *Staunton* [VA] *Leader*, February 16, 1961, 10.

42. Arnold Derlitzki, "Beside the Point," *Decatur* [IL] *Herald*, April 9, 1934, 5.

43. "Day's Sporting News and Views," *Plain*

Speaker (Hazelton, PA), April 29, 1937, 18; J.R. Schmidt, "When 'The ABC' Was Classic," United States Bowling Congress, April 4, 2012, https://bowl.com/news/when-the-abc-was-classic. From 1961 through 1979, the ABC took Andy's suggestion and created a "Classic" division for teams with two or more professionals. Due to decreasing entries in the division, the idea was scrapped in 1979. Today, the USBC Championships segregate bowlers into one of three divisions, based on average.

44. Derlitzki, "Besides the Point," 5.
45. John Lardner, "Great Duo Shoots in Pin Tourney: Marino Must Fight Bowling Jinx," *Sunday Star* (Washington, D.C.), April 18, 1937, B-10.
46. Frank, "The Falcaro Strikes Again," 38.
47. Rosensweet, "Andy Varipapa Says," 38.
48. Associated Press, "Marino Keeps Single Match Bowling Title," *Capital Times* (Madison, WI), February 1, 1937, 14.
49. Associated Press, "Ned Day Takes Pin Match Crown," *Capital Times* (Madison, WI), December 20, 1937, 12.
50. Associated Press, "Hank Marino Abdicates as Match Champ," *Decatur* [IL] *Herald*, January 15, 1938, 6.
51. "Illness of Day Postpones Bowling Series in Detroit," *Detroit Free Press*, February 24, 1938, 15.
52. Associated Press, "Bowling Crown Won by Ned Day," *Oshkosh* [WI] *Northwestern*, October 31, 1938, 15.
53. Miller, *The Bowlers' Encyclopedia*, 222, 220.
54. "Varipapa Says 'Pro Play' Would Make Bowling Spectator Sport," *Elmira* [NY] *Star-Gazette*, May 14, 1940, 13.
55. "Varipapa Says," 13.
56. "Varipapa Says," 13. Andy did not always accurately predict the future. In 1951, the ABC ran a double elimination tournament at the Memorial Auditorium in St. Paul, Minnesota, on the same lanes as the ABC Championships. The ABC Masters became one of bowling's major championships, and Andy finished second in 1952 at age 61.
57. Ruffolo, "The Andy Varipapa Story," 8–1.
58. Joe Spinella's cousins were the famous Spinella brothers. Barney owned Barney Spinella's Bowling and Billiards, and Phil (who invited Andy to the 1925 ABC championships) still owned the New Orpheum Bowling Academy. When it came to bowling, the Spinella's had Brooklyn covered.
59. Ruffolo, "The Andy Varipapa Story," 8–2, 8–3.
60. Ruffolo, "The Andy Varipapa Story," 8–2.
61. Ruffolo, "The Andy Varipapa Story," 8–3.

Chapter 11

1. Ralph Brackbill, "Bowling Alleys: Age, 27 Hours," *Evening Sun* (Baltimore, MD), January 31, 1940, 18. Because lanes could not stay on the floor of an arena indefinitely, the BPAA had to disassemble the lanes and store them for next year's event. The labor-intensive process of disassembling, storing, and reinstalling the lanes the following year cost at least $7,500.
2. Arch Ward, "Chicago Gets National Bowling Tournament," *Chicago Tribune*, September 16, 1941, 21.
3. Ward, 21; John C. Thomas, "Star-Crossed: The Colorful History of the Chicago Coliseum," *Owlcation!*, July 14, 2022, https://owlcation.com/humanities/Star-Crossed-The-Colorful-History-of-the-Chicago-Coliseum.
4. Ron Grossman, "Meet Arch Ward: The Sports Editor Who Created MLB's All-Star Game," *Chicago Tribune*, July 17, 2022, 17.
5. John C. Eberhart and Raymond A. Bauer, "An Analysis of the Influences on Recall of a Controversial Event: The Chicago Tribune and the Republic Steel Strike," *The Journal of Social Psychology* 14, no. 1 (1941): 211, https://doi.org/10.1080/00224545.1941.9921507. Only the New York *Daily News* had a higher U.S. circulation than the *Tribune*.
6. To create greater geographical diversity among the contestants, the tournament committee encouraged newspapers to sponsor city-wide elimination tournaments. These events guaranteed cities like Omaha and Dayton an entrant.
7. C.H. Beukema, "Andy Varipapa Enters 10 Pin All-Star Meet," *Chicago Tribune*, November 9, 1941, part 2, 8.
8. Beukema, part 2, 8.
9. C.H. Beukema, "Lay Alleys for 10 Pin Series, Tickets Go Fast," *Chicago Tribune*, November 13, 1941, 29.
10. Jason Gordon, "Asymmetric Information—Explained," The Business Professor, last updated March 27, 2023, https://thebusinessprofessor.com/communications-negotiations/asymmetric-information-definition.
11. Vox, "The Hidden Oil Patterns on Bowling Lanes," Vox Almanac, YouTube video, July 13, 2017, https://www.youtube.com/watch?v=t-osG0F2MZM. Balls tend to skid where the lane has oil and hook where the lane is dry.
12. Petersen Classic, *Louis P. Petersen Classic*.
13. The Pete benefited from its reputation for low scores, so much so that a folklore developed around the methods tournament organizers used to keep them that way. See Schmidt, *The Bowling Chronicles*, 181–184; Suheil Jammal, "Petersen Classic Has Quirky Charms," *Orlando Sentinel*, August 4, 1996, K-9; George Walsh, "The Classic: Sweat, Misery and Cash," *Sports Illustrated*, May 8, 1961, 56, https://vault.si.com/vault/1961/05/08/the-classic-sweat-misery-and-cash. The Pete moved out of Archer Recreation in 1994, and after being held in the Chicago suburb of Hoffman Estates for many years, is now held in the Milwaukee suburb of Wauwatosa.
14. C.H. Beukema, "Field of 80 Named to Bowl in All-Star Tourney," *Chicago Tribune*, November 19, 1941, 23. Despite their claim of wanting geographical diversity among the entrants, the committee (60 percent of whom were from the Chicago

area) went ahead and invited 15 bowlers from Chicago, far more than any other city. Competitors hailed from 19 different states, but 54 percent were from just five metropolitan areas—Chicago, Detroit, New York, Cleveland, and St. Louis.

15. C.H. Beukema, "Put Finishing Touches on 10 Alleys Today," *Chicago Tribune*, December 2, 1941, 23.

16. C.H. Beukema, "All-Star Bowling Tourney Starts Today," *Chicago Tribune*, December 7, 1941, part 2, 1.

17. Falcaro still bowled competitively but strategically sat out the All-Star. If he did not win, he had to drop his "Undefeated Match Game Champion" title.

18. "U.S. and Japs at War," *Chicago Tribune*, December 8, 1941, 1.

19. Mike Conklin, "Odds & Ins," *Chicago Tribune*, December 6, 1991, sec. 4, 9. The Bears-Cardinals was still an intra-city rivalry because the Chicago Cardinals had not yet moved to St. Louis.

20. J.R. Schmidt, "Crimmins Wins All-Star #1 at the Start of World War II," *Bowlers Journal International*, January 2020, 33.

21. Conklin, "Odds & Ins," sec. 4, 9

22. Since someone must have been offended at being referred to as a "loser," losing bowlers now move to the "contenders' bracket."

23. For example: Player A bowls games of 225, 180, 200, 250, 200 for a 1,055 series. Player B bowls 205, 175, 190, 275, 250 for a 1,095 series. Player A earned 21.1 points for pinfall and three points or winning games one, two and three for a total of 24.1 Petersen points. Player B earned 21.9 points for pinfall, three points for winning games four and five, and one point for having a higher series having won fewer games for a total of 24.9 Petersen points. Without computer-aided scoring, keeping track of where a player precisely stood during match play was challenging.

24. Associated Press, "Day Leads Jackson by 29 Points," *St. Louis Post-Dispatch*, November 10, 1941, 2B.

25. Bruce Bohle, "Jackson's Strong Finish Cuts Day's Lead in Title Pin Match," *St. Louis Star Times*, December 1, 1941. Why insurmountable? If Jackson somehow won 35 of the remaining 40 games, that would make up 30 of his 62-point deficit. To make up the other 32 points, Jackson needed to beat Day by 1600 pins. It was unlikely that Jackson could beat Day by 10 pins a game, let alone 40.

26. Associated Press, "Jackson In Match-Play Round of Individual 10 Pin Tournament," *St. Louis Post-Dispatch*, December 11, 1941, 12.

27. C.H. Beukema, "Joe Sinke's 1,030 Leads All-Star Bowling," *Chicago Tribune*, December 8, 1941, 27.

28. "All-Star Scores," *Chicago Tribune*, December 8, 1941, 27.

29. C.H. Beukema, "Crimmins Regains Lead in Bowling Meet," *Chicago Tribune*, December 10, 1941, 33.

30. C.H. Beukema, "Two Detroit Bowlers Lead All-Star Field," *Chicago Tribune*, December 11, 1941, 27. Field average calculated by author.

31. Estimating the cut is easy: Newton averaged 194.4 for 15 games which projects to a 3888 total for 20 games (194.4 × 20). But if the lanes play significantly harder or easier during the final squad, the estimate may change substantially.

32. "All-Star Bowling Scores," *Chicago Tribune*, December 11, 1941, 30.

33. I learned addition long before kindergarten by keeping my bowling score, achieved by rolling a toy ball knocking down plastic pins in my basement. My ever-patient grandma Anna checked my math and served as my pinboy.

34. "All-Star Bowling Scores," December 11, 1941, 30.

35. Beukema, "Two Detroit Bowlers Lead," 27.

36. "Crimmins Earns Right to Bowl Day for Title," *Chicago Tribune*, December 15, 1941, 29.

37. C.H. Beukema, "Widen Scope of All-Star Tenpin Play for 1942," *Chicago Tribune*, December 16, 1941, 25.

38. Dick Davis, "Well, Bowl Me Over," *Appleton* [WI] *Post-Crescent*, December 16, 1941, 15.

39. C.H. Beukema, "Andy Varipapa, National Star, Is in Charge," *Chicago Tribune*, February 18, 1942, 21; "Varipapa Scores Bowling Success," *Chanute Field Wings* (Champaign, IL), November 28, 1942, 18; C.H. Beukema, "Andy at Great Lakes," *Chicago Tribune*, November 26, 1942, 41. The Hale American campaign was designed to improve the overall physical fitness of Americans,

40. "War-Bond Sales Top All Marks," *Sunday Herald-Leader* (Lexington, KY), November 1, 1942, 7; Lou E. Cohen, "Stars of Diamond in Pin Exhibition," *Brooklyn Eagle*, September 18, 1942, 15; Lou E. Cohen, "Varipapa Opens Benefit Bowling Series Tonight," *Brooklyn Eagle*, June 5, 1942, 17.

Chapter 12

1. Sports Reference LLC, "Yearly League Leaders & Records for Oldest," Baseball-Reference.com, 2023, https://www.baseball-reference.com/leaders/Oldest_leagues.shtml; Sports Reference LLC, "Yearly League Leaders & Records for Youngest," Baseball-Reference.com, 2023, https://www.baseball-reference.com/leaders/Youngest_leagues.shtml. A total of 538 players appeared in MLB games in 1944: 33 were age 38 or older, 11 were age 17 or under. Forty-six-year-old pitcher Horace Lisenbee appeared in 31 games for the Reds in 1945, a year after 15-year-old Joe Nuxhall appeared for them. Most famously, outfielder Pete Gray, who lost his left arm in a childhood accident, played in 77 games for the St. Louis Browns in 1945.

2. Gary Bedingfield, "Baseball in World War II," Baseball in Wartime, 2022, https://www.baseballinwartime.com/baseball_in_wwii/baseball_in_wwii.htm; Todd Neikirk, "These 8

Notes—Chapter 12

Baseball Hall of Famers Served During World War II," *War History Online*, March 4, 2022, https://www.warhistoryonline.com/war-articles/hall-of-famers-wwii.html.

3. Gary Bedingfield, "Baseball's Greatest Sacrifice—World War II Deaths," Baseball in Wartime, 2018, https://www.baseballsgreatestsacrifice.com/world_war_ii.html.

4. Pro Football Hall of Fame, "Football's Wartime Heroes," Pro Football Hall of Fame, 2021, https://www.profootballhof.com/news/2005/01/footballs-wartime-heroes; Thalia Ertman, "Football and the NFL During World War II," Friends of the National WWII Memorial, September 13, 2019, https://www.wwiimemorialfriends.org/blog/football-and-the-nfl-during-world-war-ii.

5. Ray Nelson, "Pin Boy Shortage Biggest Bowling Worry," *St. Louis Star-Times*, October 14, 1943, 22.

6. Associated Press, "War Marks Strike on Bowling Gear," *New York Times*, January 31, 1943

7. Ed Olly, "Of All Things," *Daily Home News* (New Brunswick, NJ), September 30, 1943, 10.

8. Olly, "Of All Things," 10.

9. Olly, "Of All Things," 10.

10. "Varipapa Entertains Big Crowd," *Battle Creek Enquirer and News*, February 5, 1942, 19; C.H. Beukema, "School Opens Tomorrow for Chicago Bowlers," *Chicago Tribune*, March 1, 1942, part 2, 5; C.H. Beukema, "Varipapa Will Open Bowling Classes Today," *Chicago Tribune*, November 23, 1942, 23.

11. Miller, *The Bowlers' Encyclopedia*, 32–33.

12. "Crimmins Gets 1,801; Shatters Day's ABC Mark," *Chicago Tribune*, May 10, 1942, 26. At 202.62, Andy's 10-year average was less than a pin behind Johnny Crimmins (203.38) and Ned Day (203.12).

13. Miller, *The Bowlers' Encyclopedia*, 38.

14. Fritz Howell, "ABC to Cut 1943 Tourney to 4,500 Teams," *Dayton Sunday Journal-Herald*, April 19, 1942, sports, 3.

15. United Press International, "Call Off Bowling Congress for Duration," *Akron Beacon Journal*, November 19, 1942, 31.

16. Miller, *The Bowlers' Encyclopedia*, 32–33.

17. "Chicago Says Sad Farewell to Auditorium," *Chicago Tribune*, August 1, 1941, 1.

18. "Chicago Says Sad Farewell," 1.

19. "City to Operate Auditorium as Service Center," *Chicago Tribune*, August 31, 1942, 13.

20. C.H. Beukema, "All-Star Tourney to Open Service Alleys," *Chicago Tribune*, September 4, 1942, 25.

21. C.H. Beukema, "Bowling Centers Await Start of All-Star Trials," *Chicago Tribune*, October 23, 1942, 23.

22. Lou E. Cohen, "Stars of Diamond in Pin Exhibition," *Brooklyn Eagle*, September 18, 1942.

23. Ruffolo, "The Andy Varipapa Story," 8–6.

24. Ruffolo, "The Andy Varipapa Story," 8–6.

25. Clifford Kirkpatrick, *Can War Marriages Be Made to Work?* (Washington, D.C.: United States Army Division of Information and Education, 1944), https://www.historians.org/about-aha-and-membership/aha-history-and-archives/gi-roundtable-series/pamphlets/em-30-can-war-marriages-be-made-to-work-(1944).

26. "Constance Varipapa Weds Lt. Cornacchia," *Brooklyn Eagle*, October 18, 1942, 15.

27. Ruffolo, "The Andy Varipapa Story," 8–6, 8–7.

28. C.H. Beukema, "Andy at Great Lakes," *Chicago Tribune*, November 26, 1942, 41.

29. C.H. Beukema, "Bomar Leads All-Star Field into Bowling Tourney Today," *Chicago Tribune*, December 11, 1942, 33.

30. C.H. Beukema, "Schwoegler Wins National Bowling Title," *Chicago Tribune*, December 14, 1942, 23.

31. C.H. Beukema, "Bowlers Wend Thumb-Sore Homeward Way," *Chicago Tribune*, December 15, 1942, 25.

32. Carl Baumgartner, "Tenpin Topics," *Cincinnati Enquirer*, January 11, 1942, 26.

33. Jimmy Smith, "Jimmy Smith Tells How to Care for the Hands While Bowling," *St. Louis Post-Dispatch*, November 29, 1925, 21; Joe Wilman, "How to Treat Sore Thumb to Prevent Infections," *Rochester Democrat and Chronicle*, February 27, 1960, 13; Dick Weber and Patty Costello, "Bowling Tips: The Sore Thumb," *Scrantonian* (Scranton, PA), January 20, 1980, D8.

34. Jack Patterson, "'Raw' Talent Making Roth Real Dreamer," *Akron Beacon Journal*, February 7, 1975, 18; Chuck Pezzano, "Roth Shreds His Thumb . . . and the Bowling Pins," *Courier-News* (Bridgewater, NJ), February 18, 1978, B-27; Associated Press, "Ugly Thumb, Beautiful Bankroll," *Sunday Call-Chronicle* (Allentown, PA), December 31, 1978, C-8.

35. Pezzano, "Roth Shreds His Thumb," B-27.

36. "Strikes to Spare," *Lexington [KY] Leader*, October 23, 1942, 8. Thanks to Chris Keller's "Bowlers Tape," patented in 1982, today bowlers use pre-cut tape to make micro-adjustments to their thumbhole.

37. Petersen Classic, *Louis P. Petersen Championship*.

38. Schmidt, *The Bowling Chronicles*, 18; "Koepp Captures Diamond Medal Bowling Meet," *Chicago Tribune*, November 9, 1943, 25.

39. "Varipapa Wins," *Daily News* (New York), May 25, 1943, 45.

40. J.R. Schmidt, "Landgraf Classic," *Dr. Jake's Bowling History Blog*, May 14, 2020, https://bowlinghistory.wordpress.com/2020/05/14/landgraf-classic-bowling-tournament-new-york-list-of-champions/.

41. Paul Gould, "Life Is Just One Grand Tour After Another for Andy Varipapa, Bowling's Ambassador," *Brooklyn Eagle*, April 11, 1943, 26.

42. Andy Varipapa II, email message to author, March 18, 2023.

43. Ruffolo, "Andy Varipapa Biography," 6–2.

44. Ruffolo, "Andy Varipapa Biography," 6–3.

45. Beukema, "School Opens Tomorrow," part 2, 5; "Final Class Sets Attendance Record for Bowling School," *Nassau Daily Review-Star* (Freeport, NY), April 2, 1941, 16.
46. Lester Rose, "Andy the Great," *Daily News* (New York), August 8, 1943, 31.
47. Gordon J. White, Jr., "Bowling's Gentle Man," *New York Times*, September 8, 1959, 47.
48. Ed Buckley, "Down the Alley," *Newsday* (Hempstead, NY), November 4, 1943, 32. Like many top bowlers employed by Long Island aerospace companies, Young's duties included representing Liberty Aircraft at bowling tournaments during the year.
49. Grasso and Hartman, *Historical Dictionary of Bowling*, 308.
50. Ed Buckley, "Down the Alley," *Newsday* (Hempstead, NY), November 9, 1943, 20.
51. "Varipapa Defeats Young in Match by 755 Pins," *Newsday* (Hempstead, NY), November 30, 1943, 20.
52. Charles Bartlett, "All-Star Pin Meet Attracts Nation's Best," *Chicago Tribune*, September 30, 1943, 30.
53. That year, bowlers still rolled 100 games, but a three-game position round roll off was added to accommodate television. In 1971, the BPAA renamed the tournament the U.S. Open. Qualifying and match play rounds were cut to 56 games and the traditional five-person stepladder decided the champion.
54. "All-Star Bowling Scores," *Chicago Tribune*, December 8, 1943, 33.
55. "All-Star Bowling Scores," *Chicago Tribune*, December 9, 1943, 28.
56. Mort Luby, "Three Detroiters Fail to Survive 12-Game Play," *Detroit Times*, December 9, 1943, 21. Modern bowling centers use infrared lights to detect fouls, but back in 1943, a judge sat in a chair perpendicular to the foul lines and called fouls as needed.
57. Fred Bujack accepted the alternate position and joined the finals after Mort Lindsey was forced to withdraw due to a sore thumb. Bujack averaged 206.6, higher than everyone but champion Ned Day. He collected $200, and had it not been for the 25-point penalty assessed to the alternate, would have finished second. See Mort Luby, "'King Ned' Tops All," *Detroit Evening Times*, December 13, 1943, 20.
58. Charles Bartlett, "Ned Day Regains National Bowling Crown," *Chicago Tribune*, December 13, 1943, 25.
59. Grasso and Hartman, *Historical Dictionary of Bowling*,
60. "Dies in Auto Crash," *Daily News* (New York), December 18, 1943, 5.
61. Ed Buckley, "Down the Alley," *Newsday* (Hempstead, NY), January 29, 1944, 15.
62. "Where To Go Bowling," advertisement, *Newsday* (Hempstead, NY), September 29, 1944, 30.
63. Ruffolo, "Andy Varipapa Biography," 6–4.
64. Ruffolo, "Andy Varipapa Biography," 6–4.
65. Ruffolo, "Andy Varipapa Biography," 6–4.
66. Lorraine V. Ruffolo, "Summers" (unpublished manuscript, 1960), 1, Varipapa Family Papers, private collection.
67. J.R. Schmidt, "Complete All-Americans to 1950," *Dr. Jake's Bowling History Blog*, March 9, 2011, https://bowlinghistory.wordpress.com/2011/03/09/complete-all-americans/; "Burton on All-America," *St. Louis Post-Dispatch*, April 27, 1944, 20.
68. "Titlists to Contest in Benefit Match," *Daily Argus* (Mount Vernon, NY), May 11, 1944, 16.
69. Charles Bartlett, "Ned Day Will Open Bowling School Oct. 12," *Chicago Tribune*, September 22, 1944, 29
70. United Press International, "Ned Day Trails Paul Krumske," *Kenosha Evening News*, November 20, 1944, 8; Charles Bartlett, "Krumske Wins National Pin Duel with Day," *Chicago Tribune*, November 27, 1944, 19.
71. "Gibson Paces Qualifiers in Bowling Tourney in Chicago," *Herald-News* (Passaic, NJ), December 7, 1944, 25
72. Charles Bartlett, "Small Leads All-Star Meet for 16 Games," *Chicago Tribune*, December 8, 1944, 27.
73. Charles Bartlett, "Buddy Bomar Wins All-Star Bowling Title," *Chicago Tribune*, December 11, 1944, 17.
74. Schmidt, *The Bowling Chronicles*, 48.
75. Grasso and Hartman, *Historical Dictionary of Bowling*, 79.
76. Charles Bartlett, "3 Ring Tenpin Marathon Will End Tomorrow," *Chicago Tribune*, February 10, 1945, 18.
77. Al Del Greco, "At Random in Sportdom," *Bergen Evening Record* (Hackensack, NJ), February 16, 1945, 16.
78. Harold Kahl, "Sparing No Pins," *Detroit Times*, April 1, 1945, part 2, 3.
79. Associated Press, "Varipapa Takes Lead," *Nashville Banner*, March 19, 1945, 10
80. "Buddy Bomar Whips Varipapa in Match," *Capital Times* (Madison, WI), April 2, 1945, 12.
81. "Varipapa, Young Outbowl Morris and Bud Bomar," *Binghamton [NY] Press*, May 19, 1945, 11; W.W. Edgar, "Norris and Bomar Watch Deficit Mount to 849 Pins," *Detroit Free Press*, May 21, 1945, 12. Bomar did come back to average 200 for the 21 remaining games at Baldwin.
82. "Varipapa and Young Finish in Tie for N.B.A. Classic Title," *Nassau Daily Review-Star*, May 24, 1945, 20.
83. United Press International, "Norris Rolls 300—Varipapa, Young, Pick Up Marbles," *Brooklyn Eagle*, May 28, 1945, 11.
84. Lorraine V. Ruffolo, "Long Island Championship" (unpublished manuscript, 1960), Varipapa family papers, private collection.
85. Bob Stirrat, "Varipapa Beats Young by 3 Pins for N.B.A. Crown," *Nassau Daily Review-Star*, June 11, 1945, 12.

Chapter 13

1. Sports Reference LLC, "Major League Miscellaneous Year-by-Year Averages and Totals," Baseball-Reference.com, 2023, https://www.baseball-reference.com/leagues/majors/misc.shtml; Sports Reference LLC, "1946 NFL Attendance Data," Pro-Football-Reference.com, 2023, https://www.pro-football-reference.com/years/1946/attendance.htm; Sports Reference LLC, "1945 NFL Attendance Data," Pro-Football-Reference.com, 2023, https://www.pro-football-reference.com/years/1945/attendance.htm.
2. "1946 NFL Attendance Data."
3. Charles Bartlett, "World Series in Bowling Starts Next Saturday," *Chicago Tribune*, November 25, 1945, part 2, 5.
4. "All-Star Bowling Scores," *Chicago Tribune*, December 3, 1945, 24.
5. Charles Bartlett, "Ohio Bowler Takes Lead in Tribune Meet," *Chicago Tribune*, December 4, 1945, 19; Charles Bartlett, "Walter Ward Keeps All-Star Bowling Lead," *Chicago Tribune*, December 5, 1945, 31.
6. Charles Bartlett, "Bomar Begins Title Defense This Morning," *Chicago Tribune*, December 6, 1945, 27.
7. Charles Bartlett, "Joe Wilman Bowls into All-Star Lead," *Chicago Tribune*, December 7, 1945, 35.
8. Bartlett, "Joe Wilman Bowls into All-Star Lead," 35.
9. Charles Bartlett, "Wilman Increases Lead in Pin Tourney," *Chicago Tribune*, December 8, 1945, 17.
10. Charles Bartlett, "Wilman Leads; Decide Pin Title Today," *Chicago Tribune*, December 9, 1945, 33.
11. In a four-game Petersen Point match, a bowler who beats their opponent by 100 pins and wins all four games picks up six points.
12. Charles Bartlett, "Wilman Takes All-Star Bowling Crown," *Chicago Tribune*, December 10, 1945, 27.
13. Bartlett, "Wilman Takes All-Star Bowling Crown," 27.
14. "Cassio Meets Ferrara at Thierry's Thursday," *Sunday Times* (New Brunswick, NJ), February 24, 1946, 15; "Walter Ward Hits 217 Average in Defeating Andy Varipapa by 737," *Sandusky* [OH] *Register Star-News*, February 25, 1946, 11.
15. James Segreti, "Carlson's 1,652 Leads Pin Meet for Third Day," *Chicago Tribune*, February 5, 1946, 20.
16. "Sparando Captures Bowling Sweepstakes," *Sunday Times* (New Brunswick, NJ), March 4, 1946, 8.
17. "Wilman in Eastern Debut Here Saturday," *Nassau Daily Review-Star* (Freeport, NY), March 6, 1946, 16.
18. "Final Standings in A.B.C.," *Detroit Free Press*, May 8, 1940, 22; Lester P. Koelling, "Bowling with Koelling," *Indianapolis News*, March 27, 1945, 9.
19. Franz Wippold, "Champ Wins Top Money in Bowling Event Here," *St. Louis Star-Times*, February 18, 1946, 18.
20. Grasso and Hartman, *Historical Dictionary of Bowling*, 206.
21. Nicholas Hirshon, "A Forgotten Pioneer in Sports Television: Phillies Jackpot Bowling (1959–1960," *American Journalism* 36, no. 2 (2019): 205–207, https://doi.org/10.1080/08821127.2019.1602419.
22. Tom Kouros, "The Other Side of Andy Varipapa," *Bowlers Journal*, October 1984, 28.
23. Maxwell Stiles, "Varipapa's 257 Key to 2nd Crown," *Philadelphia Inquirer*, June 23, 1959, 35.
24. Charlie Tiano, "In the Pocket," *Kingston* [NY] *Daily Freeman*, March 11, 1946, 9.
25. "Varipapa, Sparando Claim 284 Pin Lead," *Nassau Daily Review-Star* (Freeport, NY), April 8, 1946, 13; "Too Tough Twosome," *Nassau Daily Review-Star* (Freeport, NY), April 15, 1946, 15.
26. Chuck Pezzano, "Varipapa—Bowling's All-Time Best," *News Beacon* (Fair Lawn, NJ), September 21, 1984, 14.
27. "New York, Hempstead, Geneva Get Pin Titles," *Rochester Democrat and Chronicle*, May 20, 1946, 30; "Varipapa Steals Bowling Laurels at A.B.C. Meet," *Brooklyn Eagle*, April 30, 1946, 14.
28. Ken Johnson, "Hitting the Headpin," *Windsor* [Ontario, Canada] *Daily Star*, December 12, 1945, 22.
29. "Jersey Kegler Averages 203.6 for 10 ABCs," *Bradford* [PA] *Era*, September 18, 1946, 8. This was Cassio's 10th ABC Championships, so he was previously ineligible for the 10-year-average list.
30. Ed Buckley, "Around the Alleys," *Newsday* (Hempstead, NY), May 28, 1946, 35.
31. Ed Buckley, "Around the Alleys," *Newsday* (Hempstead, NY), June 4, 1946, 29.
32. Buckley, "Around the Alleys," June 4, 1946, 29.
33. "Top Keglers in $1,000 Event," *Tucson Daily Citizen*, August 3, 1946, 8.
34. "Young Annexes $1,000 Prize," *Tucson Daily Citizen*, August 5, 1946, 14.
35. Bob Brachman, "One Prize Pin Event," *San Francisco Examiner*, August 14, 1946, 22.
36. Bob Stirrat, "Sports in Review," *Nassau Daily Review-Star* (Freeport, NY), October 30, 1946, 14.
37. "Wins Bethlehem $1,000 Sweeps with 1,132," *Morning Call* (Allentown, PA), November 11, 1946, 11.
38. Charles Bartlett, "Everything Set in 6th All-Star Bowling Series," *Chicago Tribune*, November 15, 1946, 34.
39. "All-Star Bowling Scores," *Chicago Tribune*, December 2, 1946, 30; "All-Star Bowling Scores," *Chicago Tribune*, December 3, 1946, 36; "Scores in National All-Star Bowling Meet," *Chicago Tribune*, December 4, 1946, 39.
40. Charles Bartlett, "Varipapa Tops All-Star Field Thru First Day," *Chicago Tribune*, December 6, 1946, 37.

41. Bartlett, "Varipapa Tops All-Star Field Thru First Day," 37.
42. Gordon J. White, Jr., "Long-Staying Record," *New York Times*, March 15, 1960, 50. White suggested that Brandt's record was unbreakable, but he could not have foreseen the technological changes that made scoring easier (see Chapter 19). Through the 2021–22 season there have been 40 perfect 900 series and likely hundreds of others that surpassed Brant's once revered 886. See United States Bowling Congress, "Individual Records," USBC Records, accessed January 17, 2023, https://bowl.com/getmedia/915d5f03-543c-4b19-823a-c11e9135cce0/ptindividualrecords-3.pdf.
43. Charles Bartlett, "Brandt Leads All-Star Meet by Four Points," *Chicago Tribune*, December 7, 1946, 22.
44. "Leo Rollick Clings to Fifth Spot," *Los Angeles Times*, December 8, 1946, 22.
45. "All-Star Bowling Scores," *Chicago Tribune*, December 9, 1946, 38
46. "Alley Title to Varipapa," *Lansing State Journal*, December 9, 1946, 11; "You Don't Say," *Dunkirk [NY] Evening Observer*, January 6, 1947, 10.
47. Kalman, "All-Star Andy," 58.
48. Associated Press, "Varipapa Beats Brandt to Win Bowling Title," *St. Louis Post-Dispatch*, December 9, 1946, 20.
49. James Segreti, "Victory Earns Salary Raise for Varipapa," *Chicago Tribune*, December 10, 1946, 37.
50. Segreti, 37.
51. Robertson, "Champion U.S. Trick Shot Bowler," 15. Andy was 41 in 1934 but the article mentions that he is 38.
52. Fay, "Bowling's Talking Machine," 6.
53. Dick Evans, "Best Bowlers in History? Andy Varipapa Belongs," *Miami Herald*, October 24, 1982, 15C.
54. Charles Bartlett, "Varipapa Wins National Bowling Crown," *Chicago Tribune*, December 9, 1946, 37.
55. Associated Press, "Varipapa Beats Brandt," 20.
56. Charles Einstein, "Varipapa Wins Pin Meet," *Hammond [IN] Times*, December 9, 1946, 9; Daniel, "Varipapa Arrives," 18.
57. Hinteroff, "He Couldn't Make the Dodgers," E1.
58. Daniel, "Varipapa Arrives," 18.
59. Billy Sixty, "Better Bowling," *Cincinnati Enquirer*, January 10, 1947, 19.
60. "Billy Sixty," USBC Hall of Fame, accessed January 18, 2023, https://bowl.com/usbc-hall-of-fame/hall-of-famers/billy-sixty.
61. "NBPA Members Honor Varipapa," *Newsday* (Hempstead, NY), December 23, 1946, 41.

Chapter 14

1. Cummins, Tait, "Red Peppers: Hot Sport Chatter," *Cedar Rapids Evening Gazette*, December 22, 1946, sec. 2, 1.
2. "Jersey Kegler Averages 203.6 for Ten ABC's," *Bradford [PA] Era*, September 18, 1946.
3. Andy Varipapa, "Improve Your Bowling," *Morning Call* (Paterson, NJ), February 24, 1947, 20; Andy Varipapa, "Improve Your Bowling," *Morning Call* (Paterson, NJ), February 25, 1947, 20.
4. Varipapa, "Improve Your Bowling," 20.
5. "Flesch Takes Ritz Classic with 1779," *Salt Lake Tribune*, April 28, 1947.
6. "Detroit Keglers Triumph in Ogden Classic," *Ogden [UT] Standard-Examiner*, April 28, 1947, 11.
7. Chuck Pezzano, "Down My Alley," *Morning Call* (Paterson, NJ), October 7, 1953, 28.
8. Chuck Pezzano, "Down My Alley," *Morning Call* (Paterson, NJ), September 2, 1964, 16; "Grazio Castellano," USBC Hall of Fame, accessed March 17, 2023, https://bowl.com/usbc-hall-of-fame/hall-of-famers/grazio-castellano.
9. Don Snyder, "Calm Returns to A.B.C. Following Big Week-End," *Los Angeles Times*, April 8, 1947, 6.
10. Associated Press, "N.Y. Mineralites Capture Lead in American Bowling Congress," *Courier-News* (Bridgewater, NJ), April 18, 1947, 24.
11. United States Bowling Congress, "Andy Varipapa Open Championship History."
12. Don Snyder, "A.B.C. Champs Crowned as Pin Tourney Ends," *Los Angeles Times*, May 13, 1947, 14.
13. "A.B.C. Leaders," *Los Angeles Times*, May 13, 1947, 14.
14. Hampson, "Sports Slants," 14.
15. Stan Cardinet, "Clicking the Maples," *Valley Times* (North Hollywood, CA), April 21, 1947, 8.
16. Hollywood Walk of Fame, "Dave O'Brien," Official Website of the Hollywood Walk of Fame, October 25, 2019, https://walkoffame.com/dave-obrien/.
17. Ruffolo, "Andy Varipapa Biography," 7–3.
18. "Los Angeles Business Men Plan Huge Recreation Center," *Los Angeles Times*, May 23, 1937, part V, 5.
19. *Bowling Tricks*, directed by David Barclay (Culver City, CA: Metro-Goldwyn-Mayer, 1948), 0:30 to 0:49, https://www.youtube.com/watch?v=fzjPcVZRCxA.
20. Ruffolo, "Andy Varipapa Biography," 7–4.
21. *Bowling Tricks*, 8:25 to 9:22.
22. Jim Miley, "Bowler, 81, Still Gets Perfect Strike," *The Long-Islander* (Huntington, NY), January 18, 1973, 6.
23. Bob Brachman, "Varipapa, Bowling King, Arrives; Speaks His Piece," *San Francisco Examiner*, July 31, 1947, 25.
24. Bob Brachman, "Pin Theory Upheld," *San Francisco Examiner*, August 5, 1947, 25.
25. Brachman, "Pin Theory Upheld," 25.
26. "The Greatest," 79.
27. Andy Varipapa, "Letters," *Time*, May 19, 1947, 6, https://time.com/vault/issue/1947-05-19/page/8/.
28. Varipapa, "Letters," 6.
29. "Varipapa, Norris Make All Star Team Again," *Bayonne [NJ] Times*, June 9, 1947, 8.

30. "Buddy Bomar Voted 'Bowler of the Year' With Junie McMahon Occupying 6th Slot," *Bergen Evening Record* (Hackensack, NJ), August 27, 1947, 17.
31. Howard V. Millard, "Bait for Bugs," *Decatur* [IL] *Herald*, August 31, 1947, 14.
32. Art McMahon, "The Sportsman's Corner," *Herald-News* (Passaic, NJ), August 6, 1947, 16.
33. Ed Maurer, "Down the Alley," *Journal-News* (Nyack, NY), August 30, 1947, 6.
34. Robert Phipps, "Jackie's Not First Negro," *Evening World-Herald* (Omaha, NE), September 2, 1947, 11.
35. J.R. Schmidt, "Wrong Foot Louie," *Dr. Jake's Bowling History Blog*, October 12, 2016, https://bowlinghistory.wordpress.com/2016/10/12/wrong-foot-louie-lou-campi-famous-bowler/.
36. Associated Press, "Bowling Marks Set in Tourney," *Tucson Daily Citizen*, November 1, 1947, 6.
37. "Varipapa, Campi Move to First in Pin Doubles," *Chicago Tribune*, November 3, 1947, 35.
38. Associated Press, "Lou and Andy Win Doubles," *Bergen Evening Record* (Hackensack, NJ), November 3, 1947, 20.
39. Associated Press, 20.
40. Bob Brachman, "Champion Pin Entry," *San Francisco Examiner*, May 28, 1946, 18.
41. Ruffolo, "Andy Varipapa Biography," 7–5.
42. "Auditorium Is Bought by College," *Chicago Tribune*, August 6, 1946, 1.
43. Charles Bartlett, "All-Star's 12 Alleys Take Form," *Chicago Tribune*, November 26, 1947, 15.
44. Edgar Williams, "Champion of All Bowlers," *Philadelphia Inquirer*, January 19, 1947, 12.
45. Associated Press, "Johnson Tops Pinmen Gaining 'World Series' Final in Bowling," *Evening Star* (Washington, D.C.), December 11, 1947, C-3.
46. Associated Press, "Johnson Tops Pinmen Gaining 'World Series' Final in Bowling," C-3.
47. Charles Bartlett, "Andy Leads Final Field in Pin Meet," *Chicago Tribune*, December 12, 1947, 41.
48. Associated Press, "Wilman Holds Slim Lead Over Varipapa in Tourney," *Bergen Evening Record* (Hackensack, NJ), December 13, 1947, 13.
49. Associated Press, "Joe Wilman Keeps Lead," *San Francisco Examiner*, December 14, 1947, 28.
50. Byron Schoeman, "Andy the Great," *Bowling*, January 1982, 6.
51. "I'm a Man, Huh?" 58.
52. Schoeman, "Andy the Great," 6.
53. *Dreamer*, dir. by Noel Nosseck (Hollywood: Twentieth Century Fox, 1979), https://www.youtube.com/watch?v=ZDZO-Qm0OzE, was Hollywood drama about bowling. Unlike comedies *Kingpin* and *The Big Lebowski*, *Dreamer* was a critical and financial flop. In the climactic scene, young Harold Nuttingham (played by Tim Matheson), throws a strike to defeat reigning champion Johnny Watkin (played by Dick Weber) to win the "Grand Championship." Why Dick Weber did not appear as himself is one of cinema's great mysteries.
54. Andy Varipapa with Lorraine V. Ruffolo, "The Championship Crown" (unpublished manuscript, 1960), 24–25, Varipapa Family Papers, private collection.
55. Charles Curtis, "Here's the Story Behind Pete Weber's Famous 'Who Do You Think You Are? I Am!' Moment," *For the Win* (blog), February 26, 2020, https://ftw.usatoday.com/2020/02/pete-weber-who-do-you-think-you-are-origin; "I'm a Man, Huh?" 58.
56. Varipapa with Ruffolo, "The Championship Crown," 25.
57. The BPAA renamed the All-Star the U.S. Open in 1971.

Chapter 15

1. Berni Fisher, "Champ Varipapa to Get Hometown Honors Monday," *Newsday* (Hempstead, NY), December 26, 1947, 2.
2. Dick Clemente, "Around the Alleys," *Newsday* (Hempstead, NY), February 21, 1948, 17.
3. Dick Clemente, "Around the Alleys," *Newsday* (Hempstead, NY), February 24, 1948, 36.
4. S&Q Clothiers, "World Famous Bowler Andy Varipapa Picks a Winner," advertisement, *Enid* [OK] *Morning News*, October 9, 1951, 2.
5. "Wansa's 1716 Wins Petersen Tenpin Classic," *St. Louis Post-Dispatch*, February 9, 1948, 8.
6. Associated Press, "Varipapa Fails in A.B.C. Tourney," *Herald-News* (Passaic, NJ), April 26, 1948, 19.
7. Associated Press, 19; "Varipapa Fails to Roll a 600," *Racine* [WI] *Journal-Times*, April 26, 1948; Associated Press, "Varipapa Blows Chance in ABC," *Shreveport* [LA] *Journal*, April 26, 1948, 11.
8. Miller, *The Bowlers' Encyclopedia*, 38.
9. Bob Zellner, "The-Right-Angle," *Newsday* (Hempstead, NY), May 5, 1948, 48.
10. "Varipapa Accepts Falcaro Challenge," *Newsday* (Hempstead, NY), May 14, 1948, 60.
11. Ed Maurer, "Down the Alley," *Journal-News* (Nyack, NY), May 8, 1948, 6.
12. Dick Clemente, "Varipapa Declares Match Conditions," *Newsday* (Hempstead, NY), June 1, 1948, 33.
13. Dick Clemente, "Around the Alleys," *Newsday* (Hempstead, NY), June 14, 1949, 44.
14. Clemente, 44.
15. A few years later, Heineman's was renamed Mid-Isle Lanes and stood on Peninsula Boulevard until it closed in the early 1990s. A self-storage facility now occupies the site.
16. Dick Clemente, "Graz Wins Open Tourney; Tops Sis in Climax Text," *Newsday* (Hempstead, NY), June 14, 1948, 12.
17. Dick Clemente, "Sis Mantovani Hits 300; 298 for Frank Varipapa," *Newsday* (Hempstead, NY), May 28, 1948, 62.
18. Dick Clemente, "'Like Father, Like Son,' Proverb True in Frank Varipapa's Case," *Newsday* (Hempstead, NY), April 12, 1951, 58.

19. Clemente, "Graz Wins Open Tourney," 12.
20. "Miss Lorraine Varipapa Weds Robert R. Ruffolo," *Newsday* (Hempstead, NY), June 13, 1949, 31.
21. "Varipapa Only Bowler Again on All-America," *St. Louis Post-Dispatch*, June 13, 1948, 2D.
22. "Varipapa Named Bowler of Year; Wilman Second," *St. Louis Post-Dispatch*, August 31, 1948, 2B.
23. BPAA and Tribune Charities, "Where's Andy?" advertisement, *Chicago Tribune*, December 6, 1948, part 4, 2.
24. "All-Star Bowling Scores," *Chicago Tribune*, December 16, 1948, part 4, 3.
25. "All-Star Bowling Scores," December 15, 1948, part 4, 4; "All-Star Bowling Scores," *Chicago Tribune*, December 16, 1948, part 4, 3.
26. "All-Star Bowling Scores," *Chicago Tribune*, December 16, 1948, part 4, 3.
27. "All-Star Bowling Scores," *Chicago Tribune*, December 17, 1948, part 4, 1.
28. Schmidt, *The Bowling Chronicles*, 17–18.
29. Roy Edwards, "74-Year-Old Plans Long Bowling Tour," *Fort Worth Star-Telegram*, March 29, 1957, 19.
30. Schmidt, *The Bowling Chronicles*, 17–18.
31. Charles Bartlett, "Varipapa Gains All-Star Tourney Lead," *Chicago Tribune*, December 18, 1948, part 2, 1.
32. "Schwoegler Still in Second Place," *Wisconsin State Journal* (Madison), December 19, 1948, 37.
33. "All-Star Bowling Scores," *Chicago Tribune*, December 20, 1948, part 3, 2.
34. Gianmarc Manzione, "The Gambler: John Handegard," United States Bowling Congress News, May 17, 2010, https://bowl.com/news/the-gambler-john-handegard.
35. Dick Clemente, "Hempstead Alleys Sold to Kuskys by Varipapa," *Newsday* (Hempstead, NY), December 24, 1948, 29.
36. Clemente, "Hempstead Alleys Sold to Kuskys by Varipapa," 29.
37. Charles Bartlett, "Son Shines but Papa Varipapa Rolls Only 1365," *Chicago Tribune*, February 1, 1949, part 3, 2.
38. "Campi and Varipapa to Face Bomar-Day Combination in Doubles Match," *Bergen Evening Record* (Hackensack, NJ), February 5, 1949, 13.
39. "Varipapa, Campi Lead," *Detroit Free Press*, February 6, 1949, C-3.
40. "Newark Pair Wins U.S. Title," *Philadelphia Inquirer*, February 7, 1949, 25.

Chapter 16

1. Ila Callaway, "Varipapa Wins 3 Games, Loses 2 in Match Test," *Miami Herald*, March 7, 1949, 18; "Varipapa May Bowl Worthington," *Tampa Daily Times*, March 11, 1949, 14; Clarence Kunick, "World Champion Bowler at YMCA Tonight for Show," *Bogalusa* [LA] *Bulletin*, March 21, 1949, 1.

2. "Vacation and Sports Show at Milwaukee April 2–10," *Kenosha* [WI] *Evening News*, March 31, 1949, 26.
3. Milwaukee Sentinel Sports and Entertainment Show, "Milwaukee's Outstanding Entertainment Value," advertisement, *Wisconsin State Journal* (Madison), April 1, 1949, 33.
4. Associated Press, "Varipapa, Hexed by 10-Pin, Rolls 1,767 All-Events Total," *Rochester Democrat and Chronicle*, April 7, 1949, 36.
5. Associated Press, "Varipapa, Hexed by 10-Pin, Rolls 1,767 All-Events Total," 36.
6. Joe Anzivino, "Up Front in the Sports World," *Honolulu Star-Bulletin*, April 15, 1949, 21.
7. "Varipapa Has Tonight Off; Wahiawa Next Step," *Honolulu Star-Bulletin*, April 16, 1949, 13.
8. Joe Anzivino, "Up Front in the Sports World," *Honolulu Star-Bulletin*, May 9, 1949, 12.
9. Grumman Athletic Association, *Industrial Bowling Tournament Championship 1962* (Bethpage, NY: Grumman Athletic Association, 1962), 5.
10. Grumman Athletic Association, 10–13. Frank's record was shattered the following year by Herbie Player of Liberty who rolled 2,705 (an average of 225.4).
11. "Bowlers Start Match Round," *Cincinnati Post*, October 1, 1947, 21; Charles Bartlett, "Women Accept Bowling Bid," *Chicago Tribune*, October 5, 1949, part 3, 1.
12. Bartlett, "Women Accept Bowling Bid," part 3, 1.
13. "Men's All-Star Bowling Scores," *Chicago Tribune*, December 8, 1949, part 4, 6.
14. Charles Bartlett, "McMahon Keeps Bowling Lead," *Chicago Tribune*, December 9, 1949, part 4, 1.
15. Charles Bartlett, "McMahon Wins Tenpin Title," *Chicago Tribune*, December 12, 1949, part 4, 1.
16. James Segreti, "Mrs. Ladewig Wins Women's Pin Title," *Chicago Tribune*, December 9, 1949, part 4, 1.
17. Schmidt, *The Bowling Chronicles*, 185.
18. Bruce Manell, "Ladewig Leads Top Female Bowlers of the Century," *Post-Star* (Glens Falls, NY), January 6, 2000, C-7; Grasso and Hartman, *Historical Dictionary of Bowling*, 328.
19. Associated Press, "Tom Hennessey's 1651 Stands Up for First Prize of $5000 in Petersen Bowling Classic," *St. Louis Post-Dispatch*, February 6, 1950, 14; "Hennessey, Lippe Retain Tenpin Leads," *Chicago Tribune*, February 4, 1950, part 2, 2.
20. "200 at Boys Town Watch Varipapa," *Evening World-Herald* (Omaha, NE), February 10, 1950, 31; Dick Clemente, "Around the Alleys," *Newsday* (Hempstead, NY), January 3, 1950, 37.
21. Jerry McNerney, "Lubanski, Easter Win Crown," *Courier-Journal* (Louisville, KY), March 27, 1950, sec. 2, 4.
22. Kevin Allen and Del Reddy, *King of the Pins* (Wayne, MI: Victory Entertainment, 2010),

103–106; Ed Lubanski, *Championship Bowling Special*, "Ed Lubanski Goes for Back-to-Back 300s on Live TV" (WPST-TV Miami, June 22, 1959), https://www.youtube.com/watch?v=FXHJL7Gk1sI.

23. Sports Reference LLC, "Ed Lubanski," Baseball-Reference.com, 2023, https://www.baseball-reference.com/register/player.fcgi?id=lubans001edw.

24. Allen and Reddy, *King of the Pins*, 9.

25. Associated Press, "New Tricks Needed by Varipapa," *Cincinnati Enquirer*, May 25, 1950, 22.

26. International News Service, "Varipapa Hits 592 in ABC Bowling," *Herald-News* (Passaic, NJ), May 24, 1950, 37.

27. Carl Reich, "Bowling Notes," *San Francisco Examiner*, July 4, 1950, 21.

28. Art Knighton, "Keg Champ Shows Fans," *Oakland Tribune*, July 8, 1950, 12.

29. "Tow Modestans Top Doubles in Peach Bowling Tourney," *Modesto [CA] Bee*, July 10, 1950, 17.

30. "Large Crowd Sees Opening of New Bowling Layout," *Plainfield [NJ] Courier-News*, August 2, 1950, 54.

31. "Schwoegler and Varipapa Take 331-Pin Lead," *Wisconsin State Journal* (Madison), September 18, 1950, 11.

32. Dick Peters, "Easter, 67, and Lubanski, 21, Retain Pin Laurels," *Detroit Free Press*, September 25, 1950, 27.

33. "Campi, Mrs. Tencza Out of National Pin Finals," *Herald-News* (Passaic, NJ), December 14, 1950, 47.

34. Charles Bartlett, "Hoover Wins National Pin Title," *Chicago Tribune*, December 18, 1950, part 6, 1.

35. Charles Bartlett, "All-Star Pin Meet 10 Year Marks Listed," *Chicago Tribune*, December 6, 1951, part 6, 6. The article incorrectly stated that Andy made eight finals, but he made only seven. He missed the cut in 1941, 1943, and 1950.

36. Lou Erb, "Colorful Andy Varipapa Singled Out for Third All-Star Award of Merit," *Sunday Call-Chronicle* (Allentown, PA), January 13, 1963, D-6.

37. "Varipapa Disappoints with 1,763 at A.B.C.," *Brooklyn Eagle*, April 16, 1951, 15.

38. "Varipapa Thrills Nearly 500 With Pin Demonstration," *Mason City [IA] Globe-Gazette*, April 20, 1950, 9.

39. "Wilman Honored in Bowling 'Hall,'" *St. Cloud [MN] Times*, April 23, 1951, 13.

40. "Wilman Honored in Bowling 'Hall,'" 13.

41. "Marino Voted Bowler of Half Century," *Wisconsin State Journal* (Madison), May 10, 1951, sec. 2, 9.

42. Writers listed 15 bowlers on their ballot; first place was worth 15 points, second 14, and so on. To earn 995 votes, Marino must have received at least 43 first-place votes and 25 seconds. If some voters ranked him third or lower, he received more than 43 first-place votes.

43. "Joe, Andy Among 'Greatest,'" *Nassau Daily Review-Star* (Freeport, NY), May 12, 1951, 8.

44. Bill Hengen, "Leading State Bowlers Match 'Champs' Monday," *Minneapolis Tribune*, May 27, 1951, S-5.

45. "5 Mill Citians Survive in ABC Tourney," *Minneapolis Tribune*, May 29, 1951, 15; "Harich Upsets Day; Local Keglers Star," *Minneapolis Tribune*, May 30, 1951, 18.

46. Ted Peterson, "Jouglard Topples Wilman 662–612," *Minneapolis Tribune*, June 3, 1951, 37.

47. United Press International, "Lee Hailed as Bowler of the Year," *Detroit Free Press*, June 5, 1951, 20.

48. Andy Varipapa II, email message to author, March 18, 2023.

49. Kogan, *Brunswick: The Story*, 70.

50. International Bowling Museum & Hall of Fame, "Get a Grip," Behind the Scenes of Bowling, accessed April 13, 2023, https://www.bowlingheritage.com/item/get-a-grip/.

51. Jerry McNerney, "Schwoegler's Form Makes a Hit Here," *Courier-Journal* (Louisville), December 18, 1949, sec. 2, 6.

52. Dick Hyland, "Behind the Line," *Los Angeles Times*, August 19, 1940, 23.

53. International Bowling Museum & Hall of Fame, "Doc's Diagram," Behind the Scenes of Bowling, accessed April 13, 2023, https://www.bowlingheritage.com/item/docs-diagram/.

54. Dick Clemente, "Around the Alleys," *Newsday* (Hempstead, NY), May 5, 1951, 25.

55. "ABC Sec Heads Over-Seas Clinic," *Sidney [OH] Daily News*, August 13, 1951, 8.

56. Pezzano, "Andy Varipapa: Hero or Villain," 23.

57. Andy Varipapa with Lorraine V. Ruffolo, "Varipapa Bowls Abroad" (unpublished manuscript, 1960), 1, Varipapa Family Papers, private collection.

58. Hank Fishbach, "Top U.S. Bowlers, Varipapa, Norris to Tour EUCOM," *Stars and Stripes*, August 24, 1951, European edition, 11; "Local Bowler Overseas," *Montgomery [AL] Advertiser*, September 23, 1951, C-4. Andy always made it a point to say he performed in Africa, and this article proves that he did so, for at least a day.

59. Schmidt, *The Bowling Chronicles*, 177.

60. Varipapa with Ruffolo, "Varipapa Bowls Abroad," 3.

61. Varipapa with Ruffolo, "Varipapa Bowls Abroad," 3.

62. Schmidt, *The Bowling Chronicles*, 177.

63. "Joe Falcaro Dead," 88.

64. Ed Comerford, "Around the Alleys," *Newsday* (Hempstead, NY), September 8, 1951, 24.

65. Ed Maurer, "Down the Alley," *Journal-News*, September 15, 1951, 20; Charles J. Tiano, "Sports," *Kingston [NY] Daily Freeman*, September 11, 1951, 14; Al Del Greco, "For the Record," *Bergen Evening Record* (Hackensack, NJ), September 10, 1951, 8.

66. Comerford, "Around the Alleys," 24.

67. "Varipapa Still Clings to All-Star Chance,"

Newsday (Hempstead, NY), December 12, 1951, 96.

68. Charles Bartlett, "Mrs. Ladewig, McMahon Win All-Star Titles," *Chicago Tribune*, December 17, 1951, part 4, 1.

69. Tony Wurzer, "Blazing Finish Wins Bowling Event, Title Chance for McMahon, Brosius," *Buffalo Evening News*, March 31, 1952, 28.

70. Aaron Smith, "Glenn Allison Makes 71st Appearance at USBC Open Championships," USBC News, May 16, 2023, https://bowl.com/news/glenn-allison-makes-71st-appearance-at-usbc-open-championships. Through the 2023 Open Championships, Glenn Allison trails Lillard by just 1,134 pins. If Allison participates in the 2024 tournament—he will be 93 at the time—he can break Lillard's record.

71. Keith Brehm, "It's This Way," *Racine* [WI] *Journal-Times*, April 14, 1952, 13.

72. Brehm, "It's This Way," 13.

73. Andy Varipapa and Nick Tronsky, *Andy Varipapa's Quick Way to Better Bowling*, ed. Tom McLaughlin (Garden City, NY: Garden City Books, 1952).

Chapter 17

1. Early Television Foundation, "Postwar American Television: Estimated U.S. TV Sets and Stations," Early Television Museum, accessed April 18, 2023, https://www.earlytelevision.org/us_tv_sets.html.

2. United States Department of Commerce, *Statistical Abstract of the United States: 1960* (Washington, D.C.: U.S. Government Printing Office, 1960), 520, https://www.census.gov/library/publications/1960/compendia/statab/81ed.html.

3. Hirshon, "Bowling Headliners," 3.

4. Jim Krupka, "From a Humble Start on TV in 1947," *Morning Call* (Paterson, NJ), February 11, 1990, C12.

5. Mort Luby, Jr., "The Golden Eye of TV," *Bowlers Journal*, November 1983, 126.

6. Bartlett, "Varipapa Gains All-Star Tourney Lead," part 2, 1.

7. "Television," *Chicago Tribune*, December 11, 1949, 10.

8. Early Television Foundation, "Postwar American Television."

9. Hirshon, "Bowling Headliners," 7–11.

10. Hirshon, Bowling Headliners," 12–13.

11. "Day, Andy Pin Champs," *Detroit Free Press*, January 31, 1950, 15.

12. United Press International, "Nagy Rolls Against McMahon," *Daily Times* (Davenport, IA), May 30, 1952, 4-B.

13. "Connie Schwoegler Gains Second Round of ABC Masters," *Wisconsin State Journal* (Madison), June 2, 1952, 11; Associated Press, "Nagy Misses 300 Game in The Masters," *Bergen Evening Record* (Hackensack, NJ), June 3, 1952, 26; United Press International, "Eight Bowlers Undefeated in Masters at ABC," *Portage* [WI] *Daily Register*, June 4, 1952; Associated Press, "Masters Pin Test Looks Like All-Star Classic," *Oshkosh* [WI] *Northwestern*, June 5, 1952, 30.

14. "Tenpin Chatter," *Shreveport* [LA] *Journal*, June 6, 1952, 15.

15. Associated Press, "McMahon, Nagy Are Beaten in Bowling Meet," *St. Louis Post-Dispatch*, June 6, 1952, 3C.

16. Associated Press, "McMahon Needs 3 Wins in a Row," *Bergen Evening Record* (Hackensack, NJ), June 7, 1952, 13.

17. United Press International, "Junie McMahon Upset in Masters Meet," *St. Louis Post-Dispatch*, June 8, 1952, 5E.

18. A.L. Hardman, "Carbide Kegler Describes Fight to Win Masters Title," *Charleston* [WV] *Gazette*, June 15, 1952, 11M.

19. Associated Press, "Taylor Defeats Varipapa for Masters Title," *Chicago Tribune*, June 8, 1952, part 2, 6.

20. Dick Clemente, "Around the Alleys," *Newsday* (Hempstead, NY), June 17, 1952, 51.

21. Hardman, "Carbide Kegler Describes Fight," 11M.

22. Hardman, "Carbide Kegler Describes Fight, 11M.

23. Dick Clemente, "Horn Turns on Blazing Finish to Dethrone Sparando," *Newsday* (Hempstead, NY), June 30, 1952, 39.

24. Al Del Greco, "For the Record," *Bergen Evening Record* (Hackensack, NJ), September 14, 1953, 24.

25. "Signing Contract for Pin Exhibitions," *Montclair* [NJ] *Times*, March 26, 1953, 35.

26. "Eastern Classic Bowling," *Plainfield* [NJ] *Courier-News*, January 2, 1954, 13.

27. Lou Marks, "Andy Varipapa, the Krueger Brewery, and $15,000," *Palm Beach* [FL] *Post*, October 21, 1984, D17.

28. Marks, "Andy Varipapa, the Krueger Brewery, and $15,000."

29. Pezzano, "Down My Alley," October 7, 1953, 28

30. Don Zamarelli, "Right Up Our Alley," *Plainfield* [NJ] *Courier-News*, January 4, 1956, 31.

31. J.R. Schmidt, "Watching a Different Sport," *Bowlers Journal International*, February 2014, 10.

32. J.R. Schmidt, email message to author, April 21, 2023.

33. Sports Reference LLC, "1955 Major League Attendance and Team Age," Baseball-Reference.com, 2023, https://www.baseball-reference.com/leagues/majors/1955-misc.shtml.

34. Sports Reference LLC, "1955 Cincinnati Redlegs Schedule," Baseball-Reference.com, 2023, https://www.baseball-reference.com/teams/CIN/1955-schedule-scores.shtml.

35. Lou Smith, "Reds Rally to Hand St. Louis 7–4 Defeat," *Cincinnati Enquirer*, August 21, 1955, 62.

36. Sports Reference LLC, "1955 Cincinnati Redlegs Schedule."

37. Max McCombs, "Kulick Claims Major Crown," *Reno Gazette-Journal*, June 28, 2012, 1D.
38. Bob Johnson, "The Great Outdoors: Not So Great for Bowling," *Bowlers Journal International*, November 2013, 267.
39. Lucas Wiseman, "U.S. Women's Open Champion Crowned," USBC News, June 27, 2012, https://bowl.com/news/u-s-women-39;s-open-champion-crowned.
40. TWC Product and Technology, "Erlanger, KY Weather History," Weather Underground, 2023, https://www.wunderground.com/history/daily/KCVG/date/1955-8-20.
41. John Small, "Varipapa Recalls a Hot Day in Cincinnati," *Cincinnati Enquirer*, March 20, 1974, 32.
42. Don Zamarelli, "Right Up Our Alley," *Plainfield* [NJ] *Courier-News*, November 21, 1955, 29.
43. Steve Hoffman, "Andy's Up to Old Tricks," *Cincinnati Enquirer*, March 29, 1968, 25; Paul Munsey and Cory Suppes, "Crosley Field," Ballparks, last updated October, 2004, https://ballparks.com/baseball/national/crosle.htm.
44. Hoffman, "Andy's Up to Old Tricks," 25; Evans, "Best Bowlers in History?" 1C.
45. Earl Lawson, "Reckless Andy," *Cincinnati Times-Star*, November 9, 1955, 30.
46. Andy Varipapa with Lorraine V. Ruffolo, "The Iron Man" (unpublished manuscript, 1960), 1, Varipapa Family Papers, private collection; Associated Press, "Varipapa in Hospital for Abdominal Exam," *Philadelphia Inquirer*, November 12, 1955, 22.
47. Lorraine V. Ruffolo, "Varipapa vs. the Medical Profession" (unpublished manuscript, 1960), 1, Varipapa Family Papers, private collection.
48. Dick Clemente, "Around the Alleys," *Newsday* (Hempstead, NY), January 14, 1956, 33.
49. "Sports & Medicine: Bowling Champ Still Going Strong at 65," *Scope Weekly* (Kalamazoo, MI), February 20, 1957, 15.
50. Varipapa and Ruffolo, "The Iron Man," 1.
51. Varipapa and Ruffolo, "The Iron Man," 1.
52. Hoffman, "Andy's Up to Old Tricks," 25.
53. Varipapa and Ruffolo, "The Iron Man," 3.
54. Al Palmer, "Try Varipapa's A, B, C of Bowling," *Pensacola* [FL] *News-Journal*, June 13, 1971, 6C.
55. Susan Varipapa, in discussion with the author, March 20, 2023.
56. Andy Varipapa II, in discussion with the author, June 29, 2023.
57. "Sports & Medicine," *Scope Weekly*, 15.
58. Andy Ruffolo, discussion. Gablinger's is forgotten today; most people assume that Miller Lite was the first light beer.
59. Jeff R. Lonto, "Who Was the Man on the Gablinger's Can? Or: The Real 'Father' of Light Beer," *Jeff R. Lonto's Chronicles from the Analog Age* (blog), April 5, 2015, http://theanalogage.blogspot.com/2015/04/who-was-man-on-gablingers-can-or-real.html.
60. Varipapa II, discussion, June 29, 2023.
61. Roger R. Remington, "Scope Magazine, Will Burton and Lester Beall," in *Hidden Treasure: The National Library of Medicine*, ed. Michael Sappol (New York: Blast Books, 2012), 210–13, https://circulatingnow.nlm.nih.gov/2018/11/29/scope-magazine-1941-1957/.
62. "Sports & Medicine," *Scope Weekly*, 15.
63. "Sports & Medicine," 15.
64. "Sports & Medicine," 15.
65. United Press International, "675 is Best Effort in ABC Competition," *Cincinnati Enquirer*, May 7, 1956, 47.
66. Don Zamarelli, "Right Up Our Alley," *Plainfield* [NJ] *Courier-News*, March 21, 1956, 30.
67. Chuck Pezzano, "Down My Alley," *Morning Call* (Paterson, NJ), March 12, 1956, 14; Chuck Pezzano, "Down My Alley," *Morning Call* (Paterson, NJ), April 12, 1956, 22.
68. Lester P. Koelling, "Bowling with Koelling," *Indianapolis News*, January 29, 1957, 13.
69. Associated Press, "Andy Varipapa Elected to Bowling Hall of Fame," *Racine* [WI] *Journal-Times*, February 17, 1957, 31.
70. Dick Clemente, "Around the Alleys," *Newsday* (Hempstead, NY), February 16, 1957, 42.
71. Clemente, 42.
72. Van Fleet, "At 69, He's Still Hot," 15.

Chapter 18

1. Andrew Hurley, *Diners, Bowling Alleys, and Trailer Parks: Chasing the American Dream in Postwar Consumer Culture* (New York: Basic Books, 2001), 140.
2. Complete accounts of the pinsetter revolution are in Hurley, *Diners, Bowling Alleys*, 139–150; Weiskopf, *The Perfect Game*, 66–77; and Kogan, *Brunswick: The Story*, 60–67.
3. Weiskopf, *The Perfect Game*, 72.
4. Mort Luby, Jr., "Farewell to the Pinboys," *Bowlers Journal*, November 1983, 125.
5. Barry Sparks, *Earl: The Greatest Bowler of All Time* (Chicago: Luby, 2019), 20; Kogan, *Brunswick: The Story*, 96. AMF leased pinsetters for 12 cents per game, roughly the same as what pinboys earned.
6. Hurley, *Diners, Bowling Alleys*, 143.
7. Worth Gatewood, "Set 'Em Up for the Ladies," *Daily News* (New York), March 6, 1955, 94.
8. Gatewood, 95.
9. Victor Kalman, "Starlight on the Alleys," *Sports Illustrated*, December 11, 1955, 52–57, https://vault.si.com/vault/1955/12/12/42387.
10. Andy Varipapa with Lorraine V. Ruffolo, "Passing of the Pinboy" (unpublished manuscript, 1960), 1, Varipapa Family Papers, private collection.
11. Van Fleet, "At 69, He's Still Hot," 15.
12. Varipapa with Ruffolo, "Passing of the Pinboy," 2–3.
13. Miller, *The Bowlers' Encyclopedia*, 220–222.
14. United States Bowling Congress, "History,"

High School, accessed May 10, 2023, https://bowl.com/youth/high-school/history.

15. William R. Conklin, "Tenpin Bowling Finds a Tonic in Electronics," *New York Times*, January 2, 1958, 40.

16. Brunswick, "Brunswick Is Proud," advertisement, *Billboard*, August 26, 1957, 19–20, https://books.google.com/books?id=YSEEAAAAMBAJ.

17. Hirshon, "A Forgotten Pioneer," 197.

18. Hirshon, "A Forgotten Pioneer," 202.

19. Hirshon, "A Forgotten Pioneer," 208.

20. Grasso and Hartman, *Historical Dictionary of Bowling*, 100.

21. Grasso and Hartman, *Historical Dictionary of Bowling*, 327.

22. Associated Press, "Million Dollar Pact," 16.

23. Michael Haupert, "MLB's Annual Salary Leaders Since 1874," *Outside the Lines* 18, no. 1 (Fall 2012): 6, http://sabr.box.com/shared/static/neai4hhtj2j3oaclgzlh.pdf.

24. Pezzano, "The Birth, Rebirth of Andy Varipapa," 30.

25. Hirshon, "A Forgotten Pioneer," 209.

26. "Varipapa Takes $8,000 Jackpot with 9 Strikes," *Bergen Evening Record* (Hackensack, NJ), April 18, 1959, 13. A righthanded bowler aims for the space between the number 1 and 3 pins (the "pocket") to throw a perfect strike. If the ball crosses over to the other side of the headpin and strikes, that is considered a lucky break.

27. Schoeman, "The Fabulous Varipapa," 7.

28. Pezzano, "Andy Varipapa: Hero or Villain," 22.

29. Hirshon, "A Forgotten Pioneer," 209.

30. Hirshon, "A Forgotten Pioneer,"216.

31. Hirshon, "A Forgotten Pioneer," 213–214.

32. William B. Loftus, "Evening Chatter," *Evening News* (Wilkes-Barre, PA), January 25, 1937, 13.

33. "J. Wilbert Sims 1st Negro in World Bowling Meet," *Jet*, December 17, 1959, 56, https://books.google.com/books?id=xa4DAAAAMBAJ.

34. Patricia L. Dooley, "Jim Crow Strikes Again: The African American Press Campaign Against Segregation in Bowling During World War II," *The Journal of African American History* 97, no. 3 (2012): 271, https://doi.org/10.5323/jafriamerhist.97.3.0270.

35. Dooley, "Jim Crow Strikes Again," 286. While dropping the racially exclusionary language, women were not welcome to compete in ABC leagues and tournaments until 1993. Just like the clause pertaining to non-whites, it took the threat of legal action for force the change.

36. "A Shot at $25,000," *Ebony*, April 1960, 85, https://books.google.com/books?id=atLRL7epvskC.

37. Schmidt, *The Bowling Chronicles*, 154–156.

38. Paul Wachter, "He's the Only Active Black Bowler to Have Won a Major Pro Tournament," Andscape, March 21, 2018, https://andscape.com/features/gary-faulkner-only-active-black-pba-bowler-to-have-won-a-major-pro-tournament/.

39. Paul Atkinson, "Varipapa Proves Strikes—Not Age—That Count," *Atlanta Constitution*, November 30, 1960, 38; Jack Kelly, "Sport Topics," *Scranton [PA] Times*, December 17, 1960, 7-A.

40. Schmidt, *The Bowling Chronicles*, 121–122; Bob Sakamoto, "Aurora Bowler Strikes It Rich," *Chicago Tribune*, August 7, 1983, sec. 3, 2. In 1983, pharmacy clerk Scott Mouis won $250,000 ($757,620 in 2023 dollars) in the 1983 American Dream Classic. The tournament paid the record quarter-million-dollar first prize through 1988.

41. Hirshon, "A Forgotten Pioneer," 217.

42. Andy Varipapa II, "Bowl Mart Log, Version 4" (unpublished data, November 27, 2022), Excel file.

43. Varipapa II, "Bowl Mart Log, Version 4."

44. The Bowling Corporation of America, American International Bowling Corporation, and American Recreation Centers were the first of the large multi-unit owners of bowling centers. See Dave Williams, "The Bowling Chain That Started Them All," *California USBC News!* (blog), July 25, 2021, https://calusbc.wordpress.com/2021/07/25/the-bowling-chain-that-started-them-all/.

45. Mort Luby, Jr., "The Professional Influence," *Bowlers Journal*, November 1983, 138.

46. John Archibald, "Eddie Elias: Giving the Pro a Chance to Make a Real Living," *Bowlers Journal*, December 1988, S27.

47. Associated Press, "'Wrong Foot' Campi Wins Empire State Bowling Title," *Poughkeepsie [NY] New Yorker*, May 25, 1959, 14.

48. Grasso and Hartman, *Historical Dictionary of Bowling*, 327.

49. Larry Paladino, "Whatever It Takes," *Bowling Digest*, June 2001, 36–37.

50. Dick Evans, "78 Bowling Leaders Receive Votes in Survey to Pick a Top 20 of All Time," *Bowling Digital* (blog), July 31, 2009, https://www.bowlingdigital.com/bowl/node/6905. Rankings are fickle. *Bowling Digest*, which ranked only bowlers, placed Carter first, Joe Norris second and Andy third. Evans' list dropped Andy to fifth and left out Norris altogether. Don Carter, ninth in the *Bowling Digest* ranking, move to third on Evans' list.

51. Dick Evans, "Dick Weber: This Legend is a Fountain of Youth," *Bowlers Journal*, January 1988, S43.

52. Frank Litsky, "Dick Weber, Early Star and Ambassador of Bowling, Dies at 75," *New York Times*, February 16, 2005, B-9, https://www.nytimes.com/2005/02/16/sports/othersports/dick-weber-early-star-and-ambassador-of-bowling-dies-at.html.

53. Melissa Isaacson, "In Bowling's Heyday, He Was the Kingpin," *Chicago Tribune*, February 15, 2005, 1.

54. Joan Taylor, "Chester Twp. 13-Year-Old Kicks in Door to 700 Club," *Daily Record* (Parsippany, NJ), February 20, 2005, B6.

55. "Varipapa Says," *Elmira [NY] Star-Gazette*, 13.

56. Ben Borowsky, "Hoover, Bluth, Carter 1-2-3," *Bristol* [PA] *Daily Courier*, May 19, 1960, 23.
57. Ben Borowsky, "Lubanski Leads at Fairlanes," *Bristol* [PA] *Daily Courier*, May 18, 1960, 16.
58. Borowsky, "Hoover, Bluth, Carter," 23.
59. Mac Russo, "Sports Review," *Morgan City* [LA] *Review*, August 4, 1960, sec. 2, 6.
60. "Varipapa Injures Leg," *Kansas City Star*, August 21, 1960, 5B.
61. "Record Field to Compete in Bowling Championships," *Arlington Heights* [IL] *Herald*, September 8, 1960, 34.
62. "Hitting the Headpin," *Jersey Journal* (Jersey City, NJ), September 16, 1960, 14.
63. Carl Reich, "Down the Alley," *San Francisco Examiner*, October 27, 1960, sec 4, 4.
64. Ruffolo, "Andy Varipapa Biography."
65. Lorraine V. Ruffolo, letter to George W. Jones, August 11, 1960, Varipapa Family Papers, private collection.
66. George W. Jones, letter to Lorraine V. Ruffolo, October 7, 1960, Varipapa Family Papers, private collection.
67. George W. Jones, letter to Lorraine V. Ruffolo, December 20, 1960, Varipapa Family Papers, private collection.
68. John Walter, letter to Lorraine V. Ruffolo, March 13, 1961, Varipapa Family Papers, private collection.
69. Maly, "A Talking Machine," 15.
70. Andy Ruffolo, discussion.
71. Clyde Bolton, "Varipapa Still Draws 'Em," *Birmingham News*, March 9, 1962, 27.
72. Bolton, "Varipapa Still Draws 'Em," 27.
73. Bill Nunnelley, "Andy Grandaddy of Pro Bowlers, And Still at It," *Birmingham Post-Herald*, March 6, 1962, 6.
74. Gene Warren, "Bill Schaufert Sweeps Lead in Pro Tourney," *Greensboro Daily News*, March 2, 1962, B6.
75. Bolton, "Varipapa Still Draws 'Em," 27.
76. "Andy Varipapa Hurt in Crash," *Cincinnati Post*, March 19, 1962, 4.

Chapter 19

1. Kogan, *Brunswick: The Story*, 96.
2. Kogan, *Brunswick: The Story*, 76.
3. Varipapa II, "Bowl Mart Log, Version 4." The Franklin Square and West Babylon stores remained open but were no longer owned by Varipapa and Lewis.
4. Boyle, "A Guy Named Smith," 36.
5. Jares, "The Poor Man's Tour," 112.
6. Altshul, "Andy Varipapa at 81," 42.
7. Andy Varipapa II, email message to author, June 12, 2023.
8. Nunnelley, "Andy Granddaddy," 6.
9. Jack Altshul, "Heads and Tales," *Newsday* (Hempstead, NY), November 18, 1963, 33.
10. Altshul, "Heads and Tales," 33.
11. "The Hidden Oil Patterns on Bowling Lanes," Vox Almanac.
12. Hy Pesner, "Bowling Is for the Young," *Journal-News* (Nyack, NY), October 24, 1964, 11.
13. Dick Clemente, "Around the Alleys," *Newsday* (Hempstead, NY), April 4, 1950, 55.
14. Charlie Smith, "No Wonder 200-Average Bowlers Are Rare Here," *Miami Herald*, March 13, 1949, 4-D.
15. To accommodate television the top five bowled a single-elimination PBA stepladder format.
16. Jeff Richgels, "Would Winning the 2022 USBC Masters on Sunday Make Norm Duke Bowling's GOAT?" 11thframe.com (blog), April 2, 2022, https://www.11thframe.com/news/article/13448. Richgels is a latter-day Billy Sixty, a veteran bowling writer elected to the USBC Hall of Fame for superior performance.
17. Aaron Smith, "Anthony Simonsen Wins Second USBC Masters Title at 2022 Event," USBC News, April 3, 2022, https://bowl.com/news/anthony-simonsen-wins-second-usbc-masters-title-at-2022-event.
18. Mark London, "Just Paying Attention," *Bowling News*, November 3, 2022, 13, http://www.thebowlingnews.net/uploads/3/4/7/8/34783484/11-03-22_bowling_news-web.pdf.
19. London, "Just Paying Attention," 13.
20. Duke, discussion.
21. United States Bowling Congress, "ABC Honor Scores" (unpublished data, March 8, 2006), Excel file. The data represent certified 300s only. Calculations by author, assuming 100 games per year per member.
22. Dan Barry, "Perfection Made Easy," *New York Times*, April 21, 2000, 25; Michael Salfino, "Bowling Equipment Helps Amateurs Close the Gap With the Pros," *Wall Street Journal*, February 21, 2011, https://www.wsj.com/articles/SB10001424052748704476604576158633690927352.
23. United States Bowling Congress, *The 2021 Annual Report of the United States Bowling Congress* (Arlington, TX: United States Bowling Congress, 2022), https://bowl.com/getmedia/2f76c863-1da1-42e0-8cee-15d2cb6f8c3b/2021_usbcannualreport.pdf; Aaron Smith, email message to author, July 5, 2023.
24. "Andy Varipapa Bowls Perfect Score," A-3; Steve Nagy, Andy Varipapa, and Fred Wolf, *Championship Bowling*, "Andy Varipapa vs Steve Nagy" (NBC, February 15, 1957), 1:45–2:00, https://www.facebook.com/watch/?v=1832085733614094.
25. "Varipapa Rolls 300 Game as Lawler Brothers Win," *Brooklyn Daily Times*, January 6, 1931, 2A; "Five Bowlers Will Get '300' Medals, Varipapa Among Them," *Brooklyn Citizen*, March 31, 1931, 6; Dick Carmody, "Varipapa Was Truly the Kingpin of the Sport," *Newsday* (Melville, NY), September 9, 1984, sports, 26.
26. Some years ago, the USBC replaced the punitive-sounding phrase "sanctioned" with "certified."

27. In Andy's prime, bowling balls were a solid mass of composite material (*Mineralite* was Brunswick's brand name) covered with hard rubber. Modern bowling balls are manufactured with of a variety of materials and are designed with the help of mechanical and chemical engineers. See Phil Regan, "Building a Bowling Ball—Part I," *Bowling This Month*, May 2019, https://www.bowlingthismonth.com/bowling-tips/building-a-bowling-ball-part-1/; United States Bowling Congress, "How a Bowling Ball is Made," accessed December 8, 2022, https://bowl.com/welcome/how-a-bowling-ball-is-made.

28. United States Bowling Congress, "Individual Records," USBC Records, accessed January 17, 2023, https://bowl.com/getmedia/915d5f03-543c-4b19-823a-c11e9135cce0/ptindividualrecords-3.pdf.

29. Adams, "Pin Champ Varipapa," 14B.

30. "Wolf Spreads Out His 3 Straight Perfectos," *Kenosha* [WI] *News*, March 27, 2013, B3.

31. Dick Clemente, "Andy Varipapa—One Bowler to Remember," *Florida Today* (Cocoa, FL), April 7, 1979, 1C.

32. Willie Theis, "Mesquite Bowler Darren Simonds Rolls Up Two Straight Huge Scores," *Spectrum and Daily News* (St. George, UT), October 19, 2021, B1.

33. Evans, "Best Bowlers in History," 15C.

34. Chuck Pezzano, "Allison Getting Benefits from Shooting 900 Series," *Record* (Hackensack, NJ), March 27, 1983, S18.

35. Pezzano, "Allison Getting Benefits from Shooting 900 Series," S18.

36. Salvino, discussion.

37. Jeff Richgels, "Ray Orf was Glenn Allison a Decade Before Allison Became Mr. 900: The Story of the Stunning 890 ABC Turned Down but Paid Off," *11thframe.com* (blog), July 9, 2020, https://11thframe.com/news/article/12203/Ray-Orf-was-Glenn-Allison-a-decade-before-Allison-became-Mr-900.

38. John J. Archibald, "Part-Time Pro Orf Gets Second Shot at $25,000," *St. Louis Post-Dispatch*, December 12, 1974, 32.

39. Archibald, "Part-Time Pro Orf Gets Second Shot at $25,000," 32.

40. Richgels, "Ray Orf was Glenn Allison."

41. "Death Notices: Cardamone—Concetta," *Newsday* (Hempstead, NY), March 14, 1964, 70.

42. Jim Dressel, "Write On!" *Long Island Bowling News* (Levittown, NY), April 4, 1984, 3.

43. "State Recalls Many Borough Auto Licenses," *Standard Union* (Brooklyn, NY), July 25, 1925, 5; "Fined $50 for Drunk Driving," *Newsday* (Hempstead, NY), March 25, 1947, 5.

44. John LaSpina, in discussion with the author, September 22, 2022.

45. "Joseph 'Josh' Veripapa (1893–1965)," Find a Grave, March 28, 2017, https://www.findagrave.com/memorial/177842962/joseph-veripapa.

46. Eric Lees, "Tenpin Bowling," *Liverpool* [UK] *Daily Post*, November 6, 1965, 15; "Andy Keeps on Bowling Along," *Manchester* [UK] *Evening News*, October 26, 1965, 10.

47. Lees, "Tenpin Bowling," 15.

48. Andy Varipapa, "Archive Film 1049422," Huntley Film Archives, filmed 1965, https://www.huntleyarchives.com/preview.asp?image=1049422.

49. "ABC Hall of Famer Looks at London," *Bowling*, April 1966, 42.

50. Chuck Pezzano, "Down My Alley," *Morning Call* (Paterson, NJ), April 1, 1966, 24.

51. Chuck Pezzano, "Down My Alley: Outdoor Bowling," *Morning Call* (Paterson, NJ), October 25, 1968, 24.

52. "President Reorganizes Council: Lovell Named Chairman," *President's Council on Physical Fitness and Sports Newsletter*, October 1970, 1, https://www.google.com/books/edition/Newsletter_President_s_Council_on_Physic/8F1eBCE1SOYC?hl=en&gbpv=1.

53. "President Reorganizes Council," 3–4.

54. Richard Brownell, "Take the Presidents Bowling," *Medium* (blog), April 24, 2018, https://medium.com/@rickbrownell/take-the-presidents-bowling-521bbc475f83; Penny Adams to Helen Smith, "White House Bowling Alley," memorandum, August 14, 1973, box 46, Sheila Weidenfeld Files at the Gerald R. Ford Presidential Library, https://www.fordlibrarymuseum.gov/library/document/0126/1489955.pdf. Three anonymous contributors donated $40,698.95 finance the installation. But with Nixon, nothing was without controversy. One donor was Nixon's close friend, Charles "Bebe" Rebozo, a wealthy Florida real estate developer and banker with reputed mob ties.

55. Jack Leahy, "The Only Varipapa," *Daily News*, October 17, 1971, 24.

56. Palmer, "Try Varipapa's A, B, C," 6C.

57. John Kershaw, "Varipapa's Not Too Old for New Tricks," *Hartford Courant*, November 11, 1978, 9C.

58. *What's My Line?* directed by Lloyd Gross, season 4, week 145 (Viacom, taped October 7, 1971), MP4 recording.

59. Well-known celebrities appeared as "mystery guests" with the panelists blindfolded to keep their identities secret. *What's My Line?* had a diverse mystery guest roster, In the fall of 1971 guests included Ruby Keeler, Jimmy Darren, Frank Zappa, and Joe Frazier (Fandom, "*What's My Line?* [1968] Episode Guide," Mark Goodson Wiki, last modified June 17, 2023, https://markgoodson.fandom.com/wiki/What%27s_My_Line%3F_(1968)/Episode_Guide).

60. "Charles Atlas, the Body-Builder and Weightlifter, Is Dead at 79," *New York Times*, December 24, 1972, 40.

61. Tom Demoretcky, "Andy Varipapa is a Rookie Lefty at 78," *Newsday* (Garden City, NY), September 1, 1969, 48. Right-handed bowlers slide on their left leg, which bears all the bowler's bodyweight when sliding.

62. Kirsch, "For the Record," B-8.

63. Max Liberman, "Veteran Andy Varipapa in Late Switch to Rolling Left-Handed," *Hartford Courant*, July 16, 1970, 57.
64. "Varipapa, 80, and Still Bowling," *Cincinnati Post*, April 9, 1971, 26.
65. Andy Varipapa with Lorraine V. Ruffolo, "Rise of the Left-Handers" (unpublished manuscript, 1969), 1–2, Varipapa Family Papers, private collection.
66. Sparks, *Earl: The Greatest*, 45–59 contains a detailed account of the righty-lefty controversy that plagued the PBA in 1971.
67. Altshul, "Andy Varipapa at 81," 42.
68. Gary Gossett, "Youngsters Short on Time for Entering AJBC Meet," *San Antonio Express*, January 3, 1971, 7-S.

Chapter 20

1. Andy Varipapa with Lorraine V. Ruffolo, "Bowling School" 1 (unpublished manuscript, 1963), Varipapa Family Papers, private collection.
2. Andy Varipapa with Lorraine V. Ruffolo, "Novice Bowler" 1 (unpublished manuscript, 1963), Varipapa Family Papers, private collection.
3. Mike Quinn, "Ageless Andy Sounds Off," *Bowlers Journal*, November 1968, 25.
4. Billy Sixty, "Better Bowling," March 1, 1946, 28.
5. "Varipapa at 81," *Indianapolis Star*, sec. 4, 12.
6. Jack Schmid, "Ball Weight," *Bowling This Month*, October 2013, https://www.bowlingthismonth.com/bowling-tips/ball-weight/. Besides mass and velocity, the ball's angle of attack and revolutions per minute influence hitting power.
7. Varipapa and Tronsky, *Andy Varipapa's Quick Way*, 1.
8. Lou DeFichy, "Bowling Roundup," *Newsday* (Hempstead, NY), August 29, 1959, 33.
9. DeFichy, "Bowling Roundup," 33.
10. Altshul, "Andy Varipapa at 81," 42.
11. Len Ziehm, "Varipapa 'strikes' for a Living since 1904," *Herald-News* (Passaic, NJ), November 7, 1981, 34.
12. Altshul, "Andy Varipapa at 81," 42.
13. Sam Zurich, in discussion with the author, April 6, 2023.
14. Jim Lizzo, in discussion with the author, April 4, 2023.
15. Zurich, discussion.
16. Zurich, discussion.
17. Professional Bowlers Association, "All-Time PBA Tour Champions," PBA National Tour, accessed May 22, 2023, https://www.pba.com/all-time-pba-tour-champions; Professional Bowlers Association, "PBA50/Senior Tour Titles," PBA 50+ Tour, accessed May 22, 2023, https://www.pba.com/pba-tour/pba50-tour/all-time-tour-titles; Bill Vint, "Chris Warren Expands All-Time Regional Titles Lead with 55th Win," USBC News, October 25, 2019, https://bowl.com/news/chris-warren-expands-all-time-regional-titles-lead-with-55th-win.
18. Petraglia, discussion. Petraglia was unsure where the lessons were held but were probably at Mid-Isle (formerly Heineman's) or Hempstead Recreation.
19. "Drift" refers to the how far a bowler's approach deviates from a straight line. Ironically, modern bowlers rely on drift—but in the opposite direction of Petraglia's—to accommodate their big hook balls. But in 1960, instructors preferred that students walked straight to the foul line.
20. Varipapa and Tronsky, *Andy Varipapa's Quick Way*, 21, 34.
21. Petraglia, discussion.
22. Petraglia, discussion
23. Petraglia, discussion.
24. Petraglia, discussion.
25. Petraglia, discussion.
26. Professional Bowlers Association, *50 Greatest Players in PBA History* (Chicago: Luby, 2008); Grasso and Hartman, *Historical Dictionary of Bowling*, 232.
27. George Smith, "Keeping the Past in Mind," *Hartford Courant*, March 20, 1994, E2.
28. John Seaburn, "Petraglia Isn't Unshakable," *Akron Beacon Journal*, March 30, 1971, B3.
29. Smith, "Keeping the Past in Mind," E2.
30. Gianmarc Manzione, "Tale of Two Tours," *Bowlers Journal International*, August 2016, 31.
31. Bowlers to Veterans Link, "Who We Are," Bowlers to Veterans Link—Brightening Veterans Lives, 2023, https://bvl.org/about.
32. *Professional Bowlers Tour*, directed by Jim Jennette, "1978 Long Island Open" (ABC, April 1, 1978), https://www.youtube.com/watch?v=teIGvpRAch8.
33. Petraglia, discussion.
34. Petraglia, discussion.
35. Pezzano, "Andy Varipapa: Hero or Villain," 23.
36. Salvino, discussion.
37. Cal Whitmore, "Adamek Top All-American," *Sunday Dispatch* (Moline, IL), September 13, 1981, 34.
38. Carmody, "Still Bowling Them Over," 80.
39. Joe Lyou, "Fireman Spoils Varipapa's Show," *Los Angeles Mirror*, December 31, 1954, part II, 2; "Television Shows for Today, Monday, and Tuesday," *Baltimore Sun*, December 18, 1955, sec. A, 2.
40. Michael Pollak, "A Broadway Splash," *New York Times*, October 18, 2008, https://www.nytimes.com/2008/10/19/nyregion/thecity/19fyi.html; Associated Press, "46-Pound Girl Can Hoist 450 Pounds," *Asbury Park* [NJ] *Press*, September 18, 1981, D2.
41. Lizzo, discussion.
42. Lizzo, discussion.
43. Lizzo, discussion.
44. Lizzo, discussion.
45. Joe Ruffolo, in discussion with the author, June 2, 2023.
46. Ruffolo, discussion.

47. Ruffolo, discussion; Varipapa, Nagy, and Wolf, "1956 Andy Varipapa vs Steve Nagy," In this episode of *Championship Bowling*, Andy used a similar line at 48:40 when accepting the winner's check from host Fred Wolf.

48. Ratings Ryan, "Weekly Nielsen Ratings: 1981–82 TV Season," *Ratings Ryan* (blog), January 14, 2021, http://www.ratingsryan.com/2021/01/weekly-nielsen-ratings-1981-82-tv-season.html.

49. Ryan; United States Department of Commerce, *Statistical Abstract of the United States: 1982-83* (Washington, D.C.: U.S. Government Printing Office, 1983), part 2, 27, 43, https://www.census.gov/library/publications/1982/compendia/statab/103ed.html. Each rating point was worth 799,000 households, so the minimum audience was 14.1 million (17.6 × 799,000). In 1981, the average U.S. household had 2.82 residents of which 7.7 percent were under five years of age. If half of the average household's residents watched, that translates to 18.35 million viewers (14,100,000 × 1.41 × 0.923).

50. "Blood and Guts," dir. by Charles S. Dubin, *M*A*S*H* (CBS, January 18, 1982), https://www.youtube.com/watch?v=74aPuLKBixg.

51. Lizzo, discussion.

52. Lizzo, discussion.

53. Lizzo, discussion.

54. Marshall Lubin and Andrew Smith, "Twin Peaks," *Newsday* (Melville, NY), September 2, 1995, A7; United States Bowling Congress, "Oddities—Honor Scores," USBC Records, accessed January 17, 2023, https://bowl.com/getmedia/915d5f03-543c-4b19-823a-c11e9135cce0/ptindividualrecords-3.pdf. The professor's calculations may have been off; twins Paul and Patrick Bentley, Jr., duplicated the Lizzo's feat just nine years later.

Chapter 21

1. Altshul, "Andy Varipapa at 81," 42; Cherin, "Varipapa the Magnificent," 57–58.

2. Pezzano, "Andy Varipapa: Hero or Villain," 21.

3. Pezzano, "Andy Varipapa: Hero or Villain," 21.

4. Dick Carmody, "Ridolf, Baker, and Ryan Head for Hall of Fame," *Newsday* (Melville, NY), February 6, 1983, sports, 23.

5. Cherin, "Varipapa the Magnificent," 59.

6. Keller, "Varipapa Knows the Tricks," B7.

7. Chuck Pezzano, "Greats Event Going to Las Vegas," *Record* (Hackensack, NJ), March 30, 1979, C-6.

8. Dick Carmody, "The Season Climaxes with Next Week's LI Open," *Newsday* (Melville, NY), March 7, 1982, sports, 22.

9. LaSpina, discussion. AHRC, based on Long Island, was formerly known as the Association for the Help of Retarded Children.

10. Chuck Pezzano, "Petescola Gains Tourney Berth," *Record* (Hackensack, NJ), October 28, 1977, D-6.

11. Joe Dommershausen, "Bowlers Name Their 10 Greatest of All Time," *Wisconsin State Journal* (Madison), February 26, 1978, sec. 3, 8. While earning 98.6 percent of the vote, it is incomprehensible that three writers did not consider Carter among the 10 best living bowlers.

12. Lou Erb, "Bowling Ranks No. 2 in a Federal Survey," *Sunday Call-Chronicle* (Allentown, PA), May 14, 1978, C-12

13. Chuck Pezzano, "Statistics Prove Strength," *Record* (Hackensack, NJ), May 28, 1978, C-20.

14. It was ironic that Strampe and Weber teamed up given that Andy criticized both early in their careers, Strampe for his tucked pinkie and Weber for his scrawny wrists (Chapter 8).

15. "Hudson Wins Bowling Title," *Akron Beacon Journal*, September 10, 1978, D11.

16. Ken Rush, "Roth is New Bowler of the Year," *Courier-Journal* (Louisville, KY), February 12, 1978, C-12.

17. "Joe Joseph, Partner Capture Tournament," *Lansing State Journal*, September 11, 1978, D1.

18. Dick Evans, "Nostalgia Revived in 'Greatest' Bowl," *Miami Herald*, September 8, 1978, 3-F.

19. Dick Evans, "'Greatest' Tourney Thrilling for All," *Miami Herald*, September 17, 1978, 13-C.

20. Chuck Pezzano, "Old-Timers Give, Get Respect," *Record* (Hackensack, NJ), September 17, 1978, C-18.

21. Jimmy Calpin, "Patty Loses Partner," *Tribune* (Scranton, PA), May 22, 1979, 14.

22. "Roth-Ellis Team Wins Tourney," *Fort Worth Star-Telegram*, September 9, 1979, 15B.

23. Lyle Zikes, "Roots of the PBA50 Tour: A Star-Studded Debut in '81," *Bowlers Journal International*, November 2013, 259.

24. Zikes, "Roots of the PBA50 Tour," 258.

25. "Bowling: PBA Seniors Championship," *Fort Lauderdale News*, August 18, 1981, 5C.

26. The international players were rarely a factor. In 1981, none advanced to the 24-man match play round.

27. Joe Dommershausen, "ABC Tourney Is Hard to Forget," *Wisconsin State Journal* (Madison), November 4, 1979, sec. 2, 10.

28. Ziehm, "Varipapa Strikes for a Living," 34.

29. Varipapa II, discussion, June 29, 2023.

30. Bill Smith III, "Andy Steals the Show," *Lewiston* [ME] *Sun-Journal*, January 28, 1982, 11.

31. Grasso and Hartman, *Historical Dictionary of Bowling*, 200.

32. Pezzano, "Andy Varipapa: Hero or Villain," 23.

33. Bill Wolcott, "Cheers to the Man Who Did the Impossible," *Niagara Gazette* (Niagara Falls, NY), March 18, 1983, 1B.

34. Pezzano, "Andy Varipapa: Hero or Villain," 21.

35. College Point Lanes, "Senior Citizens! See Andy Varipapa in Person!!!," advertisement, *Daily News* (New York), January 5, 1983, EQ6.

36. Lou Erb, "Linda Faustner Hits it Big in Lancaster," *Sunday Call-Chronicle* (Allentown, PA), April 23, 1978, 16-C.
37. Varipapa II, discussion, June 29, 2023.
38. Kristen Kelch, "Spare These Lanes, 4,000 Bowlers Cry," *Newsday* (Melville, NY), February 2, 1983, 21.
39. "A Huntington Split," *New York Times*, February 20, 1983, sec. 8, 1.
40. United States Securities and Exchange Commission, "What Are Municipal Bonds?" SEC.gov, last modified April 6, 2023, https://www.sec.gov/munied covers the basic of tax-free bonds. The tax-free provision applies to interest paid to bondholders and allows the issuer to offer a lower interest rate than if the interest were taxable. For example, a bondholder in a 28 percent marginal tax bracket is indifferent to purchasing a taxable bond that pays 6.00 percent and a tax-free bond that pays 4.32 percent.
41. Lynn Green, "Residents, Officials Oppose IDA Bonds for Waldbaum's," *Long-Islander* (Huntington, NY), June 9, 1983, 20.
42. Rick Brand, "Bonds for Converting Bowling Alley Opposed," *Newsday* (Melville, NY), June 3, 1983, 23.
43. Bradford W. O'Hearn, "Bowl-to-Market Financing Denied," *Newsday* (Melville, NY), June 21, 1983, 23.
44. O'Hearn, "Bowl-to-Market Financing Denied," 23.
45. Brad R. Humphreys, "Should the Construction of New Professional Sports Facilities Be Subsidized?" *Journal of Policy Analysis and Management* 38, no. 1 (2019): 264–70, https://doi.org/10.1002/pam.22102.
46. Andy Varipapa II, in discussion with the author, May 26, 2023.
47. Dick Carmody, "Century Bowlers Say 'Happy Birthday' to Andy," *Newsday* (Melville, NY), March 4, 1984, sports, 24.
48. Susan Varipapa, in discussion with the author, March 24, 2023.
49. Danny Schrafel, "Huntington Tenpin Legend Pitching Wheaties," *The Long-Islander* (Huntington, NY), April 9, 2015, A43.
50. "Search for Bowling Hall Officially Under Way," *Sheboygan* [WI] *Press*, May 23, 1978, 18.
51. David Fink, "City Chosen as New Site of Bowling Hall of Fame," *St. Louis Post-Dispatch*, May 8, 1979, 1.
52. "Oldest Hall of Famers Answer Call," *Lansing State Journal*, March 23, 1980, 15.
53. Cal Whitmore, "298 Not a Bad Beginning," *Sunday Dispatch* (Moline, IL), September 9, 1984, 25.
54. Jim Dressel, in discussion with the author, May 1, 2023.
55. Jeff Richgels, "Long-Time *Bowlers Journal* Editor, Columnist Jim Dressel Retires," 11thframe.com (blog), September 30, 2013, https://www.11thframe.com/news/article/6094.
56. Dressel, discussion.
57. Dressel, discussion.
58. Cal Whitmore, "Bowling Hall Shows Off Sport," *Sunday Dispatch* (Moline, IL), August 19, 1984, 22.
59. Associated Press, "Andy Varipapa Dies at 93," *Buffalo News*, August 26, 1984, C-1.
60. Associated Press, "Andy Varipapa Dies at 93," C-1.
61. Mort Luby, Jr., "Andy and Bowling Lessons in the Cellar," *Bowlers Journal*, November 1984, 11.
62. Chuck Pezzano, "Varipapa—Bowling's All-Time Best," *News Beacon* (Fair Lawn, NJ), September 21, 1984, 14.
63. Lou Marks, "Varipapa, 'Mr. Bowling,' Will Be Missed," *Palm Beach* [FL] *Post*, September 23, 1984, D16.
64. Whitmore, "298 Not a Bad Beginning," 25.
65. Joe Krajkovich, "Death of Andy Varipapa at 93 Costs Bowling One of Its Greats," *Courier-News* (Bridgewater, NJ), September 11, 1984, C-4.
66. Carmody, "Varipapa was Truly the Kingpin," sports, 26.
67. Kouros, "The Other Side of Andy Varipapa," 28.
68. Kouros, "The Other Side of Andy Varipapa," 28.
69. Kouros, "The Other Side of Andy Varipapa," 28.
70. Kouros, "The Other Side of Andy Varipapa," 28.

Epilogue

1. Varipapa II, discussion.
2. Dave Williams, "The Bowling Chain That Started Them All," *California USBC News!* (blog), July 25, 2021, https://calusbc.wordpress.com/2021/07/25/the-bowling-chain-that-started-them-all/. The Bowling Corporation of America (BCA), American International Bowling Corporation, and American Recreation Centers were the first of the large multi-unit owners of bowling centers. When BCA sold to Bowlmor in 1986, it operated 50 locations in 14 states.
3. Bill Travers, "Tournament to Honor Varipapa, The Legend," *Daily News* (New York), August 31, 1984, 65.
4. The PBA returned to Long Island at Sayville Lanes in 1991.
5. "Amateur" has a different meaning in bowling than in most sports. Generally, athletes who earn their living playing their sport are considered professionals. Bowlers remain amateurs so long as they do not join the PBA. Non–PBA members who earn a living bowling are known by the oxymoron, "professional amateurs."
6. Dick Carmody, "Varipapa Tourney Payout Totals $75,600," *Newsday* (Melville, NY), March 15, 1987, sports, 30.
7. Andy Varipapa II, "Andy Varipapa Match Game Championships—Statistics" (unpublished data, April 2023), PDF file.

8. "2004–2005 PBA Skills Challenge," YouTube video, October 17, 2016, https://www.youtube.com/watch?v=nJ3kDBuqmM8.
9. "2004–2005 PBA Skills Challenge," 43:45 to 44:00.
10. "2004–2005 PBA Skills Challenge," 1:05:40 to 1:06:25; *Strikes and Spares*, 7:42 to 8:00.
11. *Bowling Tricks*, 2:09 to 2:28.
12. "PBA's Best Bowling Trick Shots," YouTube video, March 9, 2015. https://www.youtube.com/watch?v=dLLRg0sur6g.
13. "PBA's Best Bowling Trick Shots."
14. Gianmarc Manzione, "The Man We Refuse to Forget," *Bowlers Journal International*, July 2015, 27.
15. E.J. Schultz, "Wheaties Makes Marketing Strike with Retro Bowling Ads," *AdAge* (blog), March 27, 2015, https://adage.com/article/see-the-spot/wheaties-makes-marketing-strike-retro-bowling-ads/297793.
16. General Mills, "Wheaties Presents Andy Varipapa's Bowling Tricks," advertisement, AdForum, https://www.adforum.com/creative-work/search?brand=wheaties&keyword=varipapa.
17. General Mills, "Wheaties Presents Andy Varipapa's Bowling Tricks #1," advertisement, AdForum, https://www.adforum.com/creative-work/ad/player/34511285/wheaties-presents-andy-varipapas-bowling-tricks-1/wheaties.
18. General Mills, "Wheaties Presents Andy Varipapa's Bowling Tricks #4," advertisement, AdForum, https://www.adforum.com/creative-work/ad/player/34511279/wheaties-presents-andy-varipapas-bowling-tricks-4/wheaties.
19. Manzione, "The Man We Refuse to Forget."
20. LaSpina, discussion.
21. Bob Johnson, "Andy Varipapa Exhibit to Open at Museum," USBC News, March 1, 2018, https://bowl.com/news/andy-varipapa-exhibit-to-open-at-museum.
22. Susan Varipapa, email message to author, May 25, 2023.
23. Susan Varipapa, email.
24. Andy Varipapa II, email message to author, May 9, 2023.
25. International Bowling Museum & Hall of Fame, "Explore the Vault," International Bowling Museum & Hall of Fame, accessed June 7, 2023, https://www.bowlingheritage.com/#exploreTheVault.
26. International Bowling Museum & Hall of Fame, "Andy Varipapa," Explore the Vault, accessed June 7, 2023, https://www.bowlingheritage.com/collection/andy-varipapa/.
27. Burton Jr., discussion.
28. Burton Jr., discussion.
29. Robbie Andreu, "'King of Hill' Trucks with PBA Tour," *Sun-Sentinel* (Fort Lauderdale, FL), January 29, 1985, 8C.
30. Larry Lichstein, in discussion with the author, February 24, 2023.
31. Lichstein, discussion.
32. Lichstein, discussion.
33. Lichstein, discussion.
34. Duke, discussion.
35. Pezzano, "Andy Varipapa: Hero or Villain," 20.
36. Carmody, "Varipapa was Truly the Kingpin," sports, 26.
37. Carmen Salvino, in discussion with the author, March 16, 2023.

Bibliography

All resources cited in this book, except newspaper articles, are listed below. Included are resources consulted but not cited.

To see Andy in action, his best trick-shot performances are in the Pete Smith short film *Bowling Tricks*. His career is best summarized in the History Channel's *Stories from the Hall of Fame: Bowling*. Both are available on YouTube.

Andy Varipapa II's website (www.andyvaripapa.com) has numerous artifacts and photographs beyond what appear in this book. Readers can also find additional images and updates on my Facebook, YouTube, and Instagram pages. Search for "Andy Varipapa Superstar."

I recommend four books to anyone interested in learning more about bowling history: (1) *The Perfect Game: The World of Bowling*, filled with photographs and illustrations, spans bowling's origins in 5000 BC through the late 1970s; (2) *Diners, Bowling Alleys, and Trailer Parks* focuses on bowling's effect on American culture from the 1880s through the mid–1960s; (3) Grasso and Hartman's *Historical Dictionary of Bowling* details bowling history using an encyclopedic approach; and (4) *The Bowling Chronicles*, a collection by J.R. (Dr. Jake) Schmidt, is informative and entertaining.

For a multimedia experience, visit the International Bowling Museum and Hall of Fame website (www.bowlingmuseum.com). Like the National Baseball Hall of Fame and Museum in Cooperstown is to baseball fans, the IBMHOF in Arlington, Texas, is a required visit for anyone passionate about bowling. Also, check out Schmidt's *Dr. Jake's Bowling History Blog* (https://bowlinghistory.wordpress.com/), which is regularly updated and packed with stories, photographs, and statistics.

Audiovisual

Baltz, Jerry, Parker Bohn III, Bob Learn, Jr., George Pappas, and Johnny Petraglia. *Stories from the Hall of Fame: Bowling*. Aired on the History Channel, November 6, 2002. YouTube video posted by drrjv, July 29, 2006. https://www.youtube.com/watch?v=cZMBy2xXXKs.

Barclay, David, dir. *Bowling Tricks*. Culver City, CA: Metro-Goldwyn-Mayer, 1948. YouTube video posted by Bowling City, January 12, 2014. https://www.youtube.com/watch?v=fzjPcVZRCxA.

Dubin, Charles S., dir. *M*A*S*H*. Season 10, episode 12. "Blood and Guts." Aired on CBS, January 18, 1982. YouTube video posted by Robert Varipapa, February 8, 2013. https://www.youtube.com/watch?v=74aPuLKBixg.

Duke, Norm. "Duke 300 Game Towel Shot." YouTube video posted by jdaltorio, February 15, 2011. https://www.youtube.com/watch?v=EO11nTLqenI.

Eaton, Jack, dir. *Better Bowling*. Hollywood: Paramount, 1942. YouTube video posted by BowlingOldies, February 28, 2012. https://www.youtube.com/watch?v=UPV5drhy8Co.

Feist, Felix, dir. *Set 'Em Up*. Culver City, CA: Metro-Goldwyn-Mayer, 1939. YouTube video posted by BowlingOldies, February 26, 2012. https://www.youtube.com/watch?v=PUx5wKwo9Xc.

Feist, Felix, dir. *Strikes and Spares*. Culver City, CA: Metro-Goldwyn-Mayer, 1934. https://www.dailymotion.com/video/x32qqbp.

General Mills. "Wheaties Presents Andy Varipapa's Bowling Tricks." AdForum, April 2015. https://www.adforum.com/creative-work/search?brand=wheaties&keyword=varipapa.

Gross, Lloyd, dir. *What's My Line?* Season 4, week 145. Distributed by Viacom, taped October 7, 1971. MP4 recording.

Husing, Ted, host. *Sport Slants No. 5*. New York: Vitaphone, 1932.

Jennett, Jim, dir. *Professional Bowlers Tour*. "1978 Long Island Open." Aired on ABC, April 1, 1978. YouTube video posted by BowlingOldies, February 12, 2012. https://www.youtube.com/watch?v=teIGvpRAch8.

Lindsey, Mort. *The Super Skittler*. London: British Pathé, 1934. https://www.britishpathe.com/asset/189394/.

Lindsey, Mort. *Undercover*. New York: Pathé Exchange, 1931.

Lindsey, Mort. *Weatherproof*. New York: Pathé Exchange, 1927.

Lubanski, Ed. *Championship Bowling Special*. "Ed Lubanski Goes for Back-to-Back 300s on Live TV." Aired on WPST-TV, Miami, June 22, 1959. YouTube video posted by BowlingOldies, July

15, 2014. https://www.youtube.com/watch?v=FXHJL7Gk1sI.
Nagy, Steve, Andy Varipapa, and Fred Wolf. *Championship Bowling.* "Andy Varipapa vs Steve Nagy." Aired on NBC, February 15, 1957. Facebook video posted by King of TV Bowling, January 23, 2021. https://www.facebook.com/watch/?v=1832085733614094.
Nosseck, Noel, dir. *Dreamer.* Hollywood: Twentieth Century Fox, 1979. YouTube video posted by William O'Leary, May 16, 2015. https://www.youtube.com/watch?v=ZDZO-Qm0OzE.
Professional Bowlers Association. "PBA's Best Bowling Trick Shots." YouTube video posted by PBABowling, March 9, 2015. https://www.youtube.com/watch?v=dLLRg0sur6g.
Professional Bowlers Association. "2004–2005 PBA Skills Challenge." YouTube video posted by Niko Puhar, October 17, 2016. https://www.youtube.com/watch?v=nJ3kDBuqmM8.
Schenkel, Chris, and Nelson Burton, Jr., hosts. *Bowling: The Perfect Game.* Los Angeles: ABC Sports Home Video, 1991. YouTube video posted by IseeRobots Television, April 15, 2019. https://www.youtube.com/watch?v=D9SxHUqzT3c.
Smith, Jack, host. *You Asked for It.* "Andy Varipapa's Incredible Bowling Trick Shots." Aired on ABC, September 26, 1954. YouTube video posted by You Asked for It, October 18, 2022. https://www.youtube.com/watch?v=v0L4A9z8Kxw.
Toal, Frank, host. *Speaking of Sports.* "Interview with Andy Varipapa." Aired on WCRO, Johnstown, PA, April 24, 1950. https://andyvaripapa.com/listen-to-andy-live-speaking-of-sports-with-andy-varipapa-april-24-1950/.
United States Bowling Congress. "Retro Roll: Andy Varipapa." YouTube video posted by GrowtheSport, May 20, 2011. https://www.youtube.com/watch?v=aFl_qeTyDXI.
Varipapa, Andy. *Andy Varipapa: Bowling Legend.* Arlington, TX: International Bowling Museum and Hall of Fame, 2018. https://videos.files.wordpress.com/1ekBm1qI/andy-varipapa-hof-video_dvd.mp4.
Varipapa, Andy. "Andy Varipapa Interview." Walter J. Brown Media Archives, filmed February 4, 1972. YouTube video posted by Foggy Melson Sports, October 23, 2022. https://www.youtube.com/watch?v=jcDELkoSxyc.
Varipapa, Andy. "Archive Film 1049422." Huntley Film Archives, filmed October 1965. https://www.huntleyarchives.com/preview.asp?image=1049422.
Varipapa, Andy. *Skittle Wizardry!* London: British Pathé, 1937. https://www.britishpathe.com/asset/67241/.
Varipapa, Andy. "Story on Bowling Legend Andy Varipapa." Aired on WFAA-TV Dallas, January 26, 1973. YouTube video posted by SMU Jones Film, May 25, 2018. https://www.youtube.com/watch?v=UzmURfYuxFg.
Vox. "The Hidden Oil Patterns on Bowling Lanes." YouTube video, Vox Almanac, July 13, 2017. https://www.youtube.com/watch?v=t-osG0F2MZM.

Books

Allen, Kevin, and Del Reddy. *King of the Pins.* Wayne, MI: Victory Entertainment, 2010.
Collier, Martin. *Italian Unification 1820–71.* London: Heinemann, 2003. https://archive.org/details/italianunificati0000coll/.
Grasso, John, and Eric R. Hartman. *Historical Dictionary of Bowling.* New York: Rowman & Littlefield, 2014. EBSCOhost eBook Academic Collection.
Harris, Tim. *Players: 250 Men, Women and Animals Who Created Modern Sport.* London: Yellow Jersey, 2009. http://archive.org/details/players250menwom0000harr.
Hurley, Andrew. *Diners, Bowling Alleys, and Trailer Parks: Chasing the American Dream in Postwar Consumer Culture.* New York: Basic Books, 2001.
Kirkland, K.D. *America's Premier Gunmakers: Remington.* East Bridgewater, MA: World Publications Group, 2007. http://archive.org/details/americaspremierg0000kirk_e7w9.
Kogan, Rick. *Brunswick: The Story of an American Company from 1948 to 1985.* Skokie, IL: Brunswick, 1985.
Lloyd, Annette D'Agostino. *Harold Lloyd: Magic in a Pair of Horn-Rimmed Glasses.* Albany, GA: BearManor Media, 2016.
Marks, Lou. *The Bowling Experience.* Boynton Beach, FL: Goldmark, 1987.
McDonough, Pat. *Better Bowling.* Detroit: GM Information Rack Services, 1950.
McDonough, Pat. *Better Bowling.* Rev. ed. Bronx: Ishi Press, 2015.
McElvaine, Robert S. *The Great Depression: America, 1929–1941.* New York: Times Books, 1993. http://archive.org/details/greatdepressiona00mcel.
Miller, Mark, ed. *The Bowlers' Encyclopedia.* Greenvale, WI: American Bowling Congress, 1995.
Professional Bowlers Association. *50 Greatest Players in PBA History.* Chicago: Luby, 2008.
Remington Arms—Union Metallic Cartridge. *A New Chapter in an Old Story.* New York: Remington Arms—Union Metallic Cartridge, 1912. https://archive.org/details/cu31924016409660.
Riall, Lucy. *The Italian Risorgimento: State, Society, and National Unification.* New York: Routledge, 1994. https://archive.org/details/italianrisorgime0000rial.
Salvino, Carmen and Frederick C. Klein. *Fast Lanes.* Chicago: Bonus Books, 1988.
Schmidt, J.R. *The Bowling Chronicles: Collected Writings of Dr. Jake.* Jefferson, NC: McFarland, 2017.
Sparks, Barry. *Earl: The Greatest Bowler of All Time.* Chicago: Luby, 2019.

Varipapa, Andy, and Nick Tronsky. *Andy Varipapa's Quick Way to Better Bowling*. Edited by Tom McLaughlin. Garden City, NY: Garden City Books, 1952.

Varipapa, Andy, and Nick Tronsky. *Andy Varipapa's Quick Way to Better Bowling*. Edited by Tom McLaughlin. Rev. ed. Bronx: Ishi Press, 2015.

Weiskopf, Herman. *The Perfect Game: The World of Bowling*. Englewood Cliffs, NJ: Prentice-Hall, 1978.

Ziegler-McPherson, Christina A. *Immigrants in Hoboken: One-Way Ticket, 1845–1985*. Charleston, SC: History Press, 2011.

Book Chapters

Bucki, Cecelia. "Dilution and Craft Tradition: Munitions Workers in Bridgeport, Connecticut, 1915–19." In *The New England Working Class and New Labor History*, edited by Herbert G. Gutman and Donald H. Bell, 137–56. Urbana: University of Illinois Press, 1987. https://archive.org/details/newenglandworkin0000unse_n8b1.

Gomellini, Mateo, and Gianni Toniolo. "The Industrialization of Italy, 1861–1971." In *The Spread of Modern Industry to the Periphery Since 1871*, edited by Kevin H. O'Rourke and Jefferey G. Williamson, 115–141. New York: Oxford University Press, 2017. http://doi.org/10.1093/acprof:oso/9780198753643.001.0001.

King, Rob. "The Art of Diddling: Slapstick, Science, and Antimodernism in the Films of Charley Bowers." In *Funny Pictures: Animation and Comedy in Studio-Era Hollywood*, edited by Daniel Goldmark and Charlie Keli, 191–210. Berkley: University of California Press, 2011. ProQuest eBook Central.

Menke, Frank G. "Bowling." In *The Encyclopedia of Sports*, edited by Roger L. Treat, 3rd rev. ed., 209–38. New York: A.S. Barnes, 1963. https://archive.org/details/encyclopediaofspmen00menk/.

Remington, Roger R. "Scope Magazine, Will Burton and Lester Beall." In *Hidden Treasure: The National Library of Medicine*, edited by Michael Sappol, 210–13. New York: Blast Books, 2012. https://circulatingnow.nlm.nih.gov/2018/11/29/scope-magazine-1941-1957/.

Woolum, Janet. "Floretta Doty McCutcheon." In *Outstanding Women Athletes: Who They Are and How They Influenced Sports in America*, 150–152. Phoenix: Oryx Press, 1992. http://archive.org/details/outstandingwomen00wool.

Government Publications

United States Bureau of Economic Analysis. "Gross Domestic Product." Resources: Learning Center. April 26, 2022. https://www.bea.gov/resources/learning-center/what-to-know-gdp.

United States Census Bureau. "Introduction to NAICS." North American Industry Classification System. December 19, 2022. https://www.census.gov/naics/.

United States Department of Commerce. *Bicentennial Edition: Historical Statistics of the United States, Colonial Times to 1970*. Washington, D.C.: US Government Printing Office, 1975. https://www.census.gov/library/publications/1975/compendia/hist_stats_colonial-1970.html.

United States Department of Commerce. *1910 Census*. Vol. 3. Washington, D.C.: Government Printing Office, 1913. https://www.census.gov/library/publications/1913/dec/vol-3-population.html

United States Department of Commerce. *Statistical Abstract of the United States: 1960*. Washington, D.C.: U.S. Government Printing Office, 1960. https://www.census.gov/library/publications/1960/compendia/statab/81ed.html.

United States Department of Commerce. *Statistical Abstract of the United States: 1982–83*. Washington, D.C.: U.S. Government Printing Office, 1983. https://www.census.gov/library/publications/1982/compendia/statab/103ed.html.

United States Department of Commerce and Labor. *Census of Manufactures: 1905, Earnings of Wage-Earners*. Bulletin 93. Washington, D.C.: Government Printing Office, 1908. https://babel.hathitrust.org/cgi/pt?id=nnc1.cu56779232.

United States Department of Labor. "Union Scale of Wages and Hours of Labor May 15, 1917." *Bulletin of the United States Bureau of Labor Statistics*. Washington, D.C.: Government Printing Office, March 1919. https://fraser.stlouisfed.org/title/union-scale-wages-hours-labor-3912/union-scale-wages-hours-labor-may-15-1917-476870.

United States Department of the Interior, National Park Service. "National Register of Historic Places Registration Form: Brooklyn Navy Yard Historic District." May 22, 2014. https://npgallery.nps.gov/AssetDetail/314d2a7b-7525-4998-8a77-dd3b9dba7073.

United States National Archives and Records Administration. "Census Records." Accessed October 29, 2022. https://www.archives.gov/research/census.

United States Securities and Exchange Commission. "What Are Municipal Bonds?" SEC.gov. Last modified April 6, 2023. https://www.sec.gov/munied.

Journal Articles

Bordo, Michael D., Christopher J. Erceg, and Charles L. Evans. "Money, Sticky Wages, and the Great Depression." *American Economic Review* 90, no. 5 (December 2000): 1447–63. https://doi.org/10.1257/aer.90.5.1447.

Butsch, Richard. "American Movie Audiences of the 1930s." *International Labor and Working-Class History* 59 (2001): 106–20. https://www.jstor.org/stable/27672712.

Castiglione, G.E. di Palma. "Italian Immigration into the United States 1901–04." *American Journal of Sociology* 11, no. 2 (1905): 183–206. https://www.jstor.org/stable/2762660.

Cavaioli, Frank J. "Patterns of Italian Immigration to the United States." *The Catholic Social Science Review* 13 (2008): 213–29. https://doi.org/10.5840/cssr20081314.

Dooley, Patricia L. "Jim Crow Strikes Again: The African American Press Campaign Against Segregation in Bowling During World War II." *The Journal of African American History* 97, no. 3 (2012): 270–90. https://doi.org/10.5323/jafriamerhist.97.3.0270.

Eberhart, John C., and Raymond A. Bauer. "An Analysis of the Influences on Recall of a Controversial Event: The Chicago Tribune and the Republic Steel Strike." *The Journal of Social Psychology* 14, no. 1 (1941): 211–28. https://doi.org/10.1080/00224545.1941.9921507.

Haupert, Michael. "MLB's Annual Salary Leaders Since 1874." *Outside the Lines* 18, no. 1 (Fall 2012): 1–6. http://sabr.box.com/shared/static/neai4h-htj2j3oaclgzlh.pdf.

Hirshon, Nicholas. "Bowling Headliners, 1948–1950: The Creation of a Spectator Sport in Television's Emergent Years." *The International Journal of the History of Sport* 37, no. 11 (2020): 951–72. https://doi.org/10.1080/09523367.2020.1835868.

Hirshon, Nicholas. "A Forgotten Pioneer in Sports Television: Phillies Jackpot Bowling (1959–1960)." *American Journalism* 36, no. 2 (2019): 196–219. https://doi.org/10.1080/08821127.2019.1602419.

Holt, Richard. "Amateurism and Its Interpretation: The Social Origins of British Sport." *Innovation in Social Science Research* 5, no. 4 (1992): 19–31. https://doi.org/10.1080/13511610.1992.9968318.

Humphreys, Brad R. "Should the Construction of New Professional Sports Facilities Be Subsidized?" *Journal of Policy Analysis and Management* 38, no. 1 (2019): 264–70. https://doi.org/10.1002/pam.22102.

Pretelli, Mateo. "Italian Americans, Education, and Italian Language: 1880–1921." *Quaderni d'italianistica* 38, no. 1 (2017): 61–83. https://doi.org/10.33137/q.i..v38i1.31143.

Schuman, Michael. "History of Child Labor in the United States—Part 1: Little Children Working." *Monthly Labor Review*, January 2017. https://doi.org/10.21916/mlr.2017.1.

Small, Charles S. "The Railway of the New York and Brooklyn Bridge." *The Railway and Locomotive Historical Society Bulletin* 97 (October 1957): 7–20. https://www.jstor.org/stable/43520182.

Stambler, Moses. "The Effect of Compulsory Education and Child Labor Laws on High School Attendance in New York City, 1898–1917." *History of Education Quarterly* 8, no. 2 (1968): 189–214. https://doi.org/10.2307/367352.

Temin, Peter. "Lessons for the Present from the Great Depression." *The American Economic Review* 66, no. 2 (1976): 40–45. https://www.jstor.org/stable/1817196.

Ward, Richard. "Extra Added Attractions: The Short Subjects of MGM, Warner Brothers and Universal." *Media History* 9, no. 3 (2003): 221–44. https://doi.org/10.1080/1368880032000145542.

Magazine Articles

"ABC Hall of Famer Looks at London." *Bowling*, April 1966, 42.

"Andy the Great Proves That He Is." *Life*, December 29, 1947, 62–63. https://books.google.com/books?id=8E0EAAAAMBAJ&pg=PA62.

Archibald, John. "Eddie Elias: Giving the Pro a Chance to Make a Real Living." *Bowlers Journal*, December 1988, S27.

Bourke, Kevin. "Jimmy Smith: The Name No One Will Ever Forget." *Bowlers Journal*, December 1988, S89–90.

"Bowling: Handy Andy." *Newsweek*, December 23, 1946, 78–79. http://archive.org/details/sim_newsweek-us_1946-12-23_28_26.

Boyle, Robert. "A Guy Named Smith is Striking it Rich." *Sports Illustrated*, November 25, 1963, 36–38. https://vault.si.com/vault/1963/11/25/a-guy-named-smith-is-striking-it-rich.

Brownell, Richard. "Take the Presidents Bowling." *Medium*, April 24, 2018. https://medium.com/@rickbrownell/take-the-presidents-bowling-521bbc475f83.

Bushell, Gordon D. "Fifty Years with Varipapa." *Pageant*, April 1946, 42–44.

Cherin, Bob. "Varipapa the Magnificent." *Bowlers Journal*, December 1981, 54–59.

Collar, Mark. "Louie Petersen: Scoring Points Both Inside and Outside the System." *Bowlers Journal*, December 1988, S86–87.

Dressel, Jim. "Jimmy Blouin: A Match Play Bowler Supreme, the 'Blue Island Bomber' Retired His Crown Undefeated." *Bowlers Journal*, December 1988, S88–89.

Evans, Dick. "Bowling's Greatest Recall Days as Pin Boys." *Bowl Magazine*, September 29, 2000. http://www.ncausbca.org/bowlmag/archives/Evans000929.htm.

Evans, Dick. "Dick Weber: This Legend is a Fountain of Youth." *Bowlers Journal*, December 1988, S43–44.

"Exploit-O-Grams: Weatherproof—Rice Sportlight." *Film Daily*, March 27, 1927, 15. https://lantern.mediahist.org/catalog/filmdaily3940newy_0709.

Fay, Bill. "Bowling's Talking Machine." *Collier's*, April 10, 1948, 6–7. https://archive.org/details/colliers121aprspri/page/n87.

Frank, Stanley. "The Falcaro Strikes Again." *Saturday Evening Post*, March 2, 1946, 35–38.

Gould, Stephen Jay. "The Creation Myths of Cooperstown." *Natural History*, November 1989. https://www.naturalhistorymag.com/picks-from-the-past/02484/the-creation-myths-of-cooperstown.

"The Greatest." *Time*, May 5, 1947, 79. https://time.com/vault/issue/1947-05-05/page/81/.

Iden, George. "Touring With Andy Varipapa." *Bowling*, August 1977, 6, 41.

"I'm a Man, Huh?" *Time*, December 22, 1947, 58. https://time.com/vault/issue/1947-12-22/page/60/.

"J. Wilbert Sims 1st Negro in World Bowling Meet." *Jet*, December 17, 1959, 56. https://books.google.com/books/about/Jet.html?id=b0EDAAAAMBAJ.

Jares, Joe. "The Poor Man's Tour Begins to Strike It Rich." *Sports Illustrated*, April 19, 1965, 112–114. https://vault.si.com/vault/1965/04/19/the-poor-mans-tour-begins-to-strike-it-rich.

Johnson, Bob. "The Great Outdoors: Not So Great for Bowling." *Bowlers Journal International*, November 2013, 266–267.

Kalman, Victor. "All-Star Andy." *Sports Illustrated*, January 17, 1955, 56–57. https://vault.si.com/vault/1955/01/17/allstar-andy.

Kalman, Victor. "Falcaro the Great." *Sports Illustrated*, September 13, 1954, 76. https://vault.si.com/vault/1954/09/13/falcaro-the-great.

Kalman, Victor. "Not Dead Yet." *Sports Illustrated*, November 1, 1954, 75. https://vault.si.com/vault/1954/11/01/not-dead-yet.

Kalman, Victor. "Starlight on the Alleys." *Sports Illustrated*, December 11, 1955, 52–57. https://vault.si.com/vault/1955/12/12/42387.

Kouros, Tom. "The Other Side of Andy Varipapa." *Bowlers Journal*, October 1984, 28.

"Ladewig Was 'Pinboy.'" *Bowling*, September 1966, 35.

London, Mark. "Just Paying Attention." *Bowling News*, November 3, 2022, 13. http://www.thebowlingnews.net/uploads/3/4/7/8/34783484/11-03-22_bowling_news-web.pdf.

Luby, Mort, Jr. "Andy and Bowling Lessons in the Cellar." *Bowlers Journal*, November 1984, 11.

Luby, Mort, Jr. "Early Bowling Americana." *Bowlers Journal*, November 1983, 104–106.

Luby, Mort, Jr. "Farewell to the Pinboys." *Bowlers Journal*, November 1983, 112–125.

Luby, Mort, Jr. "The Golden Eye of TV" *Bowlers Journal*, November 1983, 126–129.

Luby, Mort, Jr. "A Legend to Count On." *Bowlers Journal*, November 1983, 112–113.

Luby, Mort, Jr. "The Million Dollar Pot." *Bowlers Journal*, November 1983, 141.

Luby, Mort, Jr. "The Professional Influence." *Bowlers Journal*, November 1983, 138–139.

Manzione, Gianmarc. "The Gambler: John Handegard." USBC News, May 17, 2010. https://bowl.com/news/the-gambler-john-handegard.

Manzione, Gianmarc. "The Man We Refuse to Forget." *Bowlers Journal International*, July 2015, 23–27.

Manzione, Gianmarc. "Tale of Two Tours." *Bowlers Journal International*, August 2016, 28–31.

Miller, Margery. "The Bowling Ambassador." *Christian Science Monitor*, May 1, 1947, 15. http://archive.org/details/per_christian-science-monitor_1947-05-01_39_132.

Neiman, Bob. "Floretta McCutcheon: Bowling Started Out as Her Therapy." *Bowlers Journal*, December 1988, S63–64.

Paladino, Larry. "Whatever It Takes." *Bowling Digest*, June 2001, 36–42.

"Person of the Century: Andy's the Man." *Bowlers Journal*, December 1988, 78.

"Pete Smith Over-Worked." *The Hollywood Reporter*, June 4, 1934, 2. https://lantern.mediahist.org/catalog/hollywoodreporte1821holl_1378.

Pezzano, Chuck. "Andy Tells It Like It Was." *Bowlers Journal*, February 1971, 39–41.

Pezzano, Chuck. "Andy Varipapa: Hero or Villain, He Astounded … Affronted … Entertained." *Bowling*, December 1982, 20–23.

Pezzano, Chuck. "Andy Varipapa: The Italian Farmboy Who Became the American Trick-Shot Master." *Bowlers Journal*, December 1988, S5.

Pezzano, Chuck. "At 83, Varipapa Sparkles as Instructor, Fitness Expert." *Sporting News*, June 22, 1974, 55.

Pezzano, Chuck. "The Birth, Rebirth of Andy Varipapa." *Bowling*, July 1976, 4, 30.

Quinn, Mike. "Ageless Andy Sounds Off." *Bowlers Journal*, November 1968, 24–25.

Regan, Phil. "Building a Bowling Ball—Part I." *Bowling This Month*, May 2019. https://www.bowlingthismonth.com/bowling-tips/building-a-bowling-ball-part-1/.

"Reviews of New Short Subjects: Weatherproof." *Film Daily*, April 10, 1927, 7. https://lantern.mediahist.org/catalog/filmdaily3940newy_0835.

"Reviews of Sound Shorts: Ted Husing in 'Sports Slants' (No. 5)." *Film Daily*, February 7, 1932, 11. https://lantern.mediahist.org/catalog/filmdailyvolume55859newy_0311.

"Reviews of Sound Shorts: Undercover." *Film Daily*, January 25, 1931, 12. https://lantern.mediahist.org/catalog/filmdailyvolume555newy_0222.

Richgels, Jeff. "Long-Time *Bowlers Journal* Editor, Columnist Jim Dressel Retires." 11thframe.com (blog), September 30, 2013. https://www.11thframe.com/news/article/6094.

Rorre, Pat. "Amazing Andy Varipapa." *National Bowlers Journal and Recreation Age*, June 1937, 20–21.

Ruffolo, Lorraine V. "My Dad Bowled Them Over in Hollywood." *Reminisce*, March/April 1995, 18.

"A Sampling of Courses at Pratt Institute 1887–2012." *Prattfolio: The Magazine of Pratt Institute*, May 2012, 14–15. https://issuu.com/prattinstitute/docs/prattfolio-125th-anniversary-2012.

Schmid, Jack. "Ball Weight." *Bowling This Month*, October 2013. https://www.bowlingthismonth.com/bowling-tips/ball-weight/.

Schmidt, J.R. "Crimmins Wins All-Star #1 at the Start of World War II." *Bowlers Journal International*, January 2020, 33.

Schmidt, J.R. "Little Wizard Voorhies Deserves Place in History." *Bowlers Journal International*, February 2021, 24.

Schmidt, J.R. "Watching a Different Sport." *Bowlers Journal International*, February 2014, 10.

Schoeman, Byron. "Andy the Great." *Bowling*, January 1982, 6; 12.

Schoeman, Byron. "The Fabulous Varipapa." *National Bowlers Journal and Billiard Revue*, July 1959, 7–8.

"Short Showmanship." *Motion Picture Herald*, July 7, 1934, 47. https://lantern.mediahist.org/catalog/motionpictureher116unse_0177.

"Short Subject Reviews: Strikes and Spares." *Film Daily*, November 5, 1934, 10. https://lantern.mediahist.org/catalog/filmdailyvolume666newy_0910.

"Short Subjects: Under Cover." *Motion Picture Review*, March 1931, 7. https://lantern.mediahist.org/catalog/motionpicturerev00wome_0_0029.

"A Shot at $25,000." *Ebony*, April 1960, 85–89. https://books.google.com/books?id=atLRL7epvskC.

"Sports & Medicine: Bowling Champ Still Going Strong at 65." *Scope Weekly*, February 20, 1957, 15.

Taylor, Robert Lewis. "Man with a Thumb." *New Yorker*, March 28, 1941, 25–34.

"The Thirties." *Prattfolio: The Magazine of Pratt Institute*, May 2012, 28–31. https://issuu.com/prattinstitute/docs/prattfolio-125th-anniversary-2012.

United States Bowling Congress. *The 2021 Annual Report of the United States Bowling Congress*. Arlington, TX: United States Bowling Congress, 2022. https://bowl.com/getmedia/2f76c863-1da1-42e0-8cee-15d2cb6f8c3b/2021_usbcannualreport.pdf.

Varipapa, Andy. "Letters." *Time*, May 19, 1947, 6. https://time.com/vault/issue/1947-05-19/page/8/.

Varipapa, Andy. "Wonderful Me." *Bowlers Journal*, May 1979, 71–73.

Varipapa, Andy, with Paul Gardner. "Raise Your Average 20 Pins." *Bluebook*, January 1955, 18–23.

Varipapa, Andy, with Mort Luby, Jr. "A Star That Will Always Sparkle." *Bowlers Journal*, October 1984, 56–57.

Wachter, Paul. "He's the Only Active Black Bowler to Have Won a Major Pro Tournament." *Andscape*, March 21, 2018. https://andscape.com/features/gary-faulkner-only-active-black-pba-bowler-to-have-won-a-major-pro-tournament/.

Walsh, George. "The Classic: Sweat, Misery and Cash." *Sports Illustrated*, May 8, 1961, 56–57. https://vault.si.com/vault/1961/05/08/the-classic-sweat-misery-and-cash.

Walter, John. "Andy Varipapa: Great Star Backs Up 'Pop Off' Reputation with Top Alley Action." *Bowling Magazine*, June 1951, 6–7, 26.

Walter, John. "Varipapa Elected to Hall of Fame." *National Bowlers Journal and Billiard Revue*, March 1957, 27–29.

Weinstein, Sam. "He Had More Talent in the Tips of His Fingers." *Bowlers Journal*, December 1988, S87.

Zikes, Lyle. "Roots of the PBA50 Tour: A Star-Studded Debut in '81." *Bowlers Journal International*, November 2013, 258–259.

Other Resources

Academy of Motion Picture Arts and Sciences. "1953 (26th) Academy Awards—Honorary Award." Academy Awards Acceptance Speech Database. 2019. http://aaspeechesdb.oscars.org/link/026-27/.

Academy of Motion Picture Arts and Sciences. "The 7th Academy Awards—1935." Oscars Ceremonies. 2022. https://www.oscars.org/oscars/ceremonies/1935.

Ancestry. Ancestry: Family Tree, Genealogy & Family History Records. 2023. http://www.ancestry.com.

Bedingfield, Gary. "Baseball in World War II." Baseball in Wartime. 2022. https://www.baseballinwartime.com/baseball_in_wwii/baseball_in_wwii.htm.

Bedingfield, Gary. "Baseball's Greatest Sacrifice—World War II Deaths." Baseball in Wartime. 2018. https://www.baseballsgreatestsacrifice.com/world_war_ii.html.

Bevis, Charlie. "Chuck Connors." Society for American Baseball Research. Accessed March 16, 2023. https://sabr.org/bioproj/person/chuck-connors/.

Bierman, Harold, Jr. "The 1929 Stock Market Crash." EH.net Encyclopedia. March 26, 2008. https://eh.net/encyclopedia/the-1929-stock-market-crash/.

Bowlers to Veterans Link. "What We Do." Bowlers to Veterans Link—Brightening Veterans Lives. 2023. https://bvl.org/what-we-do.

BowlersMart. "Bowling Terms." BowlersMart: Trusted by Bowlers Around the World Since 2004. 2023. https://www.bowlersmart.com/bowling-terms/.

Bowling2U. "Glossary." Bowling2U: Bringing the Best of Bowling to You. 2023. https://bowling2u.com/bowling-trivia/glossary/.

Brinkhoff, Thomas. "Italy: Regions and Major Cities." City Population. Last modified April 28, 2022. https://www.citypopulation.de/en/italy/cities/.

Brunswick. "Brunswick Is Proud." Advertisement. *Billboard*, August 26, 1957, 19–20. https://books.google.com/books?id=YSEEAAAAMBAJ.

Brunswick. *The 1981 Brunswick Memorial World Open Honors Andy Varipapa, Bowling's Living Legend*. Chicago: Brunswick, 1981. https://andy-varipapa.com/2015/12/20/av-t/.

Curtis, Charles. "Here's the Story Behind Pete Weber's Famous 'Who Do You Think You Are? I Am!' Moment." *For the Win* (blog), February 26, 2020. https://ftw.usatoday.com/2020/02/

pete-weber-who-do-you-think-you-are-origin.
Early Television Foundation. "Postwar American Television." Early Television Museum. Accessed April 18, 2023. https://www.earlytelevision.org/us_tv_sets.html.
Ertman, Thalia. "Football and the NFL During World War II." Friends of the National WWII Memorial. September 13, 2019. https://www.wwiimemorialfriends.org/blog/football-and-the-nfl-during-world-war-ii.
ESPN Enterprises. "Boxing Champions List." ESPN.com. Last modified July 25, 2023. https://www.espn.com/boxing/story/_/id/12370125/boxing-champions-list.
Evans, Dick. "78 Bowling Leaders Receive Votes in Survey to Pick a Top 20 of All Time." *Bowling Digital* (blog), July 31, 2009. https://www.bowlingdigital.com/bowl/node/6905.
Fandom. "What's My Line? (1968) Episode Guide." Mark Goodson Wiki. Last modified June 17, 2023. https://markgoodson.fandom.com/wiki/What%27s_My_Line%3F_(1968)/Episode_Guide
Find a Grave. "Joseph 'Josh' Veripapa (1893–1965)." Find a Grave: World's Largest Gravesite Collection. March 28, 2017. https://www.findagrave.com/memorial/177842962/joseph-veripapa.
Gordon, Jason. "Asymmetric Information—Explained." The Business Professor. Last updated March 27, 2023. https://thebusinessprofessor.com/communications-negotiations/asymmetric-information-definition.
Grumman Athletic Association. *Industrial Bowling Tournament Championship 1962*. Bethpage, NY: Grumman Athletic Association, 1962.
Hollywood Walk of Fame. "Dave O'Brien." Official Website of the Hollywood Walk of Fame. October 25, 2019. https://walkoffame.com/dave-obrien/.
Hong, Kevin. "Photography of Vintage, Classic and Retro Bowling Centers in North America." Maple + Pine: American Bowling Comes of Age. 2023. http://www.vintagebowling.net/.
IMDb. "IMDb: Ratings, Reviews, and Where to Watch the Best Movies." IMDb.com. 2023. https://www.imdb.com/.
International Bowling Museum and Hall of Fame. "Doc's Diagram." Behind the Scenes of Bowling. Accessed April 13, 2023. https://www.bowlingheritage.com/item/docs-diagram/.
International Bowling Museum and Hall of Fame. "Explore the Vault." International Bowling Museum and Hall of Fame. Accessed June 7, 2023. https://www.bowlingheritage.com/#exploreTheVault.
International Bowling Museum and Hall of Fame. "Get a Grip." Behind the Scenes of Bowling. Accessed April 13, 2023. https://www.bowlingheritage.com/item/get-a-grip/.
International Jewish Sports Hall of Fame. "Elected Members: Mort Lindsey." International Jewish Sports Hall of Fame. 2023. http://www.jewishsports.net/BioPages/MortimerLindsey.htm.
Johnson, Bob. "Andy Varipapa Exhibit to Open at Museum." USBC News, March 1, 2018. https://bowl.com/news/andy-varipapa-exhibit-to-open-at-museum.
Kirkpatrick, Clifford. *Can War Marriages Be Made to Work?* Washington, D.C.: United States Army Division of Information and Education, 1944. https://www.historians.org/about-aha-and-membership/aha-history-and-archives/gi-roundtable-series/pamphlets/em-30-can-war-marriages-be-made-to-work-(1944).
Lazy Journalist. "1979–80 Ratings History." *The TV Ratings Guide* (blog), August 15, 1991. http://www.thetvratingsguide.com/1991/08/1979-80-ratings-history.html.
Legal Information Institute. "Tying Arrangement." Cornell Law School Legal Information Institute. Accessed January 28, 2023. https://www.law.cornell.edu/wex/tying_arrangement.
Levin, Jay. "Recalling the Tornado That Ravaged River Edge 121 Years Ago." Northjersey.com. July 12, 2016. https://www.northjersey.com/story/news/2016/07/12/recalling-the-tornado-that-ravaged-river-edge-121-years-ago/92739130/.
Lonto, Jeff R. "Who Was the Man on the Gablinger's Can? Or: The Real 'Father' of Light Beer." *Jeff R. Lonto's Chronicles from the Analog Age* (blog), April 5, 2015. http://theanalogage.blogspot.com/2015/04/who-was-man-on-gablingers-can-or-real.html.
MateriaFutura. "Genealogy in Carfizzi." Italianside.com. 2023. https://www.italianside.com/calabria/crotone/carfizzi/genealogy/.
McLean, Keiran. "Embellish the Details! Exaggerated Stories Can Cultivate Closeness." *Psychology Today* (blog), February 13, 2020. https://www.psychologytoday.com/us/articles/201912/embellish-the-details.
Morse, Stephen P. "One-Step Webpages." Accessed October 29, 2022. https://stevemorse.org/.
Munsey, Paul, and Cory Suppes. "Crosley Field." Ballparks. Last updated October 2004. https://ballparks.com/baseball/national/crosle.htm.
National Weather Service. "Northeastern New Jersey Tornado Statistics." National Weather Service, National Oceanic and Atmospheric Administration. Accessed November 7, 2022. https://www.weather.gov/okx/NewJerseyTors.
NEGenWeb Project. "Railroad Job Descriptions." Iron Roads—Making Tracks Across Nebraska. Last updated July 31, 2021. http://www.usgennet.org/usa/ne/topic/railroads/job.html.
Neikirk, Todd. "These 8 Baseball Hall of Famers Served During World War II." War History Online. March 4, 2022. https://www.warhistoryonline.com/war-articles/hall-of-famers-wwii.html.
New York City Bowling Association. *Official List of Prize Winners of the 1934 Metropolitan Bowling Championships*. New York: New York City Bowling Association, 1934.

Pathe Exchange. "Weatherproof. Motion Picture Copyright Descriptions Collection. Class M, 1912–1977." January 13, 1927. https://www.loc.gov/item/s1229m03736/.

Petersen Classic. "About the Petersen Classic." Petersen Classic. Accessed February 10, 2023. http://www.petersenclassic.com/about-the-petersen-classic/.

Petersen Classic. *Louis P. Petersen Championship Bowling Classic Honor Roll.* Wauwatosa, WI: Petersen Classic, 2019. http://www.petersenclassic.com/wp-content/uploads/2019/05/Petersen-HonorRoll2018.pdf.

"President Reorganizes Council: Lovell Named Chairman." *President's Council on Physical Fitness and Sports Newsletter,* October 1970. https://www.google.com/books/edition/Newsletter_President_s_Council_on_Physic/8F1eBCE1SOYC?hl=en&gbpv=1.

Pro Football Hall of Fame. "Football's Wartime Heroes." Pro Football Hall of Fame. 2021. https://www.profootballhof.com/news/2005/01/footballs-wartime-heroes.

Professional Bowlers Association. "Bowling Lingo." Accessed July 17, 2023. https://www.pba.com/about/bowling-lingo.

Professional Bowlers Association. "Earl Anthony." PBA: Professional Bowlers Association. Accessed December 21, 2022. https://www.pba.com/players/earl-anthony.

Ratings Ryan. "Weekly Nielsen Ratings: 1981–82 TV Season." *Ratings Ryan* (blog). January 14, 2021. http://www.ratingsryan.com/2021/01/weekly-nielsen-ratings-1981-82-tv-season.html.

Richgels, Jeff. *11thframe.com* (blog). Accessed August 7, 2023. https://www.11thframe.com.

Richgels, Jeff. "Ray Orf Was Glenn Allison a Decade Before Allison Became Mr. 900: The Story of the Stunning 890 ABC Turned Down but Paid Off." *11thframe.com* (blog), July 9, 2020. https://11thframe.com/news/article/12203/Ray-Orf-was-Glenn-Allison-a-decade-before-Allison-became-Mr-900.

Richgels, Jeff. "Would Winning the 2022 USBC Masters on Sunday Make Norm Duke Bowling's GOAT?" *11thframe.com* (blog), April 2, 2022. https://www.11thframe.com/news/article/13448.

Schmidt, J.R. "An Andy Varipapa Bibliography." *Dr. Jake's Bowling History Blog.* August 6, 2009. https://bowlinghistory.wordpress.com/2009/08/06/an-andy-varipapa-bibliography/.

Schmidt, J.R. "Complete All-Americans to 1950." *Dr. Jake's Bowling History Blog.* March 9, 2011. https://bowlinghistory.wordpress.com/2011/03/09/complete-all-americans/.

Schmidt, J.R. *Dr. Jake's Bowling History Blog.* Last modified August 15, 2023. https://bowlinghistory.wordpress.com.

Schmidt, J.R. "Famous Teams." *Dr. Jake's Bowling History Blog.* Last modified August 8, 2023. https://bowlinghistory.wordpress.com/category/famous-teams/.

Schmidt, J.R. "Johnny Voorhies Bibliography." *Dr. Jake's Bowling Blog.* February 11, 2021, https://bowlinghistory.wordpress.com/2021/02/11/a-johnny-voorhies-bibliography/.

Schmidt, J.R. "Landgraf Classic." *Dr. Jake's Bowling History Blog.* May 14, 2020. https://bowlinghistory.wordpress.com/2020/05/14/landgraf-classic-bowling-tournament-new-york-list-of-champions/.

Schmidt, J.R. "Match Game Championship (Individual)." *Dr. Jake's Bowling History Blog.* January 1, 2009. https://bowlinghistory.wordpress.com/2009/01/01/match-game-championship-individual/.

Schmidt, J.R. "When 'The ABC' Was Classic." United States Bowling Congress. April 4, 2012. https://bowl.com/news/when-the-abc-was-classic.

Schmidt, J.R. "Wrong Foot Louie." *Dr. Jake's Bowling History Blog.* October 12, 2016. https://bowlinghistory.wordpress.com/2016/10/12/wrong-foot-louie-lou-campi-famous-bowler/.

Schultz, E.J. "Wheaties Makes Marketing Strike with Retro Bowling Ads." *AdAge* (blog), March 27, 2015. https://adage.com/article/see-the-spot/wheaties-makes-marketing-strike-retro-bowling-ads/297793.

"Sheila R. Weidenfeld Files, 1974–1977." Ann Arbor, MI, Box 46. Gerald R. Ford Presidential Library and Museum. https://www.fordlibrarymuseum.gov/library/guides/findingaid/weidenfeldfiles.asp.

Smith, Aaron. "Anthony Simonsen Wins Second USBC Masters Title at 2022 Event." USBC News. April 3, 2022. https://bowl.com/news/anthony-simonsen-wins-second-usbc-masters-title-at-2022-event.

Smith, Aaron. "Glenn Allison Makes 71st Appearance at USBC Open Championships." USBC News, May 16, 2023. https://bowl.com/news/glenn-allison-makes-71st-appearance-at-usbc-open-championships.

Sports Reference LLC. "Baseball-Reference.Com—Major League Statistics and Information." 2023. https://www.baseball-reference.com.

Sports Reference LLC. "Pro-Football-Reference.Com—Pro Football Statistics and History." 2023. https://www.pro-football-reference.com.

Stobo, John. "Labor History Time Line for the Brooklyn Navy Yard." The Brooklyn Navy Yard: Civil Servants Building Warships. Last modified June 2005. http://www.columbia.edu/~jrs9/BNY-Labor-Time-Line.html.

Stobo, John. "Unions at the Brooklyn Navy Yard." The Brooklyn Navy Yard: Civil Servants Building Warships. Last modified October 2005. http://www.columbia.edu/~jrs9/BNY-unions.html.

Thomas, John C. "Star-Crossed: The Colorful History of the Chicago Coliseum." *Owlcation!* July 14, 2022. https://owlcation.com/humanities/Star-Crossed-The-Colorful-History-of-the-Chicago-Coliseum.

Thompson, Ted. "Kegel's Revolutionary Slope Graphs." White Papers & Articles—Kegel, Built for Bowling. February 10, 2012. https://www.kegel.net/articles/kegels-revolutionary-slope-graphs.

Travers, Mark. "No, You Were Not Happier Way Back When. Here's Why." *Psychology Today* (blog), January 20, 2021. https://www.psychologytoday.com/us/blog/social-instincts/202101/no-you-were-not-happier-way-back-when-heres-why.

TWC Product and Technology. "Erlanger, KY Weather History." Weather Underground. 2023. https://www.wunderground.com/history/daily/KCVG/date/1955-8-20.

United States Bowling Congress. *Equipment Specifications and Certifications Manual*. Arlington, TX: United States Bowling Congress, 2022. https://images.bowl.com/bowl/media/legacy/internap/bowl/equipandspecs/pdfs/ESManual.pdf.

United States Bowling Congress. "Hall of Famers." USBC Hall of Fame. Accessed January 24, 2023. https://bowl.com/usbc-hall-of-fame/hall-of-famers.

United States Bowling Congress. "History." High School. Accessed May 10, 2023. https://bowl.com/youth/high-school/history.

United States Bowling Congress. "Individual Records." USBC Records. Accessed January 17, 2023. https://bowl.com/getmedia/915d5f03-543c-4b19-823a-c11e9135cce0/ptindividualrecords-3.pdf.

United States Bowling Congress. "Oddities—Honor Scores." USBC Records. Accessed January 17, 2023. https://bowl.com/getmedia/915d5f03-543c-4b19-823a-c11e9135cce0/ptindividualrecords-3.pdf.

United States Department of Justice. "The Paramount Decrees." United States Department of Justice, Antitrust Division. Last updated August 7, 2020. https://www.justice.gov/atr/paramount-decree-review.

Urbistat. "Municipality of Carfizzi." Aminstat Italia. Accessed October 21, 2022. https://ugeo.urbistat.com/AdminStat/en/it/demografia/popolazione/carfizzi/101003/4.

Varipapa, Andy, II. "Andy Varipapa: Bowling's Legendary Champion Showman." Last modified March 13, 2022. http://www.andyvaripapa.com.

"Varipapa Family Papers." Private collections of Joseph Ruffolo, Andy Varipapa II, and Susan Varipapa.

Vint, Bill. "Chris Warren Expands All-Time Regional Titles Lead with 55th Win." USBC News. October 25, 2019. https://bowl.com/news/chris-warren-expands-all-time-regional-titles-lead-with-55th-win.

Webster, Ian. "Inflation Calculator." U.S. Official Inflation Data, Alioth Finance. Last updated August 10, 2023. https://www.officialdata.org/.

Wheelock, David C. "The Great Depression: An Overview." Federal Reserve Bank of St. Louis. Accessed December 11, 2022. https://www.stlouisfed.org/~/media/files/pdfs/great-depression/the-great-depression-wheelock-overview.pdf.

Williams, Dave. "The Bowling Chain That Started Them All." *California USBC News!* (blog), July 25, 2021. https://calusbc.wordpress.com/2021/07/25/the-bowling-chain-that-started-them-all/.

Wiseman, Lucas. "U.S. Women's Open Champion Crowned." USBC News, June 27, 2012, https://bowl.com/news/u-s-women-39;s-open-champion-crowned.

World Pool-Billiard Association—Artistic Pool Division. "Sport History." World Pool-Billiard Association—Official Website of the Artistic Pool Division. 2017. https://www.wpa-apd.org/sports-history.

Zellner, Bob. "The Eastern Open." In *37th Annual Eastern Open*, 5. Garden City, NY: Bowling Corporation of America, 1984.

Zieroth, Tim. "Baseball and Basketball Players." Baseball Almanac. 2023. https://www.baseball-almanac.com/legendary/baseball_and_basketball_players.shtml.

Newspaper Databases

Ancestry. "Historical Newspapers from 1700s-2000s—Newspapers.Com." Newspapers.com. 2023. https://www.newspapers.com/.

Empire State Library Network. "NYS Historic Newspapers." NYS Historic Newspapers. Accessed February 9, 2023. https://nyshistoricnewspapers.org/.

New York Times. "Over 150 Years of New York Times Journalism, as it Originally Appeared." Times Machine. 2023. https://timesmachine.nytimes.com/.

NewspaperArchive. "Newspaper Archive 1700s-2023." NewspaperArchive. 2023. https://newspaperarchive.com/.

United States Library of Congress. "Chronicling America: Historic American Newspapers." Chronicling America. Accessed February 9, 2023. https://chroniclingamerica.loc.gov/.

Newspapers Cited

Afro-American (Baltimore)
Akron Beacon Journal
Albuquerque Journal
Allentown [PA] *Morning Call*
Appleton [WI] *Post-Crescent*
Arlington Heights [IL] *Herald*
Asbury Park [NJ] *Press*
Atlanta Constitution
Baltimore Sun
Battle Creek [MI] *Enquirer and News*
Bayonne [NJ] *Times*
Bergen Evening Record (Hackensack, NJ)
Binghamton [NY] *Press*
Birmingham News

Bibliography

Birmingham Post-Herald
Bogalusa [LA] *Bulletin*
Bradford [PA] *Era*
Bridgeport [CT] *Evening Farmer*
Bristol [PA] *Courier*
Bristol [PA] *Daily Courier*
Bristol [TN] *Herald Courier*
Brooklyn Citizen
Brooklyn Daily Eagle
Brooklyn Daily Times
Brooklyn Eagle
Buffalo Commercial
Buffalo Courier
Buffalo Evening News
Buffalo Express
Buffalo Times
Capital Times (Madison, WI)
Cedar Rapids Evening Gazette
Chanute Field Wings (Champaign, IL)
Charleston [WV] *Gazette*
Chicago Tribune
Cincinnati Enquirer
Cincinnati Post
Cincinnati Times-Star
Columbus [NE] *Telegram*
Coshocton [OH] *Daily Times*
Courier-Journal (Louisville)
Courier-News (Bridgewater, NJ)
Courier Post (Camden, NJ)
Daily Argus (Mount Vernon, NY)
Daily Argus Leader (Sioux Falls, SD)
Daily Home News (New Brunswick, NJ)
Daily Inter Ocean (Chicago)
Daily Journal (Franklin, IN)
Daily News (New York)
Daily Record (Parsippany, NJ)
Daily Republican (Monongahela, PA)
Daily Times (Davenport, IA)
Dayton Daily News
Dayton Herald
Dayton Journal
Dayton Sunday Journal-Herald
Decatur [IL] *Herald*
Des Moines Register
Des Moines Tribune
Detroit Free Press
Detroit News
Detroit Times
Dunkirk [NY] *Evening Observer*
Elmira [NY] *Star-Gazette*
Elwood [IN] *Call-Leader*
Enid [OK] *Morning News*
Evansville [IN] *Press*
Evening Courier (Camden, NJ)
Evening Independent (Massillon, OH)
Evening News (Wilkes-Barre, PA)
Evening Star (Washington, D.C.)
Evening Sun (Baltimore, MD)
Evening World-Herald (Omaha, NE)
Florida Today (Cocoa, FL)
Fort Lauderdale News
Fort Worth Star-Telegram
Gettysburg [PA] *Times*

Green Bay Press-Gazette
Greensboro Daily News
Hammond [IN] *Times*
Hartford Courant
Herald-News (Passaic, NJ)
Herald Statesman (Yonkers, NY)
Home News (New Brunswick, NJ)
Honolulu Star-Bulletin
Indianapolis News
Indianapolis Star
Indianapolis Times
Jersey Journal (Jersey City, NJ)
Journal-News (Nyack, NY)
Kansas City Star
Kenosha [WI] *Evening News*
Kenosha [WI] *News*
Kingston [NY] *Daily Freeman*
Lansing [MI] *State Journal*
Lewiston [ME] *Sun-Journal*
Lexington [KY] *Leader*
Lincoln [NE] *Star*
Liverpool [UK] *Daily Post*
Long Island Bowling News (Levittown, NY)
Long-Islander (Huntington, NY)
Los Angeles Mirror
Los Angeles Times
Lynwood [CA] *Tribune*
Manchester [UK] *Evening News*
Mansfield [OH] *News-Journal*
Mason City [IA] *Globe-Gazette*
Memphis Press-Scimitar
Miami Herald
Minneapolis Journal
Minneapolis Tribune
Modesto [CA] *Bee*
Monroe [LA] *News-Star*
Monrovia [CA] *Daily News*
Montclair [NJ] *Times*
Montgomery [AL] *Advertiser*
Montreal River Miner (Hurley, WI)
Morgan City [LA] *Review*
Morning Call (Allentown, PA)
Morning Call (Paterson, NJ)
Morning News (Wilmington, DE)
Nashville Banner
Nassau Daily Review-Star (Freeport, NY)
New Castle [PA] *Daily Herald*
New York Post
New York Times
News Beacon (Fair Lawn, NJ)
Newsday (Garden City, Hempstead, and Melville, NY)
Niagara Gazette (Niagara Falls, NY)
Oakland Tribune
Observer (Northport, NY)
Ogden [UT] *Standard*
Ogden [UT] *Standard-Examiner*
Orlando Sentinel
Oshkosh [WI] *Northwestern*
Palm Beach [FL] *Post*
Passaic [NJ] *Daily News*
Pensacola [FL] *News-Journal*
Philadelphia Inquirer

Pittsburgh Post
Pittsburgh Press
Pittsburgh Sun-Telegraph
Plain Speaker (Hazelton, PA)
Plainfield [NJ] *Courier-News*
Port Huron [MI] *Times Herald*
Portage [WI] *Daily Register*
Post-Register (Idaho Falls, ID)
Post-Star (Glens Falls, NY)
Pottsville [PA] *Evening Republican*
Poughkeepsie [NY] *New Yorker*
Progress-Bulletin (Pomona, CA)
Racine [WI] *Journal-Times*
Rapid City [SD] *Journal*
Record (Hackensack, NJ)
Reno Gazette-Journal
Rochester Democrat and Chronicle
St. Cloud [MN] *Times*
St. Louis Globe-Democrat
St. Louis Post-Dispatch
St. Louis Star-Times
Salt Lake Tribune
San Antonio Express
San Francisco Examiner
San Pedro [CA] *News-Pilot*
Sandusky [OH] *Register Star-News*
Scranton [PA] *Times*
Scranton [PA] *Tribune*
Scrantonian (Scranton, PA)

Sheboygan [WI] *Press*
Shreveport [LA] *Journal*
Sidney [OH] *Daily News*
South Bend [IN] *Tribune*
Spectrum and Daily News (St. George, UT)
Spokesman-Review (Spokane, WA)
Standard Sentinel (Hazelton, PA)
Standard Union (Brooklyn, NY)
Stars and Stripes (Darmstadt, Germany)
Staunton [VA] *Leader*
Sun-Sentinel (Fort Lauderdale, FL)
Sunday Call-Chronicle (Allentown, PA)
Sunday Dispatch (Moline, IL)
Sunday Herald-Leader (Lexington, KY)
Sunday Home News (New Brunswick, NJ)
Sunday Register (Shrewsbury, NJ)
Sunday Star (Washington, D.C.)
Sunday Times (New Brunswick, NJ)
Syracuse Post-Standard
Tampa Daily Times
Times Leader (Wilkes-Barre, PA)
Tribune (Scranton, PA)
Tucson Daily Citizen
Valley Times (North Hollywood, CA)
Wall Street Journal
Windsor [Ontario, Canada] *Daily Star*
Wisconsin State Journal (Madison)
The World (New York)

Index

Numbers in ***bold italics*** indicate pages with illustration

ABC (American Bowling Congress) 7, 39, 50, 55–57, 146, 189, 193n6, 202n39, 202n44, 206–207n43; Andy's Open Championships performance 30–31, 62, 78–79, 98–100, 104–***107***, 116, 122, 126, 128, 139; Classic Division 205n43; founding 7–9; Hall of Fame 36, 95, 128–129, 132, 139–***141***, 175–176, 187, 194n32; lane inspection and certification 39, 66, 83, 156–158; Masters 129, 134–135, 148, 150, Open Championships 9, 18–19, 29–31, 33, 43, 62, 75–77, 83–84, 86, 89, 91, 97, 132, 142, 145, ***159***, 178, 180, 206n56; *see also* eagle; USBC

ABC (American Broadcasting Company) 1, 10, 134, 169; *see also Professional Bowlers Tour*

Academy Awards 1, 50, 56
accent 33, 48, 159, 170
Adamek, Donna 174
Adams, Tom 179
Adelphi Academy 51, 68
Advisory Conference on Physical Fitness and Sports 1, 160, ***161***, 188
Airway Classic 107
Albemarle Lanes 79
All-American Teams *see Bowlers Journal International*
All-Star *see* BPAA All-Star
All-Star Bowling 136
Allen, Bill 163
Allen, Patrick 180
Allison, Glenn 157, 215n70
amateurs 7, 179, 180, 222n5
American Bowling Congress *see* ABC
American Dream Classic 217n40

American Junior Bowling Congress (AJBC) *see* YABA
American Machine and Foundry *see* AMF
American System *see* Western System
AMF (American Machine and Foundry) 40, 142, 159, 160, 176
Anderson Classic 99
Andy Varipapa Memorial Match Game Championship 179–180
Andy Varipapa Stars of the Future 172
Andy Varipapa 300 157, 180; *see also* 300 games
Andy Varipapa's Quick Way to Better Bowling 132, 152, 165
Anson, Cap 36, 199n15
Antenora, Joe 163
Anthony, Earl 10, 15, 47, 113, 155, 163, 169, ***170***, 173
Antler's Hotel Lanes 71
Archibald, John 180
Arnhorst, Chester 51, 76, 95
artistic pool *see* billiards
Asher, Barry 200n22
Askins, James 47
Atlas, Charles 162
Auditorium Theatre 89, 112
automatic pinsetters 8–9, 14–15, ***128***, 152, 189, 194n21, 216n2; invention 142–145
automobile accidents 64, 69–71, 152–153

Baker, Frank 130, ***131***, 158
Baldwin Modern 96, 117, 136
balls 7, 9, 14, 88, 91, ***163***, 165, custom fit 129–130, 189, 190, 191; performance 155, 184, 206n11, 219n27; specifications 7, 165, 194n17
Barclay, David *see* O'Brien, Dave

Barnes, Chris 180, 181
Bartlett, Charles 97–98, 103, 119–120
baseball 6, 8, 27, 36, 44, 50, 81, 88, 126, 129; Andy playing 6, 19–***21***, 66, 158, 162; Frank playing 51, 68; *see also* Brooklyn Dodgers; Cincinnati Reds; Crosley Field; Ebbets Field; New York Yankees
Bates, Sully 129–130
Bauer, John 57
Baumgarten, Elmer 8, 50, 57, 86, 128
Bay Ridge Athletics 20–***21***
Bay Ridge Bowling Academy 32
Beach, Bill 174
Beech-Nut 114
beer teams 62
Bell, Andy 20, 158
Belmonte, Jason 10, 113, 156
Benkovic, Frank 15, 39–40, 71, 90–91, 97
Bensinger's Randolph Recreation 75
Bergman & Trucks Casino Alleys 37
Berle, Milton ***147***–148
Berman, Len 154
Better Bowling 72, 108
"Better Bowling by Andy Varipapa" 105
bicycle accident 6, 21
billiards 8, 22, 29, 31, 41–44, 48, 67, 84, 152
Blaney's Bowling Alleys 56
Blick's Bowling Center 56
Blouin, Jimmy 30, 75–76, 78, 129
Blue, Ben 79
Bluth, Ray 136, 150, 173
BNY *see* Brooklyn Navy Yard
Bodis, Joe 58, 62
Boghosian, Brian 180

237

Bohn, Parker III 44, 47–48, 180
The Bolero 142
Bomar, Buddy 92, 96, 100, **104**, 110–111, 114, 116, 118, 120, 129, 136, **159**, 173, 184–185; All-Star performances 90, 95, 97–98, 101, 112, 119, 125–126, 128
Botten, Eddie 51, 136
Bowl Mart 129–130, 148, 154, 171, 179, 183–184
Bowl-O-Mat 150
Bowler of the Half-Century 129, 214n42; *see also* Marino, Hank
Bowler of the Year 94, 96, 99, 110, 117–118, 125, 145, 173, 187; *see also* BWAA
Bowlero Mineola 171, 179
Bowlers Journal see Bowlers Journal International
Bowlers Journal International 2, 10, 17, 43, 59, **68**, 72, 96, 99, 126, 134, 148, 177–178, 187–188; All-American Teams 95–96, 110, 117, 187; Person of the Century 10, 187
Bowlers to Veterans Link *see* BVL
bowling balls *see* balls
bowling boom 9, 15, 132, 142, 145, 154
Bowling Corporation of America 148, 179, 217n44, 222n2
Bowling Digest 126, 148, 188
Bowling Headliners 9, 59, 137
bowling leagues *see* leagues
Bowling Magazine 188
bowling pins *see* pins
Bowling Proprietors Association of America *see* BPAA
bowling schools 33, 93, 114, 119, 137; *see also* Chicago bowling school; Detroit bowling school
Bowling Stars 9, 136
Bowling Tricks 107–**109**, 114–**115**, 137, **181**, 225
Bowling Writers Association of America *see* BWAA
Bowl Lo-Mac Lanes 152
Bowlmor Recreation 92
boxing 74, 77, 81, 133–134, 205n3; Andy's career 19–20, 22
BPAA (Bowling Proprietors Association of America) 76–79, 189; Andy's dispute with 56–58, 62, 64–65, 67
BPAA All-Star 2, 9, 29, 60, 68, 85–98, 100–105, 112–114, 117, 119–120, 124–125, 127–128, 132–134, 146, 148, 150, 154, 156, 157, 169, 187, 209n53, 212n57; founding 81–85; *see also* U.S. Open (bowling)
BPAA National Match Games Championship *see* BPAA All-Star
BPAA National Match Games Doubles Championship 111, 120–121, 150
Brandt, Allie 101–103, **159**, 175, 211n42
Branham, George III 147
Braymiller, Lee 101
Brill, Frank 9, 29
Brodie, Buster 52, **55**
Brooklyn Alley Owners Tournament 32, 36, 156, 187
Brooklyn Dodgers 74, 79, 137; *see also* baseball
Brooklyn Navy Yard 25–29
Brown's Recreation 96
Brunswick 33, 40, 72, 83, **109**, 126, 134, 148, 176, 190, 194n23; Andy's sponsor **102**–103, **104–105**, 106–**107**, 110, 114, 122, **128**, 130–131, 133, 136, **143–144**, 171, 173–174, **182**, 184, 188; lane construction and maintenance 51, 72, 89, 124; pinsetters 142, 154, 166
Brunswick Memorial World Open 171, 174–175, 188
Buckley, Ed 100
Buddy Bomar Diamond Medal Classic 92
Budweiser 62
Bujack, Fred 97, 209n57
Bukowski, Chet 100–101
Buonomo, Tony 39
Burling, Catherine 125
Burton, Nelson, Jr. "Bo" 48, 72, 184–185
Burton, Nelson, Sr. 62, 64–67, 72, 85, 94, 97, 100, 106, 111
Bushwick 25, 29, 80, 92
BVL (Bowlers to Veterans Link) 169, 172
BWAA (Bowling Writers Association of America) 173, 189; *see also* Bowler of the Year

Camels 114
Campi, Lou 92, 111, 116, 120, 134, 136, 148, 187
candlepin bowling 192, 193n9
Capitol Alleys 65–66, 133; *see also* Dwyer's Broadway Academy
car accidents *see* automobile accidents
Cardamone, Carmen 13
Cardamone, Concetta 12–13, 138, 158
Cardamone, Frank Joseph 12–13, 25
Carfizzi 6, 11–12, 20, 110
Carlson, Adolph 76, 98, 101, **140**
Carmody, Dick 166, 178, 180
Carmody, Gerry 166
Carter, Don 15, 61, 113, 120, 132, 148, 150, 152, 173, 184; All-Star Lanes 174; Ebonite contract 9, 145, 154
Casey, William 32
Cassio, Marty 95, 98, 100, 107, 133, 136
Castellano, Graz 106, **107**, 109, 117, 134, 136, 174
Central Bowling Academy 100
Century Lanes 164–176, 179
Century's Huntington Lanes *see* Century Lanes
Championship Bowling 136, 145, 156
Charles Fritz Academy 39
Chicago Bowling Proprietors Association 124
Chicago bowling school 88, 90, 92–93, 95, 126, 134; *see also* bowling schools
Chicago Coliseum 75, 81, 83, 85, 89
Chicago Tribune 67, 81–86, 88–89, 92–95, 97–98, 100–101, 103, 117, 119
Cincinnati Reds 136–137; *see also* baseball
Cirillo, Al 58–59, 60, 67, 134
Clause, Frankie 146
Cleckner, Eddie 51
Clemente, Dick 116, 151, 157, 177
Club Bob-Lo Lanes **71**, 72
Coca-Cola 72, 81, 114
Cohn, Harry 30–31
Cole, Benny 19
Comerford, Ed 131
Connors, Chuck 68
Cook, Gus 30, 31
Cornacchia, Alice 111; *see also* DeForest, Alice
Cornacchia, Connie 25, 58, 89–90, 111, **151**, 163, 179
Cornacchia, Michael **151**, 176
Cornacchia, Mike 90, 111, **151**
Cornelia Baseball Club 21
Crescent Individual Sweepstakes 116
Crimmins, Johnny 85–86, 90–91, 93, 99–101, 119
crisscross 44, **46**, 181
Crosley Field 136–137; *see also* baseball
Crover, Jim 46–47
Cummins, Tait 105

Davis, Dave 160, 163
Daw, Charley 15, 37, 39, 40, 76, 83, 85
Day, Ned 62–63, 71, 78–79, 88, **104**, 107, 111, 116, 118–120, 126, 129, 132, 134–135, **140**, 155, 165, 174–175, 184–185; All-Star performances 83–86, 90–91, 93–95, 97–101; endorsements 72, 103, 114; *Set 'Em Up 70*, 72–73, 180
Dayon, Johnny 120
Day's Recreation 85
DeForest, Alice **151**; *see also* Cornacchia, Alice
Demaree, Al 44
DeNicola, Robert 138–139
Detroit bowling school 67–68, 72, 88, 91–92, 134, 151; *see also* bowling schools
Detroit News 67, 72, 88
DeVito, Dominick 92, 100; *see also* DeVito Classic
DeVito, Ralph 51
DeVito Classic 96, 119, 126; *see also* DeVito, Dominick
DiMaggio, Joe 160, 162, 175
DiMartino, Alice *see* Varipapa, Alice
Doehrman, Bill 176
Don Carter All-Star Lanes *see* Carter, Don
double-elimination tournament 84, 129
Downtown Bowl 109
Drake, Ted **143**
Dreamer 212n53
Dressel, Jim 2, 158, 177
dressing *see* lane conditions
duckpin bowling 132, 192, 193n9
Duke, Norm 47–48, 155–156, 180–181, 185
DuMont Network 34
Dwyer, Frank 26, 62; *see also* Dwyer's Broadway Academy
Dwyer's Broadway Academy 33, 35–38, 40; *see also* Dwyer, Frank

eagle 29–30, 78, 99, 104, 106, 116, 190; *see also* ABC Open Championships
Easter, Ebber "Sarge" 92, 100, 119–120, 125–126, **127**, 129
Eastern All-Star Classic League 106, 136
Eastern Open *see* Newsday Eastern Open
Eastern Match Game Championship 71, 76
Eastern System 26–27, 197n19
Ebbets, Charles 74

Ebbets Field 6, 79
Ebonite 9, 145, 154
Eddie and Earl Linsz Five 106
Edelman, Norm 177
education 3, 11, 13–14, 23, 185
Ehler, Herman 16–18, 195n7
Elias, Eddie 148–**149**
Ellis, Don 173–174
Ellis Island 1, 12, 35
Empire Bowling and Billiards Academy 29, 31, 71
Empire State Open 111, 148
endorsements 1, 103, 114, 139
Engan, Ralph 146
Equitable Life 1, 114
European tour (1951) 130
European tour (1965) 159
Evans, Dick 103, 148, 180, 217n50
Exposition Park Armory 106

Faetz Recreation 96
Falcaro, Adeline 90
Falcaro, Joe 15, 50–51, 62, 65, 71, 73, 76–79, 83, 92, 95, 96, 100, 106, 117, 129, 155, 207n17; doubles match 37–38, 59, 75; endorsements 114; personality 34–36, 60, 76; relationship with Andy 38–40, 90, 116, 131; shooting 77; trick shots 46–47, 49–50, 133
Faliero, Mike 179
fancy billiards *see* billiards
Farragut Pool Lanes 32, 142
Faulkner, Gary, Jr. 147
Fazio, Buzz 100, 136, 145–146, 173, 174
Feller, Bob 84, 88
Fellmeth, Catherine **109**
Fifty-Plus Program 158, 162
Fiorito, Matt 180
Firestone Tournament of Champions 10, 154, 168
Fitch Hair Tonic 114
five-pin bowling 8, 192
Flatbush 79, 92
Flesch, Bill 119–120
flying dutchman 44, 50, 52, 108; *see also* flying eagle; trick shots
flying eagle 180–181; *see also* flying dutchman; trick shots
Formula 1 74
Fothergill, Dotty 174
Fraenkle, George 17
Fraternity Hall 16–17
Frideman, Leon 5–6
Fuoco, Concetta *see* Cardamone, Concetta

G. Krueger Brewing Company 136

Gablinger's Light Beer 139, 216n58
gallbladder surgery 137–139
gambling 5, 7, 8, 19, 33, 41, 131
Garden City Bowl 154, 169, 172, 179, 185; *see also* PBA Long Island Open
Geisler, Lou 92, 94
Geisler, Mary 92, 94
Gelhausen, Felix 106, **107**
General Mills 1, 181
Gengler, John "Count" 18, 34, 37, 43–44, 155, 180
George Young Memorial High Average Award 93
Gerloskie, Harry 39
Giannone, John 187
Gibson, Therm 95–99, 111, 136, 148
Gillette 72, 114
Glen Lyon Alleys 61
Gold Bond Acoustical Tiles 114
golf 7, 10, 15, 50, 74, 79, 82, 84, 97, 148, 150
Golobic, Rex 158
Goodyear 1, 114
Grantland Rice Sportlights see *Sportlights*
Grauer, Robert 28
Great and the Greatest 173–174
Great Depression 38–39, 49, 62, 79, 83
Greater Cincinnati Bowling Association 124
"The Greek" 110
Green, Garry "Dead-Center" 41–43, 180
Grossman, Max 67–**68**, 90
Grumman Aircraft 123–124, 130

Hall of Fame *see* American Bowling Congress Hall of Fame; International Bowling Museum and Hall of Fame
Handegard, John 120
handicap 28, 32, 190, 197n32
Hansly, Bill 106–**107**
Hap Morse Lanes 64
Hardwick, Billy 10, 154
Harper and Brothers 2, 150–152
Havoline 72, 114
Hawaii trip 122–**123**
Haynes, Frank 112
heckler 60
Heil Products 62, 79
Heineman, Eddie 50, 71, 92, 100; *see also* Heineman's
Heineman's 93, 98–99, 115–117, 124, 213n15; *see also* Heineman, Eddie
Hempstead 94–95, 98, 111, 114, 118–120, 122, 126, 135–136, 152

Hempstead Recreation 92–94, 96, 98, 100, 106, 116–*118*, 120, 123, 130, 157
Hennessey, Tom 173
Hermann's Undertakers 62
High Roller 180
Himmler, Brian 180
Hinkley, Robert "Doc" 130
Hoboken 23, 25
Hoefner, Butch 39
Hollywood 22, 49–56, 72–73, 107–108, *147*–148, 170
Holman, Marshall 173–174, 200n22
Honolulu Bowling Center 122
Hoover, Dick 127, 129, 148, 150, 173
Hubert, Mary Jane 62
Hudson, Tommy 173
Huntington 169, 171, 176
Huntington Bay 163–165, 177
Husted, Dave 113

immigrants 5–7, 12; Andy's experience 1, 12–13; attitudes towards 13, 23
"Improve Your Bowling by Andy Varipapa" 68
Industrial Revolution 6–7, 11
International Bowling Federation 8, 190
International Bowling Museum and Hall of Fame 176–*177*, 183–184
International Jewish Sports Hall of Fame 43, 200n22
Italy 1, 6, 11–13, 23, 66, 110, 159, 186, 188

Jackson, Lowell 79, 84–85
Joe Thum's White Elephant Alleys 16, 43, 50
Johnny Unitas' Colt Lanes 9, 154
Johns, Lee 27
Johnson, Charley, Jr. 112
Johnson, Don 154
Johnson, Earl 147
Johnson, Walter 101
Jones, Windy *see* Cirillo, Al
Jordan, Michael 10, 181
Jordan, Tom 101
Joseph, Joe 173
Jouglard, Lee 129

Kalman, Victor 36, 76, 142
Kapiolani Lanes 122
Kartheiser, Frank 76
Kasimakis, Rudy "Revs" 180
Kawolics, Ed 85, 100, 110, 119
Keating, Jim 67
Keller, Chris 208n36
Keller, Pearl 180

Kelly, Edward 89
Kelsey, George 43
Kenmore Bowling Center 79–80, 89–90, 92–94
Kennedy, Robert 78
Kissoff, Joe 33, 106
Kistenmacher, Fred 31
Knickerbocker Alleys 7
Knox, Billy 43, 78
Koepp, Eddie 92, 106
Koster, John 19, 42
Kouros, Tom 99, 178
Kraft, Dick 32
Krajkovich, Joe 178
Kraus, Charlie 148
Kretzer, Brian 18
Krumske, Paul 90, 94–95, 97, 101, 118
Krupa, Joe 65
Kudlik, Louis 182–183, *184*
Kulick, Kelly 137
Kusky, Tony 92, 119–120, 154
Kusky, Walt 120

lacquer 88, 154–155, 190; *see also* lane conditions
Ladewig, Marion 15, 125–126, 184
Lafayette College 92, 117
Lambert, J.D. Wooster 62
Landgraf, Bill 92, 187
Landgraf Classic 9, 92–93, 116, 185, 187
lane conditions 66, 79, 83, 86, 91, 110, 155–157, 163, 184, 204n13; *see also* lacquer; polyurethane; shellac
Lange, Herb *140*
Las Vegas 108, 155, 173, 180
LaSpina, John 158, 169, 172, 183–184
Lattin, Al 65–66
Lauman, Hank 110
Lawford, Peter *147*
Lawler, Ed 31, 32, 35
Lawler, Jim 31
Lawler Brothers Bowling and Billiards Academy 29, 31–34, 36–37, 40, 67, 156
Lawler's *see* Lawler Brothers Bowling and Billiards Academy
leagues 9, 18, 26–27, 56, 74, 79, 154, 156, 190; *see also* Brooklyn Alley Owners Tournament; Eastern All-Star Classic League; Metal Trades League; National Bowling League; PBA League
Learn, Bob, Jr. 47
Leavy, Harry 30–31
Ledene, Harry, Jr. 62
Lee's Lanes 128

left-handed bowlers 162–163, 220n66
leg injury *see* bicycle accident
Lewis, Stan 129–130, 148, 179
Liberty Aircraft 93, 124, 209n48
Lichstein, Larry 185
Lillard, Bill 132, 136, 173–174
Lindemann, Tony 128
Lindsey, Mort 34, 39, 46–47, 51, 62, 75, 78, 83, 106, *140*, 201n31; trick shots 34, 42–44, 50, 180
lineup 27–28, 30
Lizzo, Jeff 171
Lizzo, Jim 167, 170–171, 179
Llo-Da-Mar Bowl 72, 85
Lloyd, Harold 72, 85
Long Island Championship 32, 96, 187
Long Island Industrial Championship 93, 123–124
Long Island Open 169, 172, 185
Louis P. Petersen System *see* Petersen Point System
Lown, Roy 163
Lubanski, Ed 126–*127*, 148
Luby, Mort, Jr. 177–178
Luby, Mort, Sr. 95, 110, 177
Lucke, Leo 31, 35
Luft, Mel 32
Lustig, Jim 179
Lynwood Lanes 51

machinist 23–25, 103
Madison Square Garden *160*, 169
Madison Street Armory 112, 124, 134
Make It and Take It 134
Make That Spare 9
Malverne Bowling Center 93
Mantovani, Sis 117
Manzione, Gianmarc 182
Maple Lanes 158, 169, 184
Marathon Match Game Champion 65
Marino, Hank 58, 62, 72–73, 83, 85, 129, *140*, *159*, 174–175; world champion 77, 79; *see also* Bowler of the Half-Century
Marino Classic 119
Marks, Lou 136, 178
Markus, Lew 65–66
Marshall, Dottie *see* Varipapa, Dottie
Marshall, Frederick *124*
Marshall, Madeline *124*
Martin, Steve 174–175
*M*A*S*H* 171
Masters *see* ABC Masters
Masters (golf tournament) 10, 73, 154, 205n2

Index

match points 197n31
Mathias, Warren 148
Maurer, Ed 110
Mayer, Louis B. 49–50
Mayfair Bowling Academy 32
Mays, Willie 9, 145
Mazzola, Frank 177
McCutcheon, Floretta 33, 117, 126
McDermott, John 9
McDonough, Charlie 100
McKee, Sally 52–53, **55**
McMahon, Art 110
McMahon, Junie 78, 98–99, 110, 117, 129, 132, 134–136, 174; All-Star performances 101, 125, 128
Melillo, James *see* Smith, Jimmy
Messina, Jerry 148
Metal Trades League 25–29
Metro-Goldwyn-Mayer *see* MGM
MGM (Metro-Goldwyn-Mayer) 49, 53, 72, 108, 114
Michaels, Mickey 133
Mid-Isle Lanes *see* Heineman's
Millard, Howard 110
Miller, Joe 58, 62, 76–77, 79
Miller High Life Classic 10
Mineola 2, 116 122, 124–125, 130, 148, 154, 171, 179
Mineola Trophy and Awards **163**, 179
Mingaud, François 41
Mosconi, Willie 130–***131***
Muller, Chris 31
Munn, Bill "Whitey" 64–65, 67
Murgie, Jim 37–38, 40, 58, 62, 75

Nagy, Steve 92, 97, 112, 119–120, 135–136, 174
NASCAR 14, 74, 81
Nassau County Bowling Proprietors Association 104
Nassau Professionals 20
Nassau-Suffolk Bowling Proprietors Association 129–130
Nassau Sweepstakes Carnival 100
National Bowling Association 8, 194n16
National Bowling Champions 9, 136
National Bowling Council 158, 162, 190
National Bowling Hall of Fame and Museum *see* International Bowling Hall of Fame and Museum

National Bowling League (1904) 17
National Bowling League (1961) 145, 195n9
National Bowling Writers Association (NBWA) *see* BWAA
National Guard Armory 106, **107**
National Italian American Sports Hall of Fame 186, 188
NBA *see* National Bowling Association
NBC *see* National Bowling Council
NBC (National Broadcasting Company) 145, 148
NBL *see* National Bowling League
Neuer, Andy 156–157
Neumann, Mike 180
New Park Lanes 185
New York State Bowling Association 99, 187, 188
New York Yankees 79–80, 90, 165, 175; *see also* baseball
Newark Recreation 65, 106, 136
Newsday 94, 116–117, 120, 124, 139, 166, 171, 175, 180
Newsday Eastern Open 5, 99, 106, 117, 136, 179
Nicklaus, Jack 2, 10, 154
nine-pin bowling 8, 192
Nixon, Pat ***161***
Nixon, Richard 1, 160, ***161***–162, 219n54
Nolen, Ray 51, 62
Norris, Joe 78, 96, ***104***, 106, 110, 114, 120, 129, 132, ***140***, 148, ***159***, 173, 175, 184, 186, 217n50; All-Star performances 84–86, 101, 111, 119; Europe trip 130–131; matches against Andy **71**–72, 96.
North American Industry Classification System 199n39
Northwest Armory 124, 134
Notre Dame *see* University of Notre Dame

O'Brien, Dave 107, ***109***
O'Donnell, Chuck 46, 176
Ogden Doubles Classic 106
open play *see* Eastern System
Orf, Ray 157–158
Orpheum Five 29–31
Orpheum Lanes 27, 29, 31, 32
Ostroski, Joe 100
outdoor bowling 136–137, 160

Pabst Blue Ribbon 134
Palace Recreation 96
Palermaa, Osku 181

Palmer, Arnold 148, 160, 162
Pan Pacific Bowling Lanes 108–***109***
Park Manor Recreation 92
pawn shop special ***181***
PBA (Professional Bowlers Association) 9, 10, 93, 111, 137, 141, 145–150, 155, 163, 167–168, 172–175, 185, 191; Andy's performances 149–150, 152–153; founding 9, 148–149; National Championship 154, 168–169, 185; PBA League 181; Skills Challenge 180–181; Trick Shot Challenge ***181***–182; *see also* PBA50 Tour; *Professional Bowlers Tour*
PBA Senior Tour *see* PBA50 Tour
PBA50 Tour 167, 174
Peach Bowling Tournament 126
Pearl Harbor attack 84
Peninsula Lanes 100
Pennzoil 1, 114
Pepsi-Cola 1, 114
perfect game *see* 300 games
Peterford, John 148
Petersen, Ernie 179
Petersen, Louis 57–58, 62, 75–76, 80, 81, 83, 89–90; *see also* Petersen Classic; Petersen Point System
Petersen Classic 9, 36, 43, 62, 83–84, 91–92, 95–96, 98, 100, 116, 120, 126, 192, 206n13; *see also* Louis Petersen
Petersen Point System 75, 85, 86, 111, 117, 191, 207n23, 210n11; *see also* Louis Petersen
Peterson, Charlie 41
Petraglia, Johnny 2, 106, 117, 150, 163, 169, 173, 176; lesson with Andy 167–168
Pezzano, Chuck 10, 60, 139, 145–146, 175, 177, 178, 180
Phillies Jackpot Bowling 9, 95, 99, 145–148
Phipps, Robert 111
pinboys 14–16, **17**, 27, 37, 52–53, 75–76, 88, 93, ***128***, 142, 144–145, 191, 195n29; influencing play 19, 75, 82–83; pay 15, 20, 26, 216n5; replaced by automatic pinsetters 15, 142, 144–145
pins 37, 93, 194n21; materials 31, 88, 192; specifications 7–9, 116, 156; use in trick shots 42–46, 52, 54, 58, 108, 180–181
pinsetters *see* automatic pinsetters

Pittsburgh Joe *see* Cole, Benny
Point Lookout 94–95, 136
polyurethane 155, 163, 191; *see also* lane conditions
pool *see* billiards
Pratt Institute 23, 25
President's Council on Physical Fitness and Sports 1, 160
Professional Bowlers Association *see* PBA
Professional Bowlers Tour (television show) 10, 184; *see also* PBA
Prohibition 27

Quaker City Lanes 65
Quinn, Jack 106

Rational Recreation 26–28
Reddy, Ed 60
Reese, Pee Wee 79
Reilly, Charlie 37–38, 40, 75
Remington UMC 23–25, 196n3
Republic Aviation 124
retirement 141, 153
Reynolds, Frank 30
Rheingold Beer 114
Richgels, Jeff 155, 177, 218n16
Richmond Hill High School 51, 68
Ridgewood 18, 25, 31, 196n19
Ridolf, Fred 172
Ripley's Believe It or Not 39, 169
Ripple, Robert 61
Ritter, Charley 32, 187
Rizzuto, Phil 68, 79, 90, 165
Rogers, Will 56, 140
Rollick, Leo 100–101
Rossman, Tom 41, 48
Roth, Mark 91, 113, 117, 169, 173–174, 200n22
round-robin tournament 50, 79, 84–85
Ruffing, Red 79, 90
Ruffolo, Andy 71, *151*
Ruffolo, Bob 117, 122, **125**, *151*, 152, 163
Ruffolo, Joe *151*, 170–171
Ruffolo, Joseph **125**
Ruffolo, Lorraine 51, 58, 70, 79, 89–90, 108, 111, 120, 122 **125**, *151*, 163, 172, 179; Andy's biographer 2, 46, 112, 150–152; bowler 117–**118**
Ruffolo, Mae **125**
Ruffolo, Robert, Jr. *151*
Rutz, Frank 40
Rutz Bowling Hall 40
Ryan, John 83
Ryan, Roy 148

Sabolowski, Ann 133
St. Patrick's School 13, 17

Salvino, Carmen 10, 66, 157, 169, 173, 186
Salvino, Ginny 186
San Su San 122, 124, 125
sandbagging 191, 197n32
SS *Sardegna* 12
Schackett, Walter 39
Schafer Beer 114
Schenkel, Chris 169
Schmidt, J.R. 111, 225
Schoeman, Byron 59
Schueneman, Leo 57–58, 62, 64
Schwoegler, Connie 96, 100, 114, 119, 122, 126–**127**, 128, 130; All-Star performances 85–86, 90–91, 93–94, 97, 111, 119, 125
Schwoegler, Tony 119
Schwoegler's Lanes 119, 127
Scott, Don 146
Scribner, Joe 36, 76
Seivert, Al 28
Serpico, Frank 65, 136
Set 'Em Up **69–70**, 72–73, 108, 180
shellac 37, 72, 82–83, 88, 154–155, 163, 191, 204n13; *see also* lane conditions
Sheridan Academy *see* Sheridan Bowl
Sheridan Bowl 2, 116, 122, 130, 166, 171, 179
Sherman, Sid 35
Shirghio, Mike 51
short films 49–50, 202n2
Showboat Hotel Lanes 173
showgirls 1, 52–**54**, 185
Shultz, Ray 40
Simonsen, Anthony 155
Sims, J. Wilbert 146–147
Sinke, Joe 85–86, 97, 100–101
Sixty, Billy 76, 103–104, **159**, 174, 177
Sloan, Jack 19, 28
Slomenski, Stan 112, 119–120
Smith, Harry 9, 154
Smith, Jimmy 6, 16–**17**, 18–19, 30, 33–37, 42–43, 65, 78, 84, 91, 129, 155, 195n6; World's Champion 17, 33, 74–75, 205n4
Smith, Pete 49–52, 53, **54**, 56, 72, 107–108, **109**, 110, 225
soccer 204n1
Soest, Ernie 100
Somerset Recreation 127
Sparando, Tony 66, 88, 92, 95, 98–99, 101, 107, 112, 133–134, 136
Spinella, Barney 39, 46, 66, 76, 83, 95, 206n58
Spinella, Joe 79, 93–94, 206n58

Spinella, Phil 29–32, 66, 206n58
Sport Slants No. 5 47, 49
Sportlights 43–44, 47, 72
Sports Illustrated 22, 36, 76, 142
State Fair Recreation **127**
Stavich, Semo 101
Steers, Harry **140**
Stein, Otto 57–58, 62, 77, 79
Stelter, George 32
Stock Market Crash *see* The Great Depression
Strampe, Bob 60, 173
Strikes and Spares 1, 2, 46, 50–54, 55–57, 59, 108, 180
Subway Bowling Academy 16–**17**
Sun Bowl 91
The Super Skittler 50
Superba Bowling Parlors 16, 74
switchman 20, 23

T-Bowl 99, 146
Tavener Alleys 64
Taylor, F. Chase 72
Taylor, Joan 150
Taylor, Willard 135
Teacher's Scotch 114
tennis 7, 9–10, 74, 79, 84, 97
Tepedino, Mike 29, 187
That's Incredible! 1, 169–171
300 games 29, 30, 33, 35, 61, 96, 106, 117, 119, 126, 136, 171, 184, 191, 192; by Andy 31, 40, 107, 110, 156–157; proliferation 156–157; *see also* Andy Varipapa 300
Thum, Joe 50
thumbs, sore 19, 91, 209n57
Thum's Individual Classic 40, 50–51, 187
Top Star Bowling 136
topography 171, 192, 201n36
tornado 5
Travaglia, Joe 29
trick shots 1–2, 43, 58–59, 91, 98, 114, 133, 137, 160, 165, 169–170, 172, 185; Andy's development 34, 40–48, diagrams **45–46**, *181*; in films and television 51, 72, 107–108, 225; *see also* crisscross; flying dutchman; flying eagle; pawn shop special; PBA Skills Challenge; tunnel shot
Tronsky, Nick 132
Trucks, Charley 37
tunnel shot 44, 47, 50, 52, **54**, 180, 202n29; *see also* trick shots
Turner, Ray 52–**54**
212th Coast Artillery Armory 78

Undercover 44
United States Bowling Congress *see* USBC
U.S. Open (bowling) 2, 91, 113, 163, 168, 209*n*53, 212*n*57; *see also* BPAA All-Star
U.S. Open (golf) 2, 205*n*2
University of Illinois 68, 89
University of Notre Dame 92, *143*
USBC (United States Bowling Congress) 7, 137, 156, 190, 192, 193*n*6, 205*n*43, 218*n*23; *see also* ABC
USBC Open Championships *see* ABC Open Championships

Vallos, George 97–98
Varipapa, Alice *24*–25, 31, 33, 50–51, 67, 70, 79–80, 90, 92, 94, 117, 120, *124-125*, 150–*151*, 152, 179; traveling with Andy 64–66, 106–108, 111, 122–*123*, 126
Varipapa, Andy II 2, 138 *151*, 174–177, 179, 184, 225
Varipapa, Concetta *see* Cardamone, Concetta
Varipapa, Connie *see* Cornacchia, Connie
Varipapa, Dottie 122, *124*, 126, *151*, 184
Varipapa, Francesco 11
Varipapa, Frank 2, 25, 51, 58, 68–70, 59, 92, 96, 105, 113, 116, 122–*124*, 138, *151*, 172, 173, 177–179, 184; bowler 111, 117, 119–120, 135–136, 174; owner of Bowl Mart 129–130, 148, 179
Varipapa, Josh 13, 158
Varipapa, Lorraine *see* Ruffolo, Lorraine

Varipapa, Susan 2, 126, 138, 150–*151*, 176, 184
Varone, Richie 179
Viale, Chris 180
Vitola, Sam 100
Voelpel, Fred 65, 92
Vogue Individual Classic 9
Voorhies, Johnny 17, 19, 42, 74–75, 84, 205*n*6

Waibel Singles Classic 9, 99
Waldbaum's Supermarkets 175–176
Walter, John 67, 151, 177
Wansa, Emil 116
Ward, Walter 61, 97–98, 112, 120
Warmbier, Marie 58, 62
Warshafsky, Barry 179
Wasdell, Jimmy 79
Watson, Stewart 77
Wayne Club 21
Weatherproof 44
Weber, Dick 10, 15, 91–92, 117, 152–153, 160, 162, 169, 173, 184, 212*n*53; All-Star performances 113, 120; bowling's ambassador 148–150, 175; wrists 60–61
Weber, Pete 113
Weinstein, Sam 173
Welu, Billy 92, 150
Wene, Sylvia 200*n*22
Werner, Val 106–*107*
Western System 26–27, 197*n*19
What's My Line 162
Wheaties 1, 72, 180–182
Wheatley Hills Golf Club 169–*170*
Whitaker, Jim 130
White Elephant Alleys *see* Joe Thum's White Elephant Alleys
White House *161*-162, 184

Whitmore, Cal 177–178
WIBC (Women's International Bowling Congress) 117, 124–125, 146, 156, 176, 192, 193*n*6, 194*n*32
Will Rogers Civic Center *140*
Williams, Walter Ray, Jr. 10, 47, 113
Williamsburg 6, 13–14, 25
Wilman, Joe 78, 88, 91, 95, *104*, 105, 107, 110, 114, 120, 128–129, 134–136, *140,* 174; All-Star performances 86, 97–101, 111–113, 119
Windy Jones *see* Cirillo, Al
Wolf, Phil 75
Women's BPAA All-Star 124–125; *see also* Women's U.S. Open
Women's International Bowling Congress *see* WIBC
Women's U.S. Open 137, 160; *see also* Women's BPAA All-Star
Woods, Tiger 148, 175, 181
World Classic 75–77, 81, 83, 85
World War I 23–25, 28, 31, 87
World War II 36, 88–90, 96–97, 128

YABA (Young American Bowling Alliance) 189, 193*n*6
Yonkers Bowl 172
You Asked for It! 169
Young, George 90, 92–93, 96, 99–101, 111, 124, 174, 209*n*48
Young American Bowling Alliance *see* YABA
Youngman, Henny 79

Zellner, Bob 116, 169
Zlokovich, Milan 109–110
Zunker, Gil 78
Zurich, Sam 167

www.ingramcontent.com/pod-product-compliance
Lightning Source LLC
Chambersburg PA
CBHW060340010526
44117CB00017B/2897